A Documentary History

of American Thought

and Society

edited by CHARLES CROWE

WESTERN RESERVE UNIVERSITY

Allyn and Bacon, Inc.   *Boston, 1965*

For Joyce and Lisa

Cover illustration: Jefferson's
drawing of the University of
Virginia. Reproduced from the
Collection of the Library of
Congress.

PREFACE

MY GOAL HAS BEEN TO PREPARE A ONE-VOLUME TEXTBOOK WHICH COM-
bines brevity with extensive coverage, and which is both concise and
comprehensive. I hope that this book will be useful in social and intellectual history courses and in those survey courses which stress social
and intellectual history. Students on all levels should have the
opportunity to examine documents in their context and to understand
their purport. To serve these needs I have emphasized the general
structure and the basic patterns of American thought and life as I
understand them. I have included Pragmatism and other abstract
philosophical movements as well as pervasive political forces from
early nationalism to recent liberalism, attempting all the while to work
both kinds of movements into a framework which includes the basic
national experiences through the generations down to the Cold War
and the Civil Rights movement. At least brief notice has been taken
of the major events in the intellectual, social, and political history of
the United States. If the scientific selections are limited to scattered
excerpts in biology, psychology, and geology, it is because of space
limitations and the great difficulty in presenting to a general audience
the basic ideas of physics, chemistry, and related disciplines.

In writing chapter introductions and choosing selections I wished
to preserve maximum flexibility in order to pursue more effectively
the several purposes of this volume. Some of the selections are
presented as no more than brief abstracts, samples, and representations, to encourage the student to read more, to illustrate a trend, or to
enable the instructor to make a reference. No attempt has been made
to keep the chapter introductions even in length: when the selections
in Chapter I and elsewhere displayed a wide range of thought and
action I held the introductions to a few pages, but in chapters such
as the last one where it seemed nearly impossible to cover all the
major categories through the readings, I used longer introductions to
carry a more substantial portion of the burden of explanation. The
format for the section introductions has been a concise paragraph
or two limited to a few important background facts, the identification
of the author, and the source of the selection. Here and there a

significant figure, not included in the readings, has appeared for a sentence or a paragraph in the introductions. I have thought of the book as an organic unit with both introductions and texts serving to express the various parts of the general structure. The book is so arranged as to allow the instructor to use some chapters and delete others. Those who stress social history may wish to delete the chapter on Pragmatism; those who give a larger voice to intellectual currents may wish to omit several of the sections devoted to social and political history; and the instructor may delete or stress as he pleases the chapters on literary history. I hope that this volume may be useful either as a "core" textbook supplemented with paperbacks and reserve shelves or as a book of supplementary readings. No textbook is passive before the "facts" and "documents" and I have not tried to pursue that illusory goal. Instead I have attempted to provide a considered framework of presentation and interpretation. When the instructor does not agree with a particular interprctation, I hope that he will create the kind of lecture-textbook dialectic which I have often found useful.

I suppose that I must confess to being impressed by both the concept of cultural pluralism and by the great human variety revealed in American history. Catholicity is one of the central concepts in a volume which would exclude no significant persons or aspects of national life. On whatever terms they are to be admitted, Frederick Douglass and Jefferson Davis, John Dewey and Josiah Royce, immigrant rabbi and nativist spokesman, must enter our gallery. The American scene belongs to all those who have inhabited it. I wish to give voice to the life of the Yankee sharper and to the dilemmas of Irish peasants, to the Southern rhetoric and to the Negro in his long bitter struggle, to the master of New England letters and to the child of the backwoods, and to a great many others.

Professor Milton Cantor of the University of Massachusetts participated fully in the initial planning and early preparation of this book. While I would not hold him responsible for interpretations used in the final version, I do wish to thank him for his very substantial contribution. I am also indebted to Mrs. Frances Slocumb for assisting in the preparation of the manuscript. Finally, my wife provided invaluable assistance by serving many long hours as typist, editorial assistant, and general critic.

Charles Crowe

ACKNOWLEDGMENTS

The author wishes to thank the following copyright owners and publishers for permission to reprint certain selections:

CHAPTER 8:

Harcourt, Brace & World, Inc. for Preface to *Main Street* by Sinclair Lewis. Reprinted by permission of Harcourt, Brace & World, Inc.

The World Publishing Company for four pages from *An American Tragedy* by Theodore Dreiser. Copyright 1925 by Horace Liveright, Inc. Copyright 1926 by Theodore Dreiser. Copyright 1953 by Helen Dreiser. Reprinted by permission of the World Publishing Company.

CHAPTER 11:

"Anarchism Is the Only Philosophy" from *Anarchism* by Emma Goldman.

The Viking Press Inc. for "Engineer vs. Captain of Industry" from *The Engineers and the Price System* by Thorstein Veblen. Reprinted by permission of The Viking Press Inc.

Charles Scribner's Sons for the selection from Volume XVII, *The Works of Theodore Roosevelt*, Charles Scribner's Sons, Publishers.

Executors of the Estate of Edith Bolling Wilson for the excerpt "No Compromise with Monopoly" from *The New Freedom* by Woodrow Wilson.

CHAPTER 12:

Charles Scribner's Sons for excerpts from "A Protestant Return to Pessimism" from *The Nature and Destiny of Man* by Reinhold Niebuhr. Reprinted by permission of Charles Scribner's Sons.

"Orthodox, Reform, and Conservative Judaism" by Solomon Grayzel in Harry Schneiderman, ed., *Two Generations in Perspective*.

University of Notre Dame Press for "A Curious Kind of Religion" by Will Herberg in Thomas T. McAvoy, *Roman Catholicism and the American Way of Life*. Reprinted by permission of the University of Notre Dame Press.

CHAPTER 13:

W. W. Norton & Company, Inc. for the excerpt from *Autobiography of an Idea* by Louis Sullivan. Reprinted by permission of W. W. Norton & Company, Inc.

Duell, Sloan & Pearce, Inc. for the excerpt from *An Autobiography* by Frank Lloyd Wright, by permission of Duell, Sloan & Pearce, Inc.

Faber and Faber Ltd., London, for the excerpt from *The New Architecture and the Bauhaus* by Walter Gropius. Reprinted by permission of Faber and Faber Ltd.

Houghton Mifflin Company for the excerpt from *Some Imagist Poems*. Reprinted by permission of Houghton Mifflin Company.

Marguerite F. Fetcher (Mrs. E. S. Fetcher) for the excerpt from *Introduction to the New Poetry* by Harriet Monroe.

CHAPTER 14:

Holt, Rinehart and Winston, Inc. for the excerpt from *Characters and Events* by John Dewey. Reprinted from *Characters and Events*, Vol. II, by John Dewey, edited by Joseph Ratner, 1929, 1957, with the permission of Holt, Rinehart and Winston, Inc.

School and Society for the excerpt from "Democracy and Educational Administration" by John Dewey. Reprinted from Vol. 45 (April, 1937), pp. 457–458, by permission of *School and Society*.

Mrs. John Dewey for the excerpt from *Interest and Effort in Education* by John Dewey. Copyright 1913 by John Dewey. Copyright renewed 1941 by John Dewey. Reprinted by permission of Mrs. John Dewey.

The Philosophical Library for the excerpt from "Logical Empiricism" by Herbert Feigl in Dagobert D. Runes, ed., *Twentieth Century Philosophy*. Reprinted by permission of The Philosophical Library.

CHAPTER 15:

Charles Scribner's Sons for the excerpt from *A Farewell to Arms* by Ernest Hemingway. Reprinted by permission of Charles Scribner's Sons. Alfred A. Knopf Inc. for the excerpt from *An American Scandal: The Scopes Trial* by Henry L. Mencken. Reprinted by permission of Alfred A. Knopf, Inc.

The Hogarth Press Ltd. and W. W. Norton & Co. Inc. for the excerpt from *Civilization and Its Discontents* by Sigmund Freud, from Volume XXI of the Standard Edition of Freud's *Complete Psychological Works*, ed. James Strachey.

Harcourt, Brace & World, Inc. for the excerpt from *The Modern Temper* by Joseph Wood Krutch. Reprinted by permission of Harcourt, Brace & World.

John Dos Passos for the excerpt from *U.S.A.* Copyright by John Dos Passos. Published by the Houghton Mifflin Company.

Harper & Row, Publishers, Inc. for the excerpt from *You Can't Go Home Again* by Thomas Wolfe. Harper and Brothers, 1940.

Randall Jarrell for the excerpt from *Losses* by Randall Jarrell.

Beacon Press for the excerpt from *The Unadjusted Man* by Peter Viereck. Reprinted by permission of the Beacon Press, copyright © 1956.

City Lights Books for the excerpt from Allen Ginsberg's *Howl*. Copyright © 1956 by Allen Ginsberg. Reprinted by permission of City Lights Books.

Simon and Schuster, Inc. for the excerpt from *The Organization Man* by William H. Whyte, Jr. Reprinted by permission of Simon and Schuster, Inc.

Oxford University Press, Inc. for the excerpt from *White Collar* by C. Wright Mills. Reprinted by permission of Oxford University Press, Inc.

CHAPTER 16:

The Viking Press Inc. for the excerpt from *Up to Now* by Alfred E. Smith. Reprinted by permission of The Viking Press Inc.

Random House, Inc. for excerpts from "An Economic Declaration of Rights" from Roosevelt's Acceptance Speech of 1932, from *The Public Papers and Addresses of Franklin Delano Roosevelt*. Copyright, reprinted by permission of Random House, Inc.

Allan Hoover for excerpts from *State Papers* by Herbert Hoover, Volumes I and II. Doubleday and Company, Inc. Reprinted by permission of Allan Hoover.

International Publishers for the excerpt from *Communism in the United States* by Earl Browder. Reprinted by permission of International Publishers.

Harper & Row, Publishers, Incorporated for the excerpt from *The Coming American Fascism* by Lawrence Dennis (Harper and Brothers, 1936). Reprinted by permission of Harper & Row, Publishers, Incorporated.

Harper & Row, Publishers, Incorporated for the excerpt from "Who is Loyal in America?" by Henry S. Commager from *Living Ideas in America*, edited by Henry S. Commager (Harper & Brothers, 1951). Reprinted by permission of Harper & Row, Publishers, Incorporated.

W. W. Norton & Company, Inc. for the excerpt from *Anthropology and Modern Life* by Franz Boas. Copyright 1928 by W. W. Norton & Company, Inc. Renewed 1956 by Norman Boas. Copyright 1932 by W. W. Norton & Company, Inc. Renewed 1960 by Helene Boas Yampolsky. Copyright © 1962 by W. W. Norton & Company, Inc. Reprinted by permission of W. W. Norton & Company, Inc.

Fortune Magazine for the excerpt from "The Republican Party" by Robert A. Taft, 1949. Courtesy of *Fortune* Magazine.

Harper & Row, Publishers, Incorporated for the excerpt from John F. Kennedy's address to the United Nations of 1961 in *To Turn the Tide* (Harper and Brothers, 1962). Reprinted by permission of Harper & Row, Publishers, Incorporated.

CONTENTS

CHAPTER I. PURITANISM AND THE ORIGINS OF
AMERICAN SOCIETY   1

1. THE NEW ENGLAND ZION   3
    Motives for Immigration (1629): John Winthrop   3
    The Holy Commonwealth (1630): John Winthrop   4
    The Puritan Place in Christian History (1702): Cotton
        Mather   5

2. COVENANT THEOLOGY   6
    God's Sovereignty Over the World (1677): Urian Oakes   7
    The Covenant of Grace; God's Compact With Man (1651):
        Thomas Shepard   8

3. PURITANISM AND POLITICS   10
    Democracy an Evil (1636): John Cotton   10
    Aristocracy Ordained by God (1630): John Winthrop   11
    The Development of a Natural Rights Ideology (1717):
        John Wise   12

4. HERESY AND WITCHCRAFT   13
    Against Toleration (1647): Nathaniel Ward   14
    The Antinomian Heresy of Anne Hutchinson (1637): John
        Winthrop   15
    Against Persecution (1644): Roger Williams   17
    Remarkable Providence (1684): Increase Mather   17
    Against the Salem Witchcraft Trials (1692): Thomas Brattle   18
    The Puritan Conscience; A Judge of Witches Repents
        (1697): Samuel Sewall   19

5. THE ARTS, THE SCIENCES, AND PURITANISM   20
    The Plain Style (1648): Thomas Hooker   21
    Humanism and Puritanism (1726): Cotton Mather   21
    Natural Philosophy Friendly to Religion (1721): Cotton
        Mather   22

6. TWO PURITAN OFFSPRING: REVIVALISM AND RATIONALISM   23
    Religious Experiences (1740): Jonathan Edwards   24

Contents

A Revival Sermon During the Great Awakening (1741):
Jonathan Edwards   25
Affections Are the Seat of Religion (1746): Jonathan
Edwards   26
A Rationalist Attack on Revivalism (1743): Charles Chauncy   28

7. PURITANISM AND CAPITALISM   30
Wage, Price, and Profit Controls (1633, 1639): John
Winthrop   30
Puritanism and the Development of Commercial Ethics
(1701): Cotton Mather   32

8. THE PURITAN BECOMES A YANKEE   33
On Doing Good (1710–1726): Cotton Mather   34
A Debt to Cotton Mather (1784): Benjamin Franklin   35
How to Get Rich (1748): Benjamin Franklin   35
How to Seek Moral Perfection (1771): Benjamin Franklin   36
How to Deal With the Poor (1760): Benjamin Franklin   37

CHAPTER II. THE ENLIGHTENMENT AND THE
NEW NATION   39

1. SCIENCE   39
Experiments in Electricity (1749): Benjamin Franklin   44
Science, A Great Friend to Man (1797): Samuel Harrison
Smith   45

2. PHILOSOPHIC TRENDS   46
The Principles of Action in Matter (1751): Cadwallader
Colden   47
The Faculty of the Moral Sense (1814): Thomas Jefferson   48
Toward an American Philosophy of Education (1806):
Benjamin Rush   49
The Idea of Progress (1787): Joel Barlow   51

3. HUMANITARIANISM   52
A Plea for the Poor and the African Stranger (1793): John
Woolman   52
Against the Oppression of Women (1775): Thomas Paine   54
Let the Punishment Fit the Crime (1779): Thomas Jefferson   54

4. NATURAL LAW   55
The Natural Rights of the Colonists (1765): James Otis   56

The Great Social Compact: The Declaration of Independence
   (1776): Thomas Jefferson   57
The Virtues of "A Little Rebellion" (1787): Thomas
   Jefferson   58
5. THE STATE, SOCIETY, AND THE NEW NATION   59
   Virtuous Happiness, The End of Government (1776):
     John Adams   61
   Allow Power to Property (1787): Alexander Hamilton   61
   Human Frailty and the Primacy of Local Interests Make the
     Constitution a Doubtful Enterprise (1787, 1789):
     Samuel Adams   62
   A Defense of the New Constitution (1787): Alexander
     Hamilton   63
   The Descent of Obligations Through the Generations
     (1790): James Madison Debates Thomas Jefferson   64
   Republican Unity With Diversity and Toleration (1801):
     Thomas Jefferson   65
   Against "The Tyranny of the Many" (1805): Fisher Ames   66
   The Democratic Gentlemen (1838): James Fenimore Cooper   67

6. ECONOMIC GOALS OF THE NEW NATION   68
   Farmers "The Chosen People of God" (1784): Thomas
     Jefferson   68
   Manufacturing Valuable to America (1791): Alexander
     Hamilton   69

7. RELIGION IN THE AGE OF REASON   70
   Religious Credo (1790): Benjamin Franklin   70
   Religious Credo (1823): Thomas Jefferson   71
   Camp Meeting (1805): Peter Cartwright   72

CHAPTER III: THE CONDITIONS OF AMERICAN
EXPERIENCE   75

1. THE WEST: PROMISE AND THREAT   78
   The Western Promise (1616): John Smith   78
   Frontier Democracy (1775): Richard Henderson to the
     Kentucky Convention   79
   The Menace of the West (1821): Timothy Dwight   80
   The West Defended (1816): Timothy Flint   81

2. FRONTIER WARFARE   83
   An Indian Raid (1676): Mary Rowlandson White   83

Massacre by the Paxton Boys (1763): Benjamin Franklin   84
The Indians: Savages Deserving Extermination (1782):
    Hugh Henry Brackenridge   86
3. SLAVERY AND CASTE   87
    Negro Petitions and Protests (1774, 1778)   88
    For the Emancipation and Expulsion of Negroes (1784):
       Thomas Jefferson   88
    Radical Protest Against Slavery and Caste (1829): David
       Walker   90

4. EARLY SOUTHERN SOCIETY   91
    Southern Idlers and Wilderness Aristocrats (1728, 1732):
       William Byrd   92

5. FROM DIVERSITY AND CONFLICT; TOWARD TOLERATION AND
   UNITY   94
    Politics and Religion in Maryland (1666): George Alsop   94
    From Diverse Origins, a New Man, the American (1782):
       St. Jean de Crèvecoeur   95

CHAPTER IV: THE QUEST FOR UTOPIA IN
JACKSONIAN AMERICA   97

1. JACKSONIANS AND LOCOFOCOS   100
    Jackson's War on "Privilege" (1832): The Bill to Recharter
       the Bank of the United States Vetoed   101
    History and Nature of the Democratic Party (1846–1847):
       Walt Whitman   102
    The Government of the People Is Godlike (1842): George
       Bancroft   103
    A Radical Democrat on the Class Struggle (1840):
       Orestes A. Brownson   105

2. ECONOMIC THOUGHT   106
    The Harmony of Economic Interests (1859): Henry C. Carey   106

3. REFORMERS AND HUMANITARIANS   107
    The Chardon Street Reform Convention (1841): Ralph
       Waldo Emerson   108

    The Perishing Classes (1846): Theodore Parker   109
    The Need for Mass Education in a Republic (1849): Horace
       Mann   109

A Woman's Declaration of Independence (1848): Elizabeth
   Cady Stanton   110
The Temperance Cause (1842): Marching Song of the Cold
   Water Army   111
4. RELIGION AND REFORM   112
   Religious Motives for Reform (1835): Charles G. Finney   112

5. THE ABOLITIONISTS   113
   The Barbarism of Slavery (1860): Charles Sumner   114
   A Plea for Captain John Brown (1859): Henry David
   Thoreau   115

6. UTOPIAN SOCIALISM   116
   Origins of the Brook Farm Community (1840): George
   Ripley   117
   Socialist Communion in Utopia (1844): John Sullivan
   Dwight   118

CHAPTER V. TRANSCENDENTALISM   121

1. RELIGIOUS ASPECTS   123
   A Forerunner: William Ellery Channing on Unitarian
   Christianity (1826)   124
   Man's Religious Sense (1838): Ralph Waldo Emerson   125
   Evolving Religion: The Religious Radicalism of Theodore
   Parker (1841)   126

2. ETHICAL AND AESTHETIC IDEALS   127
   A Transcendentalist Manifesto (1840): The Editors of *The
   Dial*   128
   Individualism and Spontaneity in the Good Life: Thoreau at
   Walden Pond (1845–1847)   129

3. POLITICAL THOUGHT   131
   Civil Disobedience (1849): Henry David Thoreau   131

4. NATURE   133
   Hamatreya (1847): Ralph Waldo Emerson   133

   Theories and Perceptions of Nature (1836): Ralph Waldo
   Emerson   135

CHAPTER VI. THE ROMANTIC TEMPER 140

1. ON LITERATURE IN AMERICA 143
   Few Materials for Romance in America (1828): James
   Fenimore Cooper 144
   The Proper Subjects for American Literature (1837): Ralph
   Waldo Emerson 145
   How to Write an American Romance (1835): William
   Gilmore Simms 145

2. THE ROMANTIC SCENE 146
   The Painter as Explorer of Nature (1825): Thomas Cole on
   Landscape Painting 147
   Romantic Nature (1826): Thomas Cole in the Catskills 148
   The Romance of History (1850): Nathaniel Hawthorne in
   Old Salem 149
   The Romance of the West (1818): James Kirke Paulding 150
   The Romance of the Gothic Scene (1839): Edgar Allan Poe 152

3. THE ROMANTIC DREAM OF ESCAPE AND FLIGHT 153
   The Noble Savage in the South Seas (1846): Herman
   Melville 153

4. THE ROMANTIC HERO 155
   The Yankee Hero in Homespun (1786): Royall Tyler 156
   The Hero as Noble Redskin (1822): Lydia Hunt Sigourney 157
   The Seduced Maid as "Heroine" (1791): Susanna Rowson 158
   The Hero as Reformer (1841): Ralph Waldo Emerson 159
   The Hero as Cosmic Rebel (1851): Herman Melville 160

CHAPTER VII: THE STRUGGLE FOR AMERICAN
NATIONALITY 162

1. CULTURAL NATIONALISM 167
   The Mightiest People in History (1824): Edward Everett 168
   A National University for Science and Republican Virtue
   (1805): Joel Barlow 169
   The Need for an American Language (1789): Noah Webster 170
   The Republic Needs the Fine Arts (1811): Benjamin Latrobe 171

2. POLITICAL NATIONALISM   173
    The Supremacy of the National Government (1819): John
        Marshall   174
    Nationalism and Manifest Destiny (1839, 1845): John
        L. O'Sullivan   175
    For the Preservation of the Union (1850): Daniel Webster   176
    The Union Is Perpetual (1861): Abraham Lincoln   178

3. THE ANTI-NATIONALIST OPPOSITION: STATES RIGHTS AND
    SOUTHERN NATIONALISM   179
    Origins of "States Rights" Doctrines: The Kentucky
        Resolutions (1798)   179
    Maturation of "States Rights" Doctrines (1831): John C.
        Calhoun   181
    Southern Nationalism (1861): Henry Timrod's
        "Ethnogenesis"   182

4. THE PERPLEXITIES OF COLOR, CASTE, AND SLAVERY   185
    The Virtues of Slavery; The Impossibility of Emancipation
        (1831): Thomas R. Dew   186
    The Evils of Slavery (1848): Frederick Douglass Writes to
        His Former Master   188
    A White Man's Country (1858): Stephen A. Douglas   189
    What Are the Rights of Negroes? (1858): Abraham Lincoln   190
    A Protest Against Caste (1849): William Wells Brown   192

5. THE NATURE OF THE CIVIL WAR   192
    The Irrepressible Conflict (1858): William H. Seward   193
    The War for Southern Economic Independence (1861):
        John H. Reagan   194
    Slaveholder's Rebellion (1862): Frederick Douglass   194
    The Suppression of Rebellion Becomes a Holy Crusade
        (1862, 1865): Abraham Lincoln   195
    Conflict of the Cavalier and the Puritan (1866): Edwin A.
        Pollard   196
    The Victimized South (1881): Jefferson Davis   197

6. RECONSTRUCTION   198
    The Plan to Africanize Half the Country (1867): Andrew
        Johnson   199
    The Need for Reconstruction (1867): Thaddeus Stevens   200
    The Ku Klux Terror (1879): Albion W. Tourgée   201

7. THE ROAD TO REUNION   203
    The New South: Industrialism and White Supremacy
        (1887): Henry W. Grady   204

Contents

Northern Acquiescence: *Plessy vs. Ferguson* (1896) 205
Accommodation for Limited Gains (1895): Booker T.
  Washington 206

CHAPTER VIII. REALISM AND NATURALISM 208

1. NEW APPROACHES TO LITERATURE 210
  On the Art of Fiction (1884): Henry James 211
  The Simple, the Natural, the Honest (1891): William Dean
    Howells 212

2. REVOLT AGAINST THE VILLAGE 213
  From Spoon River Anthology (1915): Edgar Lee Masters 214
  Main Street (1920): Sinclair Lewis 215

3. REALISTIC AND NATURALISTIC LITERATURE 215
  A Coldly Indifferent Universe (1895, 1899): Stephen Crane 216
  An American Tragedy (1925): Theodore Dreiser 219

CHAPTER IX. SOCIAL DARWINISM 222

1. THE SCIENTIFIC BACKGROUND 225
  Natural Selection (1859): Charles Darwin 225

2. THE DARWINIAN IMPACT ON RELIGION 226
  The Book of Genesis Upheld (1860): Louis Agassiz 227
  Darwinism Supports the Theistic View of Nature (1876):
    Asa Gray 228
  God Works Through Evolution (1888): James McCosh 228
  Consign the Special Creation Hypothesis to Limbo (1902):
    John Fiske 230

3. DARWINISM AND THE EVOLUTION OF CULTURES 231
  Evolutionary Origins of Civilization (1877): Lewis
    Henry Morgan 232

4. THE ECONOMIC AND SOCIAL STRUGGLE FOR EXISTENCE 233
  No Natural Rights in the Social Struggle (1883): William
    Graham Sumner 234
  Civilization Founded on Economic Competition (1889):
    Andrew Carnegie 235

5. Social Darwinism and the Law   236
    Law and the Struggle for Life (1873): Oliver Wendell
        Holmes   237
    Right of a Majority to Embody Their Opinions in Law
        (1905): Oliver Wendell Holmes   238

CHAPTER X. IMMIGRATION, RACISM, AND
    IMPERIALISM   240

1. Immigration and Nativist Reaction   242
    Economic Disaster in Eastern Europe (1910): Emily
        Green Balch   243
    Unrestricted Immigration a Threat to the American Worker
        (1902): Samuel Gompers   244
2. The Melting Pot Debate   245
    America: Refuge and "Melting Pot" to the World (1889,
        1909): Emma Lazarus and Israel Zangwill   246
    The "Melting Pot" Denounced (1926): Henry Pratt
        Fairchild   247

3. Doctrines of Caucasian Superiority   248
    The Immigrant Menace to Nordic Americans (1916):
        Madison Grant   249
    The Racial Beast (1902): Thomas Dixon, Jr.   250

4. Imperialism and Anti-Imperialism   251
    A Religious Justification for Anglo-Saxon Domination of the
        World (1885): Josiah Strong   252
    The White Man's Burden: U.S. Occupation of the
        Philippines (1900): Elihu Root   254
    Imperialism Incompatible With Christianity and American
        Democracy (1900): William Jennings Bryan   255
    A Poet's Protest (1900): William Vaughn Moody   255

CHAPTER XI. SOCIAL AND POLITICAL CRITICISM
    IN THE PROGRESSIVE ERA   259

1. The Reaction Against Social Darwinism   264
    Plutocracy and Paternalism (1895): Lester Frank Ward   264

2. The Radical Left: Socialists and Anarchists   265
    An Unscientific Socialist (1905): Jack London at the Bottom
        of the Social Pit   266

We Will Own the Mammoth Machines (1908): Eugene
    Debs   267
Anarchism Is the Only Philosophy (1910): Emma Goldman   269

3. CRITICAL ANALYSES OF COMMERCIAL AMERICA   270
    Progress and Poverty: The Single Tax (1879): Henry George   271
    Conspicuous Leisure and Consumption (1899): Thorstein
        Veblen   272
    Engineer vs. Captain of Industry (1921): Thorstein Veblen   273

4. THE SOCIAL GOSPEL   274
    Christian Social Duties (1886): Washington Gladden   275

5. THE MUCKRAKERS   276
    The Shame of the Cities (1904): Lincoln Steffens   277
    Following the Color Line North (1908): Ray Stannard Baker   278
6. POPULISM   279
    Preamble and Platform of the Populist Party (1892)   279

7. PROGRESSIVISM   281
    We Stand at Armageddon and Battle for the Lord (1912):
        Theodore Roosevelt   282
    No Compromise With Monopoly (1912): Woodrow Wilson   283
    To Make the World Safe for Democracy (1917, 1918):
        Woodrow Wilson   284

CHAPTER XII. FROM PROTESTANT POLITY TO
    RELIGIOUS PLURALISM   286

1. EVOLVING PROTESTANTISM   292
    Christian Nurture (1847): Horace Bushnell   293
    Urban Evangelism (1915): Billy Sunday   293
    The New Theology (1883): Theodore T. Munger   294
    A Protestant Return to Pessimism (1949): Reinhold Niebuhr   295

2. CATHOLICISM AND NATIVISM   297
    Early Nativism: The "Great Catholic Conspiracy" Against
        the Republic (1835): Samuel F. B. Morse   298
    Catholicism and Americanism (1857): Orestes A. Brownson   299
    Catholic Allegiance Not Divided (1882): Bishop Spalding 300

3. JUDAISM IN AMERICA   301
    Orthodox, Reform, and Conservative Judaism (1957):
        Solomon Grayzel   301

4. AMERICAN RELIGION   303
   A Curious Kind of Religion (1960): Will Herberg   303

CHAPTER XIII: THE REVOLT OF THE MODERNS   305

1. REVOLT IN CONTEMPORARY ART   308
   Panic in Art (1914): Leo Stein   308

2. THE EMERGENCE OF MODERN ARCHITECTURE   310
   Form Follows Function (1881): Louis Sullivan   311
   Organicism, Simplicity, Plasticity (1932): Frank Lloyd
      Wright   312
   The New Architecture (1935): Walter Gropius   313

3. THE NEW POETRY   315
   A Few Don'ts (1913): Ezra Pound   315
   Imagist Credo (1915): Anonymous   316
   A Remarkable Renascence (1928): Harriet Monroe   317

CHAPTER XIV: MODERN PHILOSOPHICAL
   TRENDS: IDEALISM, PRAGMATISM, AND
   POSITIVISM   319

1. IDEALISM   322
   A Defense of Idealism (1892): Josiah Royce   323

2. THE ORIGINS OF PRAGMATISM   325
   Science and Progress (1865): Chauncey Wright   326
   An Intellectual Autobiography (1897): Charles Peirce   327

3. PRAGMATISM: PROBLEMS OF MEANING AND TRUTH   328
   The Fixation of Belief (1877): Charles Peirce   329
   How to Make Our Ideas Clear (1878): Charles Peirce   332
   The Meaning of Pragmatism (1907): William James   334
   The Will to Believe (1897): William James   337
   Socializing Intelligence (1935): John Dewey   340
   Education (1922, 1934, 1938): John Dewey   341

5. LOGICAL POSITIVISM AND LOGICAL EMPIRICISM   343
   Logical Empiricism (1947): Herbert Feigl   343

CHAPTER XV. CRITICAL INTELLECTUALS IN A MASS CULTURE 348

1. A Pale, Bleeding Past and a Coarse Modernity 352
   The Exile Returns (1907): Henry James 353
   A Generation of Money Slaves (1894): George Santayana 354

2. Toward the Wasteland 355
   The Dynamo and the Virgin (1907): Henry Adams 356

3. The First World War and the Lost Generation 358
   A Farewell to Arms (1929): Ernest Hemingway 359
   An American Scandal: The Scopes Trial (1925): H. L.
   Mencken 361
4. Science and Modern Pessimism 362
   Civilization and Its Discontents (1930): Sigmund Freud 363
   The Spiritual Iconoclasm of Modern Science (1929):
   Joseph Wood Krutch 364

5. Protest and Affirmation in the Depression Years 364
   Portrait of a Hero, Eugene Debs (1930): John Dos Passos 365

6. The Threat of Authoritarianism and the Experience
   of War 367
   Thomas Wolfe in Nazi Germany (1934) 368
   A Bomber Pilot in World War II (1945): Randall Jarrell 369

7. Another Postwar Generation 369
   The New Conservatism (1956): Peter Viereck on Equality 370
   A Beatnik Protest (1957): Allen Ginsberg 372
   Conformity and the Organization Man (1956): William H.
   Whyte 373
   Problems of Personal Identity (1951): C. Wright Mills on
   the Personality Market 375

CHAPTER XVI: THE TWENTIETH CENTURY: INTERNATIONAL CONFLICTS AND INTERNAL CRISES 377

1. Civil Liberties and National Crises 386
   Espionage Act (1918) 387
   Alien Registration Act (1940) 388

Japanese Relocation Order (1942): Franklin D. Roosevelt 389
Charles Beard Resigns from the Columbia Faculty (1917) 390
Against Loyalty Tests for Teachers (1920): Alfred E. Smith 391
Free Competition in Ideas (1925): Oliver Wendell Holmes 391
Free Speech Limited Only by Clear and Imminent Danger
  (1927): Louis Brandeis 392

2. THE DEPRESSION AND THE NEW DEAL 393
A Spirit of Mutual Self-help (1931): Herbert Hoover 394
The Spread of Government Destroys Initiative (1931):
  Herbert Hoover 395
An Economic Declaration of Rights (1932): Franklin
  Delano Roosevelt 395

3. COMMUNISTS AND FASCISTS 397
A Communist Manifesto (1935): Earl Browder 397
A Case for Fascism (1936): Lawrence Dennis 398

4. THE COLD WAR AND THE LOYALTY CONTROVERSY 399
Menace of Communists and Fellow Travellers (1947):
  J. Edgar Hoover 400
Who Is Loyal to America? (1947): Henry S. Commager 401

5. THE CIVIL RIGHTS STRUGGLE 402
On the Despair and Courage of American Negroes (1902):
  W. E. B. Dubois 404
The Scientific Foundation of Modern Equalitarianism:
  Culture Not Tied to Race (1928): Franz Boas 405
Separate Facilities are Inherently Unequal: *Brown v.
  Board of Education* (1954) 406
The U.S. Commission on Civil Rights: Police Brutality
  (1961) 406
School Segregation (1963): The U.S. Commission on Civil
  Rights 407

6. THE DEMOCRATIC ORDER AND THE THREAT OF NUCLEAR WAR 408
The Choice Between the Quick and the Dead (1946):
  Bernard Baruch 410
Western Democracy vs. Soviet Communism (1949):
  Harry S. Truman 410
A Republican Version of Democracy and World Conflict
  (1949): Robert A. Taft 411
The Journey of a Thousand Miles (1961): John F. Kennedy 412

Chapter I. PURITANISM AND THE ORIGINS OF AMERICAN SOCIETY

FOR THE MOST PART THE PURITANS WERE CHRISTIANS WHO CONTINUED to accept the literal truth of Scripture, to view human history tragically as the age-old conflict of good and evil, and to believe devoutly that the world expressed God's purposes. Secondly, they were children of the Protestant Reformation, students of John Calvin's system as it was interpreted by English and European theologians such as William Ames, William Perkins, and Petrus Ramus. Stress on the doctrines of original sin and predestination created a special Calvinist version of the Christian drama: after Adam's disobedience a hopelessly corrupt humanity deserved nothing less than general damnation, but the infinitely merciful Deity relented and granted salvation through a "covenant of Grace" to men who could never have earned it through their own efforts. God's arbitrary grace made eternal bliss inevitable for a few; man's natural wickedness made hell just as certain a destination for the overwhelming majority; and the merest suggestion that either saint or sinner could alter his lot was a presumptuous denial of Divine Omnipotence and events ordained from the beginning of time.

Finally, the Puritans were Anglicans who wished to set aside the moderate Protestantism of the Elizabethan settlement and work for a "purer" ritual, a simpler church organization, and a greater acceptance of Calvinist ideas. Paradoxically, the Puritans denied that predestination allowed them the luxury of fatalism and were activists who exerted much influence in England and still more in America where their holy commonwealth was actually established. God's covenant with Abraham granted grace and salvation only to a few but it bound all men to strive for a Godly state and church. Although New England church membership was restricted to the saints, all men were obliged to attend church. The predestined damnation of the vast majority did not relieve them from obligation to observe righteous ethical and civic rules.

Puritan society as viewed by scholars bears little resemblance to many popular notions of the New England way. One common image reveals the Puritan as a somber, black-robed revivalist specializing in the prohibition of pleasures—a description that hardly fits the historical New Englander of crimson cloaks and lace collars who drank fantastic quantities of raw rum at ministerial ordinations and decorated his home as lavishly as fortune and law permitted. Patriotic orators inevitably present the Puritans as advocates of religious toleration and individual liberty. This description is even more inaccurate for an aristocratically oriented society which regulated intensively the public and private lives of all citizens and vigorously persecuted Quakers, Baptists, Antinomians, and Arminians.

Puritanism was a complex and demanding way of life with a series of very narrow paths on which men were told to seek signs of grace but were cautioned to avoid a sense of certainty about salvation, to deny the belief in man's free will (Arminianism) while rejecting "surrender" to religious intoxication (Antinomianism), to pursue their occupations vigorously without forgetting that the greater glory of God was the end of human existence, to realize that true knowledge of salvation was subjective but to attempt an objective establishment of their election through public confessions before church members, to prepare for grace while remembering the general inability to achieve it. These attitudes and tensions bred introspection, an iron self-discipline, and a sense of moral superiority.

However, Puritan piety was difficult to sustain beyond the first generation, and a slackening of religious controls became evident during the second generation (in 1662 the half-way covenant permitted the children of church members to become partial members without public confessions). Despite the decline in piety many Puritan elements persisted for generations and were extremely important in the formation of the American character. Attitudes as diverse as the extremely high popular regard for the businessman, the conception of government as a necessary evil rooted in man's faults, and popular hostility toward many forms of serious art and music all have connections with the Puritan strain. For that matter, representative government, American individualism, national styles of nonconformity and spontaneity, basic literary traditions, and a great many other elements of American life are partly derived from Puritanism.

1. The New England Zion

The verbal war of several centuries over the respective roles of economic, social, and religious motives in Puritan immigration to the New World shows no signs of ending. The immigrants themselves had a strong sense of mission and tended to stress religious motives. In America they tried to create apart from a depraved world a truly Christian commonwealth, a "new Zion," a "city set upon the hill," as an instrument of God's plans for the climax of human history and what might very well be the last act of the Christian tragedy. Later ideas about the destiny of a virtuous and democratic America in relation to a corrupt and declining Europe were derived in part from Puritan attitudes. AUTHORS: John Winthrop (1588–1649), a Suffolk squire and lawyer, was a pioneer governor of Massachusetts Bay. Cotton Mather (1663–1728), minister, teacher, scholar, scientist, a member of the Royal Society, and a grandson of a founder, wrote histories in which he celebrated the virtues of the pioneers and mourned the passing of the religious zeal which had marked the lives of the early settlers. SELECTIONS: "Motives For Immigration" from a Winthrop manuscript of 1629. "The Holy Commonwealth" from a Winthrop sermon, "A Modell of Christian Charity," preached in 1630 during the journey to the New World. "The Puritan Place in Christian History" from Mather's *Magnalia Christi Americana* (*The Ecclesiastical History of New England*, 1702).

MOTIVES FOR IMMIGRATION (1629):
JOHN WINTHROP

Particular Considerations in the case of J.W.

First It is come to that issue as the success of the plantation depends upon his going for the chief supporters (upon whom the rest depends) will not stir without him.

Secondly His means here are so shortened (now three of his sons being come to age have drawn away the one half of his estate) as he shall not be able to continue in that place and employment where he now is, his ordinary charge being still as great almost as when his means was double.

Thirdly He acknowledgeth a satisfactory calling outward from some of the chief of the plantation, [and] inward by the inclination of his own heart to the work, and both [are] approved by godly and judicious divines (whereof some have the most interest in him) and there is in this the like immediate call from the King, as was to his former employment.

Fourthly If he let pass this opportunity, That talent which God hath bestowed upon him for public service is like to be buried.

Fifthly His wife and such of his Children as are at years and discretion are voluntarily disposed to the same course.

REASONS FOR JUSTIFYING THE PLANTATION. . . .

First, It will be a service to the Church of great consequence to carry the Gospel into those parts of the world. . . .

Second, All other Churches of Europe are brought to desolation . . . for which the Lord begins already to frown upon us, do threaten us fearfully, and who knows but that god hath provided this place to be a refuge for many whom he means to save out of the general calamity, and seeing the Church hath no place left to fly into but the wilderness what better work can there be, then to go before and provide Tabernacles and food for her, against she cometh thither.

Third, This land grows weary of her Inhabitants, so as man who is the most precious of all creatures is here more vile and base then the Earth we Tread upon and of less price among us, then a horse or a sheep, masters are forced by authority to entertain servants, parents to maintain their own children. . . .

Fourth, The whole earth is the Lords Garden and he hath given it to the sons of men. . . .

Fifth, We are grown to that height of intemperance in all excess of riot, as no mans estate almost will suffice to keep sail with his equals, and he who fails herein must live in scorn and contempt, hence it comes that all arts and trades are carried in that deceitful and unrighteous course, as it is almost impossible for a good and upright man to maintain his charge and live comfortably in any of them. . . .

THE HOLY COMMONWEALTH (1630): JOHN WINTHROP

For the persons, we are a company professing ourselves fellow members of Christ, in which respect only, though we were absent from each other many miles, and had our employments as far distant, yet we ought to account ourselves knit together by this bond of love, and live in the exercise of it, if we would have comfort of our being in Christ. . . .

The end is to improve our lives to do more service to the Lord, the comfort and increase of the body of Christ whereof we are members, that ourselves and posterity may be the better preserved from the common corruptions of this evil world, to serve the Lord and work out our salvation under the power and purity of His holy ordinances. . . .

Thus stands the cause between God and us: we are entered into covenant with Him for this work; we have taken out a commission, the Lord hath given us leave to draw our own articles. We have professed to enterprise these actions upon these . . . ends; we have hereupon besought Him of favor and blessing. Now if the Lord shall please to hear us and bring us in peace to the place we desire, then hath He ratified this covenant and sealed our Commission, [and] will expect a strict performance of the articles contained in it. But if we shall neglect the observation of these articles which are the ends we have propounded, and dissembling with our God, shall fall to embrace this present world and prosecute our carnal intentions, seeking great things for ourselves and our posterity, the Lord will surely break out in wrath against us. . . .

We must delight in each other, make others' conditions our own, rejoice together, mourn together, labor and suffer together; always having before our eyes our commission and community in the work, our community as members of the same body. So shall we keep the unity of the spirit in the bond of peace, the Lord will be our God and delight to dwell among us, as His own people, and will command a blessing upon us in all our ways, so that we shall see much more of His wisdom, power, goodness, and truth than formerly we have been acquainted with. We shall find that the God of Israel is among us, when ten of us shall be able to resist a thousand of our enemies, when He shall make us a praise and glory, that men shall say of succeeding plantations: "The Lord make it like that of New England." For we must consider that we shall be as a city upon a hill, the eyes of all people are upon us. So that if we shall deal falsely with our God in this work we have undertaken, and· so cause Him to withdraw His present help from us, we shall be made a story and a byword through the world: We shall open the mouths of enemies to speak evil of the ways of God and all professors for God's sake; we shall shame the faces of many of God's worthy servants, and cause their prayers to be turned into curses upon us, till we be consumed out of the good land whither we are going. . . .

THE PURITAN PLACE IN CHRISTIAN HISTORY (1702): COTTON MATHER

I write the Wonders of the Christian Religion, flying from the Depravations of Europe, to the American Strand: And, assisted by the Holy Author of that Religion, I do, with all Conscience of Truth, required therein by Him, who is the Truth itself, Report the Wonderful Displays of His Infinite Power, Wisdom, Goodness, and Faithfulness, wherewith His Divine Providence hath Irradiated an Indian Wilderness. . . .

The Sum of the Matter is, That from the very Beginning of the Reformation in the English Nation, there hath always been a Generation of Godly Men, desirous to pursue the Reformation of Religion, according to the Word of God, and the Example of the best Reformed Churches. . . .

And there hath been another Generation of Men, who have still employed the Power which they have generally still had in their Hands, not only to stop the Progress of the Desired Reformation, but also, with Innumerable Vexations, to Persecute those that most Heartily wished well unto it. . . .

It is the History of these Protestants, that is here attempted: Protestants that highly honoured and affected The Church of England, and humbly Petition to be a Part of it: But by the Mistake of a few powerful Brethren, driven to seek a place for the Exercise of the Protestant Religion, according to the Light of their Consciences, in the Desarts of America. . . .

The First Age was the Golden Age: To return unto That, will make a Man a Protestant, and I may add, a Puritan. 'Tis possible, That our Lord Jesus Christ carried some Thousands of Reformers into the Retirements of an American Desart, on purpose, that, with an opportunity granted unto many of his Faithful Servants, to enjoy the precious Liberty of their Ministry, tho' in the midst of many Temptations all their days, He might there, To them first, and then By them, give a Specimen of many Good Things, which He would have His Churches elsewhere aspire and arise unto: And This being done, He knows not whether there be not All done, that New-England was planted for; and whether the Plantation may not, soon after this, Come to Nothing. . . .

And let us humbly speak it, it shall be Profitable for you to consider the Light, which from the midst of this Outer Darkness, is now to be Darted over unto the other side of the Atlantick Ocean. But we must therewithal ask your Prayers, that these Golden Candlesticks may not quickly be Removed out of their place!

But whether New England may Live any where else or no, it must Live in our History!. . . .

2. Covenant Theology

In the new world Zion religious thought was often described as the central human activity, and ordinary people listened for hours with close attention to extremely intricate theological reasoning. For New Englanders the conception of God's terrible power burned brightly; truly He sustained every sparrow in flight. Covenant theology (see the first page of the introduction to Chapter I) helped to span the almost paralyzing distance between a sovereign and omnipotent God and his hopelessly weak and corrupt creatures. Through the covenant (compact), God intervened in human history to prevent all men from going to the universal damnation which corrupt human nature merited as a result of Adam's original sin. Thus Abraham and all of God's Saints to the end of time, elected from amongst the masses by the inscrutable will of the Deity, were assured of irresistible and saving grace. AUTHORS: Urian Oakes (1631–1681), Harvard graduate, teacher, and President, had teaching and preaching careers in both old and New England. Thomas Shepard (1605–1649), one of the most popular and powerful ministers in early New England, was a militant champion of theological orthodoxy. SELECTIONS: "God's Sovereignty Over the World" from Oakes' *The Sovereign Efficacy of Divine Providence* (1677). "The Covenant of Grace; God's Compact with Man" from Shepard's *A Defense of the Answer made unto the Nine Questions* . . . (1651).

GOD'S SOVEREIGNTY OVER THE WORLD (1677): URIAN OAKES

Though God is able to give Being to things in an immediate way, yet it is his pleasure in the course of his Providence to use Means, and to produce many things by the mediation and Agency of second Causes, and so gives casual virtue and ability to these and those things in order to the producing of such and such Effects. It is a good observation, that the Lord is pleased, not through any defect of power in Himself but out of the abundance of his goodness to communicate casual power and virtue to his Creatures, and to honour them with that Dignity that they may be his Instruments, by which he will produce these and those Effects: whereby He takes them, as it were, into partnership and fellowship with Himself in the way of his providential Efficiency, that they may be Underworkers to, yea Co-workers with Himself. . . .

Though the Lord is pleased sometimes upon great and important Occasions, to leave the ordinary Road of Providence, and act beyond and above the usual, stated course of Things; and not to concurre with, and shine upon the endeavours of created Agents, so as to crown them with that success which according to an ordinary course of Providence, might be rationally expected; yet it is not to be imagined that He should ordinarily dispence with the course, and methods of his ordinary Providence: For why then should it be called ordinary? God who is the Lord of Hosts, the great Leader Commander and Ruler of Nature, not only permits, but also effectually commands and causes his whole Militia, ordinarily, to move and act according to their Natures and natural Properties respectively, without countermanding them.

We see here something of the Power, and Greatness, and Glory of God appearing in his Efficiency, whereby He works all in all. . . . In him we live and move, and have our Being. The Counsels of the ablest Statesmen, how rational soever, shall not prosper without him: Ministers, how sufficient soever, pious, learned, industrious, zealous, shall convert no man, edify no man, comfort and establish no man, without Him. I Cor. 3. 6, 7. Though Scholars study hard, they shall make no proficiency without the Blessing of God. The Merchant may trade, and project rationally, and yet shall not grow rich upon it, unless God give him success. . . .

THE COVENANT OF GRACE; GOD'S COMPACT WITH MAN (1651): THOMAS SHEPARD

The blessed God hath evermore delighted to reveal and communicate Himself by way of Covenant. He might have done good to man before his fall, as also since his fall, without binding Himself in the bond of Covenant; Noah, Abraham, and David, Jews, Gentiles, might have had the blessings intended, without any promise or Covenant. But the Lord's heart is so full of love (especially to His own) that it cannot be contained so long within the bounds of secrecy-viz. from God's eternal purpose to the actual accomplishment of good things intended—but it must aforehand overflow and break out into the many streams of a blessed Covenant. The Lord can never get near enough to His people, and thinks He can never get them near enough unto Himself, and therefore unites and binds and fastens them close to Himself, and Himself unto them, by the bonds of a Covenant. . . .

Oh! the depth of God's grace herein: that when sinful man deserves never to have the least good word from Him, that he should open His whole heart and purpose to him in a Covenant; that when he deserves nothing else but separation from God, and to be driven up and down the world as a vagabond, or as dried leaves fallen from our God, that yet the Almighty God cannot be content with it, but must make Himself to us, and us to Himself, more sure and near than ever before! And is not this Covenant then (Christian reader) worth thy looking into and searching after? Surely never was there a time wherein the Lords calls His people to more serious searching into the nature of the Covenant than in these days. . . .

Nay, is not the time come wherein the Lord of hosts seems to have a quarrel against all the world, and especially His churches and people, whom He goes on to waste by the sharpest sword that (almost) was ever drawn out? And is it not the duty of all that have the least spark of holy fear and trembling to ask and search diligently what should be the reason of this sore anger and hot displeasure, before they and theirs be consumed in the burning flames of it? . . .

As particular persons, when they break their Covenant, the Lord therefore breaks out against them: so, when whole churches forsake their Covenant, the Lord therefore doth sorely visit them. . . .

It is true, the Covenant effectually made can never be really broke, yet externally it may. But suppose God's churches were in greatest peace, and had a blessed rest from all their labors round about them: yet what is the child's position, but his legacy left him, written with the finger of God his father, in the New Covenant, and the blood of Jesus Christ his redeemer, in His last will and testament? What is a Christian's comfort, and where doth it chiefly lie, but in this: that the Lord hath made with him an everlasting Covenant, in all things stablished and sure? Which were the last breathing of the sweet singer of Israel, and the last bubblings up of the joy of his heart (II Sam. 23:5). . . .

As all good things are conveyed to God's people not barely by common providence but by special Covenant (Isa. 16:8, 9), so all the evils they meet with in this world (if in them the face of God's anger appears), upon narrow search, will be found to arise from breach of Covenant, more or less. So that if it be the great cause of all of the public calamities of the church and people of God, and those calamities are already begun, and God's hand is stretched out still—was there then ever a more seasonable time and hour to study the Covenant, and so see the sin, repent of it, and at last to lay hold of God's rich grace. . .

The Church of God is therefore bound to bless God much for this food in season, and for the holy judicious and learned labors of this aged, experienced and precious servant of Christ Jesus, who hath taken much pains to discover—and that not in words and allegories but in the demonstration and evidence of the Spirit—the great mystery of godliness wrapped up in the Covenant, and hath now fully opened sundry knotty questions concerning the same, which happily have not been brought so fully to light until now. Which cannot but be of singular and seasonable use, to prevent apostasies from the simplicity of the Covenant and Gospel of Christ. The sermons were preached in the remote ends of the earth and, as it were, set under a bushel, a church more remote from the numerous society of others of the saints; if now, therefore, the light be set upon a hill, 'tis where it should stand, and where Christ surely would have it put. The good Lord enlighten the minds of all those who seek for the truth by this and such like helps; and the Lord enlighten the whole world with His glory, even with the glory of His Covenant, grace and love, that His people hereby may be sealed up daily unto all fulness of assurance and peace, in these evil times. . . .

3. Puritanism and Politics

Almost as important to the Puritans as the covenant of grace were the civil covenants among men and with God which helped to create a strong sense of community. The New Englanders built an aristocratic society and took a middle course in opposition to both popular rule and absolutism. Although ministers had an enormous civil influence as political advisors, they did not hold office, and New England was not strictly speaking a theocracy. The religious aristocracy of God's saints and the political aristocracy of gentlemen (a status carefully defined by law according to birth, wealth, and occupation) were not identical; Cotton Mather's slave, for example, was a saint. Despite early aristocratic beliefs, New England's long-range development was, in a manner still imperfectly understood, toward constitutional republicanism. Some of the elements in that evolutionary process were the congregational pattern of self-rule, the gradual decline of aristocratic power, the growth of representative government in town and colonial institutions, and the development of a natural rights ideology. AUTHORS: John Cotton (1584–1652), perhaps the most learned minister in the Great Migration, recovered quickly from the taint of association with the heretical Anne Hutchinson and continued to function as a member of the ruling elite. John Winthrop (1588–1649) defended his concept of responsible, aristocratic government even after being thrust out of the governorship. John Wise (1652–1725), an able pamphleteer in the cause of congregational freedom, led a celebrated effort to resist a provincial tax in 1687. SELECTIONS: "Democracy An Evil" from a Cotton letter to Lords Say and Seal in 1636. "Aristocracy Ordained by God" from a Winthrop sermon, "A Modell of Christian Charity" (1630). "The Development Of A Natural Rights Ideology" from Wise's Vindication of the Government of New England (1717).

DEMOCRACY AN EVIL (1636): JOHN COTTON

Democracy, I do not conceyve that ever God did ordeyne as a fitt government eyther for church or commonwealth. If the people be governors, who shall be governed? As for monarchy, and aristocracy, they are both of them clearly approved, and directed in scripture, yet so as referreth the soveraigntie to himselfe, and setteth up Theocracy in both, as the best forme of government in the commonwealth, as well as in the church. . . .

The church submitteth itselfe to all the lawes and ordinances of men, in what commonwealth soever they come to dwell. But it is one thing, to submit unto what they have noe calling to reforme: another thing, voluntarily to ordeyne a forme of government, which to the best discerning of many of us (for I speake not of myselfe) is expressly contrary to rule. Nor neede your Lordship feare (which yet I speake with submission to your Lordships better judgment) that this course will lay such a foundation, as nothing but a mere democracy can be built upon it. Bodine confesseth, that though it be status popularis, *where a people choose their owne governors;** yet the government is not a democracy, if it be administred, not by the people, but by the governors, whether one (for then it is a monarchy, though elective) or by many for then (as you know) it is aristocracy. In which respect it is, that church government is justly denyed to be democratical, though the people choose their officers and rulers.

Nor neede wee feare, that this course will, in time, cast the commonwealth into distractions, and popular confusions. For (under correction) these three things doe not undermine, but doe mutually and strongly mainteyne one another (even those three which wee principally aime at) authority in magistrates, liberty in people, purity in the church. Purity, preserved in the church, will preserve well ordered liberty in the people, and both of them establish well-ballanced authority in the magistrates. God is the author of all these three, and neyther is himselfe the God of confusion, nor are his wayes the wayes of confusion, but of peace. . . .

ARISTOCRACY ORDAINED BY GOD (1630): JOHN WINTHROP

God Almightie in his most holy and wise providence hath soe disposed of the Condicion of mankinde, as in all times some must be rich some poore, some highe and eminent in power and dignitie; others meane and in subjeccion.

The Reason Hereof.

1. Reas: First, to hold conformity with the rest of his workes, being delighted to shewe forthe the glory of his wisdome in the variety and differance of the Creatures and the glory of his power, in ordering all these differances for the preservacion and good of the whole, and the glory of his

---

* The general tenor of Cotton's argument was to express his faith in "aristocracy," but these seven words suggest the entering wedge of representative government.

greatnes that as it is the glory of princes to have many officers, soe this great King will have many Stewards counting himself more honoured in dispenceing his guifts to man by man, then if hee did it by his owne immediate hand.

2. Reas: Secondly, That he might have the more occasion to manifest the worke of his Spirit: first, upon the wicked in moderating and restraineing them: soe that the riche and mighty should not eate upp the poore, nor the poore, and dispised rise upp against their superiours, and shake off theire yoake; . . . in the regenerate in exercising his graces in them, as in the greate ones, theire love, mercy, gentlenes, temperance etc., in the poore and inferiour sorte, theire faithe patience, obedience etc:

3. Reas: Thirdly, That every man might have need of other, and from hence they might be all knitt more nearly together in the Bond of brotherly affeccion: from hence it appeares plainely that noe man is made more honourable than another or more wealthy etc., out of any perticuler and singuler respect to himselfe but for the glory of his Creator and the Common good of the Creature, Man; Therefore God still rescues the propperty of these guifts to himselfe as Ezek: 16:17. he there calls wealthe his gold and his silver etc. Prov: 3:9. he claimes theire service as his due honour the Lord with theire riches etc. . . .

THE DEVELOPMENT OF A NATURAL RIGHTS IDEOLOGY (1717): JOHN WISE

I shall consider man in a state of natural being, as a freeborn subject under the crown of heaven, and owing homage to no one but God himself. . . .

That God has established the law of nature as the general rule of government is . . . illustrable from the many sanctions in providence, and from the peace and guilt of conscience in them that either obey or violate the law of nature. . . .

The native liberty of man's nature implies a faculty of doing or omitting things according to the direction of his judgment. But in a more special meaning this liberty does not consist in a loose and ungovernable freedom or in an unbounded license of acting. . . .

And so every man must be conceived to be perfectly in his own power and disposal, and not to be controlled by the authority of any other. And thus every man must be acknowledged equal to every man, since all subjection and all command are equally banished on both sides; and, considering all men thus at liberty, every man has a prerogative to judge for himself, namely, what shall be most for his behoof, happiness, and well-being.

The third capital immunity belonging to man's nature is an equality amongst men, which is not to be denied by the law of nature, till man has resigned himself with all his rights for the sake of a civil state, and then his personal liberty and equality is to be cherished and preserved to the highest degree, as will consist with all just distinctions amongst men of honor, and shall be agreeable with the public good. For man has a high valuation of himself, and the passion seems to lay its first foundation (not in pride, but) really in the high and admirable frame and constitution of human nature. The word man, says my author, is thought to carry somewhat of dignity in its sound; and we commonly make use of this as the most proper and prevailing argument against a rude insulter, namely, I am not a beast or a dog, but am a man as well as yourself. Since, then, human nature agrees equally with all persons, and since no one can live a sociable life with another that does not own or respect him as a man, it follows, as a command of the law of nature, that every man esteem and treat another as one who is naturally his equal, or who is a man as well as he. There be many popular or plausible reasons that greatly illustrate this equality, namely, that we all derive our being from one stock, the same common father of the human race. . . .

4. Heresy and Witchcraft

New Englanders, who despised religious toleration even more than political democracy, denied that heretics should be allowed to serve Satan's cause and oppose God's truth. Anne Hutchinson, Roger Williams, the Quakers, and the Salem witches were dealt with decisively and harshly. The zeal which often accompanies an ardent belief in a set of absolute truths was enhanced by the idea that God whose "general Providence" sustains the world (see the Oakes selection in Section 1), achieved His specific purposes through "special providences"—smallpox as a punishment, a broken leg as a warning, a good crop as a reward. Satan was also present in the world and the Puritans, as readily as inhabitants of the Old World, believed in witchcraft. The celebrated Salem trials of 1692 resulted in the execution of twenty persons and the terrorization of a town, but afterward many of the judges and jurors followed Samuel Sewall in apologizing for their actions. A humble public confession to so grievous a sin from so proud a man as Sewall must have been a very difficult matter. Both the Puritan conscience and Puritan intolerance left their marks on American culture. As the clashing views of Nathaniel Ward and Roger Williams suggest, the Puritans did not invariably agree. Williams and Anne Hutchinson belonged no less to Puritanism than did Ward and John Winthrop. The modern student, however, must not fall into the error of supposing that Williams held "modern" views on religious toleration or that he would have urged the toleration of doctrines known to be "false." Two points should be stressed from the complex position of Williams: men often brought great frailty to the search for truth; and secular power was too profane an instrument to rule the world of sacred things. AUTHORS: Nathaniel Ward (1578–1652), a lawyer and a minister, drew up the Massachusetts Body of Liberties in 1641. John Winthrop (1588–1649) was the leading Massachusetts governor in the first generation. Roger Williams (1604–1683) had sharp clashes with ministers and political leaders over his extreme position on the independence of each congregation, criticism of persecution for the "cause of conscience," and insistence that the settlers must buy land from the Indians. Forced to leave Salem, he founded the colony of Providence in what was to become Rhode Island. Increase Mather (1639–1723), Cotton Mather's father, a leading minister and a Harvard president, secured a renewal of the Massachusetts Charter after the Glorious Revolution of 1689. Thomas Brattle (1658–1713) was a mathematician and a Harvard treasurer. Samuel Sewall (1652–1730), businessman and jurist, served as a judge during the Salem trials. SELECTIONS: "Against Toleration" from Ward's The Simple Cobbler of Aggawam (1647). "The Antinomian Heresy of Anne Hutchinson" from Winthrop's Journals, 1637. "Against Persecution" from Williams' The Bloudy Tenant, of Persecution, for the Cause of Conscience, discussed in a Conference between Truth and Peace (1644). "Remarkable Providences" from Mather's Remarkable Providences (1684). "Against the Salem Witchcraft Trials," from a Brattle manuscript, "A Full and Candid Account of the Delusion called Witchcraft," 1692. "The Puritan Conscience: A Judge of Witches Repents" from Sewall's Diary, 1697.

AGAINST TOLERATION (1647): NATHANIEL WARD

The Truths of God are the Pillars of the world, whereon States and Churches may stand quiet if they will; if they will not, Hee can easily shake them off into delusions, and distractions enough.

Satan is now in his passions, he feeles his passion approaching; hee loves to fish in royled waters. . . . Civill Commotions make roome for uncivill practises: Religious mutations, for irreligious opinions: Change of Aire, discovers corrupt bodies; Reformation of Religion, unsound mindes.

First, such as have given or taken any unfriendly reports of us New-English, should doe well to recollect themselves. Wee have beene reputed a Colluvies of wild Opinionists, swarmed into a remote wildernes to find elbow-roome for our phanatick Doctrines and practices: I trust our diligence past, and constant sedulity against such persons and courses, will plead better things for us. I dare take upon me, to bee the Herauld of New-England so farre, as to proclaime to the world, in the name of our Colony, that all Familists, Antinomians, Anabaptists, and other Entrusiasts shall have free Liberty to keepe away from us, and such as will come to be gone as fast as they can, the sooner the better.

Secondly, I dare averre, that God doth no where in his word tolerate Christian States, to give Toleration to such adversaries of his Truth, if they have power in their hands to suppresse them.

Here is lately brought us an extract of a Magna Charta, so called, compiled between the Sub-planters of a West-Indian Island; whereof the first Article of constipulation, firmly provides free stable-room and litter for all kinde of consciences, be they never so dirty or jadish; making it actionable, yea, treasonable, to disturbe any man in his Religion, or to discommend it, whatever it be. . . .

If the devill might have his free option, I beleeve he would ask nothing else, but liberty to enfranchize all false Religions, and to embondage the true; nor should hee need: It is much to be feared, that laxe Tolerations upon State-pretences and planting necessities, will be the next subtle Stratagem he will spread to distate the Truth of God and supplant the peace of the Churches. . . .

The power of all Religion and Ordinances, lies in their purity; their purity in their simplicity; then are mixtures pernicious. I lived in a City, where a Papist preached in one Church, a Lutheran in another, a Calvinist in a third; a Lutheran one part of the day, a Calvinist the other, in the same Pulpit: the Religion of that place was but motly and meagre, their affections Leopard-like. . . .

Such as are least able, are most busie to pudder in the rubbish, and to raise dust in the eye of more steady Repayrers.

THE ANTINOMIAN HERESY OF ANNE HUTCHINSON (1637): JOHN WINTHROP

She advanced doctrines and opinions which involved the colony in disputes and contentions; and being improved, to civil as well as religious purposes, had like to have produced ruin both to church and state. . . .

Besides the meetings for public worship on the Lord's day, the stated lecture every Thursday in Boston, and other occasional lectures in other towns, there were frequent private meetings of the brethren of the churches for religious exercises. Mrs. Hutchinson thought fit to set up a meeting of the sisters also, where she repeated the sermons preached the Lord's day before, adding her remarks and expositions. Her lectures made much noise, and sixty or eighty principal women attended them. At first, they were generally approved of. After some time, it appeared she had distinguished the ministers and members of churches through the country; a small part of them under covenant of grace, the rest under a covenant of works.* The whole colony was soon divided into two parties; and however distant one party was from the other in principle, they were still more so in affection. The two capital errors, with which she was charged, were these, "That the Holy Ghost dwells personally in a justified person; and that nothing of sanctification can help to evidence to believers their justification." From these two, a great number of others were said to flow, which were enumerated and condemned at a synod held the next year. . . . The town and country were distracted with these subtleties, and every man and woman who had brains enough to form some imperfect conceptions of them inferred and maintained some other point, such as these: "a man is justified before he believes; faith is no cause of justification; and if faith be before justification, it is only a passive faith, an empty vessel, etc., and assurance is by immediate revelation only." The fear of God and love of our neighbor seemed to be laid by and out of the question. . . .

Whilst these contentions were thus increasing within, the Pequods, the most warlike of all the Indians, were plotting destruction from without. . . .

Towards the end of the year religious heats became more violent, and the civil affairs more sensibly affected by them. The people of Boston, in general, were in favour of Mr. Vane, the governor, the rest of the towns, in general, for Mr. Winthrop, the deputy governor.

Mrs. Hutchinson was next called to her trial, before the whole court and many of the elders. . . . Her sentence upon record stands thus: "Mrs. Hutchinson, the wife of Mr. William Hutchinson, being convicted for traducing the ministers and their ministry in the country, she declared voluntarily her revelations, and that she should be delivered and the court ruined with their posterity, and thereupon was banished. . . ."

---

* The "covenant of works," a very heretical doctrine, generally meant the idea that man could by good works at least partly earn his salvation. Such a notion was taken as a challenge to orthodox insistence on man's depravity and God's power.

AGAINST PERSECUTION (1644):
ROGER WILLIAMS

PEACE: Deare Truth, I have two sad Complaints:

First, the most sober of thy Witnesses, that dare to plead thy Cause, how are they charged to be mine Enemies, contentious, turbulent, seditious?

Secondly, Thine Enemies, though they speake and raile against thee, though they outragiously pursue, imprison, banish, kill thy faithfull Witnesses, yet how is all vermillion'd o're for Justice 'gainst the Heretics? . . . He that kills, and hee that's killed, they both cry out, It is for God, and for their conscience. . . .

TRUTH: Deare Peace . . . tis true. . . .

Yet strife must be distinguished: It is necessary or unnecessary, godly or ungodly, Christian or unchristian, etc.

It is unnecessary, unlawful, dishonourable, ungodly, unchristian, in most cases in the world, for there is a possibility of keeping sweet Peace in most cases, and if it be possible, it is the expresse command of God that Peace be kept, Rom. 13.

Againe, it is necessary, honourable, Godly, etc. . . . to defend the innocent . . . and to rescue the oppressed. . . .

[Peace hears] the cry of the whole earth, made drunke with the bloud of its inhabitants, slaughtering each other in their blinded zeale, for Conscience, for Religion, against the Catholickes, against the Lutherans, etc. . . .

TRUTH: Sweet Peace, what hast thou there?

PEACE: Arguments against persecution for cause of Conscience. . . . These Arguments against . . . persecution [were written] in milke, tending to soule nourishment, even for Babes and Sucklings in Christ. It was in milke, spiritually white, pure, and innocent. . . .

It was in milke, soft, meeke, peaceable, and gentle, tending both to the peace of soules, and the peace of States and Kingdomes. . . .

REMARKABLE PROVIDENCES (1684):
INCREASE MATHER

Such Divine judgements, tempests, floods, earthquakes, thunders as are unusual, strange apparitions, or whatever else shall happen that is prodigious, witchcrafts, diabolical possessions, remarkable judgements upon noted sinners, eminent deliverances, and answers of prayer, are to be reckoned among illustrious providences. . . .

And as the experience of other ages and places of the world, so the things which Divine Providence hath permitted and ordered to come to pass amongst ourselves, if the Scriptures were silent, make it manifest beyond all contradiction, that there are devils infesting this lower world. . . .

Sometimes Providence permits the devil himself (without the use of instruments) to molest the houses of some, as a punishment for sin committed, most commonly . . . for the sin of murder. . . .

That there have been . . . witches the following arguments do manifest.

1. The argument by many insisted on from the Scriptures is irrefragable: therein witchcrafts are forbidden. . . .

2. Experience has too often made it manifest that there are such in the world as hold a correspondence with hell. There have bin known wizards; yea, such as have taught others what ceremonies they are to use in maintaining communion with devils. . . .

3. There have been many in the world who have, upon conviction, confessed themselves guilty of familiarity with the devil. . . .

AGAINST THE SALEM WITCHCRAFT TRIALS (1692): THOMAS BRATTLE

The great cry of many of our neighbours now is, What, will you not believe the confessors? Will you not believe men and women who confess that they have signed to the devil's book? that they were baptized by the devil; and that they were at the mock-sacrament once and again? What! will you not believe that this is witchcraft, and that such and such men are witches, although the confessors do own and assert it? . . .

1. The afflicted persons are brought into court; and after much patience and pains taken with them, do take their oaths, that the prisoner at the bar did afflict them: And here I think it very observable, that often, when the afflicted do mean and intend only the appearance and shape of such an one, (say G. Proctor), yet they positively swear that G. Proctor did afflict them; and they have been allowed so to do; as though there was no real difference between G. Proctor and the shape of G. Proctor. . . .

2. The confessors do declare what they know of the said prisoner; and some of the confessors are allowed to give their oaths; a thing which I believe was never heard of in this world; that such as confess themselves to be witches, to have renounced God and Christ, and all that is sacred,

should yet be allowed and ordered to swear by the name of the great God! This indeed seemeth to me to be a gross taking of God's name in vain. . . .

3. Whoever can be an evidence against the prisoner at the bar is ordered to come into court; and here it scarce ever fails but that evidences, of one nature and another, are brought in, though, I think, all of them altogether alien to the matter of indictment; for they none of them do respect witchcraft upon the bodies of the afflicted, which is the alone matter of charge in the indictment.

4. They are searched by a jury; and as to some of them, the jury brought in, that on such or such a place there was a preternatural excrescence. And I wonder what person there is, whether man or woman, of whom it cannot be said but that, in some part of their body or other, there is a preternatural excrescence. The term is a very general and inclusive term.

Some . . . are very forward to censure and condemn the poor prisoner at the bar, because he sheds no tears; but such betray great ignorance in the nature of passion, and as great heedlessness as to common passages of a man's life. . . .

Now, that the justices have thus far given ear to the devil, I think may be mathematically demonstrated to any man of common sense: And for the demonstration and proof hereof, I desire, only, that these two things may be duly considered, viz.

1. That several persons have been apprehended purely upon the complaints of these afflicted, to whom the afflicted were perfect strangers, and had not the least knowledge of imaginable, before they were apprehended.

2. . . . I think it will appear evident to any one, that the devil's information is the fundamental testimony that is gone upon in the apprehending of the aforesaid people. . . .

What will be the issue of these troubles, God only knows; I am afraid that ages will not wear off that reproach and those stains which these things will leave behind them upon our land. I pray God pity us, humble us, forgive us, and appear mercifully for us in . . . our . . . distress. . . .

THE PURITAN CONSCIENCE; A JUDGE OF WITCHES REPENTS (1697): SAMUEL SEWALL

Jan. 14, 1697. Copy of the Bill I put up on the Fast day; giving it to Mr. Willard as he pass'd by, and standing up at the reading of it, and bowing when finished; in the Afternoon.

Samuel Sewall, sensible of the reiterated strokes of God upon himself and family; and being sensible, that as to the Guilt contracted upon the opening of the late commission of Oyer and Terminer at Salem (to which the order for this Day relates) he is, upon many accounts, more concerned than any that he knows of, Desires to take the Blame and shame of it [sentencing the witches], Asking pardon of men, And especially desiring prayers that God, who has an Unlimited Authority, would pardon that sin and all other his sins; personal and Relative: And according to his infinite Benignity, and Sovereignty, Not Visit the sin of him, or of any other, upon himself or any of his, nor upon the Land: But that He would powerfully defend him against all Temptations to Sin, for the future; and vouchsafe him the efficacious, saving Conduct of his Word and Spirit.

5. The Arts, the Sciences, and Puritanism

Puritan preoccupation with an intense, highly intellectualized, and carefully controlled religious life generated an atmosphere which was not very favorable to aesthetic achievement. In the fine arts the Puritans created little, appreciated little, and devised means to keep "sensual" elements out of church rituals and buildings. Still, New England craftsmen who sought only to make the most useful objects from the best available materials created houses, furniture, and kitchenware which have been much admired in recent times—probably because the attitudes of the colonial craftsman bear a resemblance to the dominant aesthetic approach of twentieth-century architects and interior designers ("form follows function"). Some of the Puritan preachers and writers were aesthetic cousins of the craftsmen in that they also created beauty as an accidental by-product of utilitarian activities. The preachers disliked "affecting carnal eloquence," wished to express themselves in simple precise language, and created America's first literary tradition, the plain style, which ultimately bore fruit in the magnificent prose of Thoreau and Emerson. Despite their dislike of "sensual" art and "carnal" eloquence (which had a profound influence on American literature and art), the Puritans did not wish to destroy the English humanism in which they had been reared. In a similar fashion, they wished to preserve existing knowledge of the physical universe and to join the important new explorations in natural philosophy (science). Increase Mather knew Newtonian physics; Cotton Mather was a member of the Royal Society; the Mathers did pioneering work in the introduction of inoculation; and other distinguished amateurs helped to make New Englanders receptive to science. AUTHORS:

Thomas Hooker (1586–1647), an eloquent preacher with a commanding personality, was the founder and virtual ruler of the early Connecticut settlements. Cotton Mather (1663–1728) had a life-long interest in natural philosophy. SELECTIONS: "The Plain Style" from Hooker's *A Survey of the Summe of Church Discipline* (1648). "Humanism And Puritanism" from Mather's *Manuductio ad Ministerium* (1726). "Natural Philosophy Friendly to Religion" from Mather's *The Christian Philosopher* (1721).

THE PLAIN STYLE (1648): THOMAS HOOKER

That the discourse comes forth in such a homely dresse and coarse habit, the Reader must be desired to consider, It comes out of the wildernesse, where curiosity is not studied. Planters if they can provide cloth to go warm they leave the cutts and lace to those that study to go fine.

As it is beyond my skill, so I professe it is beyond my care to please the nicenesse of mens palates, with any quaintnesse of language. They who covet more sauce then meat, they must provide cooks to their minde. . . .

I could not lavish out in the loosenesse of language, and as the case stands, if I could answer any mans desire in that daintinesse of speech, I would not do the matter that Injury which is now under my hand: *Ornari res ipsa negat.* The substance and solidity of the frame is that, which pleaseth the builder, its the painters work to provide varnish.

If the manner of the discourse should occasion any disrellish in the apprehension of the weaker Reader, because it may seem too Logicall, or Scholasticall, in regard of the terms I use, or the way of dispute that I proceed in, in some places: I have to professe. . . .

That plainesse and perspicuity, both for matter and manner of expression, are the things, that I have conscientiously indeavoured in the whole debate: for I have ever thought writings that come abroad, they are not to dazle, but direct the apprehension of the meanest, and I have accounted it the chiefest part of Judicious learning, to make a hard point easy and familiar in explication. . . .

HUMANISM AND PURITANISM (1726): COTTON MATHER

Poetry, whereof we have now even an Antediluvian piece in our hands, has from the beginning been in such request, that I must needs recommend unto you some acquaintance with it. Though some have had a soul so unmusical, that they have decried all verse as being but a meer playing and fiddling upon words; all versifying, as if it were more unnatural than if we should chuse dancing instead of walking; and rhyme, as if it were but a sort of morisce-dancing with bells; yet I cannot wish you a soul that shall be wholly unpoetical. An old Horace has left us an art of poetry, which you may do well to bestow a perusal on. And besides your lyric hours, I wish you may so far understand an epic poem, that the beauties of an Homer and a Virgil may be discerned with you. . . .

Nevertheless, I cannot but advise you. Withhold thy throat from thirst. Be not so set upon poetry, as to be always poring on the passionate and measured pages. Let not what should be sauce, rather than food for you, engross all your application. Beware of a boundless and sickly appetite for the reading of the poems which now the rickety nation swarms withal; and let not the Circaean cup intoxicate you. But especially preserve the chastity of your soul from the dangers you may incur, by a conversation with muses that are no better than harlots: among which are others besides Ovid's Epistles, which for their tendency to excite and foment impure flames, and cast coals into your bosom, deserve rather to be thrown into the fire, than to be laid before the eye which a covenant should be made withal. Indeed, not merely for the impurities which they convey, but also on some other accounts; the powers of darkness have a library among us, whereof the poets have been the most numerous as well as the most venomous authors. Most of the modern plays, as well as the romances, and novels and fictions, which are a sort of poems, do belong to the catalogue of this cursed library. The plays, I say, in which there are so many passages that have a tendency to overthrow all piety, They are national sins, and therefore call for national plagues; and if God should enter into judgment, all the blood in the nation would not be able to atone for them. . . .

NATURAL PHILOSOPHY FRIENDLY TO RELIGION (1721): COTTON MATHER

The Essays now before us will demonstrate, that Philosophy is no Enemy, but a mighty and wondrous Incentive to Religion: and they will exhibit that Philosophical Religion, which will carry with it a most sensible Character, and victorious Evidence of a reasonable Service. . . . In the Dispositions and Resolutions of Piety thus enkindled, a Man most effectually shews himself a Man, and with unutterable Satisfaction answers the grand End of his Being, which is, To glorify God. He discharges also the Office of a Priest for the Creation. . . . The whole world is indeed a

Temple of God, built and filled by that Almighty Architect; and in this Temple every such one . . . will speak of His Glory. . . .

THE LORD BY WISDOM HAS FOUNDED THE EARTH. A poor Sojourner on the EARTH now thinks it his Duty to behold and admire the WISDOM of his glorious Maker there.

The EARTH, which is the Basis and Support of so many Vegetables and Animals, and yields the alimentary Particles, whereof WATER is the Vehicle, for their Nourishment: . . .

The various Moulds and Soils of the Earth declare the admirable Wisdom of the Creator, in making such a provision for a vast variety of Intentions. GOD SAID, LET THE EARTH BRING FORTH!

. . . It is pretty odd; they who have written DE ARTE COMBINA-TORIA, reckon of now fewer than one hundred and seventy-nine Millions, one thousand and sixty different sorts of Earth: But we may content ourselves with Sir JOHN EVELYN's Enumeration, which is very short of that.

However the VEGETABLES owe not so much of their Life and Growth to the EARTH itself, as to some agreeable Juices or Salts log'd in it. Both Mr. BOYLE and VAN HELMONT, by Experiments, found the Earth scarce at all diminished when PLANTS even TREES, had been for divers Years growing in it.

The STRATA of the Earth, its LAYS and BEDS, afford surprizing Matters of Observation: the OBJECTS lodged in them; the USES made of them; and particularly the PASSAGE they give to SWEET WATERS, as being the COLANDERS [strainers] wherein they are sweetened. It is asserted that these are found all to lie very much according to the Laws of Gravity. . . .

6. *Two Puritan Offspring: Revivalism and Rationalism*

Many Puritan intellectual and social attitudes persisted into the eighteenth century but the decline of religious piety and a series of theological compromises combined to create crisis conditions by the seventeen-thirties. Jonathan Edwards attempted to meet a double challenge by using the physics of Newton and the psychology of John Locke to support traditional Calvinist doctrines and by encouraging emotional preaching to revive religious zeal. Edwards, perhaps the greatest of American theologians, provided new force and formulations for old dogmas after a fashion which thrust his influence through several generations; and he was one of the powerful preachers in that stormy religious revival, the Great

Awakening. Edwards represented both a pinnacle of Puritan intellectual achievement and an approach to religion which was to destroy important elements in Calvinist Congregationalism. The spiritual sons and grand-sons of Edwards were to tear his world in half: revivalists eventually attacked the stress on a complex, distinct, and firmly held set of religious dogmas with a learned ministry to interpret them; and Puritan intellec-tualism provided a path which led to Arminianism, Unitarianism, Deism, and rationalism. Charles Chauncy, appalled by what he considered to be the hysterical excesses of the Great Awakening, was alert to the menace of unlimited emotionalism, but failed to realize that an excess of his own emphasis on reason might threaten both the emotional life and the doc-trinal structure of religion. AUTHORS: Jonathan Edwards (1703–1758), undoubtedly the most able philosopher and theologian of the colonial period, was a minister and, during the closing months of his life, presi-dent of Princeton. Charles Chauncy (1705–1787) was a Boston minister and theologian with Arminian tendencies. SELECTIONS: "Religious Ex-periences" from Edwards' Personal Narrative, 1740. "A Revival Sermon During the Great Awakening" from Sinners in the Hands of an Angry God (1741). "Affections Are the Seat of Religion" from Edwards' Treatise Concerning the Religious Affections (1746). "A Rationalist At-tack on Revivalism" from Chauncy's Seasonable Thoughts (1743).

RELIGIOUS EXPERIENCES (1740):
JONATHAN EDWARDS

When I look into my heart, and take a view of my wickedness, it looks like an abyss infinitely deeper than hell. And it appears to me, that were it not for free grace, exalted and raised up to the infinite height of all the fulness and glory of the great Jehovah, and the arm of his power and grace stretched forth in all the majesty of his power, and in all the glory of his sovereignty, I should appear sunk down in my sins below hell itself; far beyond the sight of every thing, but the eye of sovereign grace, that can pierce even down to such a depth. And yet it seems to me, that my conviction of sin is exceeding small, and faint; it is enough to amaze me, that I have no more sense of my sin. . . .

From my childhood up, my mind had been full of objections against the doctrine of God's sovereignty, in choosing whom he would to eternal life, and rejecting whom he pleased; leaving them eternally to perish, and be everlastingly tormented in hell. It used to appear like a horrible doc-trine to me. . . .

Now I saw further, and my reason apprehended the justice and reasonableness of it. However, my mind rested in it; and it put an end to all those cavils and objections. And there has been a wonderful alteration in my mind, in respect to the doctrine of God's sovereignty, from that day to this; so that I scarce ever have found so much as the rising of an objection against it, in the most absolute sense, in God's shewing mercy to whom he will shew mercy, and hardening whom he will. God's absolute sovereignty and justice, with respect to salvation and damnation, is what my mind seems to rest assured of, as much as of any thing that I see with my eyes; at least it is so at times. But I have often, since that first conviction, had quite another kind of sense of God's sovereignty than I had then. I have often since had not only a conviction, but a delightful conviction. The doctrine has very often appeared exceeding pleasant, bright, and sweet. Absolute sovereignty is what I love to ascribe to God. . . .

The soul of a true Christian, as I then wrote my meditations, appeared like such a little white flower as we see in the spring of the year; Low and humble on the ground, opening its bosom to receive the pleasant beams of the sun's glory; rejoicing as it were in . . . rapture; diffusing around a sweet fragrancy; standing peacefully and lovingly, in the midst of other flowers round about; all in like manner opening their bosoms, to drink in the light of the sun. There was no part of creature holiness, that I had so great a sense of its loveliness, as humility, brokenness of heart and poverty of spirit; and there was nothing that I so earnestly longed for. My heart panted after this, to lie low before God, as in the dust; that I might be nothing, and that God might be ALL, that I might become as a little child. . . .

A REVIVAL SERMON DURING THE GREAT
AWAKENING (1741): JONATHAN EDWARDS

The use of this awful subject may be for awakening unconverted persons in this congregation. . . .

The God that holds you over the pit of hell, much as one holds a spider, or some loathsome insect over the fire, abhors you, and is dreadfully provoked: his wrath towards you burns like fire; he looks upon you as worthy of nothing else, but to be cast into the fire; he is of purer eyes than to bear to have you in his sight; you are ten thousand times more abominable in his eyes, than the most hateful venomous serpent is in ours. You have offended him infinitely more than ever a stubborn rebel did his prince; and yet it is nothing but his hand that holds you from falling into the fire every moment. It is to be ascribed to nothing else, that you did not go to hell the last night; that you was suffered to awake again in this world, after you closed your eyes to sleep. And there is no other reason to be given, why you have not dropped into hell since you arose in the morning, but that God's hand has held you up. There is no other reason to be given why you have not gone to hell, since you have sat here in the house of God, provoking his pure eyes by your sinful wicked manner of attending his solemn worship. Yea, there is nothing else that is to be given as a reason why you do not this very moment drop down into hell. . . .

God seems now to be hastily gathering in his elect in all parts of the land; and probably the greater part of adult persons that ever shall be saved, will be brought in now in a little time, and that it will be as it was on the great out-pouring of the Spirit upon the Jews in the apostles' days; the election will obtain, and the rest will be blinded. If this should be the case with you, you will eternally curse this day, and will curse the day that ever you was born, to see such a season of the pouring out of God's Spirit, and will wish that you had died and gone to hell before you had seen it. Now undoubtedly it is, as it was in the days of John the Baptist, the axe is in an extraordinary manner laid at the root of the trees, that every tree which brings not forth good fruit, may be hewn down and cast into the fire.

Therefore, let every one that is out of Christ, now awake and fly from the wrath to come. The wrath of Almighty God is now undoubtedly hanging over a great part of this congregation: Let every one fly out of Sodom: "Haste and escape for your lives, look not behind you, escape to the mountain, lest you be consumed. . . ."

AFFECTIONS ARE THE SEAT OF RELIGION (1746): JONATHAN EDWARDS

Doctrine. True religion, in great part, consists in holy affections.

God has endowed the soul with two faculties: one is that by which it is capable of perception and speculation, or by which it discerns, and views, and judges of things; which is called the understanding. The other faculty is that by which the soul does not merely perceive and view things, but is some way inclined with respect to the things it views or considers; either is inclined to them, or is disinclined and averse from them; or is the faculty by which the soul does not behold things, as an indifferent un-affected spectator, but either as liking or disliking, pleased or displeased, approving or rejecting. This faculty is called by various names; it is sometimes called the inclination: and, as it has respect to the actions that are determined and governed by it, is called the will: and the mind, with regard to the exercises of this faculty, is often called the heart. . . .

The will, and the affections of the soul, are not two faculties; the affections are not essentially distinct from the will, nor do they differ from the mere actings of the will, and inclination of the soul, but only in the liveliness and sensibleness of exercise. In every act of the will whatsoever, the soul either likes or dislikes, is either inclined or disinclined to what is in view: these are not essentially different from those affections of love and hatred: that liking or inclination of the soul to a thing, if it be in a high degree, and be vigorous and lively, is the very same thing with the affection of love; and that disliking and disinclining, if in a greater degree, is the very same with hatred. In every act of the will for, or towards something not present, the soul is in some degree inclined to that thing; and that inclination, if in a considerable degree, is the very same with the affection of desire. And in every degree of the act of the will, wherein the soul approves of something present, there is a degree of pleasedness; and that pleasedness, if it be in a considerable degree, is the very same with the affections of joy or delight. And if the will disapproves of what is present, the soul is in some degree displeased, and if that displeasedness be great, it is the very same with the affection of grief or sorrow.

Such seems to be our nature, and such the laws of the union of soul and body, that there never is in any case whatsoever, any lively and vigorous exercise of the will or inclination of the soul, without some effect upon the body, in some alteration of the motion of its fluids, and especially of the animal spirits. And, on the other hand, from the same laws of the union of the soul and body, the constitution of the body, and the motion of its fluids, may promote the exercise of the affections. But yet it is not the body, but the mind only, that is the proper seat of the affections. The body of man is no more capable of being really the subject of love or hatred, joy or sorrow, fear or hope, than the body of a tree, or than the same body of man is capable of thinking and understanding. As it is the soul only that has ideas, so it is the soul only that is pleased or displeased with its ideas. As it is the soul only that thinks, so it is the soul only that loves or hates, rejoices or is grieved at what it thinks of. Nor are these motions of the animal spirits, and fluids of the body, any thing properly belonging to the nature of the affections, though they always accompany them, in the present state; but are only effects or concomitants of the affections that are entirely distinct from the affections themselves, and no way essential to them; so that an unbodied spirit may be as capable of love and hatred, joy or sorrow, hope or fear, or other affections, as one that is united to a body. . . .

Such is man's nature, that he is very inactive, any otherwise than he is influenced by some affection, either love or hatred, desire, hope, fear, or some other. These affections we see to be the springs that set men agoing, in all the affairs of life, and engage them in all their pursuits: these are the things that put men forward, and carry them along, in all their worldly business; and especially are men excited and animated by these, in all affairs wherein they are earnestly engaged, and which they pursue with vigor. We see the world of mankind to be exceeding busy and active; and the affections of men are the springs of the motion: take away all love and hatred, all hope and fear, all anger, zeal, and affectionate desire, and the world would be, in a great measure motionless and dead; there would be no such thing as activity amongst mankind, or any earnest pursuit whatsoever. It is affection that engages the covetous man, and him that is greedy of worldly profits, in his pursuits; and it is by the affections, that the ambitious man is put forward in his pursuit of worldly glory; and it is the affections also that actuate the voluptuous man, in his pursuit of pleasure and sensual delights: the world continues, from age to age, in a continual commotion and agitation, in a pursuit of these things; but take away all affection, and the spring of all this motion would be gone, and the motion itself would cease. And as in worldly things, worldly affections are very much the spring of men's motion and action; so in religious matters, the spring of their actions is very much religious affection: he that has doctrinal knowledge and speculation only, without affection, never is engaged in the business of religion. . . .

We may hence learn how great their error is, who are for discarding all religious affections, as having nothing solid or substantial in them.

There seems to be too much of a disposition this way, prevailing in this land at this time. Because many who, in the late extraordinary season, appeared to have great religious affections, did not manifest a right temper of mind, and run into many errors, in the time of their affections, and the heat of their zeal; and because the high affections of many seem to be so soon come to nothing, and some who seemed to be mightily raised and swallowed up with joy and zeal, for a while, seem to have returned like the dog to his vomit; hence religious affections in general are grown out of credit with great numbers, as though true religion did not at all consist in them. Thus we easily and naturally run from one extreme to another. . . .

A RATIONALIST ATTACK ON REVIVALISM (1743): CHARLES CHAUNCY

The Way in which these Terrors [emotional conversions] spread themselves is a Circumstance, that does not much favour their divine Origin. They seem to be suddenly propagated, from one to another, as in a great Fright or Consternation. They often begin with a single Person, a Child, or Woman, or Lad, whose Shrieks set others a Shrieking; and so the Shrieks catch from one to another, 'till the whole Congregation is alarmed, and such an awful scene, many Times, open'd, as no Imagination can paint to the Life. . . . Some will faint away, fall down upon the

Floor, wallow and foam. Some Women will rend off their Caps, Handker-
chiefs, and other Clothes, tear their Hair down about their Ears, and
seem perfectly bereft of their Reason.

Appearances in this Kind, I have often had an Account of from
those who have been present at them; and as begun by one or two
Persona at first: And where this has been the Case, there is no great
Difficulty in finding out the Cause: 'Tis far more reasonable to look for it
in Nature, than in Grace.

It may not be amiss to observe still further, that these Terrors, with
their Effects, are uniform all over the Country; operating upon all in
whom they take Place, much in the same Way and Manner, be their
moral Character what it will. Whether the Subjects of them be great or
small Sinners, whether the Sins they have committed be more or less,
whether they have continued in Sin a longer or shorter Time, there is no
Difference as to their Fears, and the Operation of them; but they are all
indiscriminately thrown into the like horrible Circumstances; which it is
not reasonable to think would be the Case, if they were put into this
Condition by a divine Influence: Whereas, its the very Thing that might
be expected, where Nature is suddenly surpris'd, and overcome, as in a
Fright.

In fine, it's a Circumstance no Ways favouring the divine Rise of
these Out-cries, that many People now commonly make them, not as
urg'd hereto from an over-pouring Sense of their own Sins, but the Sins of
others. Having been converted themselves, their Distress, under the
Preaching of the Word, is now raised to such a Height for the unconverted Sinners in the Congregation, that they can't help screaming out;
and so many of them, sometimes at once, as that the Worship is interrupted, or greatly disturb'd. . . . But are Shriekings a suitable Expression of . . . Concern; especially in the House of GOD? And can it be
suppos'd, the GOD of Order, would, by the Exertment of his Power,
raise this Concern to such a Height, as that his own Worship should be
broke up upon the Account of it? 'Tis impossible. I never heard one
sober, solid Person speak a Word in Favour, of these Out-cries; and am
heartily sorry, any Thing has been printed, encouraging so gross an Extravagance. I hope none, from the meer Sound of some Texts, will justify
this same Distress for others, as it begins now to discover it self, among
some Persons, in another Form, in Travail-Pains and Throws. . . .

These are the Reasons, why I can't entertain so high an Opinion as
some others do, of the Terrors appearing in strange bodily Effects, which
have been so common of late in this Land. . . .

7. Puritanism and Capitalism

In New England's first century radical change came to economic attitudes as well as to religious and political aspects of Puritan life. The early immigrants believed, as most Europeans had for centuries, that communal good rather than individual gain was the end of all economic activity. Other traditional ideals were brought from old England: workers must be guided primarily by the ethics of good workmanship, merchants ought to charge no more than a just price, and civil rulers were obligated to regulate prices, wages, and profits in the interest of the community. What factors, then, were responsible for the revolution in economic attitudes; how did men come to believe that they had a natural right to buy cheaply and sell dearly? Some scholars have traced the causes to the fruition of Calvinist ethics. In his account of Protestantism and the rise of capitalism Max Weber stressed the Calvinist concept of the calling: a carpenter or a merchant as well as a clergyman had a vocation, a calling from God, and thrifty, energetic, provident men who pursued their callings well became rich while lazy, improvident, reckless men who failed to heed God's command were inevitably poor. Since God rewarded the virtuous and punished the wicked in secular affairs, some Protestants eventually came to regard wealth as a sign of divine blessing and poverty as proof of God's hostility. AUTHORS: John Winthrop (1588–1649) had an economic outlook which was much closer to the fifteenth than the nineteenth century. Cotton Mather (1663–1728) provides excellent illustrations for the relationship of Calvinism and capitalist ethics suggested by the Weber thesis. SELECTIONS: "Wage, Price, and Profit Controls" from Winthrop's Journals, 1633, 1639. "Puritanism And The Development Of Commercial Ethics" from Mather's Two Brief Discourse Directing a Christian in His Calling (1701) and Sober Sentiments (1722).

WAGE, PRICE, AND PROFIT CONTROLS
(1633, 1639): JOHN WINTHROP

The scarcity of workmen had caused them to raise their wages to an excessive rate . . . and accordingly those who had commodities to sell advanced their prices sometime double to what they cost in England, so as it grew to a general complaint, which the court, taking knowledge of, as also of some further evils, which were springing out of the excessive rates of wages, they made an order, that carpenters, masons, etc., should take but two shillings the day, and laborers but eighteen pence, and that no commodity should be sold at above four pence in the shilling more than it cost for ready money in England; oil, wine, etc., and cheese, in regard of the hazard of bringing, etc., (excepted). The evils which were springing, etc., were: 1. Many spent much time idly, etc., because they could get as much in four days as would keep them a week. 2. They spent much in tobacco and strong waters, etc., which was a great waste to the commonwealth, which, by reason of so many foreign commodities expended, could not have subsisted to this time, but that it was supplied by the cattle and corn, which were sold to new comers at very dear rates. . . . Soon after order was taken for prices of commodities, viz., not to exceed the rate of four pence in the shilling above the price in England, except cheese and liquors, etc. . . .

At a general court . . . great complaint was made of the oppression used in the country in sale of foreign commodities; and Mr. Robert Keaine, who kept a shop in Boston, was notoriously above others observed and complained of; and, being convented, he was charged with many particulars; in some, for taking above six-pence in the shilling profit; in some above eight-pence. . . .

After the court had censured him, the church of Boston called him also in question, where (as before he had done in the court) he did, with tears, acknowledge and bewail his covetous and corrupt heart, yet making some excuse for many of the particulars, which were charged upon him . . . as 1. That, if a man lost in one commodity, he might help himself in the price of another. 2. That if, through want of skill or other occasion, his commodity cost him more than the price of the market in England, he might then sell it for more than the price of the market in New England, etc. These things gave occasion to Mr. Cotton . . . to lay open . . . false principles, and to give some rules. . . .

The rules for trading were these:—

1. A man may not sell above the current price, i.e., such a price as is usual in the time and place, and as another (who knows the worth of the commodity) would give for it, if he had occasion to use it; as that is called current money, which every man will take, etc.

2. When a man loseth in his commodity for want of skill, etc., he must look at it as his own fault or cross, and therefore must not lay it upon another.

3. Where a man loseth by casualty of sea, or, etc., it is a loss cast upon himself by providence, and he may not ease himself of it by casting it upon another; for so a man should seem to provide against all providences, etc., that he should never lose; but where there is a scarcity of the commodity, there men may rise their price; for now it is a hand of God upon the commodity, and not the person.

4. A man may not ask any more for his commodity than his selling price, as Ephron to Abraham, the land is worth thus much. . . .

PURITANISM AND THE DEVELOPMENT OF COMMERCIAL ETHICS (1701): COTTON MATHER

What is your Occupation? Genesis, XLVII. 3.

'Tis taken for granted then that they had One. It was the Question that Pharaoh put unto the Sons of Jacob. And it implies that every true Israelite should be able to give a good Answer unto such a Question. The Question which we are now to Discourse upon is, How a Christian may come to give a Good Answer unto that Question? or, How a Christian may come to give a Good Account of his Occupation and of his Behaviour in it?

There are Two Callings to be minded by All Christians. Every Christian hath a General Calling, Which is to Serve the Lord Jesus Christ and Save his own Soul in the Services of Religion that are incumbent on all the Children of men. God hath called us to Believe on His son, and Repent of our Sin, and observe the Sacred Means of our Communion with Himself, and bear our Testimony to His Truths and Wayes in the World: and every man in the world should herein conform to the Calls of that God, who hath called us with this Holy Calling. But then, every Christian hath also a Personal Calling; or, a certain Particular Employment by which his Usefulness in his Neighbourhood is distinguished, God hath made man a Sociable Creature. We expect Benefits from Humane Society. It is but equal, that Humane Society should Receive Benefits from Us. We are Beneficial to Humane Society by the Works of that Special Occupation in which we are to be employ'd according to the Order of God.

A Christian, at his Two Callings, is a man in a Boat, Rowing for Heaven, the House which our Heavenly Father hath intended for us. If he mind but one of his Callings, be it which it will, he pulls the Oar but on one side of the Boat, and will make but a poor dispatch to the Shoar of Eternal Blessedness. . . .

Would a man Rise by his Business? I say, then let him Rise to his Business. It was foretold. Prov. 22:29, "Seest thou a man Diligint . . . in his Business? He shall stand before Kings"; He shall come to preferment. And it was instanced by him who foretold it; I Kings 11:28. "Solomon, seeing that the young man was industrious, he made him a Ruler." I tell you, with Diligence a man may do marvellous . . . things. Young man, work hard while you are Young; You'l Reap the effects of it when you are Old. Yea, How can you Ordinarily enjoy any Rest at Night, if you have

not been well at work in the Day? Let your Business engross the most of
your time. . . . Let every man have the Discretion to be well instructed
in, and well acquainted with, all the mysteries of his Occupation. Be a
master of your trade; count it a disgrace to be no workman. . . .

Acknowledge thy Dependence on the glorious God, for thy Thriv-
ing in the World. It is what we are minded of; Deut. VIII. 18. "Thou
shalt remember the Lord thy God; for it is He that gives thee Power to
get wealth." Be sensible of this; Riches come not always to them who are
sharpest at inventing the most probable Methods of coming at it. Be
sensible of this; The way to succeed in our Enterprizes, O Lord, I know
the way of man is not in himself! Be sensible of this; In our Occupation
we spread our Nets; but it is God who brings unto our Nets all that
comes into them. . . .

8. *The Puritan Becomes a Yankee*

The collapse of early Puritan economic attitudes and the diminution of
religious piety was accompanied by other radical changes until the society
of Winthrop and Cotton had virtually ceased to exist. Calvinist doctrines
had always tended to separate ethics and religion and as Puritan society
declined, New Englanders increasingly stressed ethics at the expense of
theology and piety. Even Cotton Mather, who had spent his early and
middle years exalting the old Puritan ideal and deploring the loss of
religious zeal, was capable of entertaining semi-heretical theological ideas
and giving unusually strong stress to ethics. Mather's later writings provide interesting evidence on some of the means by which the Puritan was
transformed into a Yankee. Benjamin Franklin, who may deserve to be
called the first Yankee, owed a great deal to his New England past.
However, the eighteenth-century English enlightenment was at least as
powerful a force in the formation of his character. Only a few aspects of
Franklin's mind are represented in this section. The crafty businessman,
the limited provincial, the cracker barrel sage became the great scientist,
the versatile inventor, the Founding Father, and the Parisian cosmopolite.
AUTHORS: Cotton Mather (1663–1728) wrote on a variety of subjects
from theology to science, history, and ethics. Benjamin Franklin (1706–
1790) had many careers as printer, postmaster, scientist, legislator, colonial agent for Pennsylvania, American diplomat, and delegate to the U.S.
Constitutional Convention. SELECTIONS: "On Doing Good" from Mather's *Manuductio ad Ministerium* (1726) and *Bonifacius, or Essays to Do
Good* (1710). "A Debt to Cotton Mather" from a Franklin letter to

Samuel Mather in 1784. "How to Get Rich" from Franklin's *Advice to a Young Tradesman* (1748). "How to Seek Moral Perfection" from Franklin's *Autobiography*, 1771. "How to Deal With the Poor" from a Franklin letter of 1760 to the *London Chronicle*.

ON DOING GOOD (1710, 1726): COTTON MATHER

Essays to do good may fill your Life, and be the very Spirit and Business of it, and the principal Delight. The Motto which an English Lord has upon his Coat of Arms, is what I propose to your continual Ambition: Ut Prosim (that I may succeed). And, My Son, My Advice to you, is, Begin betimes to take that Noble Question into Consideration, What Good may I be capable of doing in the World? Have stated and proper Times for it, and these as often as may be, to consider on the Question; and keep a Record of your Purposes. First with an humble and mournful sense how much you want [lack] that Wisdom, which is to find out well-advised Inventions, Look up to GOD YOUR SAVIOUR, that by Him (who is the Wisdom of GOD) living in you, and leading of you, you may obtain a fair View of the Opportunities to do Good, which he has put into your Hand, that they may not be a Price in the Hand of a Fool; and a clear View of the Methods to be taken that this Good may be prosecuted, and your Desire sweetly accomplished. Then proceed and Enquire.

Enquire, First, What shall I do for My Self, that I may My Self Improve in Knowledge and Goodness; and the Ends of those Means, which the Divine Cultivation employs upon me?

Enquire, next, What shall I do for my several Relatives, my Kindred according to the Flesh, that I may prove a Blessing in each of my Relations? Take a Catalogue of them; and successively bestow distinct Thoughts upon them all.

Then go on to take some Cognizance of the several societies to which you stand related; Especially the Church whereof you are a Member, (and the College, if you belong to That!) Yea, the Town, and the Land, whereof you are an Inhabitant.

Think, What Good is to be proposed and promoted here! To what an Extent, O dear Son, and pleasant Child, may thy Projections carry thee!

Particular Persons in your Neighbourhood may now also be found out as Objects that Good may be done unto; The Poor for to be relieved; The Sick for to be visited; the Sad for to be comforted; and those that are out of the Way, to be reclaimed from the Error of their Way. Many of those whom you have distinguished in thus doing of Good unto them, you will find prove Monsters of Ingratitude. But let not this dishearten you. GOD is now trying of you, Whether you will do Good for the pure sake of Good; And you will this way have Recompences ascertained unto you, in the Harvest, when, Whatsoever Good Thing any Man does, the same shall he receive of the Lord. . . .

You cannot but acknowledge that it is the sovereign God who has bestowed upon you the riches which distinguish you. A devil himself, when he saw a rich man, could not but make this acknowledgment to the God of heaven: "Thou hast blessed the work of his hands, and his substance is increased in the land. . . .

The charitable . . . very frequently . . . have been rewarded with remarkable success in their affairs, and increase of their property; and even in this world have seen the fulfillment of those promises: "Cast thy bread upon the waters"—thy grain into the moist ground—"and thou shalt find it after many days." "Honor the Lord with thy substance; so shall thy barns be filled with plenty." History has given us many delightful examples of those who have had their decimations followed and rewarded by a surprising prosperity of their affairs. Obscure mechanics and husbandmen have risen to estates, of which one they had not the most distant expectation. . . .

A DEBT TO COTTON MATHER (1784): BENJAMIN FRANKLIN

The last time I saw . . . [Cotton Mather] was in the beginning of 1724, when I visited him after my first trip to Pennsylvania. He received me in his library, and on my taking leave showed me a shorter way out of the house through a narrow passage, which was crossed by a beam over head. We were still talking as I withdrew, he accompanying me behind, and I turning partly towards him, when he said hastily, "Stoop, stoop!" I did not understand him, till I felt my head hit against the beam. He was a man that never missed any occasion of giving instruction, and upon this he said to me, "You are young, and have the world before you; Stoop as you go through it, and you will miss many hard thumps." This advice, thus beat into my head, has frequently been of use to me; and I often think of it, when I see pride mortified, and misfortunes brought upon people by their carrying their heads too high. . . .

HOW TO GET RICH (1748): BENJAMIN FRANKLIN

Remember, that time is money. He that can earn ten shillings a day by his labour, and goes abroad, or sits idle, one half of that day, though he spends but sixpence during his diversion or idleness, ought not to reckon that the only expense; he has really spent, or rather thrown away, five shillings besides.

Remember, that credit is money. . . .

Remember, that money is of the prolific, generating nature. Money can beget money, and its offspring can beget more, and so on. Five shillings turned is six, turned again it is seven and three-pence, and so on till it becomes an hundred pounds. The more there is of it, the more it produces every turning. . . .

Remember, that six pounds a year is but a groat a day. For this little sum (which may be daily wasted either in time or expense unperceived) a man of credit may, on his own security, have the constant possession and use of an hundred pounds. So much in stock, briskly turned by an industrious man, produces great advantage.

Remember, this saying, The good paymaster is lord of another man's purse. He that is known to pay punctually and exactly to the time he promises, may at any time, and on any occasion, raise all the money his friends can spare. . . .

The most trifling actions that affect a man's credit are to be regarded. The sound of your hammer at five in the morning, or nine at night, heard by a creditor, makes him easy six months longer; but, if he sees you at a billiard-table, or hears your voice at a tavern, when you should be at work, he sends for his money the next day; demands it, before he can receive it, in a lump.

It shows, besides, that you are mindful of what you owe; it makes you appear a careful as well as an honest man, and that still increases your credit. . . .

In short, the way to wealth, if you desire it, is as plain as the way to market. It depends chiefly on two words, industry and frugality; that is, waste neither time nor money, but make the best use of both. Without industry and frugality nothing will do, and with them every thing. He that gets all he can honestly, and saves all he gets (necessary expenses excepted), will certainly become rich, if that Being who governs the world, to whom all should look for a blessing on their honest endeavours, doth not, in his wise providence, otherwise determine. . . .

HOW TO SEEK MORAL PERFECTION (1771):
BENJAMIN FRANKLIN

It was about this time I conceiv'd the bold and arduous project of arriving at moral perfection. I wish'd to live without committing any fault at any time; I would conquer all that either natural inclination, custom, or company might lead me into. As I knew, or thought I knew, what was right and wrong, I did not see why I might not always do the one and avoid the other. But I soon found I had undertaken a task of more difficulty than I had imagined. While my care was employ'd in guarding against one fault, I was often surprised by another; habit took the advantage of inattention; inclination was sometimes too strong for reason. I concluded, at length, that the mere speculative conviction that it was our interest to be completely virtuous, was not sufficient to prevent our slipping; and that the contrary habits must be broken, and good ones acquired and established, before we can have any dependence on a steady, uniform rectitude of conduct. For this purpose I therefore contrived the following method. . . .

I made a little book, in which I allotted a page for each of the virtues. I rul'd each page with red ink, so as to have seven columns, one for each day of the week, marking each column with a letter for the day. I cross'd these columns with thirteen red lines, marking the beginning of each line with the first letter of one of the virtues, on which line and in its proper column, I might mark, by a little black spot, every fault I found upon examination to have been committed respecting that virtue upon that day.

I enter'd upon the execution of this plan for self-examination, and continu'd it with occasional intermissions for some time. I was surpris'd to find myself so much fuller of faults than I had imagined; but I had the satisfaction of seeing them diminish. . . .

My list of virtues contain'd at first but twelve; but a Quaker friend having kindly informed me that I was generally thought proud; that my pride show'd itself frequently in conversation; that I was not content with being in the right when discussing any point, but was overbearing, and rather insolent, of which he convinc'd me by mentioning several instances; I determined endeavouring to cure myself, if I could, of this vice or folly among the rest, and I added Humility to my list, giving an extensive meaning to the word. . . .

HOW TO DEAL WITH THE POOR (1760):
BENJAMIN FRANKLIN

I am for doing good to the poor, but I differ in opinion about the means. I think the best way of doing good to the poor, is, not making them easy in poverty, but leading or driving them out of it. In my youth, I travelled much, and I observed in different countries, that the more public provisions were made for the poor, the less they provided for themselves, and of course became poorer. And, on the contrary, the less was done for them, the more they did for themselves, and became richer. There is no country in the world where so many provisions are established for them; so many hospitals to receive them when they are sick or lame, founded and maintained by voluntary charities; so many almshouses for the aged of both sexes, together with a solemn general law made by the rich to subject their estates to a heavy tax for the support of the poor. Under all these obligations, are our poor modest, humble, and thankful? And do they use their best endeavours to maintain themselves, and lighten our shoulders of this burthen? On the contrary, I affirm, that there is no country in the world in which the poor are more idle, dissolute, drunken, and insolent. The day you passed that act, you took away from before their eyes the greatest of all inducements to industry, frugality, and sobriety, by giving them a dependence on somewhat else than a careful accumulation during youth and health, for support in age or sickness.

In short, you offered a premium for the encouragement of idleness, and you should not now wonder, that it has had its effect in the increase of poverty. Repeal that law, and you will soon see a change in their manners. Saint Monday and Saint Tuesday will soon cease to be holidays. Six days shalt thou labour, though one of the old commandments long treated as out of date, will again be looked upon as a respectable precept; industry will increase, and with it plenty among the lower people; their circumstances will mend, and more will be done for their happiness by inuring them to provide for themselves, than could be done by dividing all your estates among them. . . .

Chapter II. THE ENLIGHTENMENT
AND THE NEW NATION

SEVERAL STRANDS OF EARLY NATIONAL CULTURE CAN BE TRACED TO the evolution of New England society. Traditional ideas on communal regulation of wages, commodities, and prices gave way to laissez-faire economics which stressed the free competition of individuals; Puritan political beliefs developed in the direction of representative government; and the old conception of God's rational order moved toward the eighteenth-century conception of "Nature and Nature's God." The oldest Puritan traditions persisted with some of their original content, but the dominant voices of the age of the American Revolution usually spoke in accents more secular, tolerant, and friendly toward science and reason. Moreover, intellectual currents flowed directly from Europe to Americans who were more receptive to new ideas than the Puritans had been.

The intellectual giants of early modern times, and particularly Sir Isaac Newton, established a new cosmic order of mathematical systemization which won enthusiastic applause in the eighteenth century. Newton exerted a profound and pervasive influence, not only in "natural philosophy," but also in political and religious thought. The philosophers sought to create a science of politics, and Thomas Hobbes's call for mathematical precision in statecraft had at least a distant echo in Thomas Jefferson's assertion that the rights of man were "self-evident" and, one supposes, much like the axioms of Euclidian geometry in being propositions beyond proof, demanding acceptance from all rational men. John Locke, claiming Newtonian science as his starting point, set out to explore the implications of modern science for epistemology, politics, religion, and ethics. Lockean ideas entered the New World so forcefully that the man became for a good many "the great Mr. Locke, America's philosopher."

The "natural" and the "rational"—and the two were often made synonymous—provide the major keys to the eighteenth-century mind. The new science of politics sprang from the attempt to survey human history and society in quest of rationality; nature provided the norm and suggested the proper foundations for the legal and social order. By searching nature, Americans thought that they could discover natural laws which ruled men insofar as they were rational beings. "Irrational" and "unnatural" laws and customs which had survived from feudal times had to give way to the "natural" rights of life, liberty, property, and "the pursuit of happiness." Since kings could not invoke divine rights or aristocracies rule by right of birth, and since men were in at least some respects "equal" by the "law of nature," government must be based upon consent. The machinery of consent was the "social contract" which sanctioned and made possible the survival of the state; and no government could be created or continued without political consent. The contract and the state existed to protect the natural rights of men, and if the state failed in its functions, the voided social contract could no longer command the allegiance of citizens.

By charting nature after a scientific fashion, man could insure the observance of natural law, and do a great deal more; he could take the path of social progress and work for the improvement, possibly the perfection of all human institutions. For many Americans, to abandon the "irrational" and to embrace the "natural" was to follow humanitarian dictates: to urge commodious living for all citizens; to expand the definitions of citizenship; to advocate the humane treatment of women, prisoners, the poor, or the slaves; and perhaps to abandon slavery. Nor did men have to accept the fetters of superstition in religion and ethics. Reason led to natural religion and man's moral sense provided the promptings of conscience without resort to revelation. Many of the Founding Fathers—Franklin, Jefferson, Madison, Washington—each after his own fashion, followed the "dictates of reason." The leaders of the American Enlightenment spoke often of "natural" religion and "rational" Christianity, doubted mystery and miracle, and warned men against the evils of excessive reliance on priests and ministers. The most militant advocates of rational religion, men such as Thomas Paine, Elihu Palmer, and Ethan Allen, advocated a "pure," "simple," and "natural Deism," which rejected revelation along with the divinity of Christ and attempted to reduce religion to a few fundamentals which all men could in good conscience accept. In the new dispensation, God, benign but remote, presided over the perfectly functioning machinery of the Newtonian cosmos.

Other "irrational" and "unnatural" survivals of traditional European cultures aroused the ire of Americans. Extensive education in the classics might produce cultured gentlefolk, but men such as Benjamin Rush doubted the value of either the human product or "the dead languages" for a republican people intensely preoccupied with the task of developing a new continental nation. The American temperament tended to be less intellectual and more utilitarian, empirical with a certain aversion toward abstractions, and much prone to value the concrete, the specific, and the practical. From early times Americans admired "know-how" and tended to distrust those who paid too much attention to final purposes and ultimate explanations. Americans discovered their ideology in the eighteenth century, incorporated it into their definitions of the national society, and afterwards generally distrusted ideology.

It is not surprising that Americans, committed as they were to the philosophy of natural rights and eager to develop the continent, eventually took the road to national independence. The immediate occasion for the Revolutionary conflict was the British attempt to reorganize the Empire after 1763, when the great imperial struggle with France ended. Many Americans felt that the imperial government sought to interfere with long established rights and customs, and began to make protests which drew sustenance from the growth and application of natural rights ideology. Political philosophers of the New World contrasted the corruption of Europe and the sharp struggle in the midst of economic scarcity with the economic abundance and the power of "virtue" in America. The new society, untainted by an aristocracy or a single established national church of great power, seemed peculiarly fit to inaugurate the Age of Reason in the midst of freedom and abundance.

Through several generations of common experience and two decades of political conflict and revolution, Americans established a wide area of basic agreement, a national consensus. In the past some scholars have presented the Revolution and the creation of the Constitution as sharply contrasting events and suggested that the makers of the Constitution deprived the society of Revolutionary gains, but it may be more accurate to view the two events as closely related stages in the single process of "nation-building" which involved a large area of agreement among most of the major participants. If the Federalist, Alexander Hamilton, commented on the potential bestiality of men, Samuel Adams, an anti-Federalist, also had some negative thoughts about human nature. If many Federalists feared "the mob" and "democracy," they had enough faith in man and the American prospect to enable them to establish enduring constitutional forms for this Republic. Scholars critical of the Constitution have noted the presence of economic forces and "self-interest" in the Convention and suggested the existence of a conspiracy against popular rights. Of course, one can see the play of economic forces in the Constitutional Convention, the American Revolution, and all major events in history, but the notion of conspiracy has little value as a general theory of historical explanation, and the Constitution presents a more challenging problem in historical explanation than any conspiratorial tale of sinister interests can solve.

The Founding Fathers wished to avoid aristocracy and tyranny on the one hand and the "excesses" of social democracy on the other hand; to check all arbitrary and authoritarian government by one man, a social class, or a "tyrannical" majority; and to establish as wisely and well as they could for posterity a moderate republicanism. The idea of consensus does stress these common political goals, but it should not be used to indicate the lack of substantial issues within the general framework of agreement. Jefferson's devotion to agrarian America and Hamilton's insistence on the importance of manufacturing provided the framework for much significant debate. Once again, however, these contrasts cannot be drawn too sharply; Hamilton merely argued for the coexistence of agricultural and manufacturing interests, and Jefferson ultimately changed his mind about the value of manufacturing. The process of establishing the nation led to new issues and contending parties. Leaders of the political enlightenment disagreed over the techniques for restricting and dividing power, specific parts of the governmental machine, the pace and nature of social progress, but all of the disagreements were limited and contained by the basic consensus. If John Adams scorned the notions of many European "prophets of progress," he also remained confident in his belief that the Revolution and the establishment of the new nation opened a profoundly important chapter in world history which would carry mankind to new pinnacles of civilization. In brief, one must strike a balance between the reality of consensus in some areas and the equally real debate over issues in other areas.

The main currents of eighteenth-century thought moved across a course illuminated by intellectual beacons such as science and its social application, reason and nature, political and social progress, American nationalism, and moderate republicanism, but the closest examination of the Enlightenment will not provide a full portrait of the emergence of American society. Not even the neat, tightly drawn set of formula reasons can completely explain the basic experience of any people at a critical stage in history. The humanitarianism, which is generally ascribed to the Age of Reason, had other roots; John Woolman's deep sympathy for the afflicted, the poor, the "African stranger," owed far more to traditional Christian pietism than to the idea of progress. Moreover, cultural survivals from earlier generations continued to influence the society, and in many instances American experience fell into patterns ignored by philosophers. In the years when Jefferson penned his most articulate statements on rational Christianity, great multitudes of his fellow citizens found their religion in surrender to the emotional ecstasy of the camp meeting. For every confessed Deist a hundred men followed traditional forms of Christianity. Many Americans in the eighteenth century were truly prophets of progress, but American experience also contained conflicting tendencies, ambiguities, and paradoxes. For that matter, there were ambiguities at the very heart of the Enlightenment. The French republic which Condorcet helped to create interrupted his ardent defence of progress with the guillotine, and the great Diderot who shaped a particularly vivid vision of social progress also left us his portrait of the perverse, puzzling, and irrational protagonist of Rameau's Nephew.

1. Science

Most of the early scientific activities in America were undertaken by New Englanders such as Increase and Cotton Mather, Zabdiel Boylston, Benjamin Colman, and John Winthrop, Jr. The Puritans argued for science most frequently on the grounds that it led to a more perfect understanding of natural and divine mysteries and that it was another way of enabling man to follow his chief end in life, the glorification of God and his Creation. Time and new ideas ultimately created different motives for studying natural philosophy. Human curiosity and the high intellectual fashions of science were no doubt significant factors in the change, but Americans of the eighteenth century stressed the social utility of science. While Benjamin Franklin made contributions to the theory of electricity, he was most widely applauded for promising to enlarge human power over the elements. AUTHORS: Benjamin Franklin (1706–1790) won the admiration of learned men throughout the Western world for his experiments in electricity. Franklin's celebrated experiments with kites to demonstrate that lightning consists of a discharge of electrical energy drew popular applause from men and women who could not follow the intricacies of natural philosophy. Samuel Harrison Smith (1772–1845), the son of a Philadelphia merchant, was a banker, amateur scientist, journalist, and author who expressed common views on the utility of science. Smith's *The Universal Gazette* (1797), later *The National Intelligencer and Washington Advertiser* (1800), was an organ of Jeffersonian views. SELECTIONS: "Experiments in Electricity" (1749) from Franklin's *Autobiography* begun in 1771 and continued from 1784 to 1789. "Science, a Great Friend to Man" from Smith's *Remarks on Education* (1798).

EXPERIMENTS IN ELECTRICITY (1749):
BENJAMIN FRANKLIN

In 1746, being at Boston I met there with a Dr. Spence who was lately arrived from Scotland, and show'd me some electric experiments. They were imperfectly perform'd as he was not very expert but, being on a subject quite new to me, they equally surpris'd and pleased me. Soon after my return to Philadelphia, our library company receiv'd from Mr. P. Collinson, Fellow of the Royal Society of London, a present of a glass tube with some account of the use of it in making such experiments. I eagerly seized the opportunity of repeating what I had seen at Boston; and, by much practice, acquir'd great readiness in performing those, also, which we had an account of from England, adding a number of new ones. I say much practice, for my house was continually full, for some time, with people who came to see these new wonders.

To divide a little this incumbrance among my friends, I caused a number of similar tubes to be blown at our glasshouse, with which they furnished themselves, so that we had at length several performers. Among these, the principal was Mr. Kinnersley, an ingenious neighbor, who, being out of business, I encouraged to undertake showing the experiments for money, and drew up for him two lectures, in which the experiments were rang'd in such order, and accompanied with such explanations in such method, as that the foregoing should assist in comprehending the following. He procur'd an elegant apparatus for the purpose, in which all the little machines that I had roughly made for myself were nicely form'd by instrument-makers. His lectures were well attended and gave great satisfaction, and after some time he went thro' the colonies exhibiting them in every capital town and pick'd up some money. In the West India Islands, indeed, it was with difficulty the experiments could be made, from the general moisture of the air.

Oblig'd as we were to Mr. Collinson for his present of the tube, etc.,

I thought it right he should be inform'd of our success in using it, and wrote him several letters containing accounts of our experiments. He got them read in the Royal Society where they were not at first thought worth so much notice as to be printed in their Transactions. One paper, which I wrote for Mr. Kinnersley, on the sameness of lightning with electricity, I sent to Dr. Mitchel, an acquaintance of mine and one of the members also of that society, who wrote me word that it had been read, but was laughed at by the connoisseurs. The papers, however, being shown to Dr. Fothergill, he thought they were of too much value to be stifled, and advis'd the printing of them. Mr. Collinson then gave them to Cave for publication in his *Gentleman's Magazine*; but he chose to print them separately in a pamphlet and Dr. Fothergill wrote the preface. . . .

SCIENCE, A GREAT FRIEND TO MAN (1798): SAMUEL HARRISON SMITH

All science ought to derive its rank from its utility. The real good which it derives actually does, or is capable of doing, is the only genuine criterion of its value. Man may indulge himself in sublime reveries, but the world will forever remain uninterested in them. It is only when he applies the powers of his mind to objects of general use, that he becomes their benefactor; until he does this he is neither entitled to their gratitude or applause.

He is the best friend of man, who makes discoveries involving effects which benefit mankind the most extensively. Moral truths are therefore of importance but little short of infinite. . . . These truths, all agree, are not to be sought in the cloister. They are only acquired by united the calm and patient reflection of retirement, with the bold and penetrating observation of life.

In physics, the happiness of mankind is in the highest degree increased by discoveries and improvments connected with agriculture and manufacture. These two occupations employ nine tenths of most communities, and a much larger proportion of others. Does it not then become an interesting enquiry, whether it be not expedient in infancy and youth to communicate to the mind the leading principles of nature and art in these departments of labour, not only by a theoretic exposition of them, but also by their practical development. . . .

If almost the whole community be destined to pursue one or other of these avocations from necessity, and if it be the duty of an individual to support himself, whenever he can, by an exertion of his own powers; and if these can only yield a sure support from an ability to be acquired in youth to prosecute a particular branch of agriculture or mechanics, does it not seem to be the duty of society to control education in such a way as to secure to every individual this ability? If this ability existed, how much misery would be annihilated, how much crime would be destroyed? . . .

2. Philosophic Trends

Cadwallader Colden's writings had little influence, but they are interesting specimens of early philosphical speculation. Colden, a materialist, or a "mechanist," probably owed something to the materialism of Thomas Hobbes; his accounts of "bodies in motion" as the basic stuff and process of the cosmos bear general resemblances to the ideas of Helvetius and d'Alembert. John Locke was the most influential philosopher for the American scene, but toward the end of the eighteenth century, a growing number of thinkers turned to the Scottish "common sense" philosophers who fought scepticism by insisting that certain basic beliefs and mental processes were the "furniture" of the mind without which man could not function rationally. Eighteenth- and nineteenth-century Americans also read English moralists such as Bishop Butler and Lord Kames, who argued for existence of a special "power," "faculty," or "sense" which yielded moral truths. John Locke's faculty psychology seemed to support this line of thought, and Jefferson's essay on the moral sense contains ideas drawn both from Lockean psychology and the British moralists. No great originality can be claimed for the Joel Barlow selection, but the poem does indicate a fairly common notion of progress. AUTHORS: Cadwallader Colden (1688–1776) immigrated from Scotland in 1710 to America where he rose to the Lieutenant-Governorship of New York (1761–1766). Colden wrote prolifically on medicine, moral philosophy, and natural science. Thomas Jefferson (1743–1826) shared with many leaders of eighteenth-century thought the habit of tracing the promptings of conscience to a moral sense. Benjamin Rush (1745–1813), a Philadelphia physician, served as a delegate to the Continental Congress, surgeon-general of the Continental Army, a delegate to the Constitutional Convention, a teacher of chemistry and medicine, and a humanitarian reformer interested in temperance, anti-slavery, and other causes. Joel Barlow (1754–1812), a Connecticut-born graduate of Yale, was a teacher, editor, preacher, soldier, diplomat, and lawyer, as well as a poet. SELECTIONS: "The Principles of Action in Matter" from a Colden pamphlet of the same title (1751). "The Faculty of the Moral Sense" from Jefferson's letter of 1814 to Thomas Law. "Toward an American Philosophy of Education" from Rush's *Observation Upon the Study of the Latin and the Greek Languages* (1806). "The Idea of Progress" from Barlow's *The Vision of Columbus* (1787).

THE PRINCIPLES OF ACTION IN MATTER (1751): CADWALLADER COLDEN

SECT. I

Of the Essential Properties and Differences of Things

1. We have no knowledge of substances, or of any being, or of any thing, abstracted from the action of that thing or being. All our knowledge of things consists in the perception of the power, or force, or property, or manner of acting of that thing; that is, of the action of that thing on our senses, or of the effects of that thing on some other thing, whose action affects, or is the object of our senses, and in the perception of the relations or ratios of these actions to each other. For if any thing produce no alteration in our senses, it is impossible for us to know that any such thing exists: and every effect must be produced by some cause, or by some action.

2. Every thing, that we know, is an agent, or has a power of acting; for as we know nothing of any thing but its action, and the effects of this action, the moment any thing ceases to act it must be annihilated as to us: we can have no kind of idea of its existence. Any thing, which produces any effect or alteration in another thing, must either have its power and force of itself, or its action must be the effect of some other cause, and consequently it is not a primary agent: but in this place I only consider primary agents, and such must continually exert their force and energy. For it seems a contradiction in terms that any thing should obstruct or oppose its own force or energy: consequently every thing exerting of itself any power or force must be continually acting. Whatever stops be supposed to happen in its action, they can only be the effects of some opposite power or force, acting at the same time, and of superior or equal force in that instance, by which, tho' it continue to exert its power, its action is stopt, or rendered ineffectual.

3. If the idea or conception, which the action of any thing excites in us, be such, that at the same time we perceive that the thing itself, endowed with this power of acting, must be of some shape, or that it may be divided into parts, that its power or force may be increased by addition of parts, or lessened by the taking away of part, it is then conceived to be of some quantity. And every thing which is conceived to be of some quantity, is commonly called *matter*.

4. But if the actions of any thing do not excite in us any perception of its being of any quantity, or of any form or shape, or of its consisting of any parts, or that its force or action can be increased or lessened by the addition or taking away of part, that thing, commonly goes under the name of an *immaterial* substance, or of *spirit*.

5. Now from this manner of considering things, I hope to shew, that we may have as clear and distinct an idea or conception of spirit, as we can have of matter: and that all the difficulties or absurdities, which many have fallen into, arise from an error in the conceptions of the power, force, energy, or manner of acting, and which are commonly called the properties or qualities of things; or from the confusion which arises by the using of different terms, or words to express things, which in themselves are not different. The property, or quality of any thing, is nothing else but the action of that thing: and the different qualities or properties of any thing or substance are no other than the different actions or manner of acting of that thing. For we can have no idea or conception of the property or quality of any thing excited in us, but by the action of that thing: unless it can be supposed, that an effect is produced without a cause, and that a cause can be conceived without action. Therefore,

6. The difference of things (so far at least as we can know) consists in their different actions, or manner of acting. And if the actions of several things be such, as that we evidently perceive, that they cannot proceed from the same power or force, or kind of power or force, such things are said to be in their *nature* different, or *essentially* different. The essence of things or of substances, so far as we can discover it, consists in the power, or force, or manner of acting of those things.

It remains then, in the first place, to consider the several powers of those things, which we conceive as consisting of some quantity, and which are commonly called matter. Afterwards the action of the immaterial powers, or of intelligent beings, may be considered. . . .

THE FACULTY OF THE MORAL SENSE (1814):
THOMAS JEFFERSON

It has been said that we feed the hungry, clothe the naked, bind up the wounds of the man beaten by thieves, pour oil and wine into them, set him on our own beast and bring him to the inn, because we receive ourselves pleasure from these acts. So Helvetius, one of the best men on earth . . . after defining "interest" to mean not merely that which is pecuniary, but whatever may procure us pleasure or withdraw us from pain says "the humane man is he to whom the sight of misfortune is insupportable, and who to rescue himself from this spectacle, is forced to succor the unfortunate object." This indeed is true. But it is one step short of the ultimate question. These good acts give us pleasure, but how happens it that they give us pleasure? Because nature hath implanted in our breasts a love of others, a sense of duty to them, a moral instinct, in short, which prompts us irresistibly to feel and to succor their distresses. . . . Some men are born without the organs of sight, or of hearing, or without hands. Yet it would be wrong to say that man is born without these faculties, and sight, hearing, and hands may with truth enter into the general definition of man. The want or imperfection of the moral sense in some men, like the want or imperfection of the senses of sight and hearing in others, is no proof that it is a general characteristic of the species. When it is wanting, we endeavor to supply the defect by education, by appeals to reason and calculation, by presenting to the being so unhappily conformed, other motives to do good and to eschew evil, such as the love, or the hatred, or rejection of those among whom he lives, and whose society is necessary to his happiness and even existence; demonstrations by sound calculation that honesty promotes interest in the long run; the rewards and penalties established by the laws; and ultimately the prospects of a future state of retribution for the evil as well as the good done while here. These are the correctives which are supplied by education, and which exercise the functions of the moralist, the preacher, and legislator; and they lead into a course of correct action all those whose disparity is not too profound to be eradicated. . . . I sincerely believe, then, with you in the general existence of a moral instinct. I think it the brightest gem with which the human character is studded, and the want of it as more degrading than the most hideous of the bodily deformities. I am happy in reviewing the roll of associates in this principle which you present in your second letter, some of which I had not before met with. To these might be added Lord Kames, one of the ablest of our advocates, who goes so far as to say, in his Principles of Natural Religion, that a man owes no duty to which he is not urged by some impulsive feeling. . . .

TOWARD AN AMERICAN PHILOSOPHY OF EDUCATION (1806): BENJAMIN RUSH

I shall answer such arguments as are usually urged in favor of the Latin and Greek languages as necessary parts of an academic education.

I. The great design of a liberal education is, to prepare youth for usefulness here, and for happiness hereafter. . . .

III. From four to five years are usually spent in acquiring a competent knowledge of the Latin and Greek languages.

IV. The knowledge of things always preceeds the knowledge of words. Children discover the truth of this observation every day. . . . It is supposed that children acquire more ideas of things in the first three years of their lives, than they acquire in any thirty years afterwards.

V. The acquisition of words lessens the ability of the mind to acquire ideas. That understanding must have uncommon strength, which does not contract an oblique direction by being employed four or five years in learning the Latin or Greek languages.

VI. The difficulty of acquiring those dead languages, and the pleasure which accompanies the knowledge of them early in life, occasion the principal obstacles to teaching, in masters, and learning, in scholars. . . .

VII. Many sprightly boys of excellent capacities for useful knowledge, have been so disgusted with the dead languages, as to retreat from the drudgery of schools, to low company, whereby they have become bad members of society, and entailed misery upon all who have been connected with them. . . .

X. The study of the Latin and Greek languages is improper in . . . the United States. While Greek and Latin are the only avenues to science, education will always be confined to a few people. It is only by rendering knowledge universal, that a republican form of government can be preserved in our country. . . .

XI. The cultivation of the Latin and Greek languages is a great obstacle to the cultivation and perfection of the English language.

XII. It is likewise one of the greatest obstructions that has ever been thrown in the way of propagating useful knowledge. . . .

It has been said, that the Latin language has become a necessary part of liberal knowledge, inasmuch as the European nations have by common consent made it the vehicle of their discoveries. This argument had some weight while science consisted only in learning what was known; but since the enquiries of philosophers have been directed to new objects of observation and experiment, the Latin language has not been able to keep pace with the number and rapidity of their discoveries. Where shall we find Latin words to convey just ideas of the many terms which electricity—chemistry—navigation—and many other sciences have introduced into our modern languages? . . . It has been said that a knowledge of the Latin and Greek languages is necessary to the learned professions of law—physic—and divinity. To this I answer, that the most useful books in each of these professions are now translated, or written in English. . . . In Europe many ancient constitutions—laws—treaties—official letters—and even private deeds, are written in Latin—hence the knowledge of it has sometimes been found useful for statesmen and lawyers—but all the constitutions . . . [etc] of the United States, are written in English. . . . It is therefore as useless in America, as the Spanish greatcoat is in the island of Cuba, or the Dutch footstove, at the Cape of Good Hope. We forget further the difference of *occupation* between the inhabitants of the present, and of the fifteenth century. . . . We occupy a new country. Our principal business should be to explore and apply its resources, all of which press us to enterprize and haste. Under these circumstances, to spend four or five years in learning two dead languages, is to turn our backs upon a gold mine, in order to amuse ourselves in catching butterflies. . . .

THE IDEA OF PROGRESS (1787): JOEL BARLOW

Kind messenger of Heaven, he thus began,
Why this progressive labouring search of man?
If man by wisdom form'd hath power to reach
These opening truths that following ages teach,
Step after step, thro' devious mazes, wind,
And fill at last the measure of the mind,
Why did not Heaven, with one unclouded ray,
All human arts and reason's power display?
That mad opinions, sects and party strife
Might find no place to embitter human life.
　　To whom the Angelic power; to thee 'tis given,
To hold high converse, and enquire of heaven,
To mark uncircled ages, and to trace
The unfolding truths that wait thy kindred race.
Know then, the counsels of the unchanging Mind,
Thro' nature's range, progressive paths design'd,
Unfinish'd works the harmonious system grace,
Thro' all duration and around all space;
Thus beauty, wisdom, power, their parts unroll,
Til full perfection joins the accordant whole.
　　So the first week, beheld the progress rise,
Which form'd the earth, and arch'd the incumbent skies.
Dark and imperfect first, the unbeauteous frame,
From vacant night to crude existence came,
Light starr'd the heavens and suns were taught their bound,
Winds woke their force, and floods their centre found;
Earth's kindred elements, in joyous strife,
Warm'd the glad glebe to vegetable life,
Till sense and power and action claim'd their place,
And Godlike reason crown'd the imperial race.
　　Progressive thus, from that great Source above,
Flows the fair fountain of redeeming love.
Dark harbingers of hope, at first bestow'd,
Taught the early faith to feel her path to God;
Down the prophetic, brightening train of years,
Consenting voices rose of different seers,
In shadowy types display'd the accomplish'd plan,
While filial Godhead should assume the man.
When the pure Church should stretch her arms abroad,
Fair as a Bride and liberal as her God;

Till warm benevolence and truth refined,
Pervade the world and harmonize mankind.
    And thus fair Science, of celestial birth,
With time's long circuit, treads the gladsome earth;
By gradual steps to mark the extended road,
That leads mankind to reason and to God. . . .

3. *Humanitarianism*

Several common forms of eighteenth-century humanitarianism are represented in this section. The reader should note that John Woolman drew
his inspiration from Quaker Pietism rather than from the abstract theories of the idealogues. Paine and Jefferson were more characteristic figures of the Enlightenment, but it is interesting to note that Jefferson and
similar figures were more apt to address their anti-slavery remarks to
private letters and papers while most of the actual pioneer work in anti-
slavery remained in the hands of the Quakers for a generation. AUTHORS:
John Woolman (1720–1772), a New Jersey Quaker with little formal
education, spent his early years as a tailor's apprentice, baker, and shop-
keeper. Woolman represented the highest and best spirit of Quaker Pietism and humanitarianism. Thomas Paine (1737–1809), the English-
born son and apprentice of a corsetmaker, played a leading part in the
American and the French Revolutions as well as in English political
agitation. Thomas Jefferson (1743–1826) took justifiable pride in his
many educational and humanitarian enterprises. SELECTIONS: "A Plea for
the Poor and the African Stranger" from a Woolman pamphlet *A Word
of Remembrance and Caution to the Rich* (1793). "Against the Oppression of Women" from Paine's pamphlet *On Female Equality* (1775).
"Let the Punishment Fit the Crime" from Jefferson's draft of a Bill for
Apportioning Crimes and Punishments of 1779.

A PLEA FOR THE POOR AND THE AFRICAN STRANGER (1793): JOHN WOOLMAN

Wealth desired for its own sake Obstructs the increase of Virtue. . . .
[and by it] some [men] are necessitated to labour too hard, while others . . . want business to earn their Bread. . . .

Rents set on lands are often so high, that persons who have but small substance are straitened in hiring a plantation. . . . Many poor people are so thronged in their business, that it is difficult for them to provide Shelter suitable for their animals, in great storms. . . .

Oxen & Horses are often seen at work, when through Heat & too much labour, their eyes, and the emotion of their Bodies manifest that they are oppressed. . . .

To be busied in that which is but vanity and serves only to please the unstable mind, tends to an alliance with those who promote that vanity, and is a snare in which many poor tradesmen are entangled.

To be employed in things connected with Virtue, is most agreeable with the Character and Inclination of an honest man.

While industrious frugal people are borne down with poverty, and oppressed with too much labour in useful things, the way to apply money, without promoting pride and Vanity, remains open to such who truly sympathize with them in their various Difficulties. . . .

The Creator of the earth is the owner of it. He gave us being thereon, and our nature requires nourishment, which is the produce of it. . . .

Where all superfluities, and the desire of outward greatness laid aside, and the right use of things universally attended to, Such a number of people might be employed in things usefull, as that moderate Labour, with the Blessings of Heaven, would answer all good purposes relating to people and their Animals, and a Sufficient number have time to attend to proper Affairs of Civil Society. . . . He who with a view to self-exaltation, causeth some with their domestick Animals to labour immoderately, and, with the monys arising to him therefrom, employes others in the Luxuries of Life, Acts contrary to the Gracious designs of Him who is the true owner of the Earth, nor can any possessions, either acquired or derived from Ancestors, justify such conduct. . . .

The negroes have been a suffering people, and we as a civil society are they by whom they have suffered. . . . My heart is affected with Sorrow while I write on this Subject, on account of the great injuries committed against these Gentiles, and against their children who have been born in that Captivity which is an unrighteous Captivity. . . .

The poor Africans were people of a strange language, & not easie to converse with; & their Scituation as Slaves, too generally destroyed that brotherly freedom which frequently subsists between us and inoffensive Strangers.

In this adverse condition, how reasonable is it to suppose, that they would revolve in their distressed minds, the iniquities committed against them, and mourn! Mourn without any to comfort them! . . .

Long oppression hath not made Oppression consistent with Brotherly Love, nor length of time through several ages made recompense to the posterity of those injured Strangers. Many of them lived, and died without having their suffering cases heard and determined according to Equity, and under a degree of Sorrow on account of the wantonness, the Vanity and Superfluity too common amongst us as a Civil Society, even while a heavy load of unrighteous proceedings lies upon us, do I now under a feeling of universal Love & in a fervent concern for the real interest of my fellow members in Society, as well as the Interest of my fellow creatures in general, express these things. . . .

AGAINST THE OPPRESSION OF WOMEN (1775): THOMAS PAINE

If we take a survey of ages and of countries, we shall find the women, almost—without exception—at all times and in all places, adored and oppressed. Man, who has never neglected an opportunity of exerting his power, in paying homage to their beauty, has always availed himself of their weakness. He has been at once their tyrant and their slave.

Nature herself, in forming beings so susceptible and tender, appears to have been more attentive to their charms than to their happiness. Continually surrounded with griefs and fears, the women more than share all our miseries, and are besides subjected to ills which are peculiarly their own. They cannot be the means of life without exposing themselves to the loss of it; every revolution which they undergo, alters their health, and threatens their existence. Cruel distempers attack their beauty—and the hour which confirms their release from those is perhaps the most melancholy of their lives. It robs them of the most essential characteristic of their sex. They can then only hope for protection from the humiliating claims of pity, or the feeble voice of gratitude.

Society, instead of alleviating their condition, is to them the source of new miseries. . . .

LET THE PUNISHMENT FIT THE CRIME (1779): THOMAS JEFFERSON

Whereas, it frequently happens that wicked and dissolute men, resigning themselves to the dominion of inordinate passions, commit violations on the lives, liberties, and property of others, and, the secure enjoyment of these having principally induced men to enter into society, government would be defective in its principal purpose, were it not to restrain such criminal acts, by inflicting due punishments on those who perpetrate them; but it appears, at the same time, equally deducible from the purposes of society, that a member thereof, committing an inferior injury, does not wholly forfeit the protection of his fellow citizens, but, after suffering a punishment in proportion to his offence, is entitled to their protection from all greater pain, so that it becomes a duty in the legislature to arrange, in a proper scale, the crimes which it may be necessary for them to repress, and to adjust thereto a corresponding gradation of punishments.

And whereas, the reformation of offenders, though an object worthy the attention of the laws, is not effected at all by capital punishments, which exterminate instead of reforming, and should be the last melancholy resource against those whose existence is become inconsistent with the safety of their fellow citizens, which also weakens the State, by cutting off so many who, if reformed, might be restored sound members to society, who, even under a course of correction, might be rendered useful in various labors for the public, and would be living and long-continued spectacles to deter others from committing the like offences.

And for as much as the experience of all ages and countries hath shown, that cruel and sanguinary laws defeat their own purpose, by engaging the benevolence of mankind to withhold prosecutions, to smother testimony, or to listen to it with bias, when, if the punishment were only proportioned to the injury, men would feel it their inclination as well as their duty, to see the laws observed. . . .

4. Natural Law

American acceptance of Natural Law obviously owes something to Congregational Church polity and to the growing independence of individual churches. New England clergymen such as John Wise and Jonathan Mayhew read John Locke but they also drew upon their own experience in the struggle to maintain and expand the independence of the congregation against church councils. James Otis, like so many of his contemporaries, argued for Colonial rights in terms of social compact and a fundamental law. Jefferson's draft of the Declaration of Independence is of course a classic summary of natural rights ideology. Jefferson's good-natured toleration of Shays' Rebellion has often been cited, as it should be, to indicate his tendency to argue for a natural right of rebellion, but the reader should remember that two years later Jefferson gave rather conservative advice to French Revolutionists, and that as President he had very little patience with the Aaron Burr conspiracy. AUTHORS: James

Otis (1725–1783), a Harvard graduate and prominent Boston lawyer, was a popular champion of free speech and colonial rights. Thomas Jefferson (1743–1826) served in many capacities as a Virginia "Patriot," a delegate to the Constitutional Convention, war governor of Virginia, ambassador, Secretary of State, Vice-President, and President. Jefferson was also a distinguished amateur in science, architecture, political and moral philosophy, and other fields. SELECTIONS: "The Natural Rights of the Colonists" from Otis' *The Rights of the British Colonies* (1765). "The Great Social Compact: The Declaration of Independence" (1776). "The Virtues of a Little Rebellion" from a letter by Jefferson in 1787 to James Madison.

THE NATURAL RIGHTS OF THE COLONISTS (1765): JAMES OTIS

In order to form an idea of the natural rights of the Colonists, I presume it will be granted that they are men, the common children of the same Creator with their brethren of Great-Britain. Nature has placed all such in a state of equality and perfect freedom, to act within the bounds of the laws of nature and reason, without consulting the will or regarding the humor, the passions or whims of any other man, unless they are formed into a society or body politic. . . . The truth is . . . men come into the world and into society at the same instant. But this hinders not but that the natural and original rights of each individual may be illustrated and explained in this way better than in any other. We see here by the way a probability, that this abstract consideration of men, which has its use in reasoning on the principles of government, has insensibly led some of the greatest men to imagine, some real general state of nature, agreeable to this abstract conception, antecedent to and independent of society. This is certainly not the case in general, for most men become members of society from their birth. . . .

There is nothing mere evident, says Mr. Locke, than "that creatures of the same species and rank promiscuously born to all the same advantages of nature, and the use of the same faculties, should also be equal one among another, without subordination and subject, unless the master of them all should by any manifest declaration of his will set one above another, and confer on him by an evident and clear appointment, an undoubted right to dominion and sovereignty. The natural liberty of man is to be free from any superior power on earth, and not to be under the will or legislative authority of man, but only to have the law of nature for his rule." This is the liberty of independent states; this is the liberty of every man out of society, and who has a mind to live so; which liberty is only abridged in certain instances, not lost to those who are born in or voluntarily enter into society, this gift of God cannot be annihilated.

The Colonists being men, have a right to be considered as equally entitled to all the rights of nature with the Europeans. . . . By being or becoming members of society, they have not renounced their natural liberty. . . . They have an undoubted right to expect, that their best good will ever be consulted by their rulers, supreme and subordinate, without any partial views confined to the particular interest of one island or another. . . .

In the long run, those who fall on arbitrary measures, will meet with their deserved fate. The law of nature, was not of man's making, nor is it in his power to mend it, or alter its course. He can only perform and keep, or disobey and break it. The last is never done with impunity, even in this life, if it is any punishment for a man to feel himself depraved; to find himself degraded by his own folly and wickedness from the rank of a virtuous and good man, to that of a brute; or to be transformed from the friend, perhaps father of his country, to a devouring Lion or Tyger. . . .

THE GREAT SOCIAL COMPACT:
THE DECLARATION OF INDEPENDENCE (1776):
THOMAS JEFFERSON

When in the Course of human events it becomes necessary for one people to dissolve the political bands which have connected them with another, and to assume among the powers of the earth, the separate and equal station to which the Laws of Nature and of Nature's God entitle them, a decent respect to the opinions of mankind requires that they should declare the causes which impel them to the separation.

We hold these truths to be self-evident, that all men are created equal, that they are endowed by their creator with certain unalienable Rights, that among these are Life, Liberty and the pursuit of Happiness. —That to secure these rights, Governments are instituted among Men, deriving their just powers from the consent of the governed.—That whenever any Form of Government becomes destructive of these ends, it is the Right of the People to alter, or to abolish it, and to institute new Government, laying its foundation on such principles, and organizing its powers in such form, as to them shall seem most likely to effect their Safety and Happiness. Prudence, indeed, will dictate that Governments long established should not be changed for light and transient causes; and accordingly all experience hath shewn, that mankind are more disposed to suffer, while evils are sufferable, than to right themselves by abolishing the forms to which they are accustomed. But when a long train of abuses and usurpations, pursuing invariably the same Object, evinces a design to reduce them under absolute Despotism, it is their right, it is their duty, to throw off such Government, and to provide new Guards for their future security.—Such has been the patient sufferance of these Colonies; and such is now the necessity which constrains them to alter their former Systems of Government. The history of the present King of Great Britain is a history of repeated injuries and usurpations, all having in direct object the establishment of an absolute Tyranny over these States. To prove this, let Facts be submitted to a candid world. . . .

THE VIRTUES OF "A LITTLE REBELLION" (1787): THOMAS JEFFERSON

Those characters, wherein fear predominates over hope, may . . . conclude too hastily, that nature has formed man insusceptible of any other government than that of force, a conclusion not founded in truth nor experience. Societies exist under three forms, sufficiently distinguishable. 1. Without government, as among our Indians. 2. Under governments, wherein the will of everyone has a just influence; as is the case in England, in a slight degree, and in our States, in a great one. 3. Under governments of force; as is the case in all other monarchies, and in most of the other republics. To have an idea of the curse of existence under these last, they must be seen. It is a government of wolves over sheep. It is a problem, not clear in my mind, that the first condition is not the best. But I believe it to be inconsistent with any great degree of population. The second state has a great deal of good in it. The mass of mankind under that, enjoys a precious degree of liberty and happiness. It has its evils, too; the principal of which is the turbulence to which it is subject. But weigh this against the oppressions of monarchy, and it becomes nothing. *Malo periculosam libertatem quam quietam servitutem* (I prefer perilous liberty to quiet servitude). Even this evil is productive of good. It prevents the degeneracy of government, and nourishes a general attention to the public affairs. I hold it, that a little rebellion, now and then, is a good thing, and as necessary in the political world as storms in the physical. Unsuccessful rebellions, indeed, generally establish the encroachments on the rights of the people, which have produced them. An observation of this truth should render honest republican governors so mild in their punishment of rebellions, as not to discourage them too much. It is a medicine necessary for the sound health of government. . . .

5. The State, Society, and the New Nation

The John Adams essay suggests several great changes which remade New England thought during the century before the American Revolution: the chief end of man was no longer the glorification of God but the virtuous happiness of citizens; man existed for himself and all human institutions, including the social contract, existed for human needs. In the political struggles of the seventeen-eighties and -nineties, common notions of human destiny and American prospects united the society. The Founding Fathers were also conscious of themselves as actors in the historical drama which had brought men out the barbarous past and to the great prospects which the American Revolution offered to the world. However, the process of nation building led naturally enough to disagreements. Most American political leaders agreed on the intimate connections of property and political power; but they drew different conclusions from the assumption. Jefferson based his approach to republicanism on a wide distribution of property in the hands of self-sufficient farmers. John Adams and Alexander Hamilton argued that the difference in talents and virtues among men led to wide differences in property and required the balancing of aristocratic and democratic elements in any decently ordered government. Hamilton insisted that governments must tie themselves to the substantial property interests in order to insure strength and stability; otherwise wealth would oppose the new government which must then turn to the disorganized masses of men. In arguing for the new constitution, Hamilton moved to less controversial ground. He urged that the new government be given adequate power to act for the national interests with force and rationality. From 1787 to 1800 the Federalists did effectively establish the Union, but they failed to understand the nature of the American two-party system as it emerged in the seventeen-nineties and they did not appreciate the political aspirations of many Jeffersonian Republicans. Samuel Adams and other anti-Federalists experienced a similar failure of political imagination in opposing the Constitution of 1787, but some of the anti-Federalists lived long enough to serve the American political system in a more positive way. Jefferson and Madison grasped the idea of "a loyal opposition" which made possible opposition to an administration without disloyalty to the government. Soon the focus of political conflict shifted to the expansion of the suffrage, and men such as Fisher Ames and James Kent continued to urge Hamilton's arguments for granting more political power to larger accumulations of property. The suffrage was broadened in the eighteen-twenties and -thirties and with it came the rhetoric of mass democracy. James Fenimore Cooper's essay represents an attempt to reconcile popular democracy with the private claims of birth, wealth, and education. AUTHORS: John Adams (1735–1826), the second President of the United States, was born in Braintree, Massachusetts, educated at Harvard, and admitted to the bar in 1758. Well before the Revolution Adams emerged as a major political figure and continued to hold high office as a delegate to the Continental Convention, a constitutional "expert," a diplomat, Vice-President, and President. Alexander Hamilton (1757–1804), a graduate of King's College (Columbia) came to public attention during the American Revolution as a "Patriot" leader and brilliant young officer on Washington's staff. Hamilton married into a great New York land-owning family and rose to political fame as an architect of the Constitution, the most prominent of the early Federalists, and Washington's brilliant Secretary of the Treasury. During the pre-Revolutionary and early Revolutionary periods Samuel Adams (1722–1803) emerged as one of the major American leaders, but he tended to pass from the center of the national political stage during the seventeen-eighties except for a brief period of limited prominence as an anti-Federalist critic of the Constitution of 1787. James Madison (1751–1836), also a Revolutionary leader and an architect of the Constitution, became a Congressman, Senator, Secretary of State, and President. Thomas Jefferson (1743–1826). Fisher Ames (1758–1808), a Harvard-educated Massachusetts lawyer became a bitter opponent of the French Revolution and one of the most tenacious Federalist opponents of the Jeffersonians. James Fenimore Cooper (1789–1851), the son of a prosperous frontier judge and a strong sympathizer with many aspects of American democracy won prominence as one of the first American professional men of letters. Cooper, who spent much time in France, attempted to give due credit to French culture, American Democracy, and the "Democratic gentlemen." SELECTIONS: "Virtuous Happiness the End of Government" from Adams' *Thoughts on Government* (1776). "Allow Power to Property" from Hamilton's manuscript of 1787 The Impudence of Democracy. "Human Frailty and the Primacy of Local Interests Make the Constitution a Doubtful Enterprise" from Adams' letters to Richard Henry Lee in 1787 and 1789. "A Defense of the New Constitution" from one of Hamilton's *Federalist Papers* (1787). "The Descent of Obligations Through the Generations" from a letter to Thomas Jefferson in 1790. "Republican Unity with Diversity and Toleration" from Jefferson's First Inaugural Address of 1801. "Against the Tyranny of the Many" from an Ames letter of 1805. "The Democratic Gentleman" from Cooper's *The American Democrat* (1838).

VIRTUOUS HAPPINESS; THE END OF
GOVERNMENT (1776): JOHN ADAMS

We ought to consider what is the end of government, before we determine which is the best form. Upon this point all speculative politicians will agree, that the happiness of society is the end of government, as all divines and moral philosophers will agree that the happiness of the individual is the end of man. From this principle it will follow, that the form of government which communicates ease, comfort, security, or, in one word, happiness, to the greatest number of persons, and in the greatest degree, is the best.

All sober inquirers after truth, ancient and modern, pagan and Christian, have declared that the happiness of man, as well as his dignity, consists in virtue. Confucious, Zoroaster, Socrates, Mahomet, not to mention authorities really sacred, have agreed in this.

If there is a form of government, then, whose principle and foundation is virtue, will not every sober man acknowledge it better calculated to promote the general happiness than any other form?

Fear is the foundation of most governments; but it is so sordid and brutal a passion, and renders men in whose breasts it predominates so stupid and miserable, that Americans will not be likely to approve of any political institution which is founded on it.

Honor is truly sacred, but holds a lower rank in the scale of moral excellence than virtue. Indeed, the former is but a part of the latter, and consequently has not equal pretensions to support a frame of government productive of human happiness.

The foundation of every government is some principle or passion in the minds of the people. The noblest principles and most generous affections in our nature, then, have the fairest chance to support the noblest and most generous models of government. . . .

ALLOW POWER TO PROPERTY (1787):
ALEXANDER HAMILTON

All communities divide themselves into the few and the many. The first are the rich and well-born, the other the mass of the people. The voice of the people has been said to be the voice of God; and, however generally this maxim has been quoted and believed, it is not true in fact. The people are turbulent and changing; they seldom judge or determine right. Give, therefore, to the first class a distinct, permanent share in the government. They will check the unsteadiness of the second, and, as they cannot receive any advantage by a change, they therefore will ever maintain good government. Can a democratic Assembly, who annually revolve in the mass of the people, be supposed steadily to pursue the public good? Nothing but a permanent body can check the imprudence of democracy. Their turbulent and uncontrolling disposition requires checks. The Senate of New York, although chosen for four years, we have found to be inefficient. Will, on the Virginia plan, a continuance of seven years do it? It is admitted that you cannot have a good Executive upon a democratic plan. See the excellency of the British Executive. He is placed above temptation. He can have no distinct interests from the public welfare. Nothing short of such an executive can be efficient. The weak side of a republican government is the danger of foreign influence. This is unavoidable, unless it is so constructed as to bring forward its first characters in its support. I am, therefore, for a general government, yet would wish to go full length of republican principles. Let one body of the Legislature be constituted during good behavior or life. Let one Executive be appointed who dares execute his powers. It may be asked: Is this a republican system? It is strictly so, as long as they remain elective. And let me observe, that an Executive is less dangerous to the liberties of the people when in office during life, than for seven years. . . .

HUMAN FRAILTY AND THE PRIMACY OF LOCAL INTERESTS MAKE THE CONSTITUTION A DOUBTFUL ENTERPRISE (1787, 1789): SAMUEL ADAMS

I confess, as I enter the Building I stumble at the Threshold. I meet with a National Government instead of a Federal Union of Sovereign States. I am not able to conceive why the Wisdom of the Convention led them to give the Preference to the former before the latter. If the several States in the Union are to become one entire Nation, under one Legislature, the Powers of which shall extend to every Subject of Legislation, and its Laws be supreme & controul the whole, the Idea of Sovereignty in these States must be lost. . . . Is it to be expected that General Laws can be adapted to the Feelings of the more Eastern and the more Southern Parts of so extensive a Nation? It appears to me difficult if practicable. Hence then may we not look for Discontent, Mistrust, Disaffection to Government and frequent Insurrections, which will require standing Armies to suppress them in one Place & another where they may happen to arise. Or if Laws could be made, adapted to the local Habits, Feelings, Views & Interests of those distant Parts, would they not cause Jealousies of Partiality in Government which would excite Envy and other malignant Passions productive of Wars and fighting. . . .

I have always been apprehensive that through the weakness of the human Mind often discovered even in the wisest and best of Men, or the perverseness of the interested, and designing, in as well as out of Government; Misconstructions would be given to the federal constitution, which would disappoint the Views, and expectations of the honest among those who acceded to it, and hazard the Liberty, Independence and Happiness of the People. I was particularly afraid that unless great care should be taken to prevent it, the Constitution in the Administration of it would gradually, but swiftly and imperceptibly run into a consolidated Government pervading and legislating through all the States, not for federal purposes *only* as it professes, but in all cases whatsoever: such a Government would soon totally annihilate the Sovereignty of the several States so necessary to the Support of the confederated Commonwealth, and sink both in despotism. . . .

A DEFENSE OF THE NEW CONSTITUTION (1787): ALEXANDER HAMILTON

The principal purposes to be answered by union are these—the common defence of the members—the preservation of the public peace as well against internal convulsions as external attacks—the regulation of commerce with other nations and between the states—the superintendence of our intercourse political and commercial with foreign countries. . . .

These powers ought to exist without limitation: Because it is impossible to foresee or to define the extent and variety of national exigencies, and the correspondent extent and variety of the means which may be necessary to satisfy them. The circumstances that endanger the safety of nations are infinite; and for this reason, no constitutional shackles can wisely be imposed on . . . [these powers]. . . .

Whether there ought to be a federal government intrusted with the care of the common defence is a question, in the first instance, open to discussion; but the moment it is decided in the affirmative, it will follow, that that government ought to be cloathed with all the powers requisite to the complete execution of its trust. And unless it can be shewn, that the circumstances which may affect the public safety are reducible within certain determinate limits; unless the contrary of this position can be fairly and rationally disputed, it must be admitted as a necessary consequence, that there can be no limitation of that authority. . . .

. . . There is an absolute necessity for an entire change in the first principles of the system: That if we are in earnest about giving the union energy and duration, we must abandon the vain project of legislating upon the state in their collective capacities; we must extend the laws of the federal government to the individual citizens of America; we must discard the fallacious scheme of quotas and requisitions, as equally impracticable and unjust. The result from all this is, that the union ought to be invested with full power to levy troops—to build and equip fleets and to raise the revenues which will be required for the formation and support of an army and navy, in the customary and ordinary modes practiced in other governments. . . .

Every view we may take of the subject, as candid inquirers after truth, will serve to convince us, that it is both unwise and dangerous to deny the federal government an unconfined authority in respect to all those objects which are intrusted to its management. It will indeed deserve the most vigilant and careful attention of the people to see, that it be modified in such a manner as to admit of its being safely vested with the requisite powers. If any plan, which has been, or may be offered to our consideration should not upon a dispassionate inspection be found to answer this description, it ought to be rejected. A government, the constitution of which renders it unfit to be trusted with all the powers which a free people *ought to delegate to any government*, would be an unsafe and improper depository of the national INTERESTS. Wherever THESE can with propriety be confided, the coincident powers may safely accompany them . . . The POWERS are not too extensive for the OBJECTS of federal administration, or in other words for the management of our NATIONAL INTERESTS; nor can any satisfactory argument be framed to show that they are chargeable with such an excess. If it be true, as has been insinuated by some of the writers on the other side, that the difficulty arises from the nature of the thing, and that the extent of the country will not permit us to form a government, in which such ample powers can safely be reposed, it would prove that we ought to contract our views and resort to the expedient of separate confederacies, which will move within more practicable spheres. For the absurdity must continually stare us in the face of confiding to a government in the direction of the most essential national interests, without daring to trust it with the authorities which are indispensable to their proper and efficient management. Let us not attempt to reconcile contradictions, but firmly embrace a rational alternative. . . .

THE DESCENT OF OBLIGATIONS THROUGH THE GENERATIONS (1790): JAMES MADISON DEBATES THOMAS JEFFERSON

[*Jefferson*, according to Madison's summary]: As the earth belongs to the living, not to the dead, a living generation can bind itself only: In every society the will of the majority binds the whole: According to the laws of mortality, a majority of those ripe at any moment for the exercise of their will do not live beyond nineteen years: To that term then is limited the validity of every act of the Society; Nor within that limitation, can any declaration of the public will be valid which is not express.

[Madison]: Would not a Government [with a fundamental constitution] so often revised become too mutable to retain those prejudices in its favor which antiquity inspires, and which are perhaps a salutary aid to the most rational Government in the most enlightened age? Would not such a periodical revision engender pernicious factions that might not otherwise come into existence? . . .

If the earth be the gift of nature to the living their title can extend to the earth in its natural State only. The improvements made by the dead form a charge against the living who take the benefit of them. This charge can no otherwise be satisfyed than by executing the will of the dead accompanying the improvements.

Debts may be incurred for purposes which interest the unborn, as well as the living: such are debts for repelling a conquest, the evils of which descend through many generations. Debts may even be incurred principally for the benefit of posterity. . . .

There seems then to be a foundation in the nature of things, in the relation which one generation bears to another, for the descent of obligations from one to another. Equity requires it. Mutual good is promoted by it. . . .

Unless such laws should be kept in force by new acts regularly anticipating the end of the term, all the rights depending on positive laws, that is, most of the rights of property would become absolutely defunct; and the most violent struggles be generated between those interested in reviving and those interested in new-modelling the former state of property. . . .

REPUBLICAN UNITY WITH DIVERSITY AND TOLERATION (1801): THOMAS JEFFERSON

But every difference of opinion is not a difference of principle. We have called by different names brethren of the same principle. We are all republicans; we are all federalists. If there be any among us who would wish to dissolve this Union or to change its republican form, let them stand undisturbed as monuments of the safety with which error of opinion may be tolerated, where reason is left free to combat it. I know, indeed, that some honest men fear that a republican government cannot be strong; that this government is not strong enough. But would the honest patriot, in the full tide of successful experiment, abandon a government which has so far kept us free and firm on the theoretic and visionary fear that this government, the world's best hope, may by possibility want energy to preserve itself? I trust not. I believe this, on the contrary, the strongest government on earth. I believe it the only one where every man, at the call of the law, would fly to the standard of the law and would meet invasions of the public order as his own personal concern. Sometimes it is said that man cannot be trusted with the government of himself. Can he then be trusted with the government of others? Or have we found angels, in the form of kings, to govern him? Let history answer this question.

Let us then, with courage and confidence, pursue our own federal and republican principles, our attachment to Union and representative government. Kindly separated by nature and a wide ocean from the exterminating havoc of one quarter of the globe; too high-minded to endure the degradations of the others; possessing a chosen country, with room enough for our descendants to the hundredth and thousandth generation; entertaining a due sense of our equal right to the use of our own faculties, to the acquisitions of our own industry, to honor and confidence from our fellow citizens, resulting not from birth but from our actions and their sense of them; enlightened by a benign religion, professed indeed and practiced in various forms, yet all of them including honesty, truth, temperance, gratitude, and the love of man; acknowledging and adoring an overruling Providence which, by all its dispensations, proves that It delights in the happiness of man here and his greater happiness hereafter; with all these blessings, what more is necessary to make us a happy and a prosperous people?. . .

AGAINST "THE TYRANNY OF THE MANY" (1805): FISHER AMES

They are certainly blind who do not see, that we are descending from a supposed orderly and stable republican government into a licentious democracy, with a progress that baffles all means to resist, and scarcely leaves leisure to deplore its celerity. The institutions and the hopes that Washington raised are nearly prostrate; and his name and memory would perish, if the rage of his enemies had any power over history. But they have not—history will give scope to her vengeance, and posterity will not be defrauded.

But if our experience had not clearly given warning of our approaching catastrophe, the very nature of democracy would inevitably produce it.

A government by the passions of the multitude, or, no less correctly, according to the vices and ambition of their leaders, is a democracy. We have heard so long of the indefeasible sovereignty of the people, and have admitted so many specious theories of the rights of man, which are contradicted by his nature and experience, that few will dread at all, and fewer still will dread as they ought, the evils of an American democracy. They will not believe them near, or they will think them tolerable or temporary. Fatal delusion!

When it is said, there may be a tyranny of the many as well as of the few, every democrat will yield at least a cold and speculative assent; but he will at all times act, as if it were a thing incomprehensible, that there should be any evil to be apprehended in the uncontrolled power of the people. He will say, arbitrary power may make a tyrant, but how can it make its possessor a slave? . . .

The people, as a body, cannot deliberate. Nevertheless, they will feel an irresistible impulse to act, and their resolutions will be dictated to them by demagogues. . . . To make a nation free, the crafty must be kept in awe, and the violent in restraint. The weak and the simple find their liberty arise not from their own individual sovereignty, but from the power of law and justice over all. It is only by the due restraint of others, that I am free. . . .

THE DEMOCRATIC GENTLEMAN (1838):
JAMES FENIMORE COOPER

Social station is that which one possesses in the ordinary associations, and is dependent on birth, education, personal qualities, property, tastes, habits, and, in some instances, on caprice, or fashion. Although the latter undeniably is sometimes admitted to control social station, it generally depends, however, on the other considerations named.

Social station, in the main, is a consequence of property. So long as there is civilization there must be the rights of property, and so long as there are the rights of property, their obvious consequences must follow. All that democracies legitimately attempt is to prevent the advantages which accompany social station from accumulating rights that do not properly belong to the condition, which is effected by pronouncing that it shall have no factitious political aids.

They who have reasoned ignorantly, or who have aimed at effecting their own personal ends by flattering the popular feeling, have boldly affirmed that "one man is as good as another"; a maxim that is true in neither nature, revealed morals, nor political theory.

That one man is not as good as another in natural qualities is proved on the testimony of our sense. One man is stronger than another; he is handsomer, taller, swifter, wiser, or braver, than all his fellows. . . . An aristocrat, therefore, is merely one who fortifies his exclusive privileges by positive institutions, and a democrat, one who is willing to admit of a free competition, in all things. To say, however, that the last supposes this competition will lead to nothing, is an assumption that means are employed without any reference to an end. He is the purest democrat who best maintains his rights, and no rights can be dearer to a man of cultivation, than exemptions from unseasonable invasions on his time, by the coarse-minded and ignorant. . . .

6. Economic Goals of the New Nation

Although many Jeffersonian ideas were to be woven into the fabric of American politics, his hopes for an agrarian society were dashed by the rise of cities and factories. Hamilton proved himself to be an accurate prophet of the American economy. AUTHORS: Thomas Jefferson (1743–1826). Alexander Hamilton (1757–1804). SELECTIONS: "Farmers: 'The Chosen People of God' " from Jefferson's *Notes on the State of Virginia* (1784). "Manufacturing Valuable to America" from Hamilton's *Report on Manufactures* (1791).

FARMERS: "THE CHOSEN PEOPLE OF GOD" (1784): THOMAS JEFFERSON

The political economists of Europe have established it as a principle that every state should endeavor to manufacture for itself. . . . In Europe the lands are either cultivated, or locked up against the cultivator. Manufacture must therefore be resorted to of necessity, not of choice, to support the surplus of their people. But we have an immensity of land courting the industry of the husbandman. . . . Those who labor in the earth are the chosen people of God, if he ever had a chosen people, whose breasts he has made his peculiar deposit for substantial and genuine virtue. It is the focus in which he keeps alive that sacred fire, which otherwise might escape from the face of the earth. Corruption of morals in the mass of cultivators is a phenomenon of which no age nor nation has furnished an example. . . .

MANUFACTURING VALUABLE TO AMERICA (1791): ALEXANDER HAMILTON

1. That inasmuch as it is acknowledged that manufacturing labor reproduces a value equal to that which is expended or consumed in carrying it on and continues in existence the original stock or capital employed, it ought, on that account alone, to escape being considered as wholly unproductive. . . .

2. . . . . Augmentation of the wealth or capital of the community (except in the instances of some extraordinary dexterity or skill), can only proceed with respect to any of them, from the savings of the more thrifty and parsimonious.

3. That the annual produce of the land and labor of a country can only be increased in two ways—by some improvement in the productive powers of the useful labor which actually exists within it, or by some increase in the quantity of such labor. That, with regard to the first, the labor of artificers being capable of greater subdivision and simplicity of operation than that of cultivators, it is susceptible, in a proportionably greater degree, of improvement in its productive powers, whether to be derived from an accession of skill or from the application of ingenious machinery: in which particular, therefore, the labor employed in the culture of land can pretend to no advantage over that engaged in manufactures. . . .

II. But, without contending for the superior productiveness of manufacturing industry, it may conduce to a better judgment of the policy which ought to be pursued . . . to evince . . . that the establishment and diffusion of manufactures have the effect of rendering the total mass of useful and productive labor in a community greater than it would otherwise be. . . .

It is now proper to proceed a step further and to enumerate the principal circumstances, from which it may be inferred that manufacturing establishments not only occasion a positive augmentation of the produce and revenue of the society but that they contribute essentially to rendering them greater than they could possibly be without such establishments. These circumstances are—

1. The division of labor.
2. An extension of the use of machinery.
3. Additional employment to classes of the community not ordinarily engaged in the business.
4. The promoting of emigration from foreign countries.
5. The furnishing greater scope for the diversity of talents and dispositions, which discriminate men from each other.

6. The affording a more ample and various field for enterprise.

7. The creating, in some instances, a new, and securing, in all, a more certain and steady demand for the surplus produce of the soil.

Each of these circumstances has a considerable influence upon the total mass of industrious effort in a community; together, they add to it a degree of energy and effect which is not easily conceived. . . .

7. Religion in the Age of Reason

The religious credos of Franklin and Jefferson were characteristic products of the religious enlightenment. Deism and rational Christianity however tended to be the private beliefs of scattered individuals, without churchs, many converts, or much future in America. The vast majority of Americans were unchurched members of older Protestant churches such as the Congregational and Episcopal, or advocates of the dynamic new Methodist and Baptist churches. These two evangelical groups promised to carry a simplified restatement of Calvinist principles across the continent with devices such as the camp meeting, the revival, the circuit rider, and simple statements on sin, the threat of damnation, and the possibility of salvation. An upsurge of revivalism after 1800 aided the growth of the evangelical churches. AUTHORS: Benjamin Franklin (1706–1790). Thomas Jefferson (1743–1826). Peter Cartwright (1785–1872), a Methodist, was one of a small band of ministerial circuit riders who helped capture vast stretches of Western territory for the Methodist and Baptist churches in the early nineteenth century. SELECTIONS: "Religious Credo" from a Franklin letter of 1790 to President Ezra Stiles of Yale University. "Religious Credo" from Jefferson's letter of 1823. Cartwright's "Camp Meeting" about experiences in 1805–1806 was published in The Backwoods Preacher (1858).

RELIGIOUS CREDO (1790): BENJAMIN FRANKLIN

You desire to know something of my religion. It is the first time I have been questioned upon it. But I cannot take your curiosity amiss, and shall endeavor in a few words to gratify it. Here is my creed.

I believe in one God, creator of the universe. That he governs it by his Providence. That he ought to be worshipped. That the most acceptable service we render to him is doing good to his other children. That the soul of man is immortal, and will be treated with justice in another life respecting its conduct in this. These I take to be the fundamental principles of all sound religion, and I regard them as you do in whatever sect I meet with them.

As to Jesus of Nazareth, my opinion of whom you particularly desire, I think the system of morals, and his religion, as he left them to us, the best the world ever saw or is likely to see; but I apprehend it has received various corrupting changes, and I have, with most of the present dissenters in England, some doubts as to his divinity; tho' it is a question I do not dogmatize upon, having never studied it, and think it needless to busy myself with it now, when I expect soon an opportunity of knowing the truth with less trouble. I see no harm, however, in its being believed, if that belief has the good consequence, as it probably has, of making his doctrines more respected and better observed, especially as I do not perceive that the Supreme takes it amiss, by distinguishing the unbelievers in his government of the world with any peculiar marks of his displeasure. . . .

RELIGIOUS CREDO (1823): THOMAS JEFFERSON

. . . I can never join Calvin in addressing his God. He was indeed an athiest, which I can never be; or rather his religion was daemonism. If ever man worshipped a false God, he did. The being described in his five points, is not the God whom you and I acknowledge and adore, the creator and benevolent governor of the world; but a daemon of malignant spirit. It would be more pardonable to believe in no God at all, than to blaspheme him by the atrocious attributes of Calvin. Indeed, I think that every Christian sect gives a great handle to atheism by their general dogma, that, without a revelation, there would not be sufficient proof of the being of God . . . I hold, (without appeal to revelation) that when we take a view of the universe, in its parts, general or particular, it is impossible for the human mind not to perceive and feel a conviction of design, consummate skill, and indefinite power in every atom of its composition. The movements of the heavenly bodies, so exactly held in their course by the balance of centrifugal and centripetal forces; the structure of our earth itself, with its distribution of lands, waters and atmosphere; animal and vegetable bodies, examined in all their minutest particles; insects, mere atoms of life, yet as perfectly organized as man or mammoth; the mineral substances, their generation and uses; it is impossible, I say, for the human mind not to believe, that there is in all this, design, cause and effect, up to an ultimate cause, a fabricator of all things from matter and motion, their preserver and regulator while permitted to exist in their present forms, and their regeneration into new and other forms. We see, too, evident proofs of the necessity of a superintending power, to maintain the universe in its course and order. Stars, well known, have disappeared, new ones have come into view; comets, in their incalculable courses, may run foul of suns and planets, and require renovation under other laws; certain races of animals are become extinct; and were there no restoring power, all existences might extinguish successively, one by one, until all should be reduced to a shapeless chaos. So irresistible are these evidences of an intelligent and powerful agent, that, of the infinite numbers of men who have existed through all time, they have believed, in the proportion of a million at least to one, in the hypothesis of an external pre-existence of a creator, rather than in that of a self-existent universe. . . .

The truth is, that the greatest enemies to the doctrines of Jesus are those, calling themselves the expositors of them, who have perverted them for the structure of a system of fancy absolutely incomprehensible, and without any foundation in his genuine words. And the day will come when the mystical generation of Jesus, by the Supreme Being as his father, in the womb of a virgin, will be classed with the fable of the generation of Minerva in the brain of Jupiter. But we may hope that the dawn of reason, and freedom of thought in these United States, will do away all this artificial scaffolding, and restore to us the primitive and genuine doctrines of this the most venerated reformer of human errors. . . .

CAMP MEETING (1805): PETER CARTWRIGHT

In making my way on one occasion . . . to my Sunday appointment, I got lost and was belated, and when I arrived, there was a large assembly collected, and this minister was preaching to them, and he preached well, and I was quite pleased with the sermon so far as I heard it. When he was done, he undertook to make a public apology for a drunken spree he had got into a few days before. . . . But to excuse himself for his unaccountable love of whiskey, he stated that he had been informed by his mother that before he was born she longed for whiskey; and he supposed that this was the cause of his appetite for strong drink. . . .

I felt somewhat indignant at this; and when I rose to close after him, I stated to the congregation that I thought the preacher's apology for drunkenness was infinitely worse than the act of drunkenness itself. . . .

After I made these statements, I felt that God was willing to bless the people there and then; and raising my voice, gave them as warm an exhortation as I could command. Suddenly an awful power fell on the congregation, and they instantly fell right and left, and cried aloud for mercy. I suppose there were not less than thirty persons smitten down; the young, the old, and middle-aged, indiscriminately, were operated on in this way. My voice at that day was strong and clear; and I could sing, exhort, pray, and preach almost all the time, day and night. I went through the assembly, singing, exhorting, praying, and directing poor sinners to Christ. While I was thus engaged, the Presbyterian minister left. . . .

Our last quarterly-meeting was a camp-meeting. We had a great many tents, and a large turn-out for a new country, and perhaps, there never was a greater collection of rabble and rowdies. They came drunk, and armed with dirks, clubs, knives, and horse-whips, and swore they would break up the meeting. . . . About the time I was half through my discourse, two very fine dressed young men marched into the congregation with loaded whips, and hats on, and rose up and stood in the midst of the ladies, and began to laugh and talk. . . . I advanced toward them. They ordered me to stand off, but I advanced. One of them made a pass at my head with his whip, but I closed in with him, and jerked him off the seat. . . . The congregation by this time were all in commotion. I heard the magistrates give general orders, commanding all friends of order to aid in suppressing the riot. . . . The mob rose, and rushed to the rescue of the two prisoners, for they had taken the other young man also. An old and drunken magistrate came up to me, and ordered me to let my prisoner go. . . . Then one of my friends, at my request took hold of my prisoner, and the drunken justice made a pass at me; but I parried the stroke, and seized him by the collar and the hair of the head, and fetching him a sudden jerk forward, brought him to the ground, and jumped on him. I told him to be quiet, or I would pound him well. The mob then rushed to the scene; they knocked down seven magistrates, and several preachers and others. . . .

On Sunday, when we had vanquished the mob, the whole encampment was filled with mourning; and although there was no attempt to resume preaching until evening, yet such was our confused state, that there was not then a single preacher on the ground willing to preach, from the presiding elder, John Sale, down. Seeing we had fallen on evil times, my spirit was stirred within me, I said to the elder, "I feel a clear conscience; for under the necessity of the circumstances we have done right; and now I ask to let me preach."

"Do," said the elder; "for there is no other man on the ground can do it."

The encampment was lighted up, the trumpet blown, I rose in the stand, and required every soul to leave the tents and come into the congregation. There was a general rush to the stand. I requested the brethren, if ever they prayed in all their lives, to pray now. My voice was strong and clear, and my preaching was more of an exhortation and encouragement than anything else. My text was, "The gates of hell shall not prevail." In about thirty minutes the power of God fell on the congregation in such a manner as is seldom seen; the people fell in every direction, right and left, front and rear. It was supposed that not less than three hundred fell like dead men in mighty battle; and there was no need of calling mourners, for they were strewed all over the camp-ground; loud wailings went up to heaven from sinners for mercy, and a general shout from Christians, so that the noise was heard afar off. Our meeting lasted all night, and Monday and Monday night; and when we closed on Tuesday, there were two hundred who had professed religion, and about that number joined the Church.

Chapter III. THE CONDITIONS OF

AMERICAN EXPERIENCE

WHILE PURITANISM AND THE ENLIGHTENMENT PROVIDED THE MOST IM-
portant components in the early national mind, other strands of
thought and experience also went into the making of American culture. Certainly the struggles of Puritans and Yankees with soul, soil,
and sea had a powerful impact on the region and the nation. Other
provincial forces also played a part. The largely Protestant, English,
and Scottish population presented a semblance of unity, but the
Continent sheltered enough human diversity to suggest to Americans
that they might be something more than transplanted Englishmen.
The presence of Indians, Anglican Cavaliers, Dutch burghers, Swed-
ish woodsmen, German pietists, French explorers, and Spanish priests
affected early American history significantly. From Texas to California scattered Spanish frontier outposts of clerics, soldiers, and defeated Indians left visible traces in the American heritage. Important
islands of Indian life, French culture in Louisiana, Spanish settlements in New Mexico, and German communities in Pennsylvania
resisted the power of the general society for generations, and persisted into the twentieth century. While assimilation was the common destiny, the vanquished left to the conquerors place names,
words, and social habits; and altered in subtle ways the very nature of
the society as well as the quality of its thought. Still more significant
forces came to birth in sectionalism. Sections both provided part of
the "stuff" of nationality and posed dangers to national existence.
The West considered as a section always seemed to some Easterners
savage, untamed, and a danger to American civilization. Even New
England challenged the Union before and during the war of 1812,
and the South with its "peculiar institution" posed problems almost
perpetually for the general society.

Almost as rapidly as the New England Puritans, Southerners
developed distinctive social patterns which were most strikingly characterized in Virginia by slaves, tobacco, and large plantations. William Byrd's descriptions of the tobacco empire in the early eighteenth

century do convey sophistication and a genial humanity, and certainly Byrd suggests some of the sources of that ideal of social grace, cosmopolitan spirit, and mastery over vast acres around which the mind of the plantation South would eventually crystallize.

Still, Southern life was broader and more complex than plantation ideals ever conceded. Tidewater "aristocrats" had to share the historical stage with James Oglethorpe's religious refugees and convicts, Byrd's "shiftless" Carolinians, and nonconformist devotees of a "hell-fire" Protestant evangelism. William Byrd, the very prototype of the Southern aristocrat, lived in the backcountry and not far beyond his richly furnished drawing room lay the "howling wilderness." Even when the plantation existed in its ripest reality, the institution rested on the brutalities of slavery and caste. Savagery of origins was demonstrated in the millions of Africans killed in the slave trade; institutionalized oppression marked the victims; and thoughtful planters such as Jefferson described slavery as an invitation to the exercise of "the most boisterous passions." Moreover, slavery left a troublesome heritage for the whole society in the rituals and superstitions of caste rule, some of which persisted a century after the end of the legal institution of slavery.

Similar ambiguities could be found in frontier life. Much has been said about the West as a force for the freedom of the individual, and the economic liberation of those whom it sheltered. The frontier, in which land was most available, did bring fulfillment to many, but existence in the wilderness shaped for ill as well as good the lives of those who came there. A sparsely settled continent, social values selectively strengthened by the problem of physical survival, social isolation, the use of violence, the levelling force of the frontier—all played a part in the development of American society.

In many cases, the frontier bred particular political forms. The first formal appearance of the state was often in voluntary social contracts which reflected the needs and the independence of the frontiersmen; the Kentucky Compact, drafted in 1775, represents a long tradition which flourished from the Mayflower Compact to the California mining camp agreements. Still if the West represented political and economic promise, it also posed the gravest dangers. Too often, the most essential human institutions collapsed on the frontier. Americans who have thrown a romantic veil around these political and social aspects of Western life, tend to forget the sterner realities of the wilderness where often men who had "deserted" past personal histories lived without the basic communal amenities, and sometimes fell prey to isolation and alienation. Three centuries of often savage frontier warfare had a powerful impact on the victorious settlers as well as on the vanquished Indians. The frontier has been described as a great democratic leveller which created a free society, but it has also been regarded as a savage reaper threatening to harvest civilization itself. If the West is to be remembered for promise and fulfillment, it cannot be forgotten as a source of violence, institutional frailty, and anti-intellectualism.

In formulating a national ideology during the second half of the eighteenth century, Americans paid scant attention to frontier conflict, caste, slavery, and sectionalism. Nor was this fact surprising in view of the need for a sense of nationality and the lack of many elements which stimulated nationalism in Europe. The United States had no ancient folk, soil, or homeland, no "blood and soil" materials, no native tongue peculiarly its own. Citizens could not define American society as an arena for social conflict or the hope for union and justice in the remote future. Abstract symbols such as the Constitution, the Union, "liberty," and "equality" provided the basic stuff of nationalism. The United States was in a sense the ideal of the Enlightenment; the nation was its mission; and as Richard Hofstadter has remarked, it was the fate of America not to have an ideology but to be one. Consequently, common definitions spoke of the remnant "saved" from the corrupt Old World, the international refuge of liberty, the New World home of virtues which had little place in the dying monarchies of Europe.

Americans could hardly describe the new nation after the fashion of sociological description as a Protestant land of English and Scottish immigrants with a diverse scattering of other religious, ethnic, and racial groups; so they sought definitions such as those provided by Crèvecoeur. After this fashion of identity speculation, the American was a new man, unique in history, and very different from Englishmen or Frenchmen. In the midst of diversity and conflict, Americans not only had to insist on the belief in unity and social peace but even felt the need to assert that the nation was these conditions by definition. If America was not the land of freedom and equality, what was it? If the American was not a new man created by the fusion of many stocks, who was he?

1. The West: Promise and Threat

In the eighteen-nineties, Frederick Jackson Turner began to write of the frontier after a fashion which many modern scholars have sharply criticized. According to Turner, the frontier was the source of democracy and individualism, the area where Americans were made from European materials. The frontier did often breed the habit of political initiative and the use of devices such as the "social contract" of the Kentucky Convention in 1775, but it now seems probable that Turner was guilty of romantic exaggeration. Although most nineteenth-century Americans would have agreed with Timothy Flint's defense, the West had its critics who feared the possible loss of social stability, and even of civilization, on the frontier. AUTHORS: John Smith (1580-1631) was a soldier, adventurer, and explorer, as well as one of the chief architects of the Jamestown Colony in Virginia. Richard Henderson (1735-1785), a Virginia frontier lawyer, followed Daniel Boone across the mountains to become one of the pioneer founders of "Transylvania" (Kentucky). Timothy Dwight (1752–1817) was a poet, theologian, one of the "Hartford Wits," and a zealous Federalist enemy of the Jeffersonian Republicans. Timothy Flint (1780–1840), a Harvard graduate and a minister, became a defender of Western virtues after a missionary tour of the West in 1815. SELECTIONS: "The Western Promise" from Smith's A Description of New England (1616). "Frontier Democracy" from a Henderson speech to the Kentucky Convention of 1775. "The Menace of the West" from Dwight's Travels in New England and New York (1821). "The West Defended" (1816) from Flint's Recollections of the Last Ten Years (1826).

THE WESTERN PROMISE (1616): JOHN SMITH

Who can desire more content, that hath small meanes; or but only his merit to advance his fortune, then to tread, and plant that ground hee hath purchased by the hazard of his life? If he have but the taste of virtue and magnanimitie, what to such a minde can bee more pleasant, then planting and building a foundation for his posteritie, gotte from the rude earth, by Gods blessing and his owne industrie, without prejudice to any? If hee have any graine of faith or zeale in Religion, what can hee doe lesse hurtfull to any: or more agreeable to God, then to seeke to convert those poore Salvages to know Christ, and humanitie, whose labors with discretion will triple requite thy charge and paines? What so truly su[i]tes with honour and honestie, as the discovering things unknowne? erecting Townes, peopling Countries, informing the ignorant, reforming things unjust, teaching virtue; and gaine to our Native mother-countrie a kingdom to attend her: finde imployment for those that are idle, because they know not what to doe: so farre from wronging any, as to cause Posteritie to remember thee; and remembring thee, ever honour that remembrance with praise? . . .

And lest any should think the toile might be insupportable, though these things may be had by labour, and diligence: I assure my selfe there are who delight extreamly in vaine pleasure, that take much more paines in *England*, to enjoy it, then I should doe heere [*New England*] to gaine wealth sufficient: and yet I thinke they should not have halfe such sweet content: for, our pleasure here is still gaines; in *England* charges and losse. Heer nature and liberty affords us that freely, which in *England* we want, or it costeth us dearely. What pleasure can be more, then (being tired with any occasion a-shore, in planting Vines, Fruits, or Hearbs, in contriving their owne Grounds, to the pleasure of their owne mindes, their Fields, Gardens, Orchards, Buildings, Ships and other works, &c.) to recreate themselves before their owne doores in their owne boates upon the Sea; where man, woman and childe, with a small hooke and line, by angling, may take diverse sorts of excellent fish, at their pleasures? And is it not pretty sport, to pull up two pence, six pence, and twelve pence, as fast as you can ha[u]le and veare a line? He is a very bad fisher [that] cannot kill in one day with his hooke and line, one, two, or three hundred Cods: which dressed and dried, if they be sould there for ten shillings the hundred, though in England they will give more than twentie may not both the servant, the master, and marchant, be well content with this gaine? If a man worke but three dayes in seaven, he may get more than hee can spend, unless he will be excessive. Now that Carpenter, Mason, Gardiner, Taylor, Smith, Sailer, Forgers, or what other, may they not make this a pretty recreation though they fish but an houre in a day, to take more then they eate in a weeke? or if they will not eate it, because there is so much better choice; yet sell it, or change it, with the fisher men, or marchants, for any thing they want. And what sport doth yeeld a more pleasing content, and lesse hurt or charge then angling with a hooke; and crossing the sweete ayre from Ile to Ile, over the silent streames of a calme Sea? Wherein the most curious may finde pleasure, profit, and content. . . .

FRONTIER DEMOCRACY (1775): RICHARD HENDERSON TO THE KENTUCKY CONVENTION

Our peculiar circumstances in this remote country, surrounded on all sides with difficulties, and equally subject to one common danger, which threatens our common overthrow, must, I think, in their effects, secure to us an union of interests, and consequently, that harmony in opinion, so essential to the forming good, wise, and wholesome laws. If any doubt remain amongst you with respect to the force or efficacy of whatever laws you now, or hereafter make, be pleased to consider that all power is originally in the people; therefore make it their interest, by impartial and beneficial laws, and you may be sure of their inclination to see them enforced. For it is not to be supposed that a people, anxious and desirous of having laws made,—who approve of the method of choosing delegates, or representatives, to meet in general convention for that purpose, can want the necessary and concomitant virtue to carry them into execution.

Nay, gentlemen, for argument's sake, let us set virtue for a moment out of the question, and see how the matter will then stand. You must admit that it is, and ever will be, the interest of a large majority that the laws should be esteemed and held sacred; if so, surely this large majority can never want inclination or power to give sanction and efficacy to those very laws which advance their interest and secure their property. And now, Mr. Chairman and gentlemen of the convention, as it is indispensably necessary that laws should be composed for the regulation of our conduct, as we have a right to make such laws without giving offense to Great Britain or any of the American colonies, without disturbing the repose of any society or community under heaven; if it is probably, nay, certain, that the laws may derive force and efficacy from our mutual consent, and that consent resulting from our own virtue, interest, and convenience, nothing remains but to set about the business immediately, and let the event determine the wisdom of the undertaking. . . .

THE MENACE OF THE WEST (1821):
TIMOTHY DWIGHT

The class of men [frontiersmen] who have been the principal subject of these remarks have already straggled onward from New-England, as well as from other parts of the Union, to Louisiana. In a political view their emigration is of very serious utility to the ancient settlements. All countries contain restless inhabitants, men impatient of labour; men who will contract debts without intending to pay them, who had rather talk than work, whose vanity persuades them that they are wise and prevents them from knowing that they are fools, who are delighted with innovation, who think places of power and profit due to their peculiar merits, who feel that every change from good order and established society will be beneficial to themselves, who have nothing to lose and therefore expect to be gainers by every scramble, and who, of course, spend life in disturbing others with the hope of gaining something for themselves. Under despotic governments they are awed into quiet; but in every free community they create, to a greater or lesser extent, continual turmoil, and have often overturned the peace, liberty, and happiness of their fellow-citizens. In the Roman Commonwealth, as before in the Republics of Greece, they were emptied out as soldiers upon the surrounding countries, and left the sober inhabitants in comparative quiet at home. It is true, they often threw these States into confusion and sometimes overturned the government. But if they had not been thus thrown off from the body politic, its life would have been of a momentary duration. As things actually were, they finally ruined all these States. For some of them had, as some of them always will have, sufficient talents to do mischief, at times, very extensive. The Gracchi, Clodius, Marius, and Mark Antony were men of this character. Of this character is every demagogue, whatever may be his circumstances. Power and profit are the only ultimate objects which every such man, with a direction as steady as that of the needle to the pole, pursues with a greediness unlimited and inextinguishable. . . .

THE WEST DEFENDED (1816): TIMOTHY FLINT

The people in the Atlantic states have not yet recovered from the horror, inspired by the term "backwoodsman." This prejudice is particularly strong in New England, and is more or less felt from Maine to Georgia. . . .

When we look round these immense regions, and consider that I have been in settlements three hundred miles from any court of justice, when we look at the position of the men, and the state of things, the wonder is, that so few outrages and murders occur. The gentlemen of the towns, even here, speak often with a certain contempt and horror of the backwoodsmen. I have read, and not without feelings of pain, the bitter representations of the learned and virtuous Dr. Dwight, in speaking of them. He represents these vast regions as a grand reservoir for the scum of the Atlantic states. He characterizes in the mass of the emigrants from New England, as discontented cobblers, too proud, too much in debt, too unprincipled, too much puffed up with self-conceit, too strongly impressed that their fancied talents could not find scope in their own country, to stay there. It is true there are worthless people here, and the most so, it must be confessed, are from New England. It is true that there are gamblers, and gougers, and outlaws; but there are fewer of them, than from the nature of things, and the character of the age and the world, we ought to expect. But it is unworthy of the excellent man in question so to designate this people in the mass.

The backwoodsman of the west, as I have seen him, is generally an amiable and virtuous man. His general motive for coming here is to be a freeholder, to have plenty of rich land, and to be able to settle his children about him. . . .

You find, in truth, that he has vices and barbarisms, peculiar to his situation. His manners are rough. He wears, it may be, a long beard. He has a great quantity of bear or deer skins wrought into his household establishment, his furniture, and dress. He carries a knife, or a dirk in his bosom, and when in the woods has a rifle on his back, and a pack of dogs at his heels. An Atlantic stranger, transferred directly from one of our cities to his door, would recoil from an encounter with him. But remember, that his rifle and his dogs are among his chief means of support and profit. Remember, that all his first days here were passed in dread of the savages. Remember, that he still encounters them, still meets bears and panthers.

Enter his door, and tell him you are benighted, and wish the shelter of his cabin for the night. The welcome is indeed seemingly ungracious: "I reckon you can stay," or "I suppose we must let you stay." But this apparent ungraciousness is the harbinger of every kindness that he can bestow, and every comfort that his cabin can afford. Good coffee, corn bread and venison, pork, wild and tame fowls are set before you. His wife, timid, silent, reserved, but constantly attentive to your comfort, does not sit at the table with you, but like the wives of the patriarchs, stands and attends on you. You are shown to the best bed which the house can offer. When this kind of hospitality has been afforded you as long as you choose to stay, and when you depart, and speak about your bill, you are most commonly told with some slight mark of resentment, that they do not keep tavern. Even the flaxen-headed urchin will turn away your money. . . .

With [a] single exception, I have found the backswoodsmen to be such as I have described; a hardy adventurous, hospitable, rough, but sincere and upright race of people. I have received so many kindnesses from them, that it becomes me always to preserve a gratefull and affectionate remembrance of them. . . .

2. *Frontier Warfare*

From the seventeenth through the nineteenth century, settlers accused the Indians of savagery, treachery, and barbarism, after the fashion of Hugh Henry Brackenridge's indictment. As the narrative by Mary White indicates, Indians could indeed conduct ruthless warfare, but the settlers were also energetic in committing acts which ranged from random assassination to cannibalism. Frontier warfare tended to devaluate human life and to establish patterns of aggression, violence, and racism—some of which still linger in American life. AUTHORS: Mary Rowlandson White (1635–1678), a New England immigrant renowned for her piety, was captured in King Philip's War on February 10, 1676. Benjamin Franklin (1706–1790), who expressed so much indignation over the massacre of Indians by the Paxton boys, is often remembered for some hostile remarks about Indians which were made current by D. H. Lawrence in *Studies in Classic American Literature*. Hugh Henry Brackenridge (1748–1816), an immigrant from Scotland to the Pennsylvania frontier, studied at Princeton and became a teacher, editor, lawyer, and a leader in the Whiskey Rebellion of 1794. SELECTIONS: "An Indian Raid" (1676) from White's *The Soveraignty and Goodness of God . . . Being a Narrative of the Captivity and Restoration of Mrs. Mary Rowlandson White* (1682). "Massacre by the Paxton Boys" (1763) from Franklin's *A Narrative of the Late Massacres, in Lancaster County . . .* (1763). "The Indians: Savages Deserving Extermination" from a Brackenridge letter to *Freeman's Journal and North American Intelligencer* in 1782.

AN INDIAN RAID (1676):
MARY ROWLANDSON WHITE

On the tenth of *February* [1676] came the *Indians* with great Numbers upon *Lancaster*: Their first coming was about Sun-rising; hearing the noise of some Guns, we looked out; several Houses were burning, and the Smoke ascending to Heaven. There were five persons taken in one House, the Father, and the Mother, and a suckling Child they knockt on the head; the other two they took and carried away alive. There were two others, who being out of their Garrison upon some Occasion, were set upon; one was knockt on the head, the other escaped: Another there was who running along was shot and wounded, and fell down; he begged of them his life, promising them Money (as they told me) but they would not hearken to him, but knockt him in head, and stript him naked, and split open his Bowels. . . .

At length they came & beset our own house, and quickly it was the dolefullest Day that ever mine eyes saw. . . . Now is that dreadful hour come, that I have often heard of (in time of War, as it was the Case in others) but now mine eyes see it. Some of our House were fighting for their lives, others wallowing in their Blood, the House on fire over our heads, and the bloody Heathen ready to knock us on the head, if we stirred out. Now might we hear Mothers and Children crying out for themselves, and one another, Lord, what shall we do? Then I took my Children (and one of my Sisters, hers) to go forth and leave the house: but as soon as we came to the door and appeared, the Indians shot so thick that the bullets rattled against the House. . . . But out we must go, the fire increasing, and coming along behind us, roaring, and the *Indians* gaping before us with their Guns, Spears, and Hatchets to devour us. No sooner were we out of the House, but my Brother-in-Law (being before Wounded in defending the House, in or near the Throat) fell down dead, whereat the *Indians* scornfully shouted, and halloed, and were presently upon him, stripping off his cloaths. The bullets flying thick, one went through my side, and the same (as would seem) through the Bowels and Hand of my dear Child in my Arms. . . . When I had been at my Masters Wigwam, I took the first opportunity I could get, to go look after my dead Child: when I came, I asked them what they had done with it? they told me it was upon the Hill; and then they went and shewed me where it was, where I saw the Ground was newly digged, and where they told me they had buried it; there I left that Child in the Wilderness, and must commit it and my self also in this wilderness Condition, to him who is above all. God having taken away this dear Child, I went to see my Daughter Mary, who was at this same *Indian* Town, at a Wigwam not very far off, though we had little liberty or opportunity to see one another. She was about ten years old, and taken from the door at first by a Praying *Indian* and afterward sold for a Gun. When I came in sight, she would fall a Weeping, at which they were provoked, and would not let me come near her, but bade me be gone; which was a Heart-cutting Word to me. I had one Child dead, another in the Wilderness, I knew not where, the third they would not let me come near to: Me (as he said) *have ye bereaved of my Children: Joseph is not, and Simeon is not, and ye will take Benjamin also; all these things are against me.* I could not sit still in this Condition, but kept walking from one place to another. . . .

MASSACRE BY THE PAXTON BOYS (1763): BENJAMIN FRANKLIN

These *Indians* were the Remains of a Tribe of the *Six Nations*, settled at *Conestogoe*, and thence called *Conestogoe Indians*. On the first Arrival of the *English* in *Pennsylvania*, Messengers from this Tribe came to welcome them, with Presents of Venison, Corn, and Skins; and the whole Tribe entered into a Treaty of Friendship with the first Proprietor, William Penn, which was to last "as long as the Sun should shine, or the Waters run in the Rivers." . . . .

This little Society continued the Custom they had begun, when more numerous of addressing every new Governor, and every Descendant of the first Proprietor, welcoming him to the Province, assuring him of their Fidelity, and praying a Continuance of that Favour and Protection they had hitherto experienced. They had accordingly sent up an Address of this Kind to our present Governor, on his Arrival; but the same was scarce delivered, when the unfortunate Catastrophe happened, which we are about to relate.

On Wednesday, the 14th of *December*, 1763, Fifty-seven Men, from Frontier Townships, who had projected the destruction of this little Commonwealth, came, all well mounted, and armed with Firelocks, Hangers and Hatchets, having travelled through the Country in the Night, to *Conestogoe* Manor. There they surrounded the small Village of *Indian* Huts, and just at Break of Day broke into them all at once. Only three Men, two Women, and a young Boy, were found at home, the rest being out among the neighboring White People, some to sell the Baskets, Brooms and Bowls they manufactured, and others on other Occasions. These poor defenceless Creatures were immediately fired upon, stabbed, and hatcheted to Death! The good *Shehaes*, among the rest, cut to Pieces in his Bed. All of them were scalped and otherwise horribly mangled. Then their Huts were set on Fire, and most of them burnt down. Then the Troop, pleased with their own Conduct and Bravery, but enraged that any of the poor *Indians* had escaped the Massacre, rode off, and in small Parties, by different Roads, went home. . . .

Notwithstanding . . . [the Governor's] Proclamation, those cruel Men again assembled themselves, and hearing that the remaining fourteen *Indians* were in the Workhouse at *Lancaster*, they suddenly appeared in that Town, on the 27th of *December*. Fifty of them, armed as before, dismounting, went directly to the Workhouse, and by Violence broke open the Door, and entered with the utmost Fury in their Countenances. When the poor Wretches saw they had *no Protection* nigh, nor could possibly escape, and being without the least Weapon for Defence they divided into their little Families, the Children clinging to the Parents; they fell on their Knees, protested their Innocence, declared their Love to the *English*, and that, in their whole Lives, they had never done them Injury; and in this Posture they all received the Hatchet! Men, Women, and little Children were every one inhumanly murdered!—in cold Blood!

The barbarous Men who committed the atrocious Fact, in defiance of Government, of all Laws human and divine, and to the eternal Disgrace of their Country and Colour, then mounted their Horses, huzza'd in Triumph, as if they had gained a Victory, and rode off—*unmolested!*

The Bodies of the Murdered were then brought out and exposed in the Street, till a Hole could be made in the Earth to receive and cover them. . . .

THE INDIANS: SAVAGES DESERVING EXTERMINATION (1782): HUGH HENRY BRACKENRIDGE

A wild Indian with his skin painted red, and a feather through his nose, has set his foot on the broad continent of North and South America; a second wild Indian with his ears cut in ringlets, or his nose slit like a swine or a malefactor, also sets his foot on the same extensive tract of soil. Let the first Indian make a talk to his brother, and bid him take his foot off the continent, for he being first upon it, had occupied the whole, to kill buffaloes, and tall elks with long horns. This claim in the reasoning of some men would be just, and the second savage ought to depart in his canoe, and seek a continent where no prior occupant claimed the soil. . . .

With regard to forming treaties or making peace with this race, there are many ideas:

They have the shapes of men and may be of the human species, but certainly in their present state they approach nearer the character of Devils; take an Indian, is there any faith in him? Can you bind him by favors? Can you trust his word or confide in his promise? When he makes war upon you, when he takes you prisoner and has you in his power will he spare you? In this he departs from the law of nature, by which, according to Baron Montesquieu and every other man who thinks on the subject, it is unjustifiable to take away the life of him who submits; the conqueror in doing otherwise becomes a murderer, who ought to be put to death. On this principle are not the whole Indian nations murderers?

Many of them may have not had an opportunity of putting prisoners to death, but the sentiment which they entertain leads them invariably to this when they have it in their power or judge it expedient; these principles constitute them murderers, and they ought to be prevented from carrying them into execution, as we would prevent a common homicide, who should be mad enough to conceive himself justifiable in killing men.

The tortures which they exercise on the bodies of their prisoners, justify extermination. . . .

3. Slavery and Caste

The first century of slavery led not only to the legal system of slavery but also to a social philosophy of caste. Although "free" Negroes existed throughout the slavery period, they were restricted and repressed; and long before the American Revolution slavery and dark complexions were riveted together in the minds of white Americans. The slaves were said to be a "naturally" inferior caste subject to white rule by reason of lesser intelligence, imagination, virtue, and beauty. Benjamin Banneker, the Negro scientist and inventor, and Phyllis Wheatley, the Negro poet, were unknown to most whites, and even the few like Jefferson who knew of them did not consider that their accomplishments constituted convincing evidence of intellectual equality. The few scattered protests and petitions of slaves and "free" Negroes seem to have influenced some white men; the Negroes who fought for the Patriots and those who joined the British in quest of freedom probably provided more persuasive arguments. A substantial number of American leaders voiced their criticism of slavery, but almost all of them continued to believe in the caste superiority of the whites. Negro protest took the form of conspiracies, revolts, and run-aways, but militant written protests were rare before the eighteen-twenties. David Walker's *Appeal* represents a militant answer to caste claims and slavery. AUTHORS: Thomas Jefferson (1743-1826) throughout most of his life criticized the institution of slavery. On the issue of racial equality, he expressed several opinions and was certainly willing to con-sider the possibility that the Negroes were the potential equals of the whites. The document of 1784 used in this chapter may not do ultimate justice to Jefferson, but it provides a clear statement of commonly ac-cepted caste beliefs. David Walker (1785–1830), the son of a slave father and a free mother, fled Wilmington, North Carolina shortly before 1827. In New England he operated a used clothing business until he died under mysterious circumstances (possibly by poisoning) after completing the third revision of his pamphlet in 1830. SELECTIONS: "Negro Petitions and Protests": the first petition from a group of slaves to the Governor and General Court of Massachusetts in 1774; the second excerpt from a protest to the Massachusetts legislature in 1788. "For the Emancipation and Expulsion of Negroes" from Jefferson's *Notes on the State of Vir-ginia* (1784). "Radical Protest against Slavery and Caste" from Walker's *Appeal . . . to the Coloured Citizens of the World . . .* (1829).

NEGRO PETITIONS AND PROTESTS (1774, 1788)

That your Petitioners apprehind we have in common with all other men a naturel right to our freedoms without Being depriv'd of them by our fellow men as we are a freeborn Pepel and have never forfeited this Blessing by aney compact or agreement whatever. But we were unjustly dragged by the cruel hand of power from our dearest frinds and sum of us stolen from the bosoms of our tender Parents. . . .

Nither can we reap an equal benefet from the laws of the Land which doth not justifi but condemns Slavery or if there had bin aney Law to hold us in Bondage we are Humbely of the Opinion ther never was aney to inslave our children for life when Born in a free Countrey. We therfor Bage your Excellency and honours will give this its deer weight and consideration and that you will accordingly cause an act of the legislative be be pessed that we may obtain our Natural right our freedoms and our children be set at lebety at the yeare of twenty one for whoues sekes more petequeley your Petitioners is in Duty ever to pray. . . .

One thing more we would bege leve to Hint, that is that your Petetioners have for sumtime past Beheald whith greef ships cleared out from this Herber for Africa and there they ether steal or case others to steal our Brothers & Sisters fill there ships holes full of unhappy men & women crouded together, then set out to find the Best markets seal them there like sheep for the slarter and then Returne near like Honest men; after haven sported with the Lives and Lebeties fello men and at the same time call themselves Christions: Blush o Hevens at this. . . .

FOR THE EMANCIPATION AND EXPULSION OF NEGROES (1784): THOMAS JEFFERSON

It will probably be asked, Why not retain and incorporate the black into the State, and thus save the expense of supplying by importation of white settlers, the vacancies they will leave? Deep-rooted prejudices entertained by the whites; ten thousand recollections, by the blacks, of the injuries they have sustained; new provocations; the real distinctions which nature has made; and many other circumstances, will divide us into parties, and produce convulsions, which will probably never end but in the extermination of the one or the other race. To these objections, which are political, may be added others, which are physical and moral. The first difference which strikes us is that of color. . . . And is this difference of no im-

portance? Is it not the foundation of a greater or less share of beauty in
the two races? Are not the fine mixtures of red and white, the expressions
of every passion by greater or less suffusions of color in the one, preferable
to that eternal monotony which reigns in the countenances, that im-
movable veil of black which covers the emotions of the other race? Add to
these, flowing hair, a more elegant symmetry of form, their own judgment
in favor of the whites, declared by their preference of them, as uniformly
as is the preference of the Oran-utan for the black woman over those of
his own species. The circumstance of superior beauty, is thought worthy
attention in the propagation of our horses, dogs, and other domestic
animals; why not in that of man? Besides those of color, figure, and hair,
there are other physical distinctions proving a difference of race. They
have less hair. . . . They secrete less by the kidneys, and more by the
glands of the skin, which gives them a very strong and disagreeable odor.
The greater degree of transpiration, renders them more tolerant of heat,
and less so of cold than the whites. . . . They seem to require less
sleep. . . . They are at least as brave, and more adventuresome . . .
[which] may perhaps proceed from a want of forethought. . . . They
are more ardent after their female; but love seems with them to be more
an eager desire, than a tender delicate mixture of sentiment and sensation. Their griefs are transient. . . . [They] have more of sensation than
reflection. To this must be ascribed their disposition to sleep when abstracted from their diversions, and unemployed in labor. . . . [In]
memory, reason, and imagination, it appears to me that in memory they
are equal to the whites; in reason much inferior . . . in imagination
they are dull, tasteless, and anomalous. . . . Some have been liberally
educated, and all have lived in countries where the arts and sciences are
cultivated to a considerable degree, and all have had before their eyes
samples of the best works from abroad. The Indians, with no advantages
of this kind, will often carve figures . . . not destitute of design and
merit. . . . They astonish you with strokes of the most sublime ora-
tory. . . . But never yet could I find that a black had uttered a thought
above the level of plain narration; never saw even an elementary trait of
painting or sculpture. In music they are more generally gifted than the
whites with accurate ears for tune and time, and they have been found
capable of imagining a small catch. Whether they will be equal to the
composition of a more extensive run of melody, or of complicated harmony, is yet to be proved. Misery is often the parent of the most affecting
touches in poetry. Among the blacks is misery enough, God knows, but
no poetry. . . . Religion, indeed, has produced a Phyllis Whately; but it
could not produce a poet. . . . I advance it, therefore, as a suspicion
only, that the blacks, whether originally a distinct race or made distinct
by time and circumstances, are inferior to the whites in the endowments
both of body and mind. . . .

Among the Romans emancipation required but one effort. The slave, when made free, might mix with, without staining the blood of his master. But with us a second is necessary, unknown to history. When freed, he is to be removed beyond the reach of mixture. . . .

RADICAL PROTEST AGAINST SLAVERY AND CASTE (1829): DAVID WALKER

I am fully aware, in making this appeal to my much afflicted and suffering brethren, that I shall not only be assailed by those whose greatest earthly desires are, to keep us in abject ignorance and wretchedness, and who are of the firm conviction that Heaven has designed us and our children to be slaves and *beasts of burden* to them and their children. I say, I do not only expect to be held up to the public as an ignorant, impudent and restless disturber of the public peace, by such avaricious creatures, as well as a mover of insubordination—and perhaps put in prison or to death, for giving a superficial exposition of our miseries, and exposing tyrants. . . . I will ask one question here.—Can our condition be any worse?—Can it be more mean and abject? . . . . [My] object is, if possible, to awaken in the breasts of my afflicted, degraded and slumbering brethren, a spirit of inquiry and investigation respecting our miseries and wretchedness in this *Republican Land of Liberty* ! ! ! ! ! ! . . . . My beloved brethren: The Indians of North and of South America—the Greeks—the Irish, subjected under the king of Great Britain—the Jews, that ancient people of the Lord—the inhabitants of the islands of the sea—in fine, all the inhabitants of the earth, (except, however, the sons of Africa), are called *men*, and of course are, and ought to be free. But we, (coloured people) and our children are *brutes! !* and of course are, and *ought to be* SLAVES to the American people and their children forever! ! to dig their mines and work their farms; and thus go on enriching them, from one generation to another with our *blood* and *our tears* ! ! ! . . . .

    Never make an attempt to gain our freedom or *natural right*, from under our cruel oppressors and murderers, until you see your way clear when that hour arrives and you move; be not afraid or dismayed; for be you assured that Jesus Christ the King of heaven and of earth who is the God of justice and of armies, will surely go before you. And those enemies who have for hundreds of years stolen our *rights*, and kept us ignorant of Him and His divine worship, he will remove. Millions of whom, are this day, so ignorant and avaricious, that they cannot conceive how God can have an attribute of justice, and show mercy to us because it pleased Him to make us black—which colour, Mr. Jefferson calls unfortunate ! ! ! ! ! ! As though we are not as thankful to our God, for having made us as it pleased himself, as they, (the whites,) are for having made them white. They think because they hold us in their infernal chains of slavery, that we wish to be white or of their color—but they are dreadfully deceived— we wish to be just as it pleased our Creator to have made us, and no avaricious and unmerciful wretches, have any business to make slaves of and hold us in slavery. How would they like for us to make slaves of, and hold them in cruel slavery, and murder them as they do us?— . . . .

Let no man of us budge one step, and let slave-holders come to beat us from our country. America is more our country, than it is the whites— we have enriched it with our *blood and tears*. The greatest riches in all America have arisen from our blood and tears: —and will they drive us from our property and homes, which we have earned with our *blood?* They must look sharp or this very thing will bring swift destruction upon them. The Americans have got so fat on our blood and groans, that they have almost forgotten the God of armies. . . . For what is the use of living, when in fact I am dead. But remember, Americans, that as miserable, wretched, degraded and abject as you have made us in preceding, and in this generation, to support you and your families, that some of you, (whites) on the continent of America, will yet curse the day that you ever were born. You want slaves, and want us for your slaves ! ! ! My colour will yet, root some of you out of the very face of the earth! ! ! ! ! ! . . . . Now, Americans! . . . . The Americans may be as vigilant as they please, but they cannot be vigilant enough for the Lord, neither can they hide themselves, where he will not find and bring them out. . . .

4. *Early Southern Society*

Defenders of the early South might argue that if Virginia displayed the arrogant faces of slavery and caste, she could also reveal, as in the instance of William Byrd's journal, the face of urbane aristocracy. Byrd also reminds us that the plot of Southern history involved groups other than masters and slaves and that a curiously symbolic meeting ground of plantation baron and the wilderness existed. AUTHOR: William Byrd (1674–1744), educated in law at the Middle Temple in London and very much at ease in English society, spent most of his life building great plantations in Virginia. SELECTIONS: "Southern Idlers and Wilderness Aristocrats" from Byrd's *History of the Dividing Line in the Year 1728 and a Progress to the Mines in the Year 1732.*

SOUTHERN IDLERS AND WILDERNESS
ARISTOCRATS (1728, 1732): WILLIAM BYRD

16 (November, 1728). We landed at the Plantation of Cornelius Keith, where I beheld the wretchedest Scene of Poverty I had ever met with in this happy Part of the World. The Man, his Wife and Six Small Children, liv'd in a Penn, like so many Cattle, without any Roof over their Heads but that of Heaven. And this was their airy Residence in the Day time, but then there was a Fodder Stack not far from this Inclosure, in which the whole Family shelter'd themselves a night's and in bad weather.

However, 'twas almost worth while to be as poor as this Man was, to be as perfectly contented. All his Wants proceeded from Indolence, and not from Misfortune. He had good Land, as well as good Health and good Limbs to work it, and, besides, had a Trade very useful to all the Inhabitants round about. He cou'd make and set up Queen Stones very well, and had proper Materials for that purpose just at Hand, if he cou'd have taken the pains to fetch them.

There is no other kind of Mills in those remote parts, and, therefore, if the Man wou'd have Workt at his Trade, he might have liv'd very comfortably. The poor woman had a little more Industry, and Spun Cotton enough to make a thin covering for her own children's Nakedness.

I am sorry to say it, but Idleness is the general character of the men in the Southern Parts of this Colony as well as in North Carolina. The Air is so mild, and the Soil so fruitful, that very little Labour is requir'd to fill their Bellies, especially where the Woods afford such Plenty of Game. These Advantages discharge the Men from the Necessity of killing themselves with Work, and then for the other Article of Raiment, a very little of that will suffice in so temperate a Climate. But so much as is absolutely Necessary falls to the good women's Share to provide. They all Spin, weave and knit, whereby they make a good Shift to cloath the whole Family; and to their credit be it recorded, many of them do it very completely, and thereby reproach their Husband's Laziness in the most inoffensive way, that is to say, by covering a better Spirit of Industry in themselves. . . .

Visit to Governor Spotswood. (September) 27, (1732). . . .

I came into the Main County Road, that leads from Fredericksburgh to Germanna, which last place I reacht in Ten Miles more. This famous Town consists of Colo. Spotswood's enchanted Castle on one Side of the Street, and a Baker's Dozen of ruinous Tenements on the other, where so many German Familys had dwelt some Years ago; but are now remov'd ten Miles higher, in the Fork of Rappahannock, to Land of their Own.

There had also been a Chappel about a Bow-Shot from the Colonel's house, at the end of an Avenue of Cherry Trees, but some pious people had lately burnt it down, with intent to get another built nearer to their own homes. Here I arriv'd about three a'clock, and found only Mrs. Spotswood at Home, who receiv'd her Old acquaintance with many a gracious Smile. I was carry'd into a Room elegantly set off with Pier Glasses, the largest of which came soon after to an odd Misfortune. Amongst other favourite Animals that cheer'd this Lady's Solitude, a Brace of Tame Deer ran familiarly about the House, and one of them came to stare at me as a Stranger. But unluckily spying his own Figure in the Glass, he made a spring over the Tea Table that stood under it, and shatter'd the Glass to pieces, and falling back upon the Tea Table, made a terrible Fracas among the China. This Exploit was so sudden, and accompany'd with such a Noise, that it surpriz'd me, and perfectly frighten'd Mrs. Spotswood. But twas worth all the Damage to shew the Moderation and good humour with which she bore this disaster. In the Evening the noble Colo. came home from his Mines, who saluted me very civily, and Mrs. Spotswood's Sister, Miss Theky, who had been to meet him en Cavalier, was so kind too as to bid me welcome. We talkt over a Legend of old Storys, supp'd about 9, and then prattl'd with the Ladys, til twas time for a Travellour to retire. In the mean time I observ'd my old Friend to be very Uxorious, and exceedingly fond of his Children. This was so opposite to the Maxims he us'd to preach up before he was married, that I cou'd not forbear rubbing up the Memory of them. But he gave a very good-natur'd turn to his Change of Sentiments, by alleging that whoever brings a poor Gentlewoman into so solitary a place, from all her friends and acquaintance, wou'd be ungrateful not to use her and all that belongs to her with all possible Tenderness.

28. We all kept Snug in our several apartments till Nine, except Miss Theky, who was the Housewife of the Family. At that hour we met over a Pot of Coffee, which was not quite strong enough to give us the Palsy. After Breakfast the Colo. and I left the Ladys to their Domestick Affairs, and took a turn in the Garden, which has nothing beautiful but 3 Terrace Walks that fall in Slopes one below another. . . . The afternoon was devoted to the ladys, who shew'd me one of their most beautiful Walks. They conducted me thro' a Shady Lane to the Landing, and by the way made me drink some very fine Water that issued from a Marble Fountain, and ran incessantly. Just behind it was a cover'd Bench, where Miss Theky often sat and bewail'd her Virginity. Then we proceeded to the River, which is the South Branch of Rappahanock, about 50 Yards wide, and so rapid that the Ferry Boat is drawn over by a Chain, and therefore called the Rapidan. At night we drank prosperity in a Bowl of Rack Punch, and then retired to our Devotions.

29. Having employ'd about 2 hours in Retirement, I Sally'd out at the first Summons to Breakfast, where our conversation with the Ladys, like Whip Sillabub, was very pretty, but has nothing in it. This it seems

was Miss Theky's Birth day, upon which I made here my Compliments, and wish'd she might live twice as long a Marry'd Woman as she had liv'd a Maid. I did not presume to pry into the Secret of her Age, nor was she forward to disclose it, for this humble Reason, lest I should think her Wisdom fell short of her Years. . . .

5. From Diversity and Conflict; Toward Toleration and Unity

George Alsop failed to describe accurately the bitter religious strife in early Maryland history among the Catholic proprietor, Anglicans, and a Puritan majority, but he was correct in asserting that the colony sheltered many defenders of religious toleration. Moreover Maryland did make an early start toward toleration and religious pluralism. Crèvecoeur suggested an important way to command national unity and to work for social peace through the concept of the American as a new man springing from but rising above Englishmen, Frenchmen, Germans, and others. AU-THORS: George Alsop (1638–1666), a tolerant Cavalier of humane views, spent four years in Maryland. St. Jean de Crèvecoeur (1735-1813) moved to Canada in 1753, to New York in 1759, served as the French Consul in New York after 1784, and returned to France in 1790. SELECTIONS: "Politics and Religion in Maryland" from Alsop's *Character of the Province of Maryland* (1666). "From Diverse Origins, a New Man, the American" from Crèvecoeur's *Letters from an American Farmer* (1782).

POLITICS AND RELIGION IN MARYLAND (1666): GEORGE ALSOP

Mary-Land, not from the remoteness of her situation, but from the regularity of her well-ordered Government, may (without sin, I think) be called *Singular*. . . .

He that desires to see the real Platform of a quiet and sober Government extant, Superiority with a meek and yet commanding power sitting at the Helme, steering the actions of State quietly, through the multitude and diversity of Opinionous waves that diversly meet, let him look on Mary-Land with eyes admiring, and he'le then judge her, *The Miracle of this Age.*

Here the *Roman Catholick*, and the *Protestant Episcopal*, (whom the world would persuade have proclaimed open Wars irrevocably against each other) contrarywise concur in an unanimous parallel of friendship, and inseparable love intayled unto one another: All Inquisitions, Martyrdom, and Banishments are not so much as named, but unexpressably abhorr'd by each other.

The several Opinions and Sects that lodge within this Government, meet not together in mutinous contempts to disquiet the power that bears Rule, but with a reverend quietness obeys the legal commands of Author-ity. . . .

The government of this Province doth continually, by all lawful means, strive to purge her Dominions from such base corroding humors, that would predominate upon the least smile of Liberty, did not the Laws check and bridle in those unwarranted and tumultuous Opinions. And truly, where a Kingdom, State or Government, keeps or cuts down the weeds of destructive Opinions, there must certainly be a blessed Harmony of quietness. And I really believe this Land or Government of *Mary-Land* may boast, that she enjoys as much quietness from the disturbance of Rebellious Opinions, as most States or Kingdoms do in the world: For here every man lives quietly, and follows his labour and imployment desiredly; and by the protection of the Laws, they are supported from those molestious troubles that ever attend upon the Commons of other States and Kingdoms, as well as from Aquafortial operation of great and eating taxes. . . .

Once every year within this Province is an Assembly called, and out of every respective County (by the consent of the people) there is chosen a number of men, and to them is deliver'd up the Grievances of the Country; and they maturely debate the matters, and according to their Consciences make Laws for the general good of the people; and where any former Law that was made, seems and is prejudicial to the good or quietness of the Land, it is repeal'd. These men that determine on these matters for the Republique, are called Burgesses, and they commonly sit in Junto about six weeks, being for the most part good ordinary Hous-holders of the several Counties, which do more by a plain and honest Conscience, then by artificial Syllogisms drest up in gilded Orations. . . .

FROM DIVERSE ORIGINS, A NEW MAN, THE AMERICAN (1782): ST. JEAN DE CRÉVECOEUR

Whence came all these people? They are a mixture of English, Scotch, Irish, French, Dutch, Germans, and Swedes. From this promiscuous breed, that race now called Americans have arisen. . . .

I could point out to you a family whose grandfather was an English-man, whose wife was Dutch, whose son married a French woman, and whose present four sons have now four wives of different nations. . . . The Americans . . . are incorporated into one of the finest systems of population which has ever appeared, and which will hereafter become distinct by the power of the different climates they inhabit. The American ought therefore to love this country much better than that wherein either he or his forefathers were born. Here the rewards of his industry follow with equal steps the progress of his labour; his labour is founded on the basis of nature, *self-interest;* Can it want a stronger allurement? Wives and children, who before in vain demanded of him a morsel of bread, now, fat and frolicsome, gladly help their father to clear those fields whence exuberant crops are to arise to feed and to clothe them all; without any part being claimed, either by a despotic prince, a rich abbot, or a mighty lord. . . .

What attachment can a poor European emigrant have for a country where he had nothing? The knowledge of the language, the love of a few kindred as poor as himself, were the only cords that tied him: his country is now that which gives him land, bread, protection, and consequence: *Ubi panis ibi patria,* is the motto of all emigrants. What then is the American, this new man? . . . *He* is an American, who leaving behind him all his ancient prejudices and manners, receives new ones from the new mode of life he has embraced, the new government he obeys, and the new rank he holds. He becomes an American by being received in the broad lap of our great *Alma Mater.* Here individuals of all nations are melted into a new race of men, whose labours and posterity will one day cause great changes in the world. Americans are the western pilgrims, who are carrying along with them that great mass of arts, sciences, vigour, and industry, which began long since in the east; they will finish the great circle. . . . The American is a new man, who acts upon new principles; he must therefore entertain new ideas, and form new opinions. From involuntary idleness, servile dependence, penury, and useless labour, he has passed to toils of a very different nature, rewarded by ample sub-sistence.—This is an American. . . .

Chapter IV. THE QUEST FOR UTOPIA IN JACKSONIAN AMERICA

THE FOUNDING FATHERS HAD THEIR RESERVATIONS ABOUT HUMAN NA-ture and the political process; they insisted that because of human greed men had to be restrained and aggregations of power balanced against each other. Still, Washington, Jefferson, John Adams, Alexander Hamilton, James Madison, and others were "Utopian" in their conception of the Revolution and the almost unlimited promise of the American future. It was the destiny of Americans in the early national period to leave behind strictures on the faults of man and society, and to extend to all areas the partial Utopianism of the Founders. The Republic in the Jacksonian era could no longer be regarded as an uncertain experiment, but merited the description of an established political reality. The storms and stresses of nation-building were over, and the sense of national self-confidence knew no bounds. Jefferson's assertion, of 1801—"We are all Republicans, We are all Federalists"—turned out to be an accurate prophecy. The one party "Era of Good Feelings" (1816–1824) was in several respects an age of factionalism in which complicated new economic and social forces struggled for political expression, but almost all the factions embraced the Republic and subscribed to a social optimism of Utopian proportions. Although a small minority clung to older notions of tying property to power through the suffrage, and a larger number were impatient with the slow pace of political and social change, the enthusiastic celebration of American progress was almost a unanimous chorus.

The will, energy, "humble" origin, and capacity for purposeful action made Andrew Jackson effective both as a symbol and an instrument of the era. Men from all classes with conflicting ambitions and ideals supported Andrew Jackson's candidacy in 1828. The special skill of the new President and his able advisors lay in gratifying the desire of mechanics, shopkeepers, frontiersmen, small farmers, and rising businessmen for a militant popular champion of the democratic rhetoric, greater economic opportunity, and a vigorous nationalism. Jackson traced his power to "the people," believed that his duty lay in executing their will, and enjoyed the adulation of self-conscious democrats from the growing towns and the expanding frontier. Although the Jacksonians were sometimes critical and restless, the temper of the age was optimistic and completely imbued with a devotion to social progress.

Some of the journalists and intellectuals who spread the gospel of "Jacksonian democracy" wished to celebrate America almost without reservations. Walt Whitman echoed a popular notion in stating that "the old and moth-eaten systems of Europe have had their day" and that America was "the glorious dawn for the down-trodden people." For Whitman and others America was by definition Utopia.

The Jacksonian orators had their critics. Many proponents of social reform shared the general faith in social progress, but insisted that more changes were needed to realize the Utopian possibilities of American society. The Jacksonians, committed to Jeffersonian hostility toward state power, could only spin the rhetoric of popular democracy and sponsor negative reforms against "monopolistic" combinations such as the Bank of the United States. Proponents of sweeping reforms turned readily enough to private instrumentalities. The stirrings of mass democracy, the victories of revivalism, and the hardships following the panic of 1837 stimulated utopian dreams so powerfully that they could no longer be ignored. Some prophets of a new order drew sustenance from the Christian past and the notion of a "saved remnant," escaping the doom of humanity to enter a special spiritual and social communion. The Shakers, the German pietists, Rappites and Zoarites, and Christian perfectionists such as John Humphrey Noyes' group, all wished to build the godly social order. More commonly, the remakers of society expounded a "liberal" Christian theology in conjunction with a confident belief in human goodness and social progress.

For the spread-eagle Jacksonian orator, America was an existing Utopia; for the "one-idea" humanitarian reformer the nation was an "almost Utopia"; for the communitarians America was a possible Utopia; and even for the Shakers and Zoarites the Republic was at least a gate to God's true millennial Utopia.

The largest category of reformers did not think the democratic millennium was so difficult to achieve as to require a complete reorganization of society. Utopia was near, and might be reached through the correction of one or several specific social evils. For these "one-idea men" on the move to perfection under the banner of progress, human horizons were unlimited, and only society was evil; men simply needed to make the appropriate institutional changes in order to achieve the full promise of American life. After the slave had been freed, the workers educated, the blind treated, and the peace congresses made supreme, the reformers were confident that all would be well.

The possibility always existed that Utopia was an inward state of soul, unrelated to all existing institutions. Accordingly, only the solitary individual could seek the inner condition; only an anarchist like Henry Thoreau could be a free man. As Emerson once suggested, proponents of the greatest reform must abjure all reformers and defy all institutions. In the end it might not be enough to "come out" of the churches to protest their sanction of slavery and other evils; one might have to "come out" of all institutions, to live by the belief that "one man is stronger than a city," indeed stronger than all cities.

On the other hand, the dream of spontaneous life, of super-individualism, could be a phantom. Even the more common dream of America as an escape from the evils of history into a new land to make new lives might be pure illusion. Perhaps, as Nathaniel Hawthorne thought, history, time and memory could not be escaped. Perhaps as Hawthorne, Herman Melville, and Edgar Allan Poe suspected, Utopia is nowhere. Still, these were solitary voices. Scepticism was a rare commodity in the eighteen-forties, and the mainstream of American thought was quite clearly Utopian.

The most celebrated single attempt to storm Utopia was made by Transcendentalists who accepted the emphasis by Emerson and Thoreau on the maximum development of the individual personality but refused to share their indifference toward projects for the improvement of American society. These "reforming" Transcendentalists, led by George Ripley, established a model reform community at Brook Farm, and in 1844 adopted the doctrines of the French socialist, Charles Fourier.

Socialism was not a novelty on the American scene. Robert Owen's secular communities of the 1820's were followed by religious communities which stressed communal ownership of property. In the 1840's religious perfectionists and millennialists constructed ideologies which sometimes led to communal ventures such as John Humphrey Noyes' celebrated experiment in biblical Communism and plural marriage at the Oneida, New York community. Neither Owenites nor religious socialists achieved the popularity of the Fourierists, who reached their zenith around 1844. In books, pamphlets, and the pages of Horace Greeley's *Tribune*, Albert Brisbane helped to create a wave of enthusiasm for Fourierism which won several hundred thousand converts. "Phalanxes" sprang up from New York to Wisconsin, and "Affiliated Unions" appeared in most major cities before the movement had run its course. By 1850 Fourierism, as well as most of the humanitarian movements, had lost the center of the social stage. During the decade to come, reform energies were to become increasingly absorbed by the anti-slavery controversy and ultimately by the ordeal of the Civil War.

1. Jacksonians and Locofocos

A complex coalition of Easterners and Westerners, businessmen and laborers, high and low tariff men brought Andrew Jackson to the White House in 1829. Jackson's "war" against the power and public functions of the privately controlled Bank of the United States won the admiration of those who feared the "money monster." The popular tone of the President's speeches and of the campaign in 1832 established for Jackson a reputation as a champion of "the people" against "the monopolists."

For more than a century historians have reflected the disagreements of Jackson's contemporaries and have added some of their own: for Arthur Schlesinger, Jr. (*The Age of Jackson*, 1946) the Democratic struggles of the 1830's were battles of workers, farmers, liberal intellectuals, and their allies against the arrogance and irresponsibility of the business community; Richard Hofstadter (*The American Political Tradition*, 1948) saw in Jackson's veto message of 1832 "the philosophy of a rising middle class" and in the entire movement a call to a struggle not for oppressed workers and debt-ridden farmers, but for "rural capitalists and village entrepreneurs" who wished to secure the road to riches against the barricades of the established upper classes; and Marvin Myers (*The Jacksonian Persuasion*, 1957) stressed the hostility of the Jacksonians toward the new capitalists and the nostalgia for an antique republicanism, for the Jeffersonian dream of an agricultural America dominated by self-sufficient yeomen rather than by "parasitic" speculators, capitalist manufacturers, and merchants. More recently Lee Benson (*The Concept of Jacksonian Democracy*, 1961) who suggested that both Whigs and Democrats accepted the equalitarian rhetoric and stressed complex "ethnocultural" politics, cast much doubt on the concept of "Jacksonian Democracy."
AUTHORS: Andrew Jackson (1767–1845) was best known as the hero of

the Battle of New Orleans (1815), an Indian fighter, a Tennessee frontier planter, the idol of the West, a firm nationalist, and the seventh President of the United States. Walt Whitman (1819–1892), printer's devil and school teacher during his youth and "the good, grey poet" of later years, spent the period between 1846 and 1855 on the staff of the *Brooklyn Eagle* and nine other newspapers and magazines as an editor and writer who used his eloquence to express a militant faith in American Democracy and its chief political instrument, the Democratic Party. George Bancroft (1800–1891), Secretary of the Navy under President Polk, diplomat, and America's first great historian, led the Democratic Party in Massachusetts from his post as the Boston Collector of Customs (1837–1845) and attempted to shape an ideology which would glorify the common man. The volatile, restless Orestes A. Brownson (1803–1876), a Universalist, a Presbyterian, a Freethinker, a Unitarian, and finally a Catholic, influenced many leading Jacksonians as a liberal editor after 1832, but in 1840 he found even the Locofoco Democrats too mild and demanded a more radical solution for industrial and commercial evils. SELECTIONS: "Jackson's War on Privilege" from the President's veto message of 1832 against the bill to recharter the Bank of the United States. "History and Nature of the Democratic Party" from Whitman's editorials in the *Brooklyn Eagle* (November 7, 1846, April 20, 1847, and July 26, 1847). "The Government of the People is Godlike" (1842) from Bancroft's *Literary and Historical Miscellanies* (1855). "A Radical Democrat on the Class Struggle" from Brownson's "The Laboring Classes," *Boston Quarterly Review* (1840).

JACKSON'S WAR ON "PRIVILEGE" (1832): THE BILL TO RECHARTER THE BANK OF THE UNITED STATES VETOED

[The bank of the United States] enjoys an exclusive privilege of banking under the authority of the General Government, a monopoly of its favor and support, and, as a necessary consequence, almost a monopoly of the foreign and domestic exchange. The powers, privileges, and favors bestowed upon it in the original charter, by increasing the value of the stock far above its par value, operated as a gratuity of many millions to the stockholders. . . . The act before me proposes another gratuity to the holders of the same stock, and in many cases to the same men, of at least seven millions more. . . . It appears that more than a fourth part of the stock is held by foreigners and the residue is held by a few hundred of our own citizens, chiefly of the richest class. For their benefit does this act exclude the whole American people. . . .

Is there no danger to our liberty and independence in a bank that in its nature has so little to bind it to our country? . . . Should its influence become concentrated, as it may under the operation of such an act as this, [for the extension of the charter,] in the hands of a self-elected directory whose interests are identical with those of the foreign stockholders, will there not be cause to tremble for the purity of our elections in peace and for the independence of our country in war? Their power would be great whenever they might choose to exert it; but if this monopoly were regularly renewed every fifteen or twenty years on terms proposed by themselves, they might seldom in peace put forth their strength to influence elections or control the affairs of the nation. . . .

It is to be regretted that the rich and powerful too often bend the acts of government to their own selfish purposes. . . . In the full enjoyment of the gifts of Heaven and the fruits of superior industry, economy, and virtue, every man is equally entitled to protection by law; but when the laws undertake to add to these natural and just advantages artificial distinctions, to grant titles, gratuities, and exclusive privileges, to make the rich richer and the potent more powerful, the humble members of society—the farmers, mechanics, and laborers—who have neither the time nor the means of securing like favors to themselves, have a right to complain of the injustice of their Government. . . .

Many of our rich men have not been content with equal protection and equal benefits, but have besought us to make them richer by act of Congress. By attempting to gratify their desires we have in the results of our legislation arrayed section against section, interest against interest, and man against man, in a fearful commotion which threatens to shake the foundations of our Union. If we can not at once, in justice to interests vested under improvident legislation, make our Government what it ought to be, we can at least take a stand against all new grants of monopoly and exclusive privileges, against any prostration of our Government to the advancement of the few at the expense of the many, and in favor of compromise and gradual reform in our code of laws and system of political economy. . . .

HISTORY AND NATURE OF THE DEMOCRATIC PARTY (1846–1847): WALT WHITMAN

The democracy of this country can never be overthrown. . . . Nor can the Democratic Party become essentially corrupt, either. For true democracy has within itself a perpetual spring of health and purity. In its very nature it is at war with all selfishness and wickedness. . . .

Why, what had Jefferson, the Columbus of our political faith, to encounter? If we are to believe the chronicles of the past, he underwent, during what was called the "reign of terror," the most provoking indignities both personal and political. . . .

From the days of Washington, the course of the Democratic Party has been a course of success and triumph. We do not mean that our party has succeeded in every *election*, . . . But we mean to say that our *principles* have advanced with a steady and sure progress. . . . The Democracy must still succeed. Even the intelligent Whigs will probably acknowledge this . . . , with all their distrust of the "common people". . . .

Thirty years from this date, America will be confessed the first *nation* on the earth. We of course mean that her power, wealth, and the happiness and virtue of her citizens will then obtain a pitch which other nations cannot favorably compare with. . . .

The progress of . . . democratic yearning for a better state bids fair to place the American people, twenty years hence—by elevating humanity itself, and disregarding mere wealth and circumstances, by a wholesome pruning of too much and too meddlesome laws—as far beyond what they now are as what they now are is beyond what they were seventy years ago. There must be continual additions to our great experiment of how much liberty society will bear. . . . And not only here, on our own beloved soil, is this democratic feeling infusing itself and becoming more and more powerful. The lover of his race, he whose good-will is not bounded by a shore or a division line, looks across the Atlantic and exults to see on the shores of Europe a restless dissatisfaction spreading wider and wider every day. . . .

THE GOVERNMENT OF THE PEOPLE IS GODLIKE (1842): GEORGE BANCROFT

There is a *spirit in man* . . . the attribute of the race . . . which is the guide to truth, is the gracious gift to each member of the human family.

Reason exists within every breast. I mean not that faculty which deduces inferences from the experience of the senses, but that higher faculty which from the infinite treasures of its own consciousness originates truth and assents to it by the force of intuitive evidence; that faculty which raises us beyond the control of time and space, and gives us faith in things eternal and invisible. There is not the difference between one mind and another which the pride of philosophers might conceive. . . .

The intellectual functions, by which relations are perceived, are the common endowments of the race. The differences are apparent, not real. The eye in one person may be dull, in another quick, in one distorted, and in another tranquil and clear; yet the relation of the eye to light is in all men the same. Just so judgment may be liable in individual minds to the bias of passion, and yet its relation to truth is immutable and is universal. . . .

You cannot discover a tribe of men, but you also find the charities of life and the proofs of spiritual existence. Behold the ignorant Algonquin deposit a bow and quiver by the side of the departed warrior, and recognize his faith in immortality. . . . He bears within him the instinct of Deity, the consciousness of a spiritual nature, the love of beauty, the rule of morality.

And shall we reverence the dark-skinned Kaffir? Shall we respect the brutal Hottentot? You may read the right answer written on every heart. . . . All are men. . . .

If it be true that the gifts of mind and heart are universally diffused, if the sentiment of truth, justice, love, and beauty exists in every one then it follows, as a necessary consequence, that the common judgment in taste, politics, and religion is the highest authority on earth and the nearest possible approach to an infallible decision. . . .

If reason is a universal faculty, the universal decision is the nearest criterion of truth. The common mind winnows opinions; it is the sieve which separates error from certainty. . . .

If wrong opinions have often been cherished by the masses, the cause always lies in the complexity of the ideas presented. Error finds its way into the soul of a nation only through the channel of truth. It is to a truth that men listen; and if they accept error also, it is only because the error is for the time so closely interwoven with the truth that the one cannot readily be separated from the other. . . .

There may be those who scoff at the suggestion that the decision of the whole is to be preferred to the judgment of the enlightened few. They say in their hearts that the masses are ignorant; that farmers know nothing of legislation; that mechanics should not quit their workshops to join in forming public opinion. But true political science does indeed venerate the masses. . . . Individuals are but shadows, too often engrossed by the pursuit of shadows; the race is immortal. Individuals are of limited sagacity; the common mind is infinite in its experience. Individuals are languid and blind; the many are ever wakeful. Individuals are corrupt; the race has been redeemed. Individuals are time-serving; the masses are fearless. Individuals may be false; the masses are ingenuous and sincere. Individuals claim the divine sanction of truth for the deceitful conceptions of their own fancies; the Spirit of God breathes through the combined intelligence of the people. . . . It is the confession of an enemy to Democracy, that "all the great and noble institutions of the world have come from popular efforts." . . .

A RADICAL DEMOCRAT ON THE CLASS STRUGGLE (1840): ORESTES A. BROWNSON

No one can observe the signs of the times with much care without perceiving that a crisis as to the relation of wealth and labor is approaching. . . . The old war between the King and the Barons is well nigh ended, and so is that between the Barons and the Merchants and Manufacturers, landed capital and commercial capital. The businessman has become the peer of my Lord. And now commences the new struggle between the operative and his employer, between wealth and labor. Every day does this struggle extend further and wax stronger and fiercer; what or when the end will be God only knows.

In this coming contest there is a deeper question at issue than is commonly imagined, a question which is but remotely touched in your controversies about United States banks and sub-treasuries. . . . No popular Senator or deputy or peer seems to have any glimpse of it; but it is working in the hearts of the million, is struggling to shape itself, and one day it will be uttered, and in thunder tones. . . .

In regard to labor two systems obtain: one that of slave labor, the other that of free labor. . . . The laborer at wages has all the disadvantages of freedom and none of its blessings, while the slave, if denied the blessings, is freed from the disadvantages. We are no advocates of slavery; . . . but we say frankly that, if there must always be a laboring population . . . we regard the slave system as decidedly preferable to the system of wages. . . .

The great mass wear out their health, spirits, and morals without becoming one whit better off than when they commenced labor. . . . We know no sadder sight on earth than one of our factory villages presents when the bell, at break of day, or at the hour of breakfast or dinner, calls out its hundreds of thousands of operatives. We stand and look at these hard-working men and women hurrying in all directions and ask ourselves where go the proceeds of their labors? The man who employs them and for whom they are toiling as so many slaves is one of our city nabobs, reveling in luxury; or he is a member of our legislature, enacting laws to put money in his own pocket. . . . He shouts for liberty, stickles for equality, and is horrified at a Southern planter who keeps slaves.

One thing is certain: that, of the amount actually produced by the operative, he retains a less proportion than it costs the master to feed, clothe, and lodge his slave. Wages is a cunning device of the devil for the benefit of tender consciences who would retain all the advantages of the slave system without the expense, trouble, and odium of being slaveholders. . . .

2. Economic Thought

Most of the Jacksonians were concerned with expanding the boundaries of economic liberty at home, but they were less united on positions toward the international economic scene. After the eighteen-thirties a growing number of men like the Massachusetts manufacturer, Abbott E. Lawrence, moved from support of free trade and an open, competitive world economy to acceptance of protective tariffs. Many New England manufacturers joined Lawrence, and Southern planters hastened to defend free trade because they feared special advantage for Northern industrialists. Henry C. Carey mediated between the two doctrines by attempting to establish a truly national position based on the "harmony" of all legitimate economic interests. Carey charged that free trade meant British economic imperialism, an attempt to keep manufacturing a British monopoly; and he urged the "decentralization" of industry through the growth of manufacturing in the non-English portions of the world. The protective tariff in America, Carey argued, would not only encourage industry but would create a "balanced" and "harmonious" order of commerce, agriculture, and manufacturing. Carey was also notable for criticizing the masters of classical economics, Smith, Ricardo, Malthus, and James Mill, who had very few critics in mid-nineteenth century America. AUTHOR: Henry Charles Carey (1793–1879), the son of an Irish immigrant, was born in Philadelphia. He made a fortune as a publisher and retired from business in 1838 to write on economics and social reform. SELECTION: "The Harmony of Economic Interests" from Carey's book of the same title, 1859.

THE HARMONY OF ECONOMIC INTERESTS (1859): HENRY C. CAREY

Overpopulation is held to be a result of a great law of nature, in virtue of which men grow in numbers faster than they can grow the food that is to nourish them; and the poverty, vice, and crime that everywhere exist, are regarded as necessary consequences of this great law, emanating from an all-wise, all-powerful, and all merciful Being. War, famine, and pestilence are regarded as means provided by that Being for restraining population within the limits of subsistence. . . . Thus it is that [England] seeks to establish a system of commercial centralization, that is—as was justly said, seventy years since, by *Adam Smith*—a manifest violation of "the most sacred rights of mankind." That great man was fully possessed of the fact that, if the farmer or planter would flourish, he must bring the consumer to his side; and that if the artisan would flourish, he must seek to locate himself in the place where the raw materials were grown, and aid the farmer by converting them into the forms fitting them for the use of men, and thus facilitating their transportation to distant lands. He saw well, that when men came thus together, there arose a general harmony of interests, each profiting his neighbor, and profiting by that neighbor's success, whereas the tendency of commercial centralization was toward poverty and discord, abroad and at home. The object of protection among ourselves is that of aiding farmers in the effort to bring consumers to their sides, and thus to carry into effect this system advocated by the great author of *The Wealth of Nations*, while aiding in the annihilation of a system that has ruined Ireland, India, Portugal, Turkey, and all other countries subject to it; and the object of the following chapters is that of showing why it is that protection is needed; how it operates in promoting the prosperity of, and harmony among, the various portions of society; and how certain it is that THE TRUE, THE PROFITABLE, AND THE ONLY MEANS OF ATTAINING PERFECT FREEDOM OF TRADE, is to be found in that efficient protection which shall fully and completely carry out the doctrine of Dr. Smith, in bringing the loom and the anvil to take their natural places by the side of the plough and the harrow. . . .

3. Reformers and Humanitarians

Surely the decade from 1840 to 1850 constituted a golden age for reform in America. Emerson catalogued only a few of the participants in that incredibly diverse parade of humanitarian reformers who wished to aid the alcoholic, the convict, the slave, the blind, the ignorant, the soldier, the sailor, the woman, and a variety of other social causes. For many of the world-menders human perfectibility was a very real possibility. In no other age can so many devotees of the gospel of social progress be found. AUTHORS: Ralph Waldo Emerson (1803–1882), a Massachusetts minister until doubts about the communion service led him to resign his pulpit, was the founder of the Transcendentalist movement, a popular lecturer, and one of the most brilliant essayists of his generation. Theodore Parker (1810–1860), a Transcendentalist, a scholar versed in a dozen languages, and a thoroughly unorthodox Unitarian minister, scandalized

Boston with his fiery attacks on social evils and intellectual reaction. Horace Mann (1796–1859), a Brown University graduate who overcame the disadvantages of a secondary school education by ignorant masters in wretched schools, became a leading lawyer, legislator, and educational reformer in Massachusetts, and laid the foundations of the modern American public school system. Elizabeth Cady Stanton (1815–1902), a pioneer suffragette, attended the first Convention for Women's Rights at Seneca Falls, New York in 1848. SELECTIONS: "The Chardon Street Reform Convention," (1841) from Emerson's article in The Dial (July, 1842). "The Perishing Classes" from Parker's The Perishing Classes (1846). "The Need for Mass Education in a Republic" from Mann's Massachusetts Board of Education, Twelfth Annual Report (1849). "A Woman's Declaration of Independence," (1848) from Mrs. Stanton, Susan B. Anthony, Matilda J. Gage, eds., A History of Women's Suffrage (1881). "The Temperance Cause: Marching Song of the Cold Water Army," from the newspaper, The Cold Water Army (September 8, 1842).

THE CHARDON STREET REFORM CONVENTION (1841): RALPH WALDO EMERSON

In the month of November, 1840, a Convention of Friends of Universal Reform assembled in the Chardon Street Chapel in Boston. . . . [In 1841 a second session was held. The participants aroused] every note of hope, of sympathy, of joy, of alarm, of abhorrence and of merriment. The composition of the assembly was rich and various. The singularity and latitude of the summons drew together, from all parts of New England and also from the Middle States, men of every shade of opinion from the straitest orthodoxy to the wildest heresy, and many persons whose church was a church of one member only. A great variety of dialect and of costume was noticed; a great deal of confusion, eccentricity, . . . as well as of zeal and enthusiasm. If the assembly was disorderly, it was picturesque. Madmen, madwomen, men with beards, Dunkers, Muggletonians, Comeouters, Groaners, Agrarians, Seventh-day Baptists, Quakers, Abolitionists, Calvinists, Unitarians and Philosophers,—all came successively to the top, and seized their moment, if not their hour, wherein to chide, or pray, or preach, or protest. The faces were a study. The most daring innovators and the champions-until-death of the old cause sat side by side. The still-living merit of the oldest New England families, glowing yet after several generations, encountered the founders of families, fresh merit, emerging, and expanding the brows to a new breadth, and lighting a clownish face with sacred fire. . . .

THE PERISHING CLASSES (1846):
THEODORE PARKER

This class of men [the urban poor] are perishing; yes, perishing in the nineteenth century; perishing in Boston, wealthy, charitable Boston; perishing soul and body, contrary to God's will; and perishing all the worse because they die slow, and corrupt by inches. . . .

What shall become of the children of such men? They stand; in the fore-front of the battle, all unprotected as they are; a people scattered and peeled, only a miserable remnant reaches the age of ten. . . .

There are two classes, the victims of society, and the foes of society, the men that organize its sins, and then tell us nobody is to blame. May God deal mercifully with the foes; I had rather take my part with the victims. Yet is there one who wishes to be a foe to mankind?

Here are the sons of the poor, vagrant in your streets, shut out by their misery from the culture of the age; growing up to fill your jails, to be fathers of a race like themselves, and to be huddled into an infamous grave. Here are the daughters of the poor, cast out and abandoned, the pariahs of our civilization, training up for a life of shame and pollution, and coming early to a miserable end. Here are the poor, daughters and sons, excluded from the refining influences of modern life, shut out of the very churches by that bar of gold, ignorant, squalid, hungry and hopeless, wallowing in their death! Are these the results of modern civilization; this in the midst of the nineteenth century, in a Christian city full of churches and gold; this in Boston, which adds $13,000,000 a year to her actual wealth? Is that the will of God? . . . .

THE NEED FOR MASS EDUCATION IN A
REPUBLIC (1849): HORACE MANN

According to the European theory, men are divided into classes,—some to toil and earn, others to seize and enjoy. According to the Massachusetts theory, all are to have an equal chance for earning, and equal security in the enjoyment of what they earn. The latter tends to equality of condition; the former to the grossest inequalities. . . .

But, is it not true, that Massachusetts, in some respects, instead of adhering more and more closely to her own theory, is becoming emulous of the baneful examples of Europe? The distance between the two extremes of society is lengthening, instead of being abridged. . . .

Now, surely, nothing but Universal Education can counterwork this tendency to the domination of capital and the servility of labor. If one class possesses all the wealth and the education, while the residue of society is ignorant and poor, it matters not by what name the relation between them may be called; the latter, in fact and in truth, will be the servile dependants and subjects of the former. But if education be equably diffused, it will draw property after it. . . .

Education, then, beyond all other devices of human origin, is the great equalizer of the conditions of men. . . . It gives each man the independence and the means, by which he can resist the selfishness of other men. It does better than to disarm the poor of their hostility towards the rich; it prevents being poor. . . .

It has a higher function. Beyond the power of diffusing old wealth, it has the prerogative of creating new. . . .

The necessity of general intelligence,—that is, of education, . . . — under a republican form of government, like most other very important truths, has become a very trite one. . . .

In a republican government, legislators are a mirror reflecting the moral countenance of their constituents. And hence it is, that the establishment of a republican government, without well-appointed and efficient means for the universal education of the people, is the most rash and fool-hardy experiment ever tried by man. . . . It may be an easy thing to make a Republic; but it is a very laborious thing to make Republicans; and woe to the Republic that rests upon no better foundations than ignorance, selfishness, and passion. Such a Republic may grow in numbers and in wealth. . . . But if such a Republic be devoid of intelligence, it will only the more closely resemble an obscene giant who has waxed strong in his youth, and grown wanton in his strength; whose brain has been developed only in the regions of the appetites and passions, and not in the organs of reason and conscience; and who, therefore, is boastful of its bulk alone, and glories in the weight of his heel and in the destruction of his arm. . . .

A WOMAN'S DECLARATION OF INDEPENDENCE (1848): ELIZABETH CADY STANTON

When, in the course of human events, it becomes necessary for one portion of the family of man to assume among the people of the earth a position different from that which they have hitherto occupied, but one to which the laws of nature and of nature's God entitle them, a decent respect to the opinions of mankind requires that they should declare the causes that impel them to such a course.

We hold these truths to be self-evident; that all men and women are created equal; that they are endowed by their Creator with certain inalienable rights; that among these are life, liberty, and the pursuit of happiness; that to secure these rights governments are instituted, deriving their just powers from the consent of the governed. . . .

The history of mankind is a history of repeated injuries and usurpations on the part of man toward woman, having in direct object the establishment of an absolute tyranny over her. To prove this, let facts be submitted to a candid world.

He has never permitted her to exercise her inalienable right to the elective franchise.

He has compelled her to submit to laws, in the formation of which she had no voice. . . .

He has taken from her all right in property. . . .

He has denied her the facilities for obtaining a thorough education. . . .

He has created a false public sentiment by giving to the world a different code of morals for men and women, by which moral delinquencies which exclude women from society, are not only tolerated, but deemed of little account in man. . . .

Now, in view of this entire disfranchisement of one-half the people of this country, their social and religious degradation—in view of the unjust laws above mentioned, and because women do feel themselves aggrieved, oppressed, and fraudulently deprived of their most sacred rights, we insist that they have immediate admission to all the rights and privileges which belong to them as citizens of the United States.

THE TEMPERANCE CAUSE (1842): MARCHING SONG OF THE COLD WATER ARMY

> Limpid cooling fountain
> Springing from the mountain
> Running in the river
> Thy sweet streams were given
> By the God of Heaven
> We will leave thee never.
>
> No, not alluring wine
> Our lips shall e'er incline
> Nature's drink to leave
> Cold water cannot harm us
> No other drink will charm us,
> This cannot deceive.

From Gallia's teeming wine-press,
From Holland's streams of gin,
Where thousands in the blindness
Prepare the bait of sin,
In many a fiery river,
From many a poisonous rill,
God calls us to deliver
The victims of the still.

4. Religion and Reform

Religious impulses were fundamental to most of the humanitarian movements. Although the idea of Christian fellowship led more Chardon
Street reformers than State Street merchants into action, a few
Boston Brahmins joined abolitionist groups and a larger number fought
for other humanitarian causes. Religious perfectionism in one form or
another was a dominant force of the age, and the concept of a "practical"
Christian brotherhood governing politics, business, and society motivated
multitudes of Americans. Many popular writers advocated secular salvation in which the bliss that Christians had traditionally assigned to
heaven could be achieved on earth. Ministers such as Charles G. Finney
convinced their parishioners that Christianity was basically a religion
of social reform. Only a small radical minority joined Orestes A. Brownson
in denouncing ministers and churches as inevitable enemies of progress,
and even the embattled anti-clericals insisted that the churches represented only perverse corruptions of Christianity which, properly understood, was a gospel of reform. AUTHORS: Charles G. Finney (1792–1875)
used a revivalist and perfectionist approach as a minister in building a
national reputation. SELECTION: "Religious Motives for Reform," from
Finney's Lectures on Revivals of Religion (1835).

RELIGIOUS MOTIVES FOR REFORM (1835):
CHARLES G. FINNEY

The churches must take right ground on the subject of slavery. . . .
It is a great national sin. . . . The fact is that slavery is, preeminently,
the sin of the church. It is the very fact that ministers and professors of
religion of different denominations hold slaves, which sanctifies the whole

abomination, in the eyes of ungodly men. Who does not know that on the subject of temperance, every drunkard in the land, will skulk behind some rum-selling deacon, or wine-drinking minister? . . . . Let the churches of all denominations . . . close their doors against all who have any thing to do with the death-dealing abomination, and the cause of temperance is triumphant. A few years would annihilate the traffic. Just so with slavery.

It is the church that mainly supports this sin. Her united testimony upon this subject would settle the question. Let Christians of all denominations. . . . write on the head and front of this great abomination, SIN! and in three years, a public sentiment would be formed that would carry all before it. . . .

The church must take right ground on . . . all the subjects of practical morality which come up for decision from time to time. . . . The evils have been exhibited, the call has been made for reform. And what is to reform mankind but the truth? And who shall present the truth if not the church and the ministry? Away with the idea that Christians can remain neutral and keep still, and yet enjoy the approbation and blessing of God. . . .

5. The Abolitionists

The modern conflict between the Christian conscience and slavery began in the eighteenth century and did not end until slavery was abolished during the Civil War. The African colonization societies of the early nineteenth century failed to provide a satisfactory solution, and pioneer agitators during the eighteen-thirties and -forties made converts across the North for the radical Abolitionist point of view. Outraged Southern spokesmen attempted to combat the reform arguments with little success, and the anti-slavery cause became during the eighteen-fifties a mass movement which enlisted the services of politicians and writers such as Charles Sumner, Henry Thoreau, John Greenleaf Whittier, and Harriet Beecher Stowe. AUTHORS: Charles Sumner (1811–1874) was a leading anti-slavery Senator, a powerful advocate of a vigorous war policy during the Civil War, and one of the architects of Congressional Reconstruction. Henry Thoreau (1817–1862), Transcendentalist, poet, naturalist, and anarchist, created the masterful prose style which enabled him to speak so eloquently on nature, anarchism, and anti-slavery. SELECTIONS: "The Barbarism of Slavery" (a speech of 1860) from Sumner's Works (1879–1883). "A Plea for Captain John Brown," from Thoreau's essay of 1859.

THE BARBARISM OF SLAVERY (1860):
CHARLES SUMNER

I begin with the Law of Slavery and its Origin; and here this Barbarism sketches itself in its own chosen definition. It is simply this: Man, created in the image of God, is divested of the human character, and declared to be a "chattel,"—that is, a beast, a thing, or article of property. . . .

Sir, look at its plain import, and see the relation which it establishes. The slave is held simply for the use of his master, to whose behests his life, liberty, and happiness are devoted, and by whom he may be bartered, leased, mortgaged, bequeathed, invoiced, shipped as cargo, stored as goods, sold on execution, knocked off at public auction, and even staked at the gaming-table on the hazard of a card or a die,—all according to law. Nor is there anything, within the limit of life, inflicted on a beast, which may not be inflicted on the slave. He may be marked like a hog, branded like a mule, yoked like an ox, hobbled like a horse, driven like an ass, sheared like a sheep, maimed like a cur, and constantly beaten like a brute,—all according to law. . . .

Foremost . . . According to the Law of Nature, . . . every human being has complete title to himself direct from the Almighty. . . . Slavery tyrannically assumes power which Heaven denied,—while, under its barbarous necromancy . . . a man is changed into a chattel, a person is withered into a thing, a soul is shrunk into merchandise. . . .

Secondly. Slavery paints itself again in its complete abrogation of marriage. . . . Under the Law of Slavery no such sacrament is respected, and no such contract can exist. The ties formed between slaves are all subject to the selfish interest or more selfish lust of the master, whose license knows no check. Natural affections which have come together are rudely torn asunder: . . . the chastity of a whole race is exposed to violence, while the result is recorded in telltale faces of children, glowing with a master's blood. . . . By license of Slavery, a whole race is delivered over to prostitution and concubinage. . . .

Thirdly. Slavery paints itself again in its complete abrogation of the parental relation. . . . Sir, is not Slavery barbarous?

Fourthly. Slavery paints itself again in closing the gates of knowledge, which are also the shining gates of Civilization. . . . The law . . . positively forbids that he shall be taught to read! . . .

Fifthly. Slavery paints itself again in the appropriation of all the toil of its victims. . . . The painful injustice of this pretension is lost in its meanness. . . . Alas, by such fallacy is a whole race pauperized! . . .

If the offense of Slavery were less extended, if it were confined to some narrow region, if it had less of grandeur in its proportions, if its victims were counted by tens and hundreds instead of millions, the five-headed enormity would find little indulgence; all would rise against it, while Religion and Civilization would lavish choicest efforts in the general welfare. But what is wrong when done to one man cannot be right when done to many. If it is wrong thus to degrade a single soul, . . . it cannot be right to degrade a whole race. . . . American Slavery, as defined by existing law, stands forth as the greatest organized Barbarism on which the sun now looks. . . .

A PLEA FOR CAPTAIN JOHN BROWN (1859): HENRY DAVID THOREAU

I trust that you will pardon me for being here. I do not wish to force my thoughts upon you, but I feel forced myself. Little as I know of Captain Brown, I would fain do my part to correct the tone and statements of . . . my countrymen. . . .

He was by descent and birth a New England farmer, a man of great common sense, deliberate and practical as that class is and tenfold more so. He was like the best of those who stood at Concord Bridge once, on Lexington Common, and on Bunker Hill, only he was firmer and higher principled than any that I have chanced to hear of as there. . . .

He was one of that class of whom we hear a breat deal, but for the most part see nothing at all,—the Puritans. It would be in vain to kill him. He died lately in the time of Cromwell, but he reappeared here. Why should he not? Some of the Puritan stock are said to have come over and settled in New England. They were a class that did something else than celebrate their forefathers' day, and eat parched corn in remembrance of that time. . . .

Treason! Where does such treason take its rise? I cannot help thinking of you as you deserve, ye governments. Can you dry up the fountains of thought? High treason, when it is resistance to tyranny here below, has its origin in, and is first committed by, the power that makes and forever recreates man. When you have caught and hung all these human rebels, you have accomplished nothing but your own guilt, for you have not struck at the fountainhead. . . .

I hear many condemn these men because they were so few. When were the good and the brave ever in a majority? Would you have had him wait till that time came?—till you and I came over to him? . . . His company was small indeed, because few could be found worthy to pass muster. Each one who there laid down his life for the poor and oppressed was a picked man, culled out of many thousands, if not millions. . . . These alone were ready to step between the oppressor and the oppressed. Surely they were the very best men you could select to be hung. That was the greatest compliment which this country could pay them. . . .

It was his peculiar doctrine that a man has a perfect right to interfere by force with the slaveholder, in order to rescue the slave. I agree with him. . . .

I speak for the slave when I say that I prefer the philanthropy of Captain Brown to that philanthropy which neither shoots me nor liberates me. . . . I do not wish to kill nor to be killed, but I can forsee circumstances in which both these things would be by me unavoidable. We preserve the so-called peace of our community by deeds of petty violence every day. Look at the policemen's billy and handcuffs! Look at the jail! Look at the gallows! Look at the chaplain of the regiment! We are hoping only to live safely on the outskirts of *this* provisional army. So we defend ourselves and our henroosts, and maintain slavery. I know that the mass of my countrymen think that the only righteous use that can be made of Sharps rifles and revolvers is to fight duels with them, when we are insulted by other nations, or to hunt Indians, or shoot fugitive slaves with them, or the like. I think that for once the Sharps rifles and the revolvers were employed in a righteous cause. The tools were in the hands of one who could use them. . . .

The murderer always knows that he is justly punished; but when a government takes the life of a man without the consent of his conscience, it is an audacious government, and is taking a step towards its own dissolution. Is it not possible that an individual may be right and a government wrong? Are laws to be enforced simply because they were made? or declared by any number of men to be good, if they are *not* good? . . .

I am here to plead his cause with you. I plead not for his life, but for his character,—his immortal life; and so it becomes your cause wholly, and is not his in the least. Some eighteen hundred years ago Christ was crucified; this morning, perchance, Captain Brown was hung. . . .

I foresee the time when the painter will paint that scene, no longer going to Rome for a subject; the poet will sing it; the historian record it; and, with the Landing of the Pilgrims and the Declaration of Independence, it will be the ornament of some future national gallery, when at least the present form of slavery shall be no more here. We shall then be at liberty to weep for Captain Brown. Then, and not till then, we will take our revenge.

6. Utopian Socialism

Emerson and Thoreau, both suspicious of groups, were reluctant Abolitionists, protesting as individuals rather than as members of the anti-slavery organizations. For Thoreau "one man in the right" was "a majority of one," and Emerson proclaimed that "whoso would be a man must be a nonconformist." However, some of Emerson's disciples, men such as George Ripley, who agreed with their mentor's emphasis on individualism, insisted that American society must be reconstructed so that every man might enjoy maximum self-development.

At Brook Farm Ripley founded a Utopian Socialist community which he hoped would "stand as a Beacon light" before the entire world. He proposed to abandon corrupt social forms, to insure social equality, to unite the tasks of thinkers and workers in each person, and to allow all men education, leisure, and free choice of jobs. Brook Farm exerted a powerful attraction for New England intellectuals, but Thoreau's anarchistic nature granted nothing to the socialists. While Emerson was both attracted and repelled, he finally decided against the community and clung to the belief that "one man is stronger than a city." The Brook Farmers prospered without the support of Emerson and Thoreau, and in 1844 the community was strengthened by the adoption of a new gospel, "scientific socialism." "Fourierism" or "Associationism" was the gift of Albert Brisbane who had studied under the master himself, Charles Fourier. When the Brook Farm "Phalanx" collapsed in 1847 its leaders continued for a few years to support the cause in other communities. AUTHORS: George Ripley (1802–1880), a Unitarian minister who abandoned his church because of its social conservatism, was a pioneer Transcendentalist, an editor of The Dial, the founder of Brook Farm, and in later years a powerful literary critic for the New York Tribune and Harper's Magazine. John Sullivan Dwight (1813–1893), also a former Unitarian minister, followed Ripley to Brook Farm, and soon became a communal leader, a Fourierist lecturer, and a Christian Socialist. In later years he devoted his life to music and helped to make Boston an important music center. SELECTIONS: "Origins of the Brook Farm Community" from Ripley's letter to Emerson (1840) printed in O. B. Frothingham George Ripley (1882). "Socialist Communion in Utopia" from Dwight's Association in Its Connection with Education and Religion (1844).

ORIGINS OF THE BROOK FARM COMMUNITY (1840): GEORGE RIPLEY

We propose to take a small tract of land, which, under skillful husbandry, uniting the garden and the farm, will be adequate to the subsistence of the families; and to connect with this a school or college, in which the most complete instruction shall be given, from the first rudiments to the highest culture. Our farm would be a place for improving the race of men that lived on it; thought would preside over the operations of labor, and labor would contribute to the expansion of thought; we should have industry without drudgery, and true equality without its vulgarity. . . .

I can imagine no plan which is suited to carry into effect so many divine ideas as this. If wisely executed, it will be a light over this country and this age. If not the sunrise, it will be the morning star. As a practical man, I see clearly that we must have some arrangement, or all changes less radical will be nugatory. I believe in the divinity of labor; I wish to "harvest my flesh and blood from the land;" but to do this, I must either be insulated and work to disadvantage, or avail myself of the services of hirelings, who are not of my order, and whom I can scarce make friends; for I must have another to drive the plough, which I hold. I cannot empty a cask of lime upon my grass alone. I wish to see a society of educated friends, working, thinking, and living together, with no strife, except that of each to contribute the most to the benefit of all.

Personally, my tastes and habits would lead me in another direction. I have a passion for being independent of the world, and of every man in it. This I could do easily on the estate which is now offered, and which I could rent at a rate, that with my other resources, would place me in a very agreeable condition, as far as my personal interests were involved. I should have a city of God, on a small scale of my own; and please God, I should hope one day to drive my own cart to market and sell greens. But I feel bound to sacrifice this private feeling, in the hope of a great social good. I shall be anxious to hear from you. Your decision will do much towards settling the question with me, whether the time has come for the fulfilment of a high hope, or whether the work belongs to a future generation. All omens now are favorable; a singular union of diverse talents is ready for the enterprise; everything indicates that we ought to arise and build; and if we let slip this occasion, the unsleeping Nemesis will deprive us of the boon we seek. For myself, I am sure that I can never give so much thought to it again; my mind must act on other objects, and I shall acquiesce in the course of fate, with grief that so fair a light is put out. A small pittance of the wealth which has been thrown away on ignoble objects, during this wild contest for political supremacy [the election of 1840], would lay the cornerstone of a house, which would ere long become the desire of nations. . . .

SOCIALIST COMMUNION IN UTOPIA (1844): JOHN SULLIVAN DWIGHT

No man is himself, alone. Part of me is in you, in every fellow being. We 'live and move and have our being' in one another, as well as in God. An individual is nothing in himself. . . . We are real *persons* only entering into true relations with all other beings; we enter into our own lives and find ourselves just in proportion as we realize and make good those relations. Only so far as the electric chain of sympathies which God threw around us all, in sign that we are one . . . is kept entire and unobstructed . . . can we be said to live; and most men live, like old trees that are dying, only in a few branches, an incoherent, fragmentary, partial life; nothing continuous, fresh, and whole about it. It takes the life of all mankind to make our single life happy. The fact that poverty exists anywhere makes you poor . . . there is one life, one destiny in all humanity; . . . all men make up the one Perfect man, and . . . only all men sharing each other's life, cooperating with and completing one another, can ever realize and bring out the full meaning of the idea of man. So far as each lives not in the whole, does he lack life; so far as he is indifferent to any, does he miss a portion of himself. . . .

The system of FOURIER, though it proposes no less than a complete reorganization of society, rightly calls itself the system of 'Attractive Industry.' Its claims to the rank of a social *science* rest upon the success of its attempt to reconcile the productive industry of man with man's natural tendencies, or 'passional attractions.' . . . The tendency of our whole nature is to Unity. Every man is a lover of harmony; the very discord of his life is a crying out for harmony. The mind tends to Truth, Science; which is the perception of Unity. The heart tends to Love; which is the enjoyment of Unity. Ignorance is only another name for the mental confusion of losing one's place in the Universal Order. Selfishness and Sin, in the same manner, are only involuntary discord, unwelcome isolation; every one tries to love, tries to work his way somehow, even by his selfishness, to the central heart of things, . . . Striving to love [his neighbor] and draw near to him, he finds himself in competition with him; one succeeds by the other's failing. All these individual wills, or natures, born for harmony, and seeking it, but seeking it by private paths that lead to private ends, have only multiplied strife by all their earnestness, and failing of the Combined Order, failing of anything which can be called Society, have thus far only realized certain successive stages of a chaotic striving after society, which we call Savageism, Patriarchalism, Barbarism, Feudalism, and, finally, Civilization, with its admirable outward order cemented by individual selfishness and held together by most curious checks and balances, curious as are all its 'improvements' for the multiplication of wealth and misery at once, its machinery for producing more, that more may starve. The history of these periods is but the record of strife. And still it goes on whirling and widening, none the less under the decent, peaceful smile of what we call our Civilization. Whence came the strife? Not from man's natural passions: have we not said that their final cause is harmony, and that no heart loves discord, no mind thinks in order to get lost? Not from any mal-adaptation between our nature and our sphere:—was not the law of my individual being appointed with perfect knowledge of all the laws of the whole universe of things, and with full regard to the laws of all other individual natures like myself, so that I in my true self-development must harmonize with others, and not clash? Whence *did* it come? We are harmonies, born each into our pre-established place in an infinite system of harmonies; every man is a microcosm, or world in miniature, reflecting all the laws of all things; and each mortal child is as indispensable to the balance and completeness of the world into which he comes so small an atom, as is each planet in the system of our sun, or each sun in the celestial sphere, or each note in the great music of God. . . .

Chapter V. TRANSCENDENTALISM

BROOK FARM WAS ONLY ONE TRANSCENDENTALIST VENTURE AMONG many. Diversity became the badge of men in a movement which sheltered political opinions ranging from George Ripley's utopian socialism to Henry Thoreau's anarchism. The critics suggested that there were almost as many Transcendentalisms as Transcendentalists. Nevertheless, the movement existed. Part of the answer to the problem rests on the success of members in maintaining an area of basic agreement in the midst of diversity; and the second half of the answer can be found in the fact that the sense of unity was stronger in the eighteen-thirties than a decade later. A common cultural and religious heritage did much to hold together Emerson, Thoreau, Ripley, Bronson Alcott, Margaret Fuller, Theodore Parker, and their associates. Similar sensibilities, beliefs, and perceptions in the context of general cultural rebelliousness made the movement possible.

Transcendentalism was among other things a religious rebellion which simultaneously denied and borrowed from its "liberal" predecessors, Deism and Unitarianism. Eighteenth-century Deism had crystallized as a "rational" religion which made possible the acceptance of God along with the rejection of Divine Revelation and church traditions. For the Deist, God revealed himself largely through his creation, a universe of natural law which resembled a perfect, self-winding clock which did not require the Deity's services after Creation. Although the Unitarians moved much more cautiously and looked to the Edinburgh Enlightenment rather than to the earlier radical Deists, they nevertheless owed an intellectual debt to the eighteenth-century American religious radicals—to Jonathan Mayhew, who opposed orthodox doctrines on the Trinity; to Joseph Priestley, who established a Unitarian church in Philadelphia and aroused Thomas Jefferson's enthusiasm; and to James Freeman of the pioneer King's Chapel in Boston. The Unitarians, like the Deists, abandoned Christ's saviourhood, exalted the dignity of man, and assigned to God a lesser role in the world of physical events. William

Ellery Channing, the most eloquent of the Unitarians, placed particular stress on the goodness of human nature and on the power of man to control his destiny. With the possible exception of Channing, however, the Unitarians avoided a radical stance. They advocated reason, carefully considered ethics, theological scholarship, and good taste; and they opposed the orthodox enemy not with "wild" sectarianism and enthusiastic manifestoes but with restrained pamphlets or, more frequently, simply by ignoring the major Calvinist ideas. The Transcendentalists could never forgive their Unitarian fathers for the restrained approach to religion—Emerson loathed "the corpse-cold Unitarianism of Brattle Street and Harvard College"; Margaret Fuller was repelled by "that sea of up-turned, complacent faces"; and George Ripley left the Unitarian Church in despair over its failure as "a religion of the heart."

The young Transcendentalists also found the tight little, neo-classical intellectual world of Boston Unitarianism offensive, and set sail on all the literary seas in search of new insights. They explored German idealism, French eclecticism, English romanticism, and Hindu mysticism. The ship of inquiry eventually anchored in home waters, for the Transcendentalists also learned from seventeenth-century Puritan Pietists—from Jonathan Edwards and from the Quakers. New England tradition contained much for Emerson, who sought a mystical joy in man and nature, a powerful emanation of divinity, and a method of intuition which would enable men to find the bedrock of truth. The Transcendentalists regarded the logical and empirical tools of "the understanding" as pedestrian, useful only for lesser things, and inferior to the intuitive "reason" which led men to the higher world of wisdom. If Emerson and Thoreau wove the patterns of their thought around the rhetoric of Plato, Swedenborg, Goethe, Carlyle, and the *Bhagavad-Gita*, they also remembered the Quaker "inner light," Edwards' love of God in Nature, and that half submerged tendency toward religious "enthusiasm" in the Puritan tradition. In all of these Transcendentalist voyages of mind and heart, conservative Unitarian leaders such as Andrews Norton could find only the obscurantist rejection of an imposing heritage and a consequent collapse into pantheistic infidelity. Emerson ignored the denunciations and went his way celebrating that central reservoir of Being, the Oversoul, and explaining the law of compensation which assured universal justice. The Concord prophet wanted not only cultural independence for the nation but also a sturdy, creative self-reliance in every aspect of life for all men. The Transcendentalists united around a creed which stressed personal freedom, non-conformity, and lives restricted only by the needs of spontaneous living.

Thoreau, following the Emersonian formulas with a greater consistency than Emerson himself, searched for fundamental meanings. For this end he renounced commonly accepted values and immersed himself in nature at Walden Pond, hoping that the experience would provide spiritual enrichment through total awareness in a fresh and uncluttered life. As a result, he developed a powerful criticism of the thirsts in American life for getting, spending, and owning,—and the solitary splendors of life at Walden stood in dramatic contrast to the bustling commercialism of Boston. Commerce and politics were for Thoreau and Emerson of small consequence in comparison to the great world of nature which provided all things from food and shelter to joy, solace, and even moral assurance.

1. Religious Aspects

The Transcendentalists often had unkind words for their Unitarian forebearers, but they remembered William Ellery Channing with gratitude. Channing's liberality, broad education, and above all his rhetorical reminder, "God is within," served the young Transcendentalists well. Emerson in 1838 announced that God was within and without, and attacked past distinctions between the natural and the supernatural,—the word miracle was "monstrous" because it was "not one with the blowing clover and the falling rain." In a fashion that appalled Unitarians, who were already denouncing the new "pantheistic" heresy, Emerson insisted on the presence of a God immanent in human nature and the cosmos, and proceeded to trace all true religion to man's "reason" (i.e., intuition), an action which made religious scholar, theologian, and Bible dispensable. After arousing Cambridge to anger, Emerson quietly returned to Concord leaving Theodore Parker to continue the fight. Parker energetically attempted to prove that all past religious dogmas and rituals were merely the expendable shells of an evolving religious consciousness. AUTHORS: William Ellery Channing (1780–1842) was the foremost Unitarian minister and writer of his generation. Ralph Waldo Emerson (1803–1882) became one of the chief architects of the Transcendentalist movement. Theodore Parker (1810–1860) had a remarkable command of German theology and philosophy which he used as a source of ideas in building his own theology. SELECTIONS: "A Forerunner: William Ellery Channing on

Unitarian Christianity" from Channing's *Unitarian Christianity* (1826).
"Man's Religious Sense" from Emerson's *Divinity School Address*
(1838). "Evolving Religion: The Religious Radicalism of Theodore
Parker" from Parker's *A Discourse on the Transient and the Permanent
in Christianity* (1841).

A FORERUNNER: WILLIAM ELLERY CHANNING
ON UNITARIAN CHRISTIANITY (1826)

Unitarianism has been made a term of so much reproach, and has been
uttered in so many tones of alarm, horror, indignation, and scorn, that to
many it gives only a vague impression of something monstrous, impious,
unutterably perilous. To such, I would say, that this doctrine, which is
considered by some as the summation of . . . blasphemies, the most
cunning weapon ever forged in the fires of hell, amounts to this,—That
there is One God, even the Father; and that Jesus Christ is not this One
God, but his son and messenger, who derived all his powers and glories
from the Universal Parent, and who came into the world not to claim
supreme homage for himself, but to carry up the soul to his Father as the
Only Divine Person, the Only Ultimate Object of religious worship. To
us, this doctrine seems not to have sprung from hell, but to have descended from the throne of God, and to invite and attract us thither.
. . . We are not induced to spread our opinions by the mere conviction
that they are true; for there are many truths, historical, metaphysical,
scientific, literary, which we have no anxiety to propagate. We regard
them as the highest, most important, most efficient truths, and therefore
demanding a firm testimony, and earnest efforts to make them known. In
thus speaking, we do not mean, that we regard our peculiar views as
essential to salvation. Far from us be this spirit of exclusion, the very
spirit of antichrist, the worst of all the delusions of Popery and of Protestantism. We hold nothing to be essential, but the simple and supreme
dedication of the mind, heart, and life to God and to his will. This
inward and practical devotedness to the Supreme Being, we are assured, is
attained and accepted under all the forms of Christianity. We believe,
however, that it is favored by that truth which we maintain, as by no
other system of faith. We regard Unitarianism as peculiarly the friend of
inward, living, practical religion. For this we value it. For this we would
spread it; and we desire none to embrace it, but such as shall seek and
derive from it this celestial influence. . . . The chief purpose of Christianity undoubtedly is, to promote piety, to bring us to God, to fill our
souls with that Great Being, to make us alive to him; and a religious
system can carry no more authentic mark of a divine original, than its

obvious, direct, and peculiar adaptation to quicken and raise the mind to its Creator.—In speaking thus of Unitarian Christianity as promoting piety, I ought to observe, that I use this word in its proper and highest sense. I mean not everything which bears the name of piety, for under this title superstition, fanaticism, and formality are walking abroad and claiming respect. I mean not an anxious frame of mind, not abject and slavish fear, not a dread of hell, not a repetition of forms, not church going, not loud profession, not severe censure of others' irreligion; but filial love and reverence towards God, habitual gratitude, cheerful trust, ready obedience, and, though last not least, an imitation of the everactive and unbounded benevolence of the Creator. . . .

MAN'S RELIGIOUS SENSE (1838):
RALPH WALDO EMERSON

The intuition of the moral sentiment is an insight of the perfection of the laws of the soul. These laws execute themselves. They are out of time, out of space, and not subject to circumstance. Thus in the soul of man there is a justice whose retributions are instant and entire. He who does a good deed is instantly ennobled. He who does a mean deed is by the action itself contracted. He who puts off impurity, thereby puts on purity. If a man is at heart just, then in so far is he God; the safety of God, the immortality of God, the majesty of God do enter into that man with justice. . . .

The perception of this law of laws awakens in the mind a sentiment which we call the religious sentiment, and which makes our highest happiness. . . .

This sentiment lies at the foundation of society, and successively creates all forms of worship. . . . And the unique impression of Jesus upon mankind, whose name is not so much written as ploughed into the history of this world, is proof of the subtle virtue of this infusion.

Meantime, whilst the doors of the temple stand open, night and day, before every man, and the oracles of this truth cease never, it is guarded by one stern condition; this, namely; it is an intuition. It cannot be received at second hand. Truly speaking, it is not instruction, but provocation, that I can receive from another soul. What he announces, I must find true in me, or reject; and on his word, or as his second, be he who he may, I can accept nothing. On the contrary, the absence of this primary faith is the presence of degradation. As is the flood, so is the ebb. Let this faith depart, and the very words it spake and the things it made become false and hurtful. . . . The doctrine of inspiration is lost; the base doctrine of the majority of voices usurps the place of the doctrine of the soul.

Miracles, prophecy, merely; they are not in the belief, nor in the aspiration of society; but, when suggested, seem ridiculous. . . .

Jesus Christ belonged to the true race of prophets. He saw with open eye the mystery of the soul. Drawn by its severe harmony, ravished with its beauty, he lived in it, and had his being there. Alone in all history he estimated the greatness of man. One man was true to what is you and me. . . . He spoke of miracles; for he felt that man's life was a miracle, and all that man doth, and he knew that this daily miracle shines as the character ascends. But the word Miracle, as pronounced by Christian churches, gives a false impression; it is Monster. It is not one with the blowing clover and the falling rain. . . .

EVOLVING RELIGION: THE RELIGIOUS RADICALISM OF THEODORE PARKER (1841)

Looking at the word of Jesus, at real Christianity, the pure religion he taught, nothing appears more fixed and certain. Its influence widens as light extends; it deepens as the nations grow more wise. But, looking at the history of what men call Christianity, nothing seems more uncertain and perishable. While true religion is always the same thing, in each century and every land, in each man that feels it, the Christianity of the pulpit, which is the religion taught, the Christianity of the people, which is the religion that is accepted and lived out, has never been the same thing in any two centuries or lands, except only in name. The difference between what is called Christianity by the Unitarians in our times, and that of some ages past, is greater than the difference between Mahomet and the Messiah. The difference at this day between opposing classes of Christians, the difference between the Christianity of some sects and that of Christ himself, is deeper and more vital than that between Jesus and Plato, pagan as we call him. . . .

Such, then, is the transient, and such the permanent in Christianity. What is of absolute value never changes; we may cling round it and grow to it forever. No one can say his notions shall stand. But we may all say the truth, as it is in Jesus, shall never pass away. Yet there are always some, even religious men, who do not see the permanent element, so they rely on the fleeting, and, what is also an evil, condemn others for not doing the same. They mistake a defense of the truth for an attack upon the holy of holies; the removal of a theological error for the destruction of all religion. Already men of the same sect eye one another with suspicion and lowering brows that indicate a storm, and, like children who have fallen out in their play, call hard names. Now, as always, there is a collision between these two elements. The question puts itself to each man, "Will you cling to what is perishing, or embrace what is eternal?" This question each must answer for himself.

My friends, if you receive the notions about Christianity which chance to be current in your sect or church, solely because they are current, and thus accept the commandment of men instead of God's truth, there will always be enough to commend you for soundness of judgment, prudence, and good sense, enough to call you Christian for that reason. But if this is all you rely upon, alas for you! The ground will shake under your feet if you attempt to walk uprightly, and like men. You will be afraid of every new opinion, lest it shake down your church; you will fear "lest if a fox go up, he will break down your stone wall." The smallest contradiction in the New Testament or Old Testament, the least disagreement between the law and the gospel, any mistake of the apostles, will weaken your faith. It shall be with you "as when a hungry man dreameth, and behold, he eateth; but he awaketh, and his soul is empty."

If, on the other hand, you take the true word of God, and live out this, nothing shall harm you. Men may mock, but their mouthfuls of wind shall be blown back upon their own face. If the master of the house were called Beelzebub, it matters little what name is given to the household. The name Christian, given in mockery, will last till the world go down. He that loves God and man, and lives in accordance with that love, needs not fear what man can do to him. His religion comes to him in his hour of sadness, it lays its hand on him when he has fallen among thieves, and raises him up, heals and comforts him. If he is crucified, he shall rise again.

My friends, you this day receive, with the usual formalities, the man you have chosen to speak to you on the highest of all themes—what concerns your life on earth, your life in heaven. It is a work for which no talents, no prayerful diligence, no piety is too great; an office that would dignify angels, if worthily filled. If the eyes of this man be holden, that he cannot discern between the perishing and the true, you will hold him guiltless of all sin in this; but look for light where it can be had, for his office will then be of no use to you. But if he sees the truth and is scared by worldly motives, and will not tell it, alas for him! If the watchman see the foe coming and blow not the trumpet, the blood of the innocent is on him. . . .

2. Ethical and Aesthetic Ideals

The oversoul had its limits as an emotional substitute for a personal Deity, and the religious impulses of the Transcendentalists frequently

found ethical and aesthetic outlets. In ethics and art the Transcendentalists demanded above all else enthusiasm, and they were extremely vexed
by both the gentlemanly moral "complacency" and the aesthetic "blindness" of polite Bostonians who still lived in an eighteenth-century world
governed by Locke in philosophy, Paley and Butler in ethics, and the neo-
classical writers in literature. Emerson and Thoreau rejected what was for
them a dead heritage. English and German romantics, French eclectics,
Neo-Platonists, and the great Hindu writers were all grist for the new
mills which would grind out a democratic aesthetics appropriate to the
experiences of the New World. As the *Dial* manifesto suggested, the early
Transcendentalist writers married the good to the beautiful, displayed a
strong vein of ethical utilitarianism in literature, and granted only a
limited value to *belles lettres*. Emerson and Thoreau were first of all
prophets of the good life whose best works were autobiographical records
of the whole man thinking, feeling, and living. For the Transcendentalists
the life of a man was the life of a nonconformist who cast aside all
superstitions of the tribe to live concretely and creatively in the present.
This was Thoreau's major purpose in going to live at Walden Pond.
AUTHORS: Emerson (1803–1882); George Ripley (1802–1880); and
Margaret Fuller (1810–1850), a critic, reformer, editor, and advocate of
women's rights. All three served as editors and contributors to *The Dial*.
Henry Thoreau (1817–1862) sent several significant manuscripts to *The
Dial*. SELECTIONS: "A Transcendentalist Manifesto" from the editorial
statement in the first issue of *The Dial* (1840). "Individualism and
Spontaneity in the Good Life: Thoreau at Walden Pond" (1845–1847)
from Thoreau's *Walden* (1854).

A TRANSCENDENTALIST MANIFESTO (1840):
THE EDITORS OF *THE DIAL*

We invite the attention of our countrymen to a new design. . . . No
one can converse much with different classes of society in New England,
without remarking the progress of a revolution. Those who share in it
have no external organization, no badge, no creed, no name. They do not
vote, or print, or even meet together. They do not know each other's faces
or names. They are united only in a common love of truth, and love of its
work. They are of all conditions and constitutions. . . . In literature,
this influence appears not yet in new books so much as in the higher tone
of criticism. The antidote to all narrowness is the comparison of the
record with nature, which at once shames the record and stimulates to
new attempts. Whilst we look at this, we wonder how any book has been
thought worthy to be preserved. There is somewhat in all life untrans-
latable into language. . . . If our Journal share the impulses of the time,

it cannot now prescribe its own course. It cannot foretell in orderly propositions what it shall attempt. All criticism should be poetic; unpredictable; superseding, as every new thought does, all foregone thoughts, and making a new light on the whole world. Its brow is not wrinkled with circumspection, but serene, cheerful, adoring. It has all things to say, and on less than all the world for its final audience.

Our plan embraces much more than criticism; were it not so, our criticism would be naught. Everything noble is directed on life, and this is. We do not wish to say pretty or curious things, or to reiterate a few propositions in varied forms, but, if we can, to give expression to that spirit which lifts men to a higher platform, restores to them the religious sentiment, brings them worthy aims and pure pleasures, purges the inward eye, makes life less desultory, and, through raising man to the level of nature, takes away its melancholy from the landscape, and reconciles the practical with the speculative powers. . . .

As we wish not to multiply books, but to report life, our resources are therefore not so much the pens of practised writers, as the discourse of the living, and the portfolios which friendship has opened to us. From the beautiful recesses of private thought; from the experience and hope of spirits which are withdrawing from all old forms, and seeking in all that is new somewhat to meet their inappeasable longings; from the secret confession of genius afraid to trust itself to aught but sympathy; from the conversation of fervid and mystical pietists; from tearstained diaries of sorrow and passion; from the manuscripts of young poets; and from the records of youthful taste commenting on old works of art; we hope to draw thoughts and feelings, which being alive can impart life.

And so with diligent hands and good intent we set down our *Dial* on the earth. We wish it may resemble that instrument in its celebrated happiness, that of measuring no hours but those of sunshine. Let it be one cheerful rational voice amidst the din of mourners and polemics. . . . Or to abide by our chosen image, let it be such a *Dial*, not as the dead face of a clock . . . but rather such a *Dial* as is the Garden itself, in whose leaves and flowers and fruits the suddenly awakened sleeper is instantly apprised not what part of dead time, but what state of life and growth is now arrived and arriving. . . .

INDIVIDUALISM AND SPONTANEITY IN THE GOOD LIFE: THOREAU AT WALDEN POND (1845–1847)

I went to the woods because I wished to live deliberately, to front only the essential facts of life, and see if I could not learn what it had to teach, and not, when I came to die, discover that I had not lived. I did not wish to live what was not life, living is so dear; nor did I wish to practise resignation, unless it was quite necessary. I wanted to live deep and suck out all the marrow of life, to live so sturdily and Spartan-like as to put to rout all that was not life, to cut a broad swath and shave close, to drive life into a corner, and reduce it to its lowest terms, and, if it proved to be mean, why then to get the whole and genuine meanness of it, and publish its meanness to the world; or if it were sublime, to know it by experience, and be able to give a true account of it in my next excursion. For most men, it appears to me, are in a strange uncertainty about . . . whether it is of the devil or of God, and have somewhat hastily concluded that it is the chief end of man here to "glorify God and enjoy him forever."

Still we live meanly, like ants; though the fable tells us that we were long ago changed into men; like pygmies we fight with cranes; it is error upon error, and clout upon clout, and our best virtue has for its occasion a superfluous and evitable wretchedness. Our life is frittered away by detail. An honest man has hardly need to count more than his ten fingers, or in extreme cases he may add his ten toes, and lump the rest. Simplicity, simplicity, simplicity! I say, let your affairs be as two or three, and not a hundred or a thousand; instead of a million count half a dozen, and keep your accounts on your thumb-nail. In the midst of this chopping sea of civilized life, such are the clouds and storms and quicksands and thousand-and-one items to be allowed for, that a man has to live, if he would not founder and go to the bottom and not make his port at all, by dead reckoning, and he must be a great calculator indeed who succeeds. Simplify, simplify. Instead of three meals a day, if it be necessary eat but one; instead of a hundred dishes, five; and reduce other things in proportion. Our life is like a German Confederacy, made up of petty states, with its boundary forever fluctuating, so that even a German cannot tell you how it is bounded at any moment. The nation itself, with all its so-called internal improvements, which, by the way, are all external and superficial, is just such an unwieldy and overgrown establishment, cluttered with furniture and tripped up by its own traps, ruined by luxury and heedless expense, by want of calculation and a worthy aim, as the million households in the land; and the only cure for it, as for them, is in a rigid economy, a stern and more than Spartan simplicity of life and elevation of purpose. It lives too fast. Men think that it is essential that the Nation have commerce, and export ice, and talk through a telegraph, and ride thirty miles an hour, without a doubt, whether they do or not; but whether we should live like baboons or like men, is a little uncertain. If we do not get out sleepers, and forge rails, and devote days and nights to the work, but go to tinkering upon our lives to improve them, who will build railroads? And if railroads are not built, how shall we get to Heaven in season? But if we stay at home and mind our business, who will want railroads? We do not ride on the railroad; it rides upon us. Did you ever think what those sleepers are that underlie the railroad? Each one is a man, an Irishman, or a Yankee man. The rails are laid on them, and they are covered with sand and the cars run smoothly over them. They are sound sleepers, I assure you. And every few years a new lot is laid down and run over; so that, if some have the pleasure of riding on a rail, others have the misfortune to be ridden upon. And when they run over a man that is walking in his sleep, a supernumerary sleeper in the wrong position, and wake him up, they suddenly stop the cars, and make a hue and cry about it, as if this were an exception. I am glad to know that it takes a gang of men for every five miles to keep the sleepers down and level in their beds as it is, for this is a sign that they may sometime get up again.

Why should we live with such hurry and waste of life? . . . Be it life or death, we crave only reality. If we are really dying, let us hear the rattle in our throats and feel cold in the extremities; if we are alive, let us go about our business. . . .

3. *Political Thought*

Emerson defended the idea that only the creative, spontaneously living, individual self represented the ultimate social good. Thoreau developed Emersonian ideas into a more articulate and persuasive argument for anarchism. Throughout the eighteen-thirties the Transcendentalists, with the single exception of Orestes A. Brownson, turned a deaf ear to the clamor of politics. The state, political parties, reformers—all were institutions and people with whom the Transcendentalists wished to have as little to do as possible. Still, time and new issues brought most of the Transcendentalists to some form of political action. Orestes A. Brownson became an energetic Locofoco editor and politician; George Ripley led a Transcendentalist contingent to Brook Farm and socialism in 1840; and even Emerson and Thoreau eventually joined the public debate against slavery. AUTHOR: Henry David Thoreau (1817–1862) presented the concept of civil disobedience which was to influence Tolstoy and Gandhi and play a part in the American civil rights struggles of the nineteen-sixties. SELECTION: "Civil Disobedience" from Thoreau's famous essay of 1849.

CIVIL DISOBEDIENCE (1849):
HENRY DAVID THOREAU

I heartily accept the motto,—"That government is best which governs least;" and I should like to see it acted up to more rapidly and systematically. Carried out, it finally amounts to this, which I also believe,—

"That government is best which governs not at all;" and when men are prepared for it, that will be the kind of government which they will have. Government is at best but an expedient; but most governments are usually, and all governments are sometimes, inexpedient. . . .

After all, the practical reason why, when the power is once in the hands of the people, a majority are permitted, and for a long period continue, to rule is not because they are most likely to be in the right, nor because this seems fairest to the minority, but because they are physically the strongest. But a government in which the majority rule in all cases cannot be based on justice, even as far as men understand it. Can there not be a government in which majorities do not virtually decide right and wrong, but conscience?—in which majorities decide only those questions to which the rule of expediency is applicable? Must the citizen ever for a moment, or in the least degree, resign his conscience to the legislator? Why has every man a conscience, then? I think that we should be men first, and subjects afterward. It is not desirable to cultivate a respect for the law, so much as for the right. . . .

How does it become a man to behave toward this American government today? I answer, that he cannot without disgrace be associated with it. I cannot for an instant recognize that political organization as my government which is also the slave's government also.

All men recognize the right of revolution; that is, the right to refuse allegiance to, and to resist, the government, when its tyranny or its inefficiency are great and unendurable. But almost all say that such is not the case now. But such was the case, they think, in the Revolution of '75. . . .

Some years ago, the State met me in behalf of the Church, and commanded me to pay a certain sum toward the support of a clergyman whose preaching my father attended, but never I myself. "Pay," it said, "or be locked up in the jail." I declined to pay, But, unfortunately, another man saw fit to pay it. . . . At the request of the selectmen, I condescended to make some such statement as this in writing:—"Know all men by these presents, that I, Henry Thoreau, do not wish to be regarded as a member of any incorporated society which I have not joined." This I gave to the town clerk; and he has it. . . .

Under a government which imprisons any unjustly, the true place for a just man is also a prison. The proper place to-day, the only place which Massachusetts has provided for her freer and less desponding spirits, is her prisons, to be put out and locked out of the State by her own act, as they have already put themselves out by their principles. It is there that the fugitive slave, and the Mexican prisoner on parole, and the Indian come to plead the wrongs of his race should find them; on that separate, but more free and honorable ground, where the State places those who are not *with* her, but *against* her,—the only house in a slave State in which a free man can abide with honor. . . .

4. Nature

Emerson's metaphysics made possible his perfect faith in the virtues of the fullest expression of each individual's personality; and without a firm belief in the benevolence of the Universe and the goodness of human nature Transcendental optimism would not have been feasible. However, the wicked as well as the virtuous seek self expression, and Emerson was reminded that basic impulses may spring "from below." He replied that "They do not seem to me to be such; but if I am the Devil's child, I will live then from the Devil." Emerson could come no closer to the doubts often raised by the problem of metaphysical evil. He seems to have shared the belief of Neo-Platonists that the highest good was the fullest measure of existence and absolute evil no more than complete non-existence. According to Emerson, each individual person was an outflowing from a central reservoir of being, the Oversoul, and the goodness of man as well as the moral cast of physical nature sprang from their near identity with the Oversoul. Emerson could thus be confident of man, look to nature as a source of goodness, and know that all existing things beneath their superficial shells were identical in that their essence consisted of virtue. AUTHOR: Emerson (1803–1882) laid the foundations of his fame by writing half a dozen essays such as "Nature" during the eighteen-thirties. SELECTION: "Hamatreya" by Emerson (1847). "Theories and Perceptions of Nature" from Emerson's *Nature* (1836).

HAMATREYA (1847): RALPH WALDO EMERSON

Bulkeley, Hunt, Willard, Hosmer, Meriam, Flint,
Possessed the land which rendered to their toil
Hay, corn, roots, hemp, flax, apples, wool and wood.
Each of these landlords walked amidst his farm,
Saying, " 'Tis mine, my children's and my name's.
How sweet the west wind sounds in my own trees!
How graceful climb those shadows on my hill!
I fancy these pure waters and the flags
Know me, as does my dog: we sympathize;
And, I affirm, my actions smack of the soil."

Where are these men? Asleep beneath their grounds:
And strangers, fond as they, their furrows plough.
Earth laughs in flowers, to see her boastful boys
Earth-proud, proud of the earth which is not theirs;
Who steer the plough, but cannot steer their feet
Clear of the grave.
They added ridge to valley, brook to pond,
And sighed for all that bounded their domain;
"This suits me for a pasture; that's my park;
We must have clay, lime, gravel, granite-ledge,
And misty lowland, where to go for peat.
The land is well,—lies fairly to the south.
" 'Tis good, when you have crossed the sea and back,
To find the sitfast acres where you left them."
Ah! the hot owner sees not Death, who adds
Him to his land, a lump of mould the more.
Hear what the Earth says:—

Earth-song

"Mine and yours;
Mine, not yours.
Earth endures;
Stars abide—
Shine down in the old sea;
Old are the shores;
But where are old men?
I who have seen much,
Such have I never seen.

"The lawyer's deed
Ran sure,
In tail,
To them, and to their heirs
Who shall succeed,
Without fail
Forevermore.

"Here is the land,
Shaggy with wood,
With its old valley,
Mound and flood.
But the heritors?—
Fled like the flood's foam.
The lawyer, and the laws,
And the kingdom,
Clean swept herefrom.

"They called me theirs,
Who so controlled me;
Yet every one
Wished to stay, and is gone,
How am I theirs,
If they cannot hold me,
But I hold them?"

When I heard the Earth-song
I was no longer brave;
My avarice cooled
Like lust in the chill of the grave.

THEORIES AND PERCEPTIONS OF NATURE (1836): RALPH WALDO EMERSON

All science has one aim, namely, to find a theory of nature. We have theories of races and of functions, but scarcely yet a remote approach to an idea of creation. We are now so far from the road to truth, that religious teachers dispute and hate each other, and speculative men are esteemed unsound and frivolous. But to a sound judgment, the most abstract truth is the most practical. Whenever a true theory appears, it will be its own evidence. Its test is, that it will explain all phenomena. Now many are thought not only unexplained but inexplicable; as language, sleep, madness, dreams, beasts, sex.

Philosophically considered, the universe is composed of Nature and the Soul. Strictly speaking, therefore, all that is separate from us, all which Philosophy distinguishes as the NOT ME, that is, both nature and art, all other men and my own body, must be ranked under this name, NATURE. . . .

NATURE

When we speak of nature . . . we have a distinct but most poetical sense in the mind. We mean the integrity of impression made by manifold natural objects. It is this which distinguishes the stick of timber of the wood-cutter from the tree of the poet. The charming landscape which I saw this morning is indubitably made up of some twenty or thirty farms. Miller owns this field. Locke that, and Manning the woodland beyond. But none of them owns the landscape. There is a property in the horizon which no man has but he whose eye can integrate all the parts, that is, the poet. This is the best part of these men's farms, yet to this their warranty-deeds give no title. . . . His intercourse with heaven and earth becomes part of his daily food. . . .

COMMODITY

Under the general name of commodity, I rank all those advantages which our senses owe to nature. This, of course, is a benefit which is temporary and mediate, not ultimate, like its service to the soul. Yet although low, it is perfect in its kind, and is the only use of nature which all men apprehend. . . . The wind sows the seed; the sun evaporates the sea; the wind blows the vapor to the field; the ice, on the other side of the planet, condenses rain on this; the rain feeds the plant; the plant feeds the animal; and thus the endless circulations of the divine charity nourish man. . . .

BEAUTY

Nature is a sea of forms radically alike and even unique. A leaf, a sunbeam, a landscape, the ocean, make an analogous impression on the mind. What is common to them all,—that perfectness and harmony, is beauty. The standard of beauty is the entire circuit of natural forms,—the totality of nature; which the Italians expressed by defining beauty "il più nell' uno." Nothing is quite beautiful alone; nothing but is beautiful in the whole. A single object is only so far beautiful as it suggests this universal grace. The poet, the painter, the sculptor, the musician, the architect, seek each to concentrate this radiance of the world on one point, and each in his several work to satisfy the love of beauty which stimulates him to produce. . . .

The world thus exists to the soul to satisfy the desire of beauty. This element I call an ultimate end. No reason can be asked or given why the soul seeks beauty. Beauty, in its largest and profoundest sense, is one expression for the universe. God is the all-fair. Truth, and goodness, and beauty, are but different faces of the same All. But beauty in nature is not ultimate. It is the herald of inward and eternal beauty, and is not alone a solid and satisfactory good. It must stand as a part, and not as yet the last or highest expression of the final cause of Nature.

LANGUAGE

Language is a third use which Nature subserves to man. Nature is the vehicle of thought, and in a simple, double, and three-fold degree.

1. Words are signs of natural facts.
2. Particular natural facts are symbols of particular spiritual facts.
3. Nature is the symbol of spirit.

1. Words are signs of natural facts. The use of natural history is to give us aid in supernatural history; the use of the outer creation, to give us

language for the beings and changes of the inward creation. Every word which is used to express a moral or intellectual fact, if traced to its root, is found to be borrowed from some material appearance. *Right* means *straight; wrong* means *twisted. Spirit* primarily means *wind; transgression,* the crossing of a *line; supercilious,* the *raising of the eyebrow.* We say the *heart* to express emotion, the *head* to denote thought; and *thought* and *emotion* are words borrowed from sensible things, and now appropriated to spiritual nature.

2. But this origin of all words that convey a spiritual import,—so conspicuous a fact in the history of language,—is our least debt to nature. It is not words only that are emblematic; it is things which are emblematic. Every natural fact is a symbol of some spiritual fact. Every appearance in nature corresponds to some state of the mind, and that state of the mind can only be described by presenting that natural appearance as its picture. An enraged man is a lion, a cunning man is a fox, a firm man is a rock, a learned man is a torch. . . .

Man is conscious of a universal soul within or behind his individual life, wherein, as in a firmament, the natures of Justice, Truth, Love, Freedom, arise and shine. This universal soul he calls Reason: it is not mine, or thine, or his, but we are its; we are its property and men. And the blue sky in which the private earth is buried, the sky with its eternal calm, and full of everlasting orbs, is the type of Reason. That which intellectually considered we call Reason, considered in relation to nature, we call Spirit. Spirit is the Creator. Spirit hath life in itself. And man in all ages and countries embodies it in his language as the Father. . . .

In like manner, the memorable words of history and the proverbs of nations consist usually of a natural fact, selected as a picture or parable of a moral truth. Thus: A rolling stone gathers no moss; A bird in the hand is worth two in the bush; A cripple in the right way will beat a racer in the wrong: Make hay while the sun shines; 'Tis hard to carry a full cup even; Vinegar is the son of wine; The last ounce broke the camel's back; Long-lived trees make roots first;—and the like. . . .

This relation between the mind and matter is not fancied by some poet, but stands in the will of God, and so is free to be known by all men. . . .

DISCIPLINE

In view of the significance of nature, we arrive at once at a new fact, that nature is a discipline. This use of the world includes the preceeding uses, as parts of itself.

Space, time, society, labor, climate, food, locomotion, the animals, the mechanical forces, give us sincerest lessons, day by day, whose meaning is unlimited. They educate both the Understanding and the Reason. Every property of matter is a school for the understanding,—its solidity or resistance, its inertia, its extension, its figures, its divisibility. The understanding adds, divides, combines, measures, and finds nutriment and room for its activity in this worthy scene. Meantime, Reason transfers all these lessons into its own world of thought, by perceiving the analogy that marries Matter and Mind. . . .

It has already been illustrated, that every natural process is a version of a moral sentence. The moral law lies at the centre of nature and radiates to the circumference. . . .

IDEALISM

The advantage of the ideal theory over the popular faith is this, that it presents the world in precisely that view which is most desirable to the mind. It is, in fact, the view which Reason, both speculative and practical, that is philosophy and virtue, take. For seen in the light of thought, the world always is phenomenal; and virtue subordinates it to the mind. Idealism sees the world in God. . . .

SPIRIT

. . . The aspect of Nature is devout. Like the figure of Jesus, she stands with bended head, and hands folded upon the breast. The happiest man is he who learns from nature the lesson of worship.

Of that ineffable essence which we call Spirit, he that thinks most, will say least. We can foresee God in the coarse, and, as it were, distant phenomena of matter; but when we try to define and describe himself, both language and thought desert us, and we are as helpless as fools and savages. . . .

Idealism acquaints us with the total disparity between the evidence of our own being and the evidence of the world's being. The one is perfect; the other, incapable of any assurance; the mind is a part of the nature of things; the world is a divine dream, from which we may presently awake to the glories and certainties of day. Idealism is a hypothesis to account for nature by other principles than those of carpentry and chemistry. . . .

PROSPECTS

At present, man applies to nature but half his force. He works on the world with his understanding alone. He lives in it and masters it by a penny-wisdom; and he that works most in it is but a half-man, and whilst his arms are strong and his digestion good, his mind is imbruted, and he is a selfish savage. His relation to nature, his power over it, is through the understanding, as by manure; the economic use of fire, wind, water, and the mariner's needle; steam, coal, chemical agriculture; the repairs of the human body by the dentist and the surgeon. This is such a resumption of power as if a banished king should buy his territories inch by inch, instead of vaulting at once into his throne. . . .

It will not need, when the mind is prepared for study, to search for objects. The invariable mark of wisdom is to see the miraculous in the common. . . .

So shall we come to look at the world with new eyes. It shall answer the endless inquiry of the intellect,—What is truth? and of the affections,—What is good? by yielding itself passive to the educated Will. Then shall come to pass what my poet said: "Nature is not fixed but fluid. Spirit alters, moulds, makes it. The immobility or bruteness of nature is the absence of spirit; to pure spirit it is fluid, it is volatile, it is obedient. Every spirit builds itself a house, and beyond its house a world, and beyond its world a heaven. Know then that the world exists for you. . . ."

Build therefore your own world. As fast as you conform your life to the pure idea in your mind, that will unfold its great proportions. A correspondent revolution in things will attend the influx of the spirit. So fast will disagreeable appearances, swine, spiders, snakes, pests, mad-houses, prisons, enemies, vanish; they are temporary and shall be no more seen. The odor and filths of nature, the sun shall dry up and the wind exhale. And when the summer comes from the south the snow-banks melt and the face of the earth becomes green before it, so shall the advancing spirit create its ornaments along its path, and carry with it the beauty it visits and the song which enchants it; it shall draw beautiful faces, hearts, wise discourse, and heroic acts, around its way, until evil is no more seen. The kingdom of man over nature, which cometh not with observation,—a dominion such as now is beyond his dream of God,—he shall enter without more wonder than the blind man feels who is gradually restored to perfect sight. . . .

Chapter VI. THE ROMANTIC TEMPER

IF "TRANCENDENTALISM" IS A DIFFICULT WORD, "ROMANTICISM" OF-
fers even more perplexing problems. Definitions of the Romantic
movement are usually so general as to be almost useless, or so narrow
as to leave out much which ought to be included; and most twentieth-
century explanations tend toward a hostile stress on irrationality, ego-
centric fixations, unseemly emotions, and the flight from civilized
discipline. Yet, neither modern hostility nor the near impossibility of
making precise definitions should prevent us from dealing with realities in intellectual history. It is certainly possible to trace the major
contours of opposition to the insistence of so many seventeenth-century intellectual leaders on elegantly controlled craftsmanship and on
the total rationality of the world; one can sense the impatience with
the dominance of carefully sculpted models for life and literature
based on the observation and rational analysis of "nature" or on
imitations of Classical accomplishments. The "Philosophes" in the
"Age of Reason" carried leading concepts of the seventeenth century
into every aspect of intellectual life, and were eventually accused of
having made the mind the executioner of emotion, and formalism
the slayer of the concrete and living thing. The Romantic painters,
sculptors, and musicians had obvious reasons for refusing to continue
imitating forms which had become feeble, and Romantic writers had
an understandable reaction to what they considered to be overab-
straction and overgeneralization. Reared in a world of declining Neo-
Classicism with a sense of the precariousness of established forms, the
Romantic wished to find for man and nature new forms and images
as well as values and definitions. Most of the new writers and artists,
wishing to recapture the concrete, living world, spoke for the life of
feeling and the value of intuition. The victories of science and
mathematics over the world of the senses, the near exhaustion of Neo-
Classical and "enlightened" sensibilities, the threat of the American
and French Revolutions to almost every aspect of the established

order,—all called for novel approaches in politics, literature, and the arts.

Beyond a general spirit of rebellion common to all, the Romantics were as sharply divided in aesthetic and social thought as their predecessors had been. One large group joined experimentation in the arts with celebration of Romantic democracy and nationalism. Often painters, sculptors, and writers used representations of Graeco-Roman republicanism to lend stability and to suggest continuity with the past as well as to counteract the "aristocratic" interpretations of Classical culture. (The marble togas of Washington statues provide an interesting example.) A second school of thought expressed a nostalgia for the dying feudal world of chivalry, and mourned the passing of many life patterns from courtly love to aristocratic social orientations. Those who felt nostalgia for the remote past turned enthusiastically to folk and fairy tales; the sentimental value of crumbling castles and venerable monasteries provided one of the chief themes of the age; and Scottish, German, and French lays and tales celebrated clan loyalties and feudal noblesse. In this context of sensibility, Henry Wadsworth Longfellow borrowed liberally from German mythology in an effort to give the American Indian the romance commonly attributed to the folk creations of early German history. Washington Irving attempted to transfer the romance of ancient Spanish and German villages to the Dutch settlements on the Hudson River. And certainly popular Southern novelists tried often enough to identify the Southern planter with the romantically colored image of the gallant "Cavalier." Longfellow, Irving, and the Southern novelists scored a victory here and there, but few major writers were tempted to follow their example. A larger group of novelists and poets which included Nathaniel Hawthorne, Edgar Allan Poe, and Charles Brockden Brown systematically experimented with sensational "Gothic" settings and situations. Americans may have lacked Rhine myths and crumbling castles, but American writers managed to introduce murderous monks, dripping daggers, leering portraits, ancestral curses, religious manias, ventriloquism, and similar devices. Beyond these Gothic trappings, the Americans had an ambiguous response to several major aspects of Romanticism. Hawthorne and James Fenimore Cooper complained about the paucity of social materials in a new, democratic society which lacked a feudal past, ancient wrongs, established churches and aristocracies, and the age-old conflict and interaction of classes. Yet these two writers and most of their colleagues agreed on a firm commitment to the Republic and on a rejection of the Europeans who sustained feudal values. With the single significant exception of some Southern writers involved in the defense of slavery and Southern society, Americans had no desire to see dying European institutions rooted in the New World. We have Mark Twain's comments on the ruinous damage done to Southern culture by Sir Walter Scott, and we know that Virginians actually held "tournaments" with fighting "lords," "squires," "favors," "lances," and such accoutrements. Men like George Fitzhugh, who rejected the philosophy of the Declaration of Independence and sought new images of Southern society, turned easily enough to notions of "chivalry," "ladies," "gentlemen," "Southrons"; they tried to imagine themselves as benevolent and aristocratic squires surrounded by faithful slave "retainers" and opposed by the coarse Yankee materialism of modern times.

Most Americans were attracted to the strands of Romanticism which celebrated the politics and aesthetics of "Romantic" democracy. Romanticism in such a guise lent the cloak of dignity and sentiment not to the paternal lord but to the glories of the "people" and the commonplace. William Wordsworth wished to speak in "the language of men" and French Revolutionists described the majesty and justice of the popular will. Ralph Waldo Emerson and Walt Whitman urged the American scholar to observe carefully hearth and home, to enter the workshop and the marketplace, and to give voice to all the unsung music of democratic folk at work and play. Early images of self and society—such as Royall Tyler's "Jonathan," the simple, direct Republican Yankee of natural virtue as opposed to the foppish and vice-ridden English gentleman—sprang from both Republican theory and the romantic sensibilities which exalted the usual and the commonplace. Most of the touches which made the nineteenth-century hero recognizable then and now can be described as "Romantic." Washington and Jefferson are peculiarly the political saints of the first epoch in American history; but Jefferson, the prudent sage, the urbane philosopher, the distinguished amateur in science and the arts, seems to belong very much to his own era, and Washington appears remote, enshrined in the marble of a "Graeco-Roman-American" conception of Republican virtue. Dominant images of Jackson and Lincoln have a more dynamic existence because they were painted in romantic colors. Jackson's admirers saw, and still sometimes see, a Romantic hero of indomitable will who by force of character and Western virtue overcame great adversity as a boy in the

Revolution, a young man on the frontier, a general at New Orleans in 1815, and as President after 1828. Lincoln stands as the democratic man of destiny fated for heroic deeds and martyrdom, conclusive evidence of the enormous potential of the common clay of democracy.

Jacksonian democracy had its "Romance"; the humanitarianism and Utopianism of the age were based partly on a sentimental celebration of the "people." Moreover, the Romantic sensibilities of antebellum America guarded the gates of the American Pantheon of heroes. The pioneer, the slave, the Southern planter, the American statesman, the idealistic and virtuous American abroad in a decadent Europe—all were Romantic heroes. In the new Romance of the West, the Indian, the hunter, the savage, and others were portrayed according to Romantic notions. Leading conceptions about America's Republican mission to the world and the great democratic "cataract" of the people emerged from the minds of Romantic authors. Finally, the national landscape of turbulent rivers and mighty mountains, great streams and wild flowers, first came to the attention of Americans during the Jacksonian era.

1. On Literature in America

The first literary productions of the early national period tended to be pallid imitations of Neo-Classical literature. Poets such as Joel Barlow and Timothy Dwight attempted to express the grand themes of Republicanism and Americanism with devices such as the heroic couplet and the epic poem; and the results were usually pomposity and self-consciousness. Except for the strongly wrought utilitarian prose of the Founding Fathers, the early successes of Washington Irving and James Fenimore Cooper, and scattered lines of lyric poetry, Americans produced little literature of quality during the first generation of national existence. Cooper ascribed the low level of accomplishment to the poverty of literary materials in a new, democratic, and monotonously uniform society. Emerson disagreed sharply later, and insisted on the aesthetic wealth of the democratic scene. William Gilmore Simms tried to show very concretely how the successful American "romance" might be written. AUTHORS: James Fenimore Cooper (1789–1851), the first American novelist to establish an international reputation, grew up on a manorial estate, attended Yale University, and paid several prolonged visits to France. Cooper spent a lifetime attempting to reconcile his acceptance of democracy and his sense of distinction based on birth, wealth, and talent. Ralph Waldo Emerson (1803–1882) advocated a democratic theory of aesthetics and established a classic rationale for the nationalist American scholar. William Gilmore Simms (1806–1870) was born and lived most of his life in Charleston, South Carolina. After abandoning law and medicine he attempted to make a living as a man of letters. SELECTIONS: "Few Materials for Romance in America" from Cooper's *Notions of the Americans* (1828). "The Proper Subjects for American Literature" from Emerson's address "The American Scholar" (1837). "How To Write an American Romance" from Simms's "Introduction" to *The Yemassee* (1835).

FEW MATERIALS FOR ROMANCE IN AMERICA (1828): JAMES FENIMORE COOPER

The second obstacle against which American literature has to contend, is in the poverty of materials. There is scarcely an ore which contributes to the wealth of the author, that is found here, in veins as rich as in Europe. There are no annals for the historian; no follies (beyond the most vulgar and commonplace) for the satirist; no manners for the dramatist; no obscure fictions for the writer of romance; no gross and hardy offences against decorum for the moralist; nor any of the rich artificial auxiliaries of poetry. The weakest hand can extract a spark from the flint, but it would baffle the strength of a giant to attempt kindling a flame with a pudding-stone. I very well know there are theorists who assume that the society and institutions of this country are, or ought to be, particularly favourable to novelties and variety. But the experience of one month, in these States, is sufficient to show any observant man the falsity of their position. The effect of a promiscuous assemblage anywhere, is to create a standard of deportment; and great liberty permits every one to aim to its attainment. I have never seen a nation so much alike in my life, as the people of the United States, and what is more, they are not only like each other, but they are remarkably like that which common sense tells them they ought to resemble. No doubt, traits of character that are a little peculiar, without, however, being either very poetical, or very rich, are to be found in remote districts; but they are rare, and not always happy exceptions. . . .

THE PROPER SUBJECTS FOR AMERICAN
LITERATURE (1837): RALPH WALDO EMERSON

I read with joy some of the auspicious signs of the coming days, as they glimmer already through poetry and art, through philosophy and science, through church and state.

One of these signs is the fact that the same movement which effected the elevation of what was called the lowest class in the state, assumed in literature a very marked and as benign an aspect. Instead of the sublime and beautiful, the near, the low, the common, was explored and poetized. That which had been negligently trodden under foot by those who were harnessing and provisioning themselves for long journeys into far countries, is suddenly found to be richer than all foreign parts. The literature of the poor, the feelings of the child, the philosophy of the street, the meaning of household life, are the topics of the time. It is a great stride. It is a sign—is it not?—of new vigor when the extremities are made active, when currents of warm life run into the hands and the feet. I ask not for the great, the remote, the romantic; what is doing in Italy or Arabia; what is Greek art, or Provencal minstrelsy; I embrace the common, I explore and sit at the feet of the familiar, the low. . . . We will walk on our own feet; we will work with our own hands; we will speak our own minds. The study of letters shall be no longer a name for pity, for doubt, and for sensual indulgence. The dread of man and the love of man shall be a wall of defense and a wreath of joy around all. A nation of men will for the first time exist, because each believes himself inspired by the Divine Soul which also inspires all men. . . .

HOW TO WRITE AN AMERICAN ROMANCE
(1835): WILLIAM GILMORE SIMMS

I have entitled this story a romance and not a novel—the reader will permit me to insist upon the distinction. I am unwilling that *The Yemassee* should be examined by any other than those standards which have governed me in its composition. . . . It is only when an author departs from his own standards that he offends against propriety and deserves punishment.

The question briefly is, what are the standards of the modern romance itself? The reply is instant. Modern romance is the substitute which the people of today offer for the ancient epic. Its standards are the same. The reader who, reading *Ivanhoe*, keeps Fielding and Richardson beside him, will be at fault in every step of his progress. . . . [To such] the works of Maturin, of Scott, of Bulwer, and the rest, are only so much incoherent nonsense.

The modern romance is a poem in every sense of the word. It is only with those who insist upon poetry as rhyme, and rhyme as poetry, that the identity fails to be perceptible. Its standards are precisely those of the epic. It invests individuals with an absorbing interest—it hurries them through crowding events in a narrow space of time—it requires the same unities of plan, of purpose, and harmony of parts, and it seeks for its adventures among the wild and wonderful. It does not insist upon what is known, or even what is probable. It grasps upon the possible; and, placing a human agent into hitherto untried situations, it exercises its ingenuity in extricating him from them, while describing his feelings and his fortunes in their progress. The task has been well or ill done in proportion to the degree of ingenuity and knowledge which the romancer exhibits in carrying out the details, according to such properties as are called for by the circumstances of the story. These proprieties are the standards set up at his starting, and to which he is required religiously to confine himself. . . .

The Yemassee is proposed as an American romance. It is so styled, as much of the material could have been furnished by no other country. Something too much of extravagance—so some may think—even beyond the usual license of fiction—may enter into certain parts of the narrative. On this subject, it is enough for me to say that the popular faith yields abundant authority for the wildest of the incidents. The natural romance of our country has been my object, and I have not dared beyond it. For the rest—for the general peculiarities of the Indians, in their undegraded condition—my authorities are numerous in all the writers who have written from their own experience. My chief difficulty, I may add, has arisen from the discrimination necessary in picking and choosing than from any deficiency of the material itself. It is needless to add that the leading events are strictly true, and that the outline is to be found in the several histories devoted to the region of the country in which the scene is laid. . . .

2. *The Romantic Scene*

The remark of Samuel Johnson that to be tired of London was to be tired of life struck the Romantic temperament as a statement which was both aesthetically blind and morally perverse. Early generations had seen the utility and serenity of pastoral life, and praised nature as evidence of God's creative power; but the Romantics explored new dimensions in nature to find beauty, drama, tragedy, and virtue. Early American painting had been confined largely to the drawing room and the portraits of artists such as Gilbert Stuart and Benjamin West. The Peales of Philadelphia began to expand the scope of American painting and artists of the Jacksonian era discovered Romantic landscapes with their roaring cataracts and quiet valleys. Americans learned to value the Catskill Mountains, Niagara Falls, the Green Mountains, submerged caverns, and wild prairies. The Romantic scene extended toward the frontier and into the past, to the architectural and sculptural works of man, and to the psychological depths of the human mind. Many Americans learned to admire the form of man through Hiram Power's Greek Slave. Others learned to shape mortar and stone after the "Greek Revival" style pioneered by the architectural ideas of Thomas Jefferson and his able colleague, Benjamin Latrobe. A number of Americans even learned to appreciate the bleak and terror-ridden Gothic landscapes of Edgar Allan Poe. AUTHORS: Thomas Cole (1801–1848), an English-born immigrant to Ohio, worked with Asher Durand to establish the Hudson River School of landscape painting. Nathaniel Hawthorne (1804–1864) sprang from a Salem family which had been prominent in seventeenth-century New England. James Kirke Paulding (1778–1860), a native New Yorker and a friend of Washington Irving, was much concerned with the use of American themes such as the West and slavery in his poetry, fiction, and essays. Edgar Allan Poe (1809-1849), editor, critic, poet, was the leading American practitioner of Gothic fiction. SELECTIONS: "The Painter as Explorer of Nature" and "Romantic Nature: Thomas Cole in the Catskills" from Cole's essays of 1825 and 1826 published in The Course of Empire . . . (1853). "The Romance of History" from Hawthorne's Preface to The Scarlet Letter (1850). "The Romance of the West" from Paulding's The Backwoodsman (1818). "The Romance of the Gothic Scene" from Poe's "The Fall of the House of Usher" (1839).

THE PAINTER AS EXPLORER OF NATURE (1825): THOMAS COLE ON LANDSCAPE PAINTING

. . . You say Mr.—— has failed in his [landscape] compositions; perhaps the reason may be easily found—that he has painted from himself, instead of recurring to those scenes in nature which, formerly, he imitated with such great success. It follows that the less he studies from nature, the further he departs from it, and loses the beautiful impress, of which you speak with such justice and feeling. But a departure from nature is not a necessary consequence in the painting of compositions; on the contrary, the most lovely and perfect parts of nature may be brought together, and combined in a whole, that shall surpass in beauty and effect any picture painted from a single view. I believe with you, that it is of the greatest importance for a painter always to have his mind upon nature, as the star by which he is to steer to excellence in his art. . . .

ROMANTIC NATURE (1826): THOMAS COLE IN THE CATSKILLS

At an hour and a half before sunset, I had a steep and lofty mountain before me, heavily wooded, and infested with wolves and bears, and, as I had been informed, no house for six miles. . . . After climbing some three miles of steep and broken road, I found myself near the summit of the mountain, with (thanks to some fire of past times) a wide prospect. Above me jutted out some bare rocks; to these I clambered up, and sat upon my mountain throne, the monarch of the scene. The sun was now nearly setting, and the shadows veiled in dim obscurity the quiet valley. Here and there a stream faintly sparkled; clouds, flaming in the last glories of day, hung on the points of the highest peaks like torches lifted by the earth to kindle the lamps of heaven. Summit rose above summit, mountain rolled away beyond mountain,—a fixed, a stupendous tumult. The prospect was sublime. A hasty sketch or two, and I commenced my descent. . . .

In one of my mountain rambles, I was overtaken by a thunder storm. . . . A sudden darkness enveloped the scene, which a few moments before was beaming with sunlight, and thunders muttered in the distance. . . . The storm came on in all its majesty. Like a hoarse trumpet sounding to the charge, a strong blast roared through the forest, which stooped in its weakness, and shook off its leaves thick as in October. To this tremendous onset succeeded a death-like calm. The deep gorge below me grew darker, and the general gloom more awful: terrific clouds gathered in their black wings upon the hollow, hushed abyss closer and closer. Expectation hung on every crag. A single pass of one long blade of lightning through the silence, followed by a crash as of a cloven mountain, with a thousand echoes, was the signal for the grand conflict. A light troop of rain-drops first swept forward, footing it over the boughs with a soft and whispery sound; then came the tread of the heavy shower; squadrons of vapour rolled in,—shock succeeded shock,—thunderbolt fell on thunderbolt,—peal followed peal,—waters dashed on every crag from the full sluices of the sky. I was wrapped in the folds of the tempest, and blindfolded to every prospect beyond the rugged doorway of the cave. Then came up a thousand fancies. I fancied anything and everything. I thought myself careening, in a chariot of rock, through airy wastes beyond the reach of gravitation, with no law but my own will: now I rose over mountainous billows of mist, then plunged into the fathomless obscure: light shot athwart the darkness, darkness extinguished light: to musical murmurs succeeded quick explosions: there was no finish, no fixedness, nor rest. . . .

All at once, a blast, with the voice and temper of a hurricane, swept up through the gulf, and lifted with magical swiftness the whole mass of clouds high into the air. This was the signal for general dispersion. A flood of light burst in from the west, and jewelled the whole broad bosom of the mountain. The birds began to sing, and I saw, in a neighbouring dell, the blue smoke curling up quietly from a cottage chimney. . . .

THE ROMANCE OF HISTORY (1850): NATHANIEL HAWTHORNE IN OLD SALEM

After my fellowship of toil and impracticable schemes with the dreamy brethren of Brook Farm; after living for three years within the subtile influence of an intellect like Emerson's; after those wild, free days on the Assabeth, indulging fantastic speculations, beside our fire of fallen boughs, with Ellery Channing; after talking with Thoreau about pine trees and Indian relics, in his hermitage at Walden; after growing fastidious by sympathy with the classic refinement of Hillard's culture; after becoming imbued with poetic sentiment at Longfellow's hearth-stone,—it was time, at length, that I should exercise other faculties of my nature, and nourish myself with food for which I had hitherto had little appetite. Even the old [Customs] Inspector was desirable, as a change of diet, to a man who had known Alcott. . . . [So I took to the old Salem Custom House and learned that] the past was not dead. . . .

This old town of Salem—my native place, though I have dwelt much away from it, both in boyhood and maturer years—possesses, or did possess, a hold on my affections. . . . The sentiment is probably assignable to the deep and aged roots which my family has struck into the soil. It is now nearly two centuries and a quarter since the original Briton, the earliest emigrant of my name, made his appearance in the wild and forest-bordered settlement, which has since become a city. . . .

The figure of that first ancestor, invested by family tradition with a dim and dusky grandeur, was present to my boyish imagination, as far back as I can remember. It still haunts me, and induces a sort of home-feeling with the past, which I scarcely claim in reference to the present phase of the town. I seem to have a stronger claim to a residence here on account of his grave, bearded, sabled-cloaked and steeple-crowned progenitor,—who came so early, with his Bible and his sword, and trode the unworn street with such a stately port, and made so large a figure, as a man of war and peace,—a stronger claim than for myself, whose name is seldom heard and my face hardly known. He was a soldier, legislator, judge; he was a ruler in the Church; he had all the Puritanic traits, both good and evil. He was likewise a bitter persecutor, as witness the Quakers, who have remembered him in their histories, and relate an incident of his hard severity towards a woman of their sect, which will last longer, it is to be feared, than any record of his better deeds, although these were many. His son, too, inherited the persecuting spirit, and made himself so conspicuous in the martyrdom of the witches, that their blood may fairly be said to have left a stain upon him. So deep a stain, indeed, that his old dry bones, in the Charter Street burial-ground, must still retain it, if they have not crumbled utterly to dust! I know not whether these ancestors of mine bethought themselves to repent. . . . At all events, I, the present writer, as their representative, hereby take shame upon myself for their sakes, and pray that any curse incurred by them—as I have heard, and as the dreary and unprosperous condition of the race, for many a long year back, would argue to exist—may be now and henceforth removed.

Doubtless, however, either of these stern and black-browed Puritans would have thought it quite a sufficient retribution for his sins, that, after so long a lapse of years, the old trunk of the family tree, with so much venerable moss upon it, should have borne, as its topmost bough, an idler like myself. . . . "What is he?" murmurs one gray shadow of my forefathers to the other. "A writer of story-books? What kind of a business in life,—what mode of glorifying God, or being serviceable to mankind in his day and generation,—may that be? Why, the degenerate fellow might as well have been a fiddler!" Such are the compliments bandied between my great-grandsires and myself, across the gulf of time! And yet, let them scorn me as they will, strong traits of their nature have intertwined themselves with mine. . . .

THE ROMANCE OF THE WEST (1818): JAMES KIRKE PAULDING

> O! holy Nature! goddess ever dear,
> What a fair scene for human bliss was here!
> What pleasant rural sports, what calm delights,
> Dear happy Summer days, and Winter nights,
> Might in such tranquil nestling place be spent,

Lull'd in the downy lap of sweet Content!
But vain it is, that rich and bounteous Heav'n,
To wretched man this smiling Earth has giv'n,
And all in vain its winning face displays
Such beauties to allure his reckless gaze,
While this same rash, malignant, reas'ning worm,
Bereft of all that's human but the form,
Pollutes her bosom with his kindred blood,
Turns to rank poison all her proffer'd good,
And plays before his Maker's sick'ning eyes
The serpent of this blooming Paradise.

Here lay dark Pittsburgh, from whose site there broke
The manufacturer's black and sparkling smoke,
Where Industry and useful Science reign'd,
And man, by labour, all his wants sustain'd;
There, mid the howling forest dark and drear,
Rov'd the wild Indian, wilder than the deer,
King of the woods—who other blessings priz'd,
And arts and industry alike despis'd:
Hunting the trade, and war the sport he loved,
Free as the winds, the dauntless chieftain rov'd,
Taunting with bitter ire, the pale-fac'd slave,
Who toils for gold from cradle to the grave.
Extremes of habits, manners, time and space,
Brought close together, here stood face to face,
And gave at once a contrast to the view
That other lands and ages never knew;
Pass but the river, and that world where meet
Of bland society each courteous sweet,
Is left behind, for manners wild and rude,
And scenes of death, or deathlike solitude. . . .

Yes! the bright day is dawning, when the West
No more shall crouch before old Europe's crest,
When men who claim thy birthright, Liberty,
Shall burst their leading-strings and dare be free. . . .
Tis true—yet 'tis no pity that 'tis true,
Many fine things they neither felt nor knew. . . .

Among them was no driv'ling princely race,
Who'd beggar half a state, to buy a vase,
Or starve a province nobly to reclaim,
From mother Earth, a thing without a name,
Some mutilated trunk decay'd and worn,
Of head bereft, of legs and arms all shorn,

Worthless, except to puzzle learned brains,
And cause a world of most laborious pains,
To find if this same headless, limbless thing,
A worthless godhead was, or worthless king.

Not such were these, whose story I unfold,
Or else some other might their tale have told.
No! they were men whose minds were form'd to dare,
Whose bodies fram'd the hardest toils to bear, . . .
Of such rare spirits was that gallant band,
Who 'gainst the bloody Indian made a stand,
Through the dark pathless woods did bravely chase
The treacherous warriors to their hiding place,
Though knowing well that in the bloody field,
They spare no soul, of all that fight or yield.

O rare Kentucky! gallant Tennessee,
And young Ohio, we are bound to thee!
Though like the aged patriarch's fav'rite son,
The younger born, a glorious race ye've run.
Be this the legend on your crests engrav'd,
Like Joseph we our elder brethren sav'd.
In some more happy, not far distant day,
When that detested poison ebbs away,
That floats in our young Country's swelling veins,
And spots her face with party colour'd stains,
Chills the wild throbbing of the heart's high beat,
And cools the glowing pulse's gen'rous heat,
O! then some bard shall frame a loftier lay,
Which sung, perchance, in some far distant day,
Along Ohio's tranquil, silvery tide,
Will many a bosom swell with honest pride,
And teach to myriad mortals yet unborn,
To turn on haughty Europe scorn for scorn,
That second Afric—robb'd of liberty,
By the same cheats that set the negro free. . . .

THE ROMANCE OF THE GOTHIC SCENE
(1839): EDGAR ALLAN POE

During the whole of a dull, dark, and resoundless day in the autumn of
the year, when the clouds hung oppressively low in the heavens, I had
been passing alone, on horseback, through a singularly dreary tract of
country, and at length found myself, as the shades of evening drew on,

within view of the melancholy House of Usher. . . . I looked upon the
scene before me—upon the mere house, and the simple landscape features of the domain—upon the bleak walls—upon the vacant eye-like
windows—upon a few rank sedges—and upon a few white trunks of
decayed trees—with an utter depression of soul, which I can compare to
no earthly sensation more properly than to the after-dream of the reveller
upon opium—the bitter lapse into every-day life—the hideous dropping
of the veil.

There was an iciness, a sinking, a sickening of the heart—an unre-
deemed dreariness of thought which no goading of the imagination could
torture into aught of the sublime. . . . I reined my horse to the precipi-
tous brink of a black and lurid tarn that lay in unruffled lustre by the
dwelling, and gazed down—but with a shudder even more thrilling than
before—upon the remodelled and inverted images of the gray sedge, and
the ghastly tree-stems, and the vacant and eye-like windows. . . .

3. *The Romantic Dream of Escape and Flight*

Nature as a haven, blissfully free of the flaws of civilized life, provided
one of the most common romantic themes. James Kirke Paulding and
James Fenimore Cooper often described the frontier as an escape from
the restrictions of civilized society; Thoreau sought the solace of nature at
Walden Pond, only a few miles from Boston; and Herman Melville
located his Utopian retreat in the South Sea islands. In Melville's *Mardi*
men and women escaped hypocrisy, shame, economic exploitation, mechanized warfare, industrial poverty, and countless other evils. AUTHOR:
Herman Melville (1819–1891), a New Yorker of English and Dutch
descent, was a cabin boy, a bank clerk, and a farmer before making the
whaling voyages which provided the background for *Mardi* and *Moby
Dick*. SELECTION: "The Noble Savage in the South Seas" (1846) from
Melville's *Mardi* (1849).

THE NOBLE SAVAGE IN   THE SOUTH SEAS
(1846): HERMAN MELVILLE

. . . Among the permanent inmates of the house were likewise several
lovely damsels, who instead of strumming pianos and reading novels, like
more enlightened young ladies, substituted for these employments the
manufacture of a fine species of tappa; but for the greater portion of the

time were skipping from house to house, gadding and gossiping with their acquaintances.

From the rest of these, however, I must except the beauteous nymph Fayaway, who was my peculiar favourite. Her free pliant figure was the very perfection of female grace and beauty. Her complexion was a rich and mantling olive, and when watching the glow upon her cheeks I could almost swear that beneath the transparent medium there lurked the blushes of a faint vermilion. The face of this girl was a rounded oval, and each feature as perfectly formed as the heart or imagination of men could desire. Her full lips, when parted with a smile, disclosed teeth of a dazzling whiteness; and when her rosy mouth opened with a burst of merriment, they looked like the milk-white seeds of the "arta," a fruit of the valley, which, when cleft in twain, shows them reposing in rows on either side, imbedded in the rich and juicy pulp. Her hair of the deepest brown, parted irregularly in the middle, flowed in natural ringlets over her shoulders, and whenever she chanced to stoop, fell over and hid from view her lovely bosom. . . .

I may succeed, perhaps, in particularising some of the individual features of Fayaway's beauty, but that general loveliness of appearance which they all contributed to produce I will not attempt to describe. The easy unstudied graces of a child of nature like this, breathing from infancy an atmosphere of perpetual summer, and nurtured by the simple fruits of the earth; enjoying a perfect freedom from care and anxiety, and removed effectually from all injurious tendencies, strike the eye in a manner which cannot be portrayed. . . .

As I extended my wanderings in the valley and grew more familiar with the habits of its inmates, I was fain to confess that, despite the disadvantages of his condition, the Polynesian savage, surrounded by all the luxurious provisions of nature, enjoyed an infinitely happier, though certainly a less intellectual existence, than the self-complacent European.

The naked wretch who shivers beneath the bleak skies, and starves among the inhospitable wilds of Terra del Fuego, might indeed be made happier by civilization, for it would alleviate his physical wants. But the voluptuous Indian, with every desire supplied, whom Providence has bountifully provided with all the sources of pure and natural enjoyment, and from whom are removed so many of the ills and pains of life—what has he to desire at the hands of Civilisation? She may "cultivate his mind,"—may "elevate his thoughts,"—these I believe are established phrases—but will he be the happier? Let the once smiling and populous Hawaiian islands, with their now diseased, starving, and dying natives, answer the question. The missionaries may seek to disguise the matter as they will, but the facts are incontrovertible; and the devoutest Christian who visits that group with an unbiased mind, must go away mournfully asking—"Are these, alas! the fruits of twenty-five years of enlightening?"

In a primitive state of society, the enjoyments of life, though few and simple, are spread over a great extent, and are unalloyed; but Civilisation, for every advantage she imparts, holds a hundred evils in reserve;—the heart-burnings, the jealousies, the social rivalries, the family dissensions, and the thousand self-inflicted discomforts of refined life, which make up in units the swelling aggregate of human misery, are unknown among these unsophisticated people. . . .

The fiend-like skill we display in the invention of all manner of death-dealing engines, the vindictiveness with which we carry on our wars, and the misery and desolation that follow in their train, are enough of themselves to distinguish the white civilised man as the most ferocious animal on the face of the earth. . . .

The term "savage" is, I conceive, often misapplied, and indeed when I consider the vices, cruelties, and enormities of every kind that spring up in the tainted atmosphere of a feverish civilisation, I am inclined to think that so far as the relative wickedness of the parties is concerned, four or five Marquesan Islanders sent to the United States as missionaries might be quite as useful as an equal number of Americans dispatched to the Islands in a similar capacity. . . .

There are no battery attorneys, to foment discord, backing their clients up to a quarrel, and then knocking their heads together; no poor relations, everlastingly occupying the spare bed-chamber, and diminishing the elbow-room at the family table; no destitute widows with their children starving on the cold charities of the world; no beggars; no debtors' prisons; no proud and hard-hearted nabobs in Typee; or to sum up all in one word—no Money! . . .

In this secluded abode of happiness there were no cross old women, no cruel step-dames, no withered spinsters, no love-sick maidens, no sour old bachelors, no inattentive husbands, no melancholy young men, no blubbering youngsters, no squalling brats. All was mirth, fun, and high good humour. Blue devils, hypochondria, and doleful dumps went and hid themselves among the nooks and crannies of the rocks. . . .

The continual happiness, which so far I was able to judge appeared to prevail in the valley, sprung principally from that all-pervading sensation which Rousseau has told us he at one time experienced, the mere buoyant sense of a healthful physical existence. And indeed in this particular the Typees had ample reason to felicitate themselves, for sickness was almost unknown. . . .

4. *The Romantic Hero*

Romanticism involved an intricate network of sensibilities, emotional impressions, ideas, opinions, and symbols from which Americans constructed their images of self and society. The homespun and virtuous Yankee, the noble, manly Redskin, the sentimental heroine whose violated virtue brought tears to the eyes of thousands of readers, the reformer who longed to change the human heart, the cosmic rebel capable of defying God Himself,—these were a few of the major images of antebellum America. AUTHORS: Royall Tyler (1757–1826), a Boston-born graduate of Harvard and a lawyer, wrote one of the first successful American plays. Lydia Hunt Sigourney (1791–1865), a Connecticut poet, wrote very popular sentimental and pious verse. Susanna Rowson (c. 1762–1824), a popular writer of sentimental fiction, accompanied her father from England to Massachusetts but returned to England in 1777. Ralph Waldo Emerson (1803–1882) made of the "reformer" a romantic figure. Herman Melville (1819–1891) created in Captain Ahab one of the great figures of nineteenth-century fiction. SELECTIONS: "The Yankee Hero in Homespun" from Tyler's play *The Contrast* (1786). "The Hero as Noble Redskin" from Sigourney's *Traits of the Aborigines of America* (1822). "The Seduced Maid as 'Heroine'" from Susanna Rowson's *Charlotte Temple* (1791). "The Hero as Reformer" from Emerson's essay on "Man the Reformer" (1841). "The Hero as Cosmic Rebel" from Melville's *Moby Dick* (1851).

THE YANKEE HERO IN HOMESPUN (1786):
ROYALL TYLER

Exult each patriot heart!—this night is shewn
A piece, which we may fairly call our own;
Where the proud titles of "My Lord! Your Grace!"
To humble Mr. and Plain Sir give place.
Our Author pictures not from foreign climes
The fashions, or the follies of the times;
But has confin'd the subject of his work
To the gay scenes—the circles of New-York.
Our native themes his Muse displays her pow'rs;
If ours the faults, the virtues too are ours.
Why should our thoughts to distant countries roam,
When each refinement may be found at home?
Who travels now to ape the rich or great,
To deck an equipage and roll in state;
To court the graces or to dance with ease,
Or by hypocrisy to strive to please?
Our free-born ancestors such arts despis'd;
Genuine sincerity alone they priz'd;

Their minds, with honest emulation fir'd,
To solid good—not ornament—aspir'd;
Or, if ambition rous'd a bolder flame,
Stern virtue throve, where indolence was shame.

But modern youths, with imitative sense,
Deem taste in dress the proof of excellence;
And spurn the meanness of your homespun arts,
Since homespun habits would obscure their parts;
Whilst all, which aims at splendour and parade,
Must come from Europe, and be ready made.
Strange! we should thus our native worth disclaim,
And check the progress of our rising fame.
Yet one, whilst imitation bears the sway,
Aspires to nobler heights, and points the way,
Be rous'd, my friends! his bold example view;
Let your own Bards be proud to copy you!
Should rigid critics reprobate our play,
At least the patriotic heart will say,
"Glorious our fall, since in a noble cause,
"The bold attempt alone demands applause."
Still may the wisdom of the Comic Muse
Exalt your merits, or your faults accuse.
But think not, 'tis her aim to be severe;—
We all are mortals, and as mortals err.
If candour pleases, we are truly blest;
Vice trembles, when compell'd to stand confess'd.
Let not light Censure on your faults, offend.
Which aims not to expose them, but amend.
Thus does our Author to your candour trust;
Conscious, the free are generous, as just. . . .

THE HERO AS NOBLE REDSKIN (1822):
LYDIA HUNT SIGOURNEY

O'er the vast regions of that Western world,
Whose lofty mountains hiding in the clouds
Conceal'd their grandeur and their wealth so long
From European eyes, the Indian rov'd,
Free and unconquered. From those frigid plains
Struck with the torpor of the Arctic pole,
To where Magellan lifts his torch to light
The meeting of the waters;—from the shore

Whose smooth green line the broad Atlantic laves,
To the rude borders of that rocky strait
Where haughty Asia seems to stand and gaze
On the New Continent, the Indian reign'd
Majestic and alone. Fearless he rose,
Firm as his mountains, like his rivers, wild,

Bold as those lakes, whose wondrous chain controls
His northern coast. The forest and the wave
Gave him his food; the slight-constructed hut
Furnish'd his shelter, and its doors spread wide
To every wandering stranger. There his cup,
His simple meal, his lowly couch of skins
Were hospitably shared. Rude were his toils,
And rash his daring, when he headlong rush'd
Down the steep precipice to seize his prey;
Strong was his arm to bend the stubborn bow,
And keen his arrow. This the Bison knew,
The spotted Panther, the rough, shaggy Bear,
The Wolf dark-prowling, the eye-piercing Lynx,
The wild Deer bounding through the shadowy glade,
And the swift Eagle, soaring high to make
His nest among the stars. Cloth'd in their spoils
He dar'd the elements; with eye sedate
Breasted the wintry winds; o'er the white heads
Of angry torrents steered his rapid bark
Light as their foam, mounted with tireless speed
Those slippery cliffs, where everlasting snows
Weave their dense robes, or laid him down to sleep
Where the dread thunder of the cataract lull'd
His drowsy sense. The dangerous toils of war
He sought and lov'd. Traditions, and proud tales
Of other days, exploits of his rapid bark
Dauntless and terrible, the warrior's song,
The victor's triumph,—all conspired to raise
The martial spirit, kindling in his breast
With life's first throb. . . .

THE SEDUCED MAID AS "HEROINE" (1791): SUSANNA ROWSON

Who can form an adequate idea of the sorrow that preyed upon the mind of Charlotte? The wife, whose breast glows with affection for her husband,

and who in return meets only indifference, can but faintly conceive her anguish. . . .

She looks around and sees the smile of friendly welcome, or the tear of affectionate consolation, on the face of every person whom she favors with her esteem, and from all these circumstances she gathers comfort; but the poor girl by thoughtless passion led astray, who, in parting with honor, has forfeited the esteem of the very man to whom she has sacrificed everything dear and valuable in life, feels his indifference to be the fruit of her own folly, and laments the want of power to recall his lost affections; she knows that there is no tie but honor, and that, in a man who has been guilty of seduction, is but very feeble; he may leave her in a moment of shame and want; he may marry and forsake her forever, and should he do so, she has no redress, no friendly, soothing companion to pour into her mind the balm of consolation, no benevolent hand to lead her back to the path of rectitude; she has disgraced her friends, forfeited the good opinion of the world, and undone herself. . . .

My dear Madam, contract not your brow into a frown of disapprobation. I mean not to extenuate the faults of those unhappy women who fall victims of guilt and folly; but surely, when we reflect how many errors we ourselves are subject to, how many secret faults lie hidden in the recesses of our hearts, which we would blush to have brought into open day, and yet whose faults require the lenity and pity of a benevolent judge, or awful would be our prospect of futurity. I say, my dear madam, when we consider this, we surely may pity the faults of others.

Believe me, many an unfortunate female, who has once strayed into the thorny paths of vice, would gladly return to virtue, were any generous friend to endeavor to raise and reassure her; but alas! it cannot be, you say, the world would deride and scoff. . . .

Oh, thou benevolent Giver of all good! how shall we erring mortals dare to look up to thy mercy in the great day of retribution, if we now uncharitably refuse to overlook the errors, or alleviate the miseries of our fellow-creatures! . . .

THE HERO AS REFORMER (1841):
RALPH WALDO EMERSON

It will afford no security from the new ideas, that the old nations, the laws of centuries, the property and institutions of a hundred cities, are built on other foundations. The demon of reform has a secret door into the heart of every lawmaker, of every inhabitant of every city. The fact that a new thought and hope have dawned in your breast, should apprise you that in the same hour a new light broke in upon a thousand private hearts. . . .

But the idea which now begins to agitate society has a wider scope than our daily employments, our households, and the institutions of property. We are to revise the whole of our social structure, the State, the school, religion, marriage, trade, science, and explore their foundations in our own nature; we are to see that the world not only fitted the former men, but fits us, and to clear ourselves of every usage which has not its roots in our own mind. What is man born for but to be a Reformer, a Remaker of what man has made; a renouncer of lies, a restorer of truth and good, imitating that great Nature which embosoms us all and which sleeps no moment on an old past, but every hour repairs herself, yielding us every morning a new day, and with every pulsation a new life? Let him renounce everything which is not true to him, and put all his practices back on their first thoughts, and do nothing for which he has not the whole world for his reason. . . .

THE HERO AS COSMIC REBEL (1851):
HERMAN MELVILLE

Captain Ahab stood upon his quarter-deck.

There seemed no sign of common bodily illness about him, nor of the recovery from any. He looked like a man cut away from the stake, when the fire has overrunningly wasted all the limbs without consuming them, or taking away one particle from their compacted aged robustness. His whole high, broad form, seemed made of solid bronze, and shaped in an unalterable mould, like Cellini's cast Perseus. Threading its way out from among his grey hairs, and continuing right down one side of his tawny scorched face and neck, till it disappeared in his clothing, you saw a slender rod-like mark, lividly whitish. It resembled that perpendicular seam sometimes made in the straight, lofty trunk of a great tree, when the upper lightning tearingly darts down it, and without wrenching a single twig, peels and grooves out the bark from top to bottom, ere running off into the soil, leaving the tree still greenly alive, but branded. . . .

So powerfully did the whole grim aspect of Ahab affect me, and the livid brand which streaked it, that for the first few moments I hardly noted that not a little of this overbearing grimness was owing to the barbaric white leg upon which he partly stood. It had previously come to me that this ivory leg had at sea been fashioned from the polished bone of the sperm whale's jaw. "Aye, he was dismasted off Japan," said the old Gay-Head Indian once; "but like his dismasted craft, he shipped another mast without coming home for it. He has a quiver of 'em."

I was struck with the singular posture he maintained. Upon each side of the *Pequod*'s quarter-deck, and pretty close to the mizen shrouds, there was an auger hole, bored about half an inch or so, into the plank. His bone leg steadied in that hole; one arm elevated, and holding by a shroud; Captain Ahab stood erect, looking straight out beyond the ship's ever-pitching prow. There was an infinity of firmest fortitude, a determinate, unsurrenderable wilfulness, in the fixed and fearless, forward dedication of that glance. Not a word he spoke; nor did his officers say aught to him; though by all their minutest gestures and expressions, they plainly showed the uneasy, if not painful, consciousness of being under a troubled master-eye. And not only that, but moody stricken Ahab stood before them with a crucifixion in his face; in all the nameless regal overbearing dignity of some mighty woe. . . .

[Ahab broods:] Is, then, the crown too heavy that I wear? this Iron Crown of Lombardy. Yet is it bright with many gem; I, the wearer, see not its far flashings; but darkly feel that I wear that, that dazzlingly confounds. 'Tis iron—that I know—not gold. 'Tis split, too—that I feel; the jagged edge galls me so, my brain seems to beat against the solid metal; aye, steel skull, mine; the sort that needs no helmet in the most brain-battering fight! . . .

I thought to find one stubborn, at the least; but my one cogged circle fits into all their various wheels, and they revolve. Or, if you will, like so many ant-hills of powder, they all stand before me; and I their match. Oh, hard! that to five others, the match itself must needs be wasting! What I've dared, I've willed; and what I've willed, I'll do! They think me mad—Starbuck does, but I'm demoniac, I am madness maddened! That wild madness that's only calm to comprehend itself! The prophecy was that I should be dismembered; and —Aye! I lost this leg. I now prophesy that I will dismember my dismemberer. Now, then, be the prophet and the fulfiller one. That's more than ye, ye great gods, ever were. I laugh and hoot at ye, ye cricket-players, ye pugilists, ye deaf Burkes and blinded Bendigoes! I will not say as schoolboys do to bullies, —Take some one of your own size; don't pommel *me*! No, ye've knocked me down, and I am up again; but *ye* have run and hidden. Come forth from behind your cotton bags! I have no long gun to reach ye. Come, Ahab's compliments to ye; come and see if ye can swerve me. Swerve me? ye cannot swerve me, else ye swerve yourselves! Man has ye there. Swerve me? The path to my fixed purpose is laid with iron rails, whereon my soul is grooved to run. Over unsounded gorges, through the rifled hearts of mountains, under torrents' beds, unerringly I rush! Naught's an obstacle, naught's an angle to the iron way! . . .

Chapter VII. THE STRUGGLE FOR

AMERICAN NATIONALITY

THE ROOTS OF AMERICAN NATIONALISM EXTEND BACK TO THE VAR-
ious conceptions of religious and political mission which helped
thrust the colonists in the direction of independence during the sev-
enteen-sixties and -seventies. The very word "America" had Utopian
connotations which reminded men of several thousand years of Utopian yearning for a "lost Atlantis," a "kingdom of Prester John," or a
Western paradise; hundreds of thousands of men and women came
to America because of economic or religious visions of Utopia in the
New World. In many ways colonial experience encouraged Utopian
definitions, particularly by providing the contrast between American
abundance and the European pinch of want. If America—as so many
political leaders urged—was to be a refuge and to have a world mission, who could use this haven and how should the nature of the
mission be defined? Natural rights ideology and the abundance of
nature thrust the new society toward a definition based on Republican destiny and economic Utopia. As a refuge for the world, American society needed to welcome immigrants of diverse religious and
ethnic origins, and early definitions of the new nation were appro-
priately "open" ones. Yet Utopian aspirations often led to frustrations because of the gap between the actual conditions of experience
and the conception of Utopia, and these frustrations became a part
of the American political landscape.

Spokesmen for the new society failed to understand the tenacity
of social, cultural, and national group definitions. Modern politicians
and scholars have learned to take group definitions more seriously by
observing events of the past century. To take a few illustrative examples, Volga and Baltic Germans maintained their identity
throughout centuries of residence in Russia, Lithuania, and Poland;
Walloons and Flemings after many generations of common Belgian
citizenship were capable of mass conflict in the streets during the
early nineteen-sixties; and new Afro-Asian nations in the post World

War II era began to experience enormous difficulties in the task of building a nation from several or several dozen different cultural groups. To proclaim free access to American nationality was a relatively easy matter; to actually achieve that freedom was considerably more difficult. Americans in the eighteen-fifties frequently spoke of toleration and religious pluralism, but most citizens were Protestants who thought of "religion" after a Protestant fashion, and many of them responded to the mass migration of Irish Catholics with discrimination, hostility, and the Know-Nothing movement. In a very real sense the newly arrived Irish challenged the society to redefine its sense of experience so as to somehow include the Catholic immigrant. These challenges of redefinition run throughout most of American history.

The greatest challenge of all appeared during the antebellum period; Abolitionists demanded the recognition of Negro slaves as at least potential members of the society. This demand was doubly difficult because several centuries of bloody frontier conflict with Indians and white mastery over black men had brought powerful racist emotions to the center of American sensibilities. The historical experience of slavery had left not only slave codes but something very close to a caste system which assigned dependency to the Negro and superiority to the white man. Negroes were commonly held to be inferior in every major category from beauty to intelligence, and an elaborate set of racist rationales and identity controls supported the power of white people across the country. Abolitionists could and did stimulate the very real conflict between democratic ideology and racist realities.

The critical challenge appeared to an American nationality only recently and precariously established. The Aaron Burr conspiracy, disloyalty in New England before and during the War of 1812, the Missouri crisis of 1820, the South Carolina secession crisis of 1832, and other incidents lent a suggestion of instability to the Federal Union. Moreover, many nationalists were only too aware of the fact that in almost every area of cultural endeavor, the United States continued to be a British province long after political independence. From the seventeen-nineties forward nationalists began to demand a national university where Republican virtue might be satisfactorily taught, an American philosophy to provide the correct guidelines for Republican thought and action, national schools of art to celebrate Republican glory and virtue, and even a national language, or at least established American rules for spelling, grammar, and usage. A growing number of Americans felt that mere political independence did not give adequate voice to a national culture which ought to speak in politics, religion, art, science, education, and other fields.

Ardent nationalists had reason to fear for the stability of a national society endangered by such powerful and disruptive forces as sectionalism, slavery, and caste. After all, the Federal Union was nearly destroyed by the conflict which exploded into Civil War in 1861; and the very nature of the Union evoked heated debate from the beginning. One of the more important friends of a nationalist government, Chief Justice John Marshall, insisted that while the national government was limited in power, it was supreme within its area of competence. Marshall worked to check tendencies toward "state sovereignty" and to establish the U.S. Supreme Court as the unquestioned arbiter of the Federal system, a goal which Thomas Jefferson and James Madison wished to reject in 1798 and 1799. In the Kentucky and Virginia Resolutions passed to protest the violation of natural rights by the Alien and Sedition Acts, the legislators threatened to "interpose" state power between the Federal government and the citizens of the state. (Both Jefferson and Madison, however, pursued nationalist policies while in the White House.) Historical circumstance made it possible for John C. Calhoun to resurrect the doctrine of states rights in 1832 and to develop a more elaborate argument on state sovereignty for the "South Carolina Exposition." The attempt of Calhoun and other South Carolinians to use the threat of secession to gain their political ends met with the determined nationalist opposition of Andrew Jackson, but Southerners turned increasingly during the eighteen-forties and -fifties to Calhoun's ideas in order to defend the "peculiar institution" and other Southern interests.

While American politics in the eighteen-fifties suggest a complexity almost beyond description, it seems clear that the central clashes sprang from the issues of slavery and caste. The conflict involved more than the Northern attack on slavery and the Southern defense. Intellectual doubt, fear, and guilt played at least a modest part in Southern politics; the North was divided on the issue of slavery; and the idea of white supremacy was powerful in the North as well as in the South. Ideas on the inferiority and the necessary subjection of the Negro clearly had a national currency, and Northern Negroes lived in a world of legal discrimination and public and private violence, a world which was dramatically at odds with the official creed of the society. Most of the time, the Abolitionists operated as a small, marginal, and generally unpopular group, but they worked from a powerful sense of Negro desperation and an explosive historical crisis.

To charges of fanaticism and inflexibility, militant Abolitionists replied that slavery and color prejudice were so deeply rooted in American society as to make extirpation unlikely without social upheaval. At the least, the anti-slavery movement forced Americans to consider the issues and kept alive the hope of ending oppression. The political atmosphere crackled with the emotional electricity of black and white relations—the Lincoln-Douglas debates, a number of major Senatorial debates, the Southern secession conventions, were filled with references to racial conflict and slavery, but some Northerners and Southerners also wished to argue in terms of states rights, the conflict of "Puritan" and "Cavalier," or the economic exploitation of the South by the North. Many nationalist leaders tried to blunt the force of the Southern rhetoric: Daniel Webster urged upon Southern disunionists the glories of the Union, the Constitution, and the American past; and in the critical hour of secession Lincoln insisted that the Union, older than the Constitution itself, was perpetual and could not be destroyed.

The precise parade of events leading to the Civil War and the relative weight of the major causes are difficult to ascertain; and a fully satisfactory explanation of the war eludes scholars. Still one cannot imagine that the conflict could possibly have taken place without the existence of slavery. It is true that most of the Republican leaders rejected the Abolitionists and insisted that Lincoln merely wished to check the expansion of slavery into any new territories. It is also probable that the North counted more Negrophobes than equalitarians with a full human sympathy for the Negro. Nevertheless, the Republicans provided several key factors which in the crucible of war made emancipation possible. In 1861 few Northerners wished to fight for emancipation, and Lincoln himself, despite his compassion for the slave, repeatedly rejected the idea of social equality and proposed the colonization of Negroes in Africa or Latin America; but the Abolitionists supplied a rationale for the struggle which events were to make plausible for a growing number of Northerners, including Lincoln. The unwanted war against "our Southern brothers" gradually became a holy crusade to end slavery. The major thrust toward emancipation came from the Negroes themselves and from the necessities dictated by the struggle. The runaway slaves who fled to Union lines, the refusal of some officers to return slaves to their "disloyal" masters, General "Ben" Butler's retention of slaves as "contraband," the successful service of Negro troops (nearly two hundred thousand served by the end of the war), and the increasingly desperate need for Negro manpower—all of these things shaped the pattern of events to which Lincoln lent his stamp of approval by issuing the Emancipation Proclamation.

The War destroyed the slave codes, but it did not bring full emancipation. The most common strategy of white Southerners was the attempt to transfer rule of the Negro from the old master to state and community through the "black codes" and the systematic use of violence for social control. Most white Southerners were bitterly determined to rule the "Freedman," whatever the cost; and over a long period of time running into the first third of the twentieth century they hammered out a system of segregation. The North was divided and deeply affected by racist thought, but President Johnson's attitudes were so blatantly white supremacist and the South so free with the use of violence that much Northern sentiment gradually crystallized around the idea of granting the rudiments of citizenship to the freedmen. Congressional Reconstruction, by no means a predestined event, can be traced to Southern intransigence, the blunders of President Johnson, and the shrewd exploitation of opportunities by Congressional leaders. Just as a war of "happenstance" became a holy Crusade, an effort to "restore" the Union became an attempt to reconstruct Southern society so as to give the Negro at least a large portion of freedom. Still, Congressional leaders thought largely in terms of the suffrage and emergency education; few understood the problems of the freedman after two centuries of slavery. An authentic drive for emancipation would have involved education, property ownership, release from the white man's violence, and psychological and social rehabilitation. Even if Northerners had not been prisoners of laissez-faire ideology and innocent about the complex relationships of institutions and individuals, a drive for full Negro citizenship would have been a very difficult enterprise. As it was, the divided North had only a few militant equalitarians; and the indifference, half-heartedness, or open Negrophobia of the great majority rendered the goal of effective and enduring Reconstruction improbable. The South could offer a nearly undivided determination in support of white supremacy (although some Bourbons such as Wade Hampton of South Carolina conceded a limited political role to Negroes). In the eighteen-seventies the Supreme Court began to accept Southern contentions and by the end of the century the Court had virtually set aside the Civil Rights bills as well as the Fourteenth and Fifteenth Amendments. The culmination of a trend came with the case of *Plessy v. Ferguson* accepting the doctrine of "separate but equal," a decision which was followed in the decade to come by a great rush of segregation laws in the Southern states.

The decline of sectional animosities, "the road to reunion," was a retreat from the drive for full citizenship; an unwritten understanding between white Northerners and Southerners achieved at the expense of full freedom for the Negro. The "New South" stood first of all for segregation and subjugation, secondly for more industrialism and diversified agriculture, and finally for a decrease in Northern and Southern animosities. Few Northerners wished to oppose the New South seriously. Even Booker T. Washington, the most influential Negro leader in the first generation after slavery, accepted at least temporarily the system of segregation, and urged Negroes to work for greater prosperity and limited political gains within the prevailing system. Toward the end of Washington's life, some young Negro intellectuals grew impatient under his tutelage, and observed that the passing of time brought more violence rather than less, fewer skilled jobs and social gains, and new segregation laws. These young leaders went on to found the N.A.A.C.P., but they won little attention from the great majority of citizens, and Americans moved into the second third of the twentieth century with full emancipation still a distant goal.

1. *Cultural Nationalism*

When the English essayist Sydney Smith jeered at the lack of American writers, artists, scientists, and scholars, Americans knew very well that he was denying the existence of a significant national culture on the western side of the Atlantic. Edward Everett attempted to answer the critics and to give his fellow citizens a firmer sense of membership in a society which tended increasingly toward greatness in all aspects of life. From the time of independence American leaders clamored for social and cultural self-sufficiency. If America had no major musicians and playwrights she must produce them; if America had few scholars she must have more; if America had no national universities she must establish at least one. Noah Webster even insisted upon the need for an American language. AU-

THORS: Edward Everett (1794–1865) was a Harvard Professor and President, a Massachusetts Governor, U.S. Congressman, Senator, Minister to England, Secretary of State, scholar and lecturer. Joel Barlow (1754–1812), a Yale graduate and a chaplain in the Revolution, was a poet, propagandist, and diplomat. Noah Webster (1758–1843), "Schoolmaster to America," wrote extensively on grammar, language, and education. Benjamin Latrobe (1764–1820), who immigrated to America in 1796 and helped launch the Greek revival in architecture, directed portions of the rebuilding of Washington after the War of 1812. SELECTIONS: "The Mightiest People in History" from Everett's *An Oration . . . Before the Society of Phi Beta Kappa* (1824). "A National University for Science and Republican Virtue" from Barlow's *Prospectus of a National University to be Established in the United States* (1805). "The Need for an American Language" from Webster's *Dissertations on the English Language* (1789). "The Republic Needs the Fine Arts" from Latrobe's *Anniversary Oration* (1811).

THE MIGHTIEST PEOPLE IN HISTORY (1824): EDWARD EVERETT

Should our happy Union continue, this great continent, in no remote futurity, will be filled up with the mightiest kindred people known in history; our language will acquire an extension which no other ever possessed; and the empire of the mind, with nothing to resist its sway, will attain an expansion, of which, as yet, we can but partly conceive. The vision is too magnificent to be fully borne;—a mass of two or three hundred millions, not chained to the oar, like the same number in China, by a stupefying despotism, but held in their several orbits of nation and state, by the grand representative attraction; bringing to bear, on every point, the concentrated energy of such a host; calling into competition so many minds; uniting into one great national feeling the hearts of so many freemen, all to be guided, moved and swayed, by the master spirits of the time! . . .

I need not say that this astonishing increase of numbers is by no means the best measure of the country's growth. Arts, letters, agriculture, all the great national interests, all the sources of national wealth, are growing in a ratio still more rapid. In our cities, the intensest activity is apparent; in the country, every spring of prosperity, from the smallest improvement in husbandry, to the construction of canals and railroads across the continent, is in vigorous action. Abroad, our vessels are beating the pathways of the ocean white; on the inland frontier, the nation is moving forward with a pace more like romance than reality. . . .

One might almost think, without extravagance, that the departed wise and good, of all places and times, are looking down from their happy seats to witness what shall now be done by us; that they who lavished their treasures and their blood, of old, who spake and wrote, who labored, fought, and perished, in the one great cause of Freedom and Truth, are now hanging from their orbs on high, over the last solemn experiment of humanity. As I have wandered over the spots once the scene of their labors, and mused among the prostrate columns of their senate houses and forums, I have seemed almost to hear a voice from the tombs of departed ages; from the sepulchres of the nations which died before the sight. They exhort us, they adjure us, to be faithful to our trust. They implore us by the long trials of struggling humanity; by the blessed memory of the departed; by the dear faith which has been plighted, by pure hands, to the holy cause of truth and man; by the awful secrets of the prison houses, where the sons of freedom have been immured; by the noble heads which have been brought to the block; by the wrecks of time, by the eloquent ruins of nations, they conjure us not to quench the light which is rising on the world. . . .

Yes, my friends, such is the exhortation which calls on us to exert our powers, to employ our time, and consecrate our labors, for the honor and service of our native land. When we engage in that solemn study, the history of our race; surveying the progress of man, from his cradle in the East to these limits of his wandering; when we behold him forever flying westward from evil and religious thraldom, over mountains and seas, seeking rest and finding none, but still pursuing the flying bow of promise to the glittering hills which it spans in Hesperian climes; we cannot but exclaim, with Bishop Berkeley, the generous prelate, who bestowed his benefactions, as well as his blessings, on our country,—

> Westward the course of Empire takes its way;
> The four first acts already past,
> A fifth shall close the drama with the day;
> Time's noblest offspring is the last.

This exclamation is but the embodiment of a vision, which the ancients, from the earliest period, cherished of some favored land beyond the mountains or the seas; a land of equal laws and happy men. . . . There are no more continents to be revealed; Atlantis hath arisen from the ocean; the farthest Thule is reached; there are no more retreats beyond the sea, no more discoveries, no more hopes. . . .

A NATIONAL UNIVERSITY FOR SCIENCE AND REPUBLICAN VIRTUE (1805): JOEL BARLOW

. . . We find ourselves in possession of a country so vast as to lead the mind to anticipate a scene of social intercourse and interest unexampled in the experience of mankind. This territory presents and will present such a variety of productions natural and artificial, such a diversity of connections abroad, and of manners, habits, and propensities at home, as will create a strong tendency to diverge and separate the views of those who shall inhabit the different regions within our limits.

It is most essential to the happiness of the people and to the pres-ervation of their republican principles, that this tendency to a separation should be overbalanced by superior motives to a harmony of sentiment; that they may habitually feel that community of interest on which their federal system is founded. This desirable object is to be attained, not only by the operations of the government in its several departments, but by those of literature, sciences and arts. The liberal sciences are in their nature republican; they delight in reciprocal communication; they cherish fraternal feelings, and lead to a freedom of intercourse, combined with the restraints of society, which contribute together to our improvement. . . .

What a range is open in this country for mineralogy and botany! How many new arts arc to arise, and how far the old ones are to be advanced, by the pursuit of these two sciences, it is impossible even to imagine. Chemistry is making a rapid and useful progress, though we still dispute about its elements. Our knowledge of anatomy has laid a neces-sary and sure foundation for surgery and medicine; surgery indeed is making great proficiency; but, after three thousand years of recorded experience, how little do we know of medicine! Mechanics and hydraulics are progressing fast, and wonderful are the facilities and comforts we draw from them; but while it continues to be necessary to make use of animal force to move heavy bodies in any direction by land or water, we have a right to anticipate new discoveries. . . .

THE NEED FOR AN AMERICAN LANGUAGE
(1789): NOAH WEBSTER

As an independent nation, our honor requires us to have a system of our own, in language as well as government. Great Britain, whose children we are and whose language we speak, should no longer be our standard, for the taste of her writers is already corrupted and her language on the decline. But if it were not so, she is at too great a distance to be our model and to instruct us in the principles of our own tongue. . . .

We have . . .the fairest opportunity of establishing a national lan-guage and of giving it uniformity and perspicuity in North America that ever presented itself to mankind. Now is the time to begin the plan. The minds of the Americans are roused by the events of a revolution; the necessity of organizing the political body and of forming constitutions of government that shall secure freedom and property, has called all the faculties of the mind into exertion; and the danger of losing the benefits of independence has disposed every man to embrace any scheme that shall tend, in its future operation, to reconcile the people of America to each other and weaken the prejudices which oppose a cordial union. . . .

A *national language* is a bond of *national union*. Every engine should be employed to render the people of this country *national*, to call their attachments home to their own country, and to inspire them with the pride of national character. However they may boast of Independence and the freedom of their government, yet their *opinions* are not sufficiently independent; an astonishing respect for the arts and literature of their parent country and a blind imitation of its manners are still prevalent among the Americans. Thus an habitual respect for another country, deserved indeed and once laudable, turns their attention from their own interests and prevents their respecting themselves. . . .

Now is the time, and *this* the country, in which we may expect success in attempting changes favorable to language, science, and government. Delay, in the plan here proposed, may be fatal; under a tranquil general government, the minds of men may again sink into indolence; a national acquiescence in error will follow; and posterity be doomed to struggle with difficulties which time and accident will perpetually multiply.

Let us then seize the present moment and establish a *national* language as well as a national government. Let us remember that there is a certain respect due to the opinions of other nations. As an independent people our reputation abroad demands that in all things we should be federal, be *national*, for if we do not respect *ourselves*, we may be assured that *other nations* will not respect us. In short, let it be impressed upon the mind of every American, that to neglect the means of commanding respect abroad is treason against the character and dignity of a brave independent people. . . .

THE REPUBLIC NEEDS THE FINE ARTS (1811): BENJAMIN LATROBE

If meritorious actions, and services rendered to the state, were commemorated by a portrait, an historical picture, a bust, a statue, a monument, or a mausoleum, the emulation to excel in the fine arts, would grow out of the emulation to deserve well of the country. . . . Without the slightest favour from the nation or the state, this society has arisen on the basis of private and individual enterprize, giving to the rising artists of the country the means of support, and paving to them the road to eminence. Affection and pride have asked for portraits, literature for embellishment, and science for elucidation, and we already rival Europe in portraits and in engravings. Commerce has called for beauty in the forms and decorations of her ships and where in Europe is there a Rush? Let the national legislature honor the hero or statesman of the revolution with busts; and sculptors will not be wanting.—The genius which under exotic influence has given so high a rank to the American pencil of a West, Copley, Trumbull, and Vanderline, would, under domestic patronage, not refuse to inspire the American chisel.—And whence arises it—is it our national ingratitude, our ignorance or our apathy—that those states or municipal bodies, which have endeavoured to erect a memorial to the merits of any of their public men, have confined it to the form of the face or the person; that the majority of the states have not even gone so far, and that the national legislature has absolutely done nothing:—while four American historical painters have attained the highest eminence in Europe, where their talents have been employed in immortalizing the achievements of a Lord Heathfield, or of a Major Pearson, in the war carried on against us; and where the patriotism of Trumbull, exhibited in his admirable pictures of the death of Warren and of Montgomery, has been obliged to wear the mask of British victory. The annual expenditure which would employ these great artists upon the transactions of our own country, and which would give to them honour and independence, would be as dust in the balance of our public accounts. The national pride, which such records excite, is well worth purchasing at the expense of a few thousand dollars; and, if the example of all the republics that have preceded us, did not authorize the hope, that history will not find us guilty of ingratitude, but only of delay, the national neglect of the memory of Washington would be sufficient to repress every sentiment of patriotism and public spirit. . . .

But if in painting and sculpture the American public have as yet done nothing for the arts, our necessities and our pride has been more favourable to the advancement of our skill in architecture. It is indeed to be regretted, that instead of adapting our architecture to the age of our society and of our institutions, and exhibiting in our public edifices that republican simplicity which we profess, some of the most magnificent situations in our country and in the world, should be already irrevocably occupied by structures copied from the palaces of the corrupt age of Diocletian, or the still more absurd and debased taste of Louis the XIV. In this city however it might naturally be expected that the purest taste would prevail. Founded by a man, the beneficent effects of whose wisdom and policy will be enjoyed by a late posterity, and the simplicity of whose manners and principles have descended to a very numerous part of this community as an inheritance, influencing and correcting the character of the whole population, the city is held responsible to the whole union for the purity of her taste in the fine arts. Nor has she altogether set them an unworthy example in her architecture. The beautiful marble with which this neighbourhood abounds, and the excellence of all other building materials, give to Philadelphia great advantages in this branch of the fine arts. The first building in which marble was employed as the principal material of its front, is the Bank of the United States. Although only a copy of a European building of indifferent taste, and very defective in its execution, it is still a bold proof of the spirit of the citizens who erected it, and of the tendency of the community to *force*, rather than to *retard*, the advancement of the arts. . . .

2. *Political Nationalism*

Chief Justice John Marshall who presided over the Supreme Court for a full generation insisted that the Federal government sprang directly from the people of the United States, and was much more than a mere agent of "sovereign" states. In the Jeffersonian era Marshall's defense of a strong and effective Federal government provided an important prop for American nationalism. A more powerful and persuasive formula for nationalism was provided by the politicians, editors, scholars, and publicists of "manifest destiny," who wished to stress Republican mission and the need for territorial expansion. To carry the flag and the Constitution to Texas, California, and Oregon—perhaps to Central America, the West Indies, Canada, or into the Pacific—would both bring the blessings of American liberty to vast new territories and strengthen the Federal Union. The very acquisition of new territory, however, threatened the existence of the Republic. To passionate arguments on the exclusion or acceptance of slavery in the new territories gained in the Mexican War, Daniel Webster replied that all issues could be resolved by American institutions within the framework of the Federal Union. Webster's eloquent pleas on the advantages of the Union to all citizens were echoed by Lincoln eleven year later. Lincoln insisted that Americans *could not* separate, that the Union was perpetual and indissoluble. AUTHORS: John Marshall (1755–1835) of Virginia, before coming to the Supreme Court in 1801, served in the Continental army, as a delegate to the Constitutional Convention, and as a diplomat in the XYZ Affair. John L. O'Sullivan (1813–1895), a Jacksonian Democrat, worked as editor, essayist, and diplomat. Daniel Webster (1782–1852), lawyer, orator, and statesman, served for a generation as a Congressman, cabinet officer, and Senator, and performed his last major duties as a nationalist and an architect of the Compromise of 1850. Abraham Lincoln (1809–1865) began his rise to the Presidency as a self-educated backwoods clerk, surveyor, and lawyer. Before winning the election of 1860, he served as a Whig Congressman, and Illinois legislator, and an unsuccessful Illinois candidate for the Senate in 1858. SELEC- TIONS: "The Supremacy of the National Government" from Marshall's opinion in McCulloch v. Maryland (1819). "Nationalism and Manifest Destiny" from the O'Sullivan articles in the United States Magazine and Democratic Review (1839, 1845). "For the Preservation of the Union" from Webster's famous "Fifth of March" speech to the Senate in 1850. "The Union is Perpetual" from Lincoln's First Inaugural Address in 1861.

THE SUPREMACY OF THE NATIONAL GOVERNMENT (1819): JOHN MARSHALL

In discussing this question, the counsel for the State of Maryland have deemed it of some importance, in the construction of the constitution, to consider that instrument not as emanating from the people, but as the act of sovereign and independent States. The powers of the general govern- ment, it has been said, are delegated by the States, who alone are truly sovereign; and must be exercised in subordination to the States, who alone possess supreme dominion. . . .

No political dreamer was ever wild enough to think of breaking down the lines which separate the States, and of compounding the Amer- ican people into one common mass. Of consequence, when they act, they act in their States. But the measures they adopt do not, on that account cease to be measures of the people themselves, or become the measures of the state governments. . . .

The government proceeds directly from the people; is "ordained and established" in the name of the people; and is declared to be ordained, "in order to form a more perfect union, establish justice, insure domestic tranquility, and secure the blessings of liberty to themselves and to their posterity." The assent of the States, in their sovereign capacity, is im- plied in calling a Convention, and thus submitting that instrument to the people. But the people were at perfect liberty to accept or reject it; and their act was final. It required not the affirmance, and could not be negatived, by the State governments. The constitution, when thus adopted, was of complete obligation, and bound the State sovereign- ties. . . .

The government of the Union, then (whatever may be the influence of this fact on the case), is emphatically and truly a government of the people. In form and in substance it emanates from them, its powers are granted by them, and are to be exercised directly on them, and for their benefit.

This government is acknowledged by all to be one of enumerated powers. The principle, that it can exercise only the powers granted to it, would seem too apparent to have required to be enforced by all those arguments which its enlightened friends, while it was depending before the people, found it necessary to urge. That principle is now universally admitted. But the question respecting the extent of the powers actually granted, is perpetually arising, and will probably continue to arise, as long as our system shall exist. In discussing these questions, the conflicting powers of the State and general governments must be brought into view, and the supremacy of their respective laws, when they are in opposition, must be settled.

If any one proposition could command the universal assent of mankind, we might expect it would be this: that the government of the union, though limited in its powers, is supreme within its sphere of action. . . .

NATIONALISM AND MANIFEST DESTINY (1839, 1845): JOHN L. O'SULLIVAN

The American people having derived their origin from many other nations, and the Declaration of National Independence being entirely based on the great principle of human equality, these facts demonstrate at once our disconnected position as regards any other nation; that we have, in reality, but little connection with the past history of any of them and still less with all antiquity, its glories, or its crimes. On the contrary, our national birth was the beginning of a new history; the formation and progress of an untried political system, which separates us from the past and connects us with the future only; and so far as regards the entire development of the natural rights of man, in moral, political, and national life, we may confidently assume that our country is destined to be *the great nation* of futurity. . . .

All this will be our future history, to establish on earth the moral dignity and salvation of man—the immutable truth and beneficence of God. For this blessed mission to the nations of the world, which are shut out from the lifegiving light of truth, has America been chosen; and her high example shall smite unto death the tyranny of kings, hierarchs, and oligarchs. . . .

. . . [Texas is now ours]. . . . A population will soon be in actual occupation of California, over which it will be idle for Mexico to dream of dominion. They will necessarily become independent. . . . And they will have a right to independence—to self-government—to the possession of the homes conquered from the wilderness by their own labors and dangers, sufferings and sacrifices—a better and a truer right than the artificial title of sovereignty in Mexico a thousand miles distant, inheriting from Spain a title good only against those who have none better. Their right to independence will be the natural right of self-government belonging to any community strong enough to maintain it. . . .

Away, then, with all the idle French talk of *balances of power* on the American continent. There is no growth in Spanish America! Whatever progress of population there may be in British Canada, is only for their own early severance of their present colonial relation to the little island three thousand miles across the Atlantic; soon to be followed by annexation and destined to swell the still accumulating momentum of our progress. And whosoever may hold the balance, though they should cast into the opposite scale all the bayonets and cannon, not only of France and England, but of Europe entire, how would it kick the beam against the simple solid weight of the two hundred and fifty, or three hundred millions—and American millions—destined to gather beneath the flutter of the Stripes and Stars, in the fast hastening year of the Lord 1845! . . .

FOR THE PRESERVATION OF THE UNION
(1850): DANIEL WEBSTER

Mr. President,—I wish to speak to-day, not as a Massachusetts man, nor as a Northern man, but as an American, and a member of the Senate of the United State. . . . The East, the North, and the stormy South combine to throw the whole sea into commotion, to toss its billows to the skies, and disclose its profoundest depths. I do not affect to regard myself, Mr. President, as holding, or as fit to hold, the helm in this combat with the political elements; but I have a duty to perform, and I mean to perform it with fidelity, not without a sense of existing dangers, but not without hope. I have a part to act, not for my own security or safety, for I am looking out for no fragment upon which to float away from the wreck, if wreck there must be, but for the good of the whole, and the preservation of all; and there is that which will keep me to my duty during this struggle, whether the sun and the stars shall appear, or shall not appear for many days. I speak to-day for the preservation of the Union. "Hear me for my cause." I speak to-day out of a solicitous and anxious heart, for the restoration to the country of that quiet and that harmony which make the blessing of this Union so rich, and so dear to us all. These are the topics that I propose to myself to discuss; these are the motives, and the sole motives, that influence me in the wish to communicate my opinions to the Senate and the country; and if I can do anything, however little, for the promotion of these ends, I shall have accomplished all that I expect. . . .

Sir, I am ashamed to pursue this line of remark. I dislike it, I have an utter disgust for it. I would rather hear of natural blasts and mildews, war, pestilence, and famine than to hear gentlemen talk of secession. To break up! to break up this great government, to dismember this glorious country, to astonish Europe with an act of folly such as Europe for two centuries has never beheld in any government or any people! No, Sir! no, Sir! There will be no secession! Gentlemen are not serious when they talk of secession. . . .

And now, Mr. President, instead of speaking of the possibility or utility of secession, instead of dwelling in those caverns of darkness, instead of groping with those ideas so full of all that is horrid and horrible, let us come out into the light of day; let us enjoy the fresh air of Liberty and Union; let us cherish those hopes which belong to us; let us devote ourselves to those great objects that are fit for our consideration and our action; let us raise our conceptions to the magnitude and the importance of the duties that devolve upon us; let our comprehension be as broad as the country for which we act, our aspirations as high as its certain destiny; let us not be pygmies in a case that calls for men. Never did there devolve on any generation of men higher trusts than now devolve upon us, for the preservation of the Constitution and the harmony and peace of all who are destined to live under it. Let us make our generation one of the strongest and brightest links in that golden chain which is destined, I fondly believe, to grapple the people of all the States to this Constitution for ages to come. We have a great, popular, constitutional government, guarded by law and by judicature, and defended by the affections of the whole people. No monarchical throne presses the States together, no iron chain of military power encircles them; they live and stand upon a Government popular in its form, representative in its character, founded upon principles of equality, and so constructed, we hope, as to last for ever. In all its history it has been beneficent; it has trodden down no man's liberty; it has crushed no state. Its daily respiration is liberty and patriotism; its yet youthful veins are full of enterprise, courage, and honorable love of glory and renown. Large before, the country has now, by recent events, become vastly larger. This republic now extends, with a vast breadth, across the whole continent. The two great seas of the world wash the one and the other shore. We realize, on a mighty scale, the beautiful description of the ornamental border of the buckler of Achilles—

> Now the broad shield complete, the artist crown'd,
> With his last band, and poured the ocean round;
> In living silver seem'd the waves to roll,
> And beat the buckler's verge, and bound the whole. . . .

THE UNION IS PERPETUAL (1861):
ABRAHAM LINCOLN

Descending from these general principles, we find the proposition that in legal contemplation the Union is perpetual confirmed by the history of the Union itself. The Union is much older than the Constitution. It was formed, in fact, by the Articles of Association in 1774. It was matured and continued by the Declaration of Independence in 1776. It was further matured and the faith of all the then thirteen States expressly plighted and engaged that it should be perpetual, by the Articles of Confederation in 1778. And finally, in 1787, one of the declared objects for ordaining and establishing the Constitution was "to form a more perfect Union." . . .

It follows from these views that no State upon its own mere motion can lawfully get out of the Union; that resolves and ordinances to that effect are legally void; and that acts of violence, within any State or States against the authority of the United States, are insurrectionary or revolutionary, according to circumstances.

I therefore consider that, in view of the Constitution and the laws, the Union is unbroken; and to the extent of my ability I shall take care, as the Constitution itself expressly enjoins me, that the laws of the Union be faithfully executed in all the States. Doing this I deem to be only a simple duty on my part; and I shall perform it so far as practicable, unless my rightful masters, the American people, shall withhold the requisite means, or in some authoritative manner direct the contrary. . . .

Physically speaking, we cannot separate. We cannot remove our respective sections from each other, nor build an impassable wall between them. A husband and wife may be divorced and go out of the presence and beyond the reach of each other; but the different parts of our country cannot do this. They cannot but remain face to face, and intercourse, either amicable or hostile, must continue between them. Is it possible, then, to make that intercourse more advantageous or more satisfactory after separation than before? Can aliens make treaties easier than friends can make laws? Can treaties be more faithfully enforced between aliens than laws can among friends? Suppose you go to war, you cannot fight always; and when, after much loss on both sides, and no gain on either, you cease fighting, the identical old questions as to terms of intercourse are again upon you.

This country, with its institutions, belongs to the people who inhabit it. Whenever they shall grow weary of the existing government, they can exercise their constitutional right of amending it, or their revolutionary right to dismember or overthrow it. . . .

3. The Anti-Nationalist Opposition: States Rights and Southern Nationalism

"States Rights" doctrines as an instrument for political opposition by minority factions in American politics originated with the Virginia and Kentucky Resolutions which were drafted under the leadership of Thomas Jefferson and James Madison. Jefferson and Madison used the notion of state "sovereignty" and "rights" to speak for human freedom in opposition to the oppressive Alien and Sedition Acts of 1798, but the doctrine was to be used in a variety of political contexts. New England exploited the logic of states rights to argue against Jefferson's foreign policy and the War of 1812; anti-slavery politicians opposed the *Dred Scott* case and the Fugitive Slave Act of 1850 with the same instruments; and Southerners in the twentieth century clothed their fight to retain segregation in the garb of states rights. John C. Calhoun's generation spoke of state sovereignty almost incessantly; and the suspicion still lingers that the doctrine functioned more as a minority strategy than as a cause. The direct defense of Southern society, and the "peculiar institution" on which it rested seems to have been the real moving force behind Southern sectionalism and nationalism. If the South could not continue its institutions without the incessant hostility of the North, then Southerners would fight to establish a new nationality. AUTHORS: John C. Calhoun (1782–1850), the chief advocate of states rights and Southern sectionalism, served as a South Carolina legislator, a U. S. congressman, Senator, Vice-President, and Secretary of War. Henry Timrod (1828–1867) was a South Carolina poet and a Confederate patriot. SELECTIONS: "Origins of 'States Rights' Doctrines: The Kentucky Resolutions" of 1798 sprang from drafts by Jefferson and Madison. "Maturation of 'States Rights' Doctrines" from Calhoun's "Fort Hill" Address of July 26, 1831. "Southern Nationalism" from Timrod's poem "Ethnogenesis" of 1861.

ORIGINS OF "STATES RIGHTS" DOCTRINES: THE KENTUCKY RESOLUTIONS (1798)

Kentucky Resolutions, November 16, 1798, 1. *Resolved*, that the several States composing the United States of America, are not united on the principle of unlimited submission to their general government; but that by compact under the style and title of a Constitution for the United States and of amendments thereto, they constituted a general government for special purposes, delegated to that government certain definite powers, reserving each State to itself, the residuary mass of right to their own self-government; and that whensoever the general government assumes un-delegated powers, its acts are un-authoritative, void, and of no force: That to this compact each State acceded as a State, and is an integral party, its co-States forming, as to itself, the other party: That the government created by this compact was not made the exclusive or final judge of the extent of the powers delegated to itself; since that would have made its discretion, and not the Constitution, the measure of its powers; but that as in all other cases of compact among parties having no common Judge, each party has an equal right to judge for itself, as well of infractions as of the mode and measure of redress. . . .

III. Resolved, that it is true as a general principle, and is also ex-pressly declared by one of the amendments to the Constitution that "the powers not delegated to the United States by the Constitution, nor prohibited by it to the States, are reserved to the States respectively, or to the people"; and that no power over the freedom of religion, freedom of speech, or freedom of the press being delegated to the United States by the Constitution, nor prohibited by it to the States, all lawful powers respecting the same did of right remain, and were reserved to the States, or to the people: That thus was manifested their determination to retain to themselves the right of judging how far the licentiousness of speech and of the press may be abridged without lessening their useful freedom, and how far those abuses which cannot be separated from their use should be tolerated rather than the use be destroyed; and thus also they guarded against all abridgment by the United States of the freedom of religious opinions and exercises, and retained to themselves the right of protecting the same, as this State, by a law passed on the general demand of its citizens, had already protected them from all human restraint or interference: And that in addition to this general principle and express declaration, another and more special provision has been made by one of the amendments to the Constitution which expressly declares, that "Congress shall make no law respecting an establishment of religion, or prohibiting the free exercise thereof, or abridging the freedom of speech, or of the press," thereby guarding in the same sentence, and under the same words, the freedom of religion, of speech, and of the press inso-much, that whatever violates either, throws down the sanctuary which covers the others, and that libels, falsehoods, defamation equally with heresy and false religion, are withheld from the cognizance of Federal tribunals. That therefore [the Sedition Act], which does abridge the feedom of the press, is not law, but is altogether void and of no effect.

MATURATION OF "STATES RIGHTS" DOCTRINES (1831): JOHN C. CALHOUN

The great and leading principle is, that the General Government emanated from the people of the several States, forming distinct political communities, and acting in their separate and sovereign capacity, and not from all of the people forming one aggregate political community; that the Constitution of the United States is, in fact, a compact, to which each State is a party, in the character already described; and that the several States, or parties, have a right to judge of its infractions; and in case of a deliberate, palpable, and dangerous exercise of power not delegated, they have the right, in the last resort, to use the language of the Virginia Resolutions, *"to interpose for arresting the progress of the evil, and for maintaining, within their respective limits, the authorities, rights, and liberties appertaining to them."* This right of interposition, thus solemnly asserted by the State of Virginia, be it called what it may,—State-right, veto, nullification, or by any other name,—I conceive to be the fundamental principle of our system, resting on facts historically as certain as our revolution itself, and deductions as simple and demonstrative as that of any political or moral truth whatever; and I firmly believe that on its recognition depend the stability and safety of our political institutions.

I am not ignorant that those opposed to the doctrine have always, now and formerly, regarded it in a very different light, as anarchical and revolutionary. . . . I have examined, with the utmost care, the bearing of the doctrine in question; and, so far from anarchical or revolutionary, I solemnly believe it to be the only solid foundation of our system, and of the Union itself; and that the opposite doctrine, which denies to the States the right of protecting their reserved powers, and which would vest in the General Government (it matters not through what department) the right of determining, exclusively and finally, the powers delegated to it, is incompatible with the sovereignty of the States, and of the Constitution itself, considered as the basis of a Federal Union. As strong as this language is, it is not stronger than that used by the illustrious Jefferson, who said, to give to the General Government the final and exclusive right to judge of its powers, is to make *"its discretion, and not the Constitution, the measure of its powers"*; and that, *"in all cases of compact between parties having no common judge, each party has an equal right to judge for itself, as well of the infraction as of the mode and measure of redress."* Language cannot be more explicit, nor can higher authority be adduced. . . .

To realize its perfection, we must view the General Government and those of the States as a whole, each in the proper sphere independent; each perfectly adapted to its respective objects; the States acting separately, representing and protecting the local and peculiar interests; and acting jointly through one General Government, with the weight respectively assigned to each by the Constitution, representing and protecting the interest of the whole; and thus perfecting, by an admirable but simple arrangement, the great principle of representation and responsibility, without which no government can be free or just. To preserve this sacred distribution as originally settled, by coercing each to move in its prescribed orbit, is the great and difficult problem, on the solution of which the duration of our Constitution, of our Union, and, in all probability, our liberty depends. How is this to be effected? . . .

Should the General Government and a State come into conflict, we have a higher remedy: the power which called the General Government into existence, which gave it all its authority, and can enlarge, contract, or abolish its powers at its pleasure, may be invoked. The States themselves may be appealed to,—three fourths of which, in fact, form a power, whose decrees are the Constitution itself, and whose voice can silence all discontent. The utmost extent, then, of the power is, that a State, acting in its sovereign capacity as one of the parties to the constitutional compact, may compel the Government, created by that compact, to submit a question touching its infraction, to the parties who created it; to avoid the supposed dangers of which, it is proposed to resort to the novel, the hazardous, and, I must add, fatal project of giving to the General Government the sole and final right of interpreting the Constitution;— thereby reversing the whole system, making that instrument the creature of its will, instead of a rule of action impressed on it at its creation, and annihilating, in fact, the authority which imposed it, and from which the Government itself derives its existence. . . .

SOUTHERN NATIONALISM (1861):
HENRY TIMROD'S "ETHNOGENESIS"

Written During the Meeting of the First Southern Congress, at Montgomery, February, 1861.

I

Hath not the morning dawned with added light?
And shall not evening call another star
Out of the infinite regions of the night,
To mark this day in Heaven? At last, we are
A nation among nations; and the world

Shall soon behold in many a distant port
   Another flag unfurled!
Now, come what may, whose favor need we court?
And, under God, whose thunder need we fear?
   Thank him who placed us here
Beneath so kind a sky—the very sun
Takes part with us; and on our errands run
All breezes of the ocean; dew and rain
Do noiseless battle for us; and the Year,
And all the gentle daughters in her train,
March in our ranks, and in our service wield
Long spears of golden grain!
A yellow blossom as her fairy shield,
June flings her azure banner to the wind,
   While in the order of their birth
Her sisters pass, and many an ample field
Grows white beneath their steps, till now, behold,
   Its endless sheets unfold
The Snow of Southern Summers! Let the earth
Rejoice! beneath those fleeces soft and warm
   Our happy land shall sleep
   In a repose as deep
As if we lay intrenched behind
Whole legions of Russian ice and Arctic storm!

II

And what if, mad with wrongs themselves have wrought,
   In their own treachery caught,
   By their own fears made bold,
   And leagued with him of old,
Who long since in the limits of the North
Set up his evil throne, and warred with God—
What if, both mad and blinded in their rage,
Our foes should fling us down their mortal gage,
And with a hostile step profane our sod!
We shall not shrink, my brothers, but go forth
And overshadowed by the mighty ghosts
Of Moultrie and of Eutaw—who shall foil
Auxiliars such as these? Nor these alone,
   But every stock and stone
   Shall help us; but the very soil,
And all the general wealth it gives to toil,
And all for which we love our noble land,
Shall fight beside, and through us; sea and strand,

The heart of woman, and her hand,
Tree, fruit, and flower, and every influence,
  Gentle, or grave, or grand;
  The winds in our defence
Shall seem to blow; to us the hills shall lend
  Their firmness and their calm;
And in our stiffened sinews we shall blend
  The strength of pine and palm!

III

Nor would we shun the battle-ground,
  Though weak as we are strong;
Call up the clashing elements around,
  And test the right and wrong!
On one side, creeds that dare to teach
What Christ and Paul refrained to preach;
Codes built upon a broken pledge,
And Charity that whets a poniard's edge;
Fair schemes that leave the neighboring poor
To starve and shiver at the schemer's door,
While in the world's most liberal ranks enrolled,
He turns some vast philanthropy to gold;
Religion, taking every mortal form
But that a pure and Christian faith makes warm,
Where not to vile fanatic passion urged,
Or not in vague philosophies submerged,
Repulsive with all Pharisaic leaven,
And making laws to stay the laws of Heaven!
And on the other, scorn of sordid gain,
Unblemished honor, truth, without a stain,
Faith, justice, reverence, charitable wealth,
And, for the poor and humble, laws which give,
Not the mean right to buy the right to live,
  But life, and home, and health!
To doubt the end were want of trust in God,
  Who, if he has decreed
  That we must pass a redder sea
Than that which rang to Miriam's holy glee,
  Will surely raise at need
  A Moses with his rod!

IV

But let our fears—if fears we have—be still,
And turn us to the future! Could we climb
Some mighty Alp, and view the coming time,

The rapturous sight would fill
  Our eyes with happy tears!
Not only for the glories which the years
Shall bring us; not for lands from sea to sea,
And wealth, and power, and peace, though these shall be;
But for the distant peoples we shall bless,
And the hushed murmurs of a world's distress;
For, to give labor to the poor,
  The whole sad planet o'er,
And save from want and crime the humblest door,
Is one among many ends for which
  God makes us great and rich!
The hour perchance is not yet wholly ripe
When all shall own it, but the type
Whereby we shall be known in every land
Is that vast gulf which lips our Southern strand,
And through the cold, untempered ocean pours
Its genial streams, that far off Arctic shores
May sometimes catch upon the softened breeze
Strange tropic warmth and hints of summer seas.

4. The Perplexities of Color, Caste, and Slavery

Pro-slavery literature ran heavily toward Scriptural quotations; passages such as St. Paul's injunction, "Servants obey thy masters" were used to supplement the notion that slavery had been "especially commanded by God through Moses, and approved by Christ through his apostles." According to another argument, Negroes, cursed as the descendants of Noah's son, Ham, sometimes had the good luck to be brought from "savage" Africa to "civilized" Christian America. Presumably the slaves were prisoners of war, enslaved rather than killed on the field of battle after a common custom in history. Southerners argued that the white masters exercised a benevolent and paternal mastery over a happy, child-like, improvident, and inferior race, which must be controlled to prevent a lapse into savage brutality. Literate slaves who escaped to freedom, men such as Frederick Douglass, told a different tale of the institutionalized brutality of white masters permanently at war with Christianity, democracy, and modern Western civilization. While Douglass obviously preferred life in the North to Southern slavery, he also made it clear that he could not find real freedom anywhere in America. He stressed the existence of Northern laws which excluded Negroes from the franchise, juries, militia duty, white churches, and white schools; of states which prohibited Negroes from testifying against white persons; and of a society which segregated black men from the cradle to the grave. Douglass and other Northern Negro leaders complained about the danger of private violence and the struggle to live on the outer margins of American society. Stephen A. Douglas appealed to Negrophobe emotions by insisting during the Lincoln-Douglas debates of 1858 that America was a "white man's country." Lincoln's reply was hardly a radical one, for he rejected the idea of political and social equality for the Negro and took the Abolitionists to task for the militancy of their attacks on the South. Still, Lincoln spoke for the more humane wing of the Republican Party in opposing slavery and insisting that the Declaration of Independence granted economic rights to Negroes. AUTHORS: Thomas R. Dew (1802–1846) of Virginia, served as a Professor of Political Law and President at the College of William and Mary. Frederick Douglass (1817?–1895), the son of a slave mother and white father, fled Maryland for freedom and a life of distinguished service as an Abolitionist, lecturer, editor, worker in the underground railroad, and diplomat. Stephen A. Douglas (1813–1861), Congressman, Senator, railroad promoter, and the Democratic candidate for the Presidency in 1860, helped to shape the Compromise of 1850 and sponsored the stormily debated Kansas-Nebraska Bill. Abraham Lincoln (1809–1865). William Wells Brown (1816–1884), the son of a slave mother and a slaveholding father, got the rudiments of education while working in a St. Louis print shop; in 1834 he escaped to freedom and worked as a reformer, physician, and historian. SELECTIONS: "The Virtues of Slavery; the Impossibility of Emancipation" from Dew's *Review of the Debate in the Virginia Legislature in 1831–1832*. "The Evils of Slavery" from a Douglass letter of 1848 published in *The Liberator*. "A White Man's Country" from the Lincoln-Douglas debates, a part of a speech given at Springfield on July 17, 1858 as reported by the *Illinois State Register*. "What Are the Rights of Negroes?" from Lincoln's reply to Douglas at Ottawa on August 21, 1858 as reported by *The Press and Tribune* with the first paragraph from a text added by Lincoln. "A Protest Against Caste" from a Brown letter of 1849 published in *The Liberator*.

THE VIRTUES OF SLAVERY; THE IMPOSSIBILITY OF EMANCIPATION (1831): THOMAS R. DEW

We have now, we think, proved our position, that slave labor, in an economical point of view, is far superior to free negro labor; and have no doubt that if an immediate emancipation of negroes were to take place, the whole southern country would be visited with an immediate general famine, from which the productive resources of all the other States of the Union could not deliver them.

It is now easy for us to demonstrate the second point in our argument—that the slave is not only *economically* but *morally* unfit for freedom. And first, idleness and consequent want are, of themselves, sufficient to generate a catalogue of vices of the most mischievous and destructive character. . . .

The great evil, however, of these schemes of emancipation, remains yet to be told. They are admirably calculated to excite plots, murders and insurrections; whether gradual or rapid in their operation, this is the inevitable tendency. . . . Two totally different races, as we have before seen, cannot easily harmonize together, . . . and even when free, . . . [the Negro's] idleness will produce want and worthlessness, and his very worthlessness and degradation will stimulate him to deeds of rapine and vengeance; he will oftener engage in plots and massacres, and thereby draw down on his devoted head, the vengeance of the provoked whites. . . . [Let Virginia] liberate her slaves, and every year you would hear of insurrections and plots, and every day would perhaps record a murder. . . .

He [Jefferson] has supposed the master in a continual passion—in the constant exercise of the most odious tyranny, and the child, a creature of imitation, looking on and learning. But is not this master sometimes kind and indulgent to his slaves? . . . We may rest assured, in this intercourse between a good master and his servant, more good than evil may be taught the child; the exalted principles of morality and religion may thereby be sometimes indelibly inculcated upon his mind. . . . Look to the slaveholding population of our country, and you every where find them characterized by noble and elevated sentiments, by humane and virtuous feelings. . . . Go into our national councils, and ask for the most generous, the most disinterested, the most conscientious, and the least unjust and oppressive in their principles, and see whether the slaveholder will be past by in the selection. . . .

Let us now look a moment to the slave, and contemplate his position. Mr. Jefferson has described him as hating, rather than loving his master, and as losing, too, all that *amor patriae* which characterizes the true patriot. We assert again, that Mr. Jefferson is not borne out by the fact. We are well convinced that there is nothing but the mere relations of husband and wife, parent and child, brother and sister, which produce a closer tie, than the relation of master and servant. We have no hesitation in affirming, that throughout the whole slaveholding country, the slaves of a good master are his warmest, most constant, and most devoted friends; they have been accustomed to look up to him as their supporter, director and defender. Everyone acquainted with southern states, knows that the slave rejoices in the elevation and prosperity of his master; and the heart of no one is more gladdened at the successful debut of young master or miss on the great theatre of the world, than that of either the young slave who has grown up with them, and shared in all their sports, and even partaken of all their delicacies—or the aged one who has looked on and watched them from birth to manhood, with the kindest and most affectionate solicitude, and has ever met from them all the kind treatment and generous sympathies of feeling, tender hearts. . . .

THE EVILS OF SLAVERY (1848): FREDERICK DOUGLASS WRITES TO HIS FORMER MASTER

I have selected this day on which to address you, because it is the anniversary of my emancipation; and knowing of no better way, I am led to this as the best mode of celebrating that truly important event. Just ten years ago this beautiful September morning, yon bright sun beheld me a slave—a poor, degraded chattel—trembling at the sound of your voice, lamenting that I was a man, and wishing myself a brute. . . . The very first mental effort that I now remember on my part, was an attempt to solve the mystery, Why am I a slave? . . . When I saw the slave-driver whip a slave woman, cut the blood out of her neck, and heard her piteous cries, I went away into the corner of the fence, wept and pondered over the mystery. I had, through some medium, I know not what, got some idea of God, the Creator of all mankind, the black and the white, and that he had made the blacks to serve the whites as slaves. How could he do this and be good, I could not tell. I was not satisfied with this theory, which made God responsible for slavery, for it pained me greatly, and I have wept over it long and often. . . . The grim horrors of slavery rise in all their ghastly terror before me, the wails of millions pierce my heart, and chill my blood. I remember the chain, the gag, the bloody whip, the death-like gloom overshadowing the broken spirit of the fettered bondman, the appalling liability of his being torn away from wife and children, and sold like a beast in the market. Say not that this is a picture of fancy. You well know that I wear stripes on my back inflicted by your direction; and that you, while we were brothers in the same church, caused this right hand, with which I am now penning this letter, to be closely tied to my left, and my person dragged at the pistol's mouth, fifteen miles, from the Bay side to Easton to be sold like a beast in the market, for the alleged crime of intending to escape from your possession. All this and more you remember, and know to be perfectly true, not only of yourself, but of nearly all the slaveholders around you.

At this moment, you are probably the guilty holder of at least three of my own dear sisters, and my only brother in bondage. These you regard as your property. They are recorded on your ledger, or perhaps have been sold to human flesh mongers, with a view to filling your own ever-hungry purse. Sir, I desire to know how and where these dear sisters are. Have you sold them? or are they still in your possession? What has become of them? Are they living or dead? And my dear old grandmother, whom you turned out like an old horse, to die in the woods—is she still alive? . . . How, let me ask, would you look upon me, were I some dark night in company with a band of hardened villains, to enter the precincts of your elegant dwelling and seize the person of your own lovely daughter Amanda, and carry her off from your family, friends and all the loved ones of her youth—make her my slave—compel her to work, and I take her wages—place her name on my ledger as property—disregard her personal rights—fetter the powers of her immortal soul by denying her the right and privilege of learning to read and write—feed her coarsely—clothe her scantily, and whip her on the naked back occasionally; more and still more horrible, leave her unprotected—a degraded victim to the brutal lust of fiendish overseers, who would pollute, blight, and blast her fair soul—rob her of all dignity—destroy her virtue, and annihilate in her person all the graces that adorn the character of virtuous womanhood? I ask how would you regard me, if such were my conduct? Oh! the vocabulary of the damned would not afford a word sufficiently infernal, to express your idea of my God-provoking wickedness. Yet sir, your treatment of my beloved sisters is in all essential points, precisely like the case I have now supposed. Damning as would be such a deed on my part, it would be no more so than that which you have committed against me and my sisters. . . .

A WHITE MAN'S COUNTRY (1858):
STEPHEN A. DOUGLAS

We are told by Lincoln that he is utterly opposed to the Dred Scott decision, . . . [because] it deprives the negro of the rights and privileges of citizenship. (Laughter and applause.) That is the first and main reason which he assigns for his warfare on the Supreme Court of the United States and its decision. I ask you, are you in favor of conferring upon the negro the rights and privileges of citizenship? ("no, no.") Do you desire to strike out of our state constitution that clause which keeps slaves and free negroes out of the state and allow the free negroes to flow in, ("never,") and cover your prairies with black settlements? Do you desire to turn this beautiful state into a free negro colony, ("no, no,") in order that when Missouri abolishes slavery she can send one hundred thousand emancipated slaves into Illinois, to become citizens and voters, on an equality with yourselves? ("Never," "no.") If you desire negro citizen-ship, if you desire to allow them to come into the state and settle with the white man, if you desire them to vote on an equality with yourselves, and to make them eligible to office, to serve on juries, and to adjudge your rights, then support Mr. Lincoln and the Black Republican party, who are in favor of the citizenship of the negro. ("Never, never.") For one, I am opposed to negro citizenship in any and every form. (Cheers.) I believe this government was made on the white basis. ("Good.") I be-lieve it was made by white men, for the benefit of white men and their posterity for ever, and I am in favor of confining citizenship to white men, men of European birth and descent, instead of conferring it upon negroes, Indians and other inferior races. ("Good for you." "Douglas forever.")

Mr. Lincoln, following the example and lead of all the little Aboli-tion orators, who go around and lecture in the basements of schools and churches, reads from the Declaration of Independence. . . . He and they maintain that negro equality is guaranteed by the laws of God, and that it is asserted in the Declaration of Independence. . . . I do not question Mr. Lincoln's conscientious belief that the negro was made his equal, and hence is his brother, (laughter,) but for my own part, I do not regard the negro as my equal, and positively deny that he is my brother or any kin to me whatever. ("Never." "Hit him again," and cheers.). . . . Now, I do not believe that the Almighty ever intended the negro to be the equal of the white man. ("Never, never.") If he did, he has been a long time demonstrating the fact. (Cheers.) For thousands of years the negro has been a race upon the earth, and during all that time, in all latitudes and climates, wherever he has wandered or been taken, he has been inferior to the race which he has met there. He belongs to an inferior race, and must always occupy an inferior position. ("Good," "that's so," &c.) I do not hold that because the negro is our inferior that therefore he ought to be a slave. . . . We have provided that the negro shall not be a slave, and we have also provided that he shall not be a citizen. . . .

WHAT ARE THE RIGHTS OF NEGROES?
(1858): ABRAHAM LINCOLN

My first impulse would be to free all the slaves, and send them to Liberia,—to their own native land. But a moment's reflection would convince me, that whatever of high hope, (as I think there is) there may be in this in the long run, its sudden execution is impossible. . . . What then? Free them all, and keep them among us as underlings? Is it quite certain that this betters their condition? I think I would not hold one in slavery, at any rate; yet the point is not clear enough to me to denounce people upon. What next? Free them, and make them politically and socially, our equals? My own feelings will not admit of this; and if mine would, we well know that those of the great mass of white people will not. . . . We can not, then, make them equals. It does seem to me that systems of gradual emancipation might be adopted; but for their tardiness in this, I will not undertake to judge our brethren of the South.

When they remind us of their constitutional rights, I acknowledge them, not grudgingly, but fully, and fairly; and I would give them any legislation for the reclaiming of their fugitives, which should not, in its stringency, be more likely to carry a free man into slavery, than our ordinary criminal laws are to hang an innocent one.

But all this, to my judgment, furnishes no more excuse for permitting slavery to go into our own free territory, than it would for reviving the African slave trade by law. . . .

Now gentlemen, I don't want to read at any greater length, but this is the true complexion of all I have ever said in regard to the institution of slavery and the black race. This is the whole of it, and anything that argues me into his idea of perfect social and political equality with the negro, is but a specious and fantastic arrangement of words, by which a man can prove a horse chestnut to be a chestnut horse. (Laughter.) I will say here, while upon this subject, that I have no purpose directly or indirectly to interfere with the institution of slavery in the states where it exists. I believe I have no lawful right to do so, and I have no inclination to do so. I have no purpose to introduce political and social equality between the white and the black races. There is a physical difference between the two, which in my judgment will probably forever forbid their living together upon the footing of perfect equality, and inasmuch as it becomes a necessity that there must be a difference, I, as well as Judge Douglas, am in favor of the race to which I belong, having the superior position. I have never said anything to the contrary, but I hold that notwithstanding all this, there is no reason in the world why the negro is not entitled to all the natural rights enumerated in the Declaration of Independence, the right to life, liberty and the pursuit of happiness. (Loud cheers.) I hold that he is as much entitled to these as the white man. I agree with Judge Douglas he is not my equal in many respects—certainly not in color, perhaps not in moral or intellectual endowment. But in the right to eat the bread, without leave of anybody else, which his own hand earns, *he is my equal and the equal of Judge Douglas, and the equal of every living man.* (Great applause). . . .

A PROTEST AGAINST CASTE (1849):
WILLIAM WELLS BROWN

I observe in the American papers an elaborate discussion upon the subject of passports for colored men. . . . We may search history in vain to find a people who have sunk themselves as low, and made themselves appear as infamous by their treatment of their fellow men, as have the people of the United States. If colored men make their appearance in the slave States as seamen, they are imprisoned until the departure of the vessel. If they make their appearance at the capital of the country, unless provided with free papers, they are sold for the benefit of the Government. In most of the States we are disfranchised, our children are shut out from the public schools, and embarrassments are thrown in the way of every attempt to elevate ourselves. And after they have degraded us, sold us, mobbed us, and done everything in their power to oppress us, then if we wish to leave the country, they refuse us passports, upon the ground that we are not citizens. This is emphatically an age of discoveries; but I will venture the assertion, that none but an American slaveholder could have discovered that a man born in a country was not a citizen of it. Their chosen motto, that "all men are created equal," when compared with their treatment of the colored people of the country, sinks them lower and lower in the estimation of the good and wise of all lands. . . .

5. The Nature of the Civil War

The construction of rationales for the conflict of North and South was underway long before the Civil War actually began. In 1858 William H. Seward announced the existence of "an irrepressible conflict" between slavery and freedom; but three years later Congressman John H. Reagan of Texas attributed the "irrepressible" struggle to the economic exploitation of the agrarian South by the commercial North. For Frederick Douglass and for many other Negroes—the Civil War was a fight for black freedom and the Union against "the slaveholder's rebellion." In 1862 Lincoln insisted that the struggle was not against slavery, but a great national war for the Union. Still by the time of his second inaugural address in 1865, the "happenstance" war had become a holy crusade, and Lincoln tentatively advanced the notion that the War was both God's judgment and His means for wiping out the sinful stain of slavery. With

the exception of Reagan's concept of economic exploitation, white Southerners rejected all of these explanations in 1865 to begin the "real"
explication of the "Lost Cause." For Edwin A. Pollard, the "Cause" was
the refined and noble "Cavalier" civilization tragically broken by the
coarse material power of the Yankee "Puritan." Jefferson Davis added
essential points to the argument: the War had little if anything to do
with slavery; Southern secession had been the last desperate resort of
people driven to extremes by decades of Northern insults and aggressions.
AUTHORS: Jefferson Davis (1808–1889) as a young man moved from
Kentucky to Mississippi where he became a leading planter and politician;
he was a West Point graduate, an officer in the Mexican War, a Senator,
and Secretary of War, and finally President of the Confederacy. John H.
Reagan (1818–1905), a Texas Congressman and Senator, served as the
Confederate Postmaster-General and Secretary of the Treasury. Edwin A.
Pollard (1831–1872), a well-travelled Virginia lawyer and editor, edited
the Daily Richmond Examiner after 1861, went into exile in Europe in
1865, and returned to Virginia in 1866. William H. Seward (1801–
1872), anti-Masonic and Republican politician, was governor of New
York, Senator, contender for the Republican presidential nomination in
1860, and Secretary of State after 1861. Frederick Douglass (c. 1817–
1895) worked during the Civil War for emancipation and the use of
Negro troops. Abraham Lincoln (1809–1865). SELECTIONS: "The Irrepressible Conflict" from a Seward speech at Rochester, New York on
October 25, 1858. "The War for Southern Economic Independence"
from Reagan's speech to Congress on January 15, 1861 as reported by
The Congressional Globe. "Slaveholder's Rebellion" from a Douglass
speech in Yates County, New York on July 4, 1862. "The Suppression of
Rebellion Becomes a Holy Crusade," the first excerpt from Lincoln's
letter of August 22, 1862 to Horace Greeley, and the second excerpt from
Lincoln's Second Inaugural Address in 1865. "Conflict of the Cavalier
and the Puritan" from Pollard's The Lost Cause (1866). "The Victimized South" from Davis' The Rise and Fall of the Confederate Government (1881).

THE IRREPRESSIBLE CONFLICT (1858):
WILLIAM H. SEWARD

Our country is a theater which [has] . . . two radically different political systems: the one resting on the basis of servile labor, the other on the
basis of voluntary labor of free men. . . .

Hitherto the two systems have existed . . . side by side within the
American Union. This has happened because the Union is a confederation of States. But in another aspect the United States constitute only

one nation. Increase of population, which is filling the States out of their very borders, together with a new and extended network of railroads and other avenues, and an internal commerce which daily becomes more intimate, is rapidly bringing the States into a higher and more perfect social unity or consolidation. Thus, these antagonistic systems are continually coming into closer contact, and collision results.

Shall I tell you what this collision means? They who think it is accidental, unnecessary, the work of interested, of fanatical agitators, and therefore ephemeral, mistake the case altogether. It is an irrepressible conflict between opposing and enduring forces, and it means that the United States must and will sooner or later become either entirely a slaveholding nation or entirely a free-labor nation. . . .

THE WAR FOR SOUTHERN ECONOMIC INDEPENDENCE (1861): JOHN H. REAGAN

You are not content with the vast millions of tribute we pay you annually under the operation of our revenue law, our navigation laws, your fishing bounties, and by making your people our manufacturers, our merchants, our shippers. You are not satisfied with the vast tribute we pay you to build up your great cities, your railroads, your canals. . . . You are not satisfied that we of the South are almost reduced to the condition of overseers for northern capitalists. You are not satisfied with all this; but you must wage a relentless crusade against our rights and institutions. . . .

We do not intend that you shall reduce us to such a condition. But I can tell you what your folly and injustice will compel us to do. It will compel us to be free from your domination, and more self-reliant than we have been. It will compel us to assert and maintain our separate independence. It will compel us to manufacture for ourselves, to build up our own commerce, our own great cities, our own railroads and canals; and to use the tribute money we now pay you for these things for the support of a government which will be friendly to all our interests, hostile to none of them. . . .

SLAVEHOLDER'S REBELLION (1862): FREDERICK DOUGLASS

All but the willfully blind or the malignantly traitorous, know and confess that this whole movement which now so largely distracts the country, and threatens ruin to the nation, has its root and its sap, its trunk and its branches, and the bloody fruit it bears only from the one source of all abounding abomination, and that is slavery. It has sprung out of a malign selfishness and a haughty and imperious pride which only the practice of the most hateful oppression and cruelty could generate and develop. No ordinary love of gain, no ordinary love of power, could have stirred up this terrible revolt. . . . The monster was brought to its birth by pride, lust and cruelty which could not brook the sober restraints of law, order and justice. . . . When . . . I hear a man denouncing abolitionists on account of the war, I know that I am listening to a man who either does not know what he is talking about, or to one who is a traitor in disguise. . . .

There is something quite distinct and quite individual in the nature and character of this rebellion. In its motives and objects it stands entirely alone, in the annals of great social disturbances. . . . The pronounced and damning peculiarity of the present rebellion, is found in the fact, that it was conceived, undertaken, planned, and persevered in, for the guilty purpose of handing down to the latest generations the accursed system of human bondage. Its leaders have plainly told us by words as well as by deeds, that they are fighting for slavery. . . . Herein is the whole secret of the rebellion.—The plan is and was to withdraw the slave system from the hated light of liberty, and from the natural operations of free principles. While the slaveholders could hold the reins of government they could and did pervert the free principles of the Constitution to slavery, and could afford to continue in the union, but when they saw that they could no longer control the union as they had done for sixty years before, they appealed to the sword and struck for a government which should forever shut out all light from the southern conscience, and all hope of Emancipation from the southern slave. This rebellion therefore, has no point of comparison with that which has brought liberty to America, or with those of Europe, which have been undertaken from time to time, to throw off the galling yoke of despotism. It stands alone in its infamy. . . .

THE SUPPRESSION OF REBELLION BECOMES A HOLY CRUSADE (1862, 1865): ABRAHAM LINCOLN

I would save the Union. I would save it the shortest way under the Constitution. The sooner the National authority can be restored, the nearer the Union will be "the Union as it was." If there be those who would not save the Union unless they could at the same time save Slavery, I do not agree with them. If there be those who would not save the Union unless they could at the same time *destroy* Slavery, I do not agree with them. My paramount object in this struggle is to save the Union, and is not either to save or destroy Slavery. If I could save the Union without freeing any slave, I would do it; and if I could save it by freeing all the slaves, I would do it; and if I could do it by freeing some and leaving others alone, I would also do that. What I do about Slavery and the colored race, I do because I believe it helps to save this Union; and what I forbear, I forbear because I do not believe it would help to save the Union. I shall do less whenever I shall believe what I am doing hurts the cause, and I shall do more whenever I shall believe doing more will help the cause. . . . [1862]

The Almighty has His own purposes. "Woe unto the world because of offenses; for it must needs be that offenses come, but woe to that man by whom the offense cometh." If we shall suppose that American slavery is one of those offenses which in the providence of God, must needs come, but which, having continued through His appointed time; He now wills to remove, and that He gives to both North and South this terrible war as the woe due to those by whom the offense came, shall we discern therein any departure from those divine attributes which the believers in a living God always ascribe to Him? Fondly do we hope, fervently do we pray, that this mighty scourge of war may speedily pass away. Yet if God wills that it continue until all the wealth piled up by the bondsman's two hundred and fifty years of unrequited toil shall be sunk, and until every drop of blood drawn with the lash shall be paid by another drawn with the sword, as was said three thousand years ago, so still it must be said, "The judgments of the Lord are true and righteous altogether." . . . [1865]

CONFLICT OF THE CAVALIER AND THE PURITAN (1866): EDWIN A. POLLARD

No one can read aright the history of America, unless in the light of a North and a South: two political aliens existing in a Union imperfectly defined as a confederation of States. . . .

The North naturally found or imagined in slavery the leading cause of the distinctive civilization of the South, its higher sentimentalism, and its superior refinements of scholarship and manners. It revenged itself on the cause, diverted its envy in an attack upon slavery, and defamed the institution as the relic of barbarism and the sum of all villainies. But, whatever may have been the defamation of the institution of slavery, no man can write its history without recognizing contributions and naming prominent results beyond the domain of controversy. . . .

In the ante-revolutionary period, the difference between the populations of the Northern and Southern colonies had already been strongly developed. . . . There could be no congeniality between the Puritan exiles who established themselves upon the cold and rugged and cheerless soil of New England, and the Cavaliers who sought the brighter climate of the South, and drank in their baronial halls in Virginia confusion to roundheads and regicides. . . .

Slavery established in the South a peculiar and noble type of civilization. It was not without attendant vices; but the virtues which followed in its train were numerous and peculiar, and asserted general good effect of the institution on the ideas and manners of the South. . . . The South had an element in its society—a landed gentry—which the North envied, and for which its substitute was a coarse ostentatious aristocracy that smelt of the trade, and that, however it cleansed itself and aped the elegance of the South, and packed its houses with fine furniture, could never entirely subdue a sneaking sense of its inferiority. . . .

The civilization of the North was coarse and materialistic. That of the South was scant of shows, but highly refined and sentimental. . . . The agricultural pursuits of the South fixed its features; and however it might decline in the scale of gross prosperity, its people were trained in the highest civilization, were models of manners for the whole country, rivalled the sentimentalism of the oldest countries of Europe, established the only schools of honour in America, and presented a striking contrast in their well-balanced character to the conceit and giddiness of the Northern people. . . .

THE VICTIMIZED SOUTH (1881):
JEFFERSON DAVIS

The Southern States and Southern people have been sedulously represented as "propagandists" of slavery, and the Northern as the defenders and champions of universal freedom. . . .

Sectional hostility which exhibited itself in 1820, on the application of Missouri for admission into the Union, which again broke out on the proposition for the annexation of Texas in 1844, and which reappeared after the Mexican war, never again to be suppressed until its fell results had been fully accomplished, was not the consequence of any difference on the abstract question of slavery. It was the offspring of sectional rivalry and political ambition. It would have manifested itself just as certainly if slavery had existed in all the States. . . . The halls of Congress afforded the vantage-ground from which assaults were made upon these [constitutional] guarantees. The Legislatures of various Northern States enacted laws to hinder the execution of the provisions made for the rendition of fugitives from service; State officials lent their aid to the work of thwarting them; and city mobs assailed the officers engaged in . . . enforcing them. . . .

It was not the passage of the "personal liberty laws," it was not the circulation of incendiary documents, it was not the raid of John Brown, it was not the operation of unjust and unequal tariff laws, nor all combined, that constituted the intolerable grievance, but it was the systematic and persistent struggle to deprive the Southern States of equality in the Union —generally to discriminate in legislation against the interests of their people; culminating in their exclusion from the Territories, the common property of the States, as well as by the infraction of their compact to promote domestic tranquillity. . . .

What resource for justice—what assurance of tranquillity—what guarantee of safety—now remained for the South? Still forbearing, still hoping, still striving for peace and union, we waited until a sectional President, nominated by a sectional convention, elected by a sectional vote—and that the vote of a minority of the people—was about to be inducted into office. . . .

No alternative remained except to seek the security out of the Union which they had vainly tried to obtain within it. The hope of our people may be stated in a sentence. It was to escape from injury and strife in the Union, to find prosperity and peace out of it. . . .

6. Reconstruction

Andrew Johnson was a reasonably representative slaveholder and Southerner except for two significant differences: a childhood of grinding poverty which left a residue of hostility toward the great planters, and his refusal to countenance secession in 1861. Johnson loved his native state, always cherished states rights doctrines, and regarded the Negro as both constitutionally inferior and dangerous to the white man. Thaddeus Stevens, impressed by the services of Negro troops, made a relatively rare act of political imagination in suggesting extensive legislation to bring full emancipation to the freedman. The "Radical" Republican drive to bring at least partial citizenship to freedmen met with a measure of immediate success, but for a complex set of reasons ended in failure.

The Civil War did bring the legal institution of slavery to an end, and it now seems probable that only such a revolutionary situation brought about by national conflict could have accomplished the task. The collapse of slavery did not mean the substitution of freedom as the common status. The path to freedom was lined with many obstacles, not the least of which turned out to be the President. False or misleading popular stereotypes about Reconstruction are too numerous to be dealt with here, but a few are worth touching upon: at no time in any state did Negroes control all major branches of the government; Reconstruction regimes cannot be described as more "corrupt" than Northern state governments during the same era; in no state did Reconstruction governments seriously attempt to gain full political and social equality for Negroes; the average length of Reconstruction was two to three years and in several states only one year; Southern society was not and could not have been effectively controlled by the 20,000 Union soldiers scattered from Virginia to Texas; the system of segregation did not exist under slavery and was not compatible with the institution; segregation as an organized system of racial control did not come into existence immediately after the removal of Federal troops, but was rather the product of the great expanse of time between 1865 and the nineteen-thirties with a particularly intense period of activity taking place between 1895 and 1910. AUTHORS: Andrew Johnson (1808–1875) rose from poverty to Congress, the Senate, and slave-holding affluence. He elected to remain with the Union in 1861, and afterward served as War Governor of Tennessee, Vice-President, and President. Thaddeus Stevens (1792–1868), an anti-Mason and a Pennsylvania legislator, as a Congressman from 1858–1868 was an implacable enemy of slavery and race subjugation; during the last three years of his life he was a major author of Congressional Reconstruction policies. Albion W. Tourgée (1838–1905), an Ohio lawyer and Union soldier who served as a North Carolina judge during Reconstruction, alienated white Southerners by his efforts to execute his office. SELECTIONS: "The Plan to Africanize Half the Country" from Johnson's Third Annual Message to Congress, December 3, 1867. "The Need For Reconstruction" from Stevens' speech to Congress on January 3, 1867 as printed in *The Congressional Globe*. "The Ku Klux Terror" from Tourgée's *A Fool's Errand* (1879).

THE PLAN TO AFRICANIZE HALF THE COUNTRY (1867): ANDREW JOHNSON

To me the process of restoration seems perfectly plain and simple. It consists merely in a faithful application of the Constitution and laws. The execution of the laws is not now obstructed or opposed by physical force. There is no military or other necessity, real or pretended, which can prevent obedience to the Constitution, either North or South. All the rights and all the obligations of States and individuals can be protected and enforced by means perfectly consistent with the fundamental law. The courts may be everywhere open, and if open their process would be unimpeded. Crimes against the United States can be prevented or punished by the proper judicial authorities in a manner entirely practicable and legal. . . .

The plan of putting the Southern States wholly and the General Government partially into the hands of negroes is proposed at a time peculiarly unpropitious. The foundations of society have been broken up by civil war. Industry must be reorganized, justice reestablished, public credit maintained, and order brought out of confusion. To accomplish these ends would require all the wisdom and virtue of the great men who formed our institutions originally. I confidently believe that their descendants will be equal to the arduous task before them, but it is worse than madness to expect that negroes will perform it for us. Certainly we ought not to ask their assistance till we despair of our own competency.

The great difference between the two races in physical mental, and moral characteristics will prevent an amalgamation or fusion of them together in one homogeneous mass. If the inferior obtains the ascendancy over the other, it will govern with reference only to its own interests—for it will recognize no common interest—and create such a tyranny as this continent has never yet witnessed. Already the negroes are influenced by promises of confiscation and plunder. They are taught to regard as an enemy every white man who has any respect for the rights of his own race. If this continues it must become worse and worse, until all order will be subverted, all industry cease, and the fertile fields of the South grow up into a wilderness. Of all the dangers which our nation has yet encountered, none are equal to those which must result from the success of the effort . . . [now being made] to Africanize the half of our country. . . .

THE NEED FOR RECONSTRUCTION (1867):
THADDEUS STEVENS

. . . May I ask, without offense, will Congress have the courage to do its duty? Or will it be deterred by the clamor of ignorance, bigotry, and despotism from perfecting a revolution begun without their consent, but which ought not to be ended without their full participation and concurrence? Possibly the people would not have inaugurated this revolution to correct the palpable incongruities and despotic provisions of the Constitution; but having it forced upon them, will they be so unwise as to suffer it to subside without erecting this nation into a perfect Republic?

Since the surrender of the armies of the Confederate States of America a little has been done toward establishing this Government upon the true principles of liberty and justice; and but a little if we stop here. We have broken the material shackles of four million slaves. . . . But in what have we enlarged their liberty of thought? In what have we taught them the science and granted them the privilege of self-government? We have imposed upon them the privilege of fighting our battles, of dying in defense of freedom, and of bearing their equal portion of taxes; but where have we given them the privilege of ever participating in the formation of the laws for the government of their native land? By what civil weapon have we enabled them to defend themselves against oppression and injustice? Call you this liberty? Call you this a free Republic where four millions are subjects but not citizens? . . .

To reconstruct the nation, to admit new States, to guaranty republican governments to old States are all legislative acts. The President claims the right to exercise them. Congress denies it and asserts the right to belong to the legislative branch. They have determined to defend these rights against all usurpers. They have determined that while in their keeping the Constitution shall not be violated with impunity. . . . This I take to be the great question between the President and Congress. . . .

But it will be said, as it has been said, "This is negro equality"! . . . It means, as understood by honest Republicans, just this much, and no more: every man, no matter what his race or color; every earthly being who has an immortal soul, has an equal right to justice, honesty, and fair play with every other man; and the law should secure him those rights. The same law which condemms or acquits an African should condemn or acquit a white man. . . . Such is the law of God and such ought to be the law of man. This doctrine does not mean that a negro shall sit on the same seat or eat at the same table with a white man. That is a matter of taste which every man must decide for himself. The law has nothing to do with it. If there be any who are afraid of the rivalry of the black man in office or in business, I have only to advise them to try and beat their competitor in knowledge and business capacity, and there is no danger that his white neighbors will prefer his African rival to himself. . . .

THE KU KLUX TERROR (1879):
ALBION W. TOURGÉE

This new Reign of Terror had come so stilly and quietly upon the world, that none realized its fearfulness and extent. . . .

Oh! a strange, sad story is that which fills the thirteen volumes of testimony, documents and conclusions, reported by that [congressional] committee; a strange commentary upon Christian civilization; a strange history of peaceful years. . . .

Of the slain there were enough to furnish forth a battlefield . . . all killed with deliberation, overwhelmed by numbers, roused from slumber at . . . midnight, in the hall of public assembly, upon the river-brink, on the lonely woodsroads, in simulation of the public execution,—shot, stabbed, hanged, drowned, mutilated beyond description, tortured beyond conception.

And almost always by an unknown hand! Only the terrible mysterious fact of *death* was certain. Accusation by secret denunciation; sentence without hearing; execution without warning, mercy, or appeal. . . .

And then the wounded,—those who escaped the harder fate,—the whipped, the mangled, the bleeding, the torn! Men despoiled of manhood! Women gravid with dead children! bleeding backs! broken limbs! Ah! the wounded in this silent warfare were more thousands than those who groaned upon the slopes of Gettysburg! Dwellings and schools and churches burned! People driven from their homes, and dwelling in the woods and fields. . . . Well did it name itself "The Invisible Empire." Unseen and unknown! In one State ten thousand, in another twenty thousand, in another forty thousand; in all an army greater than the Rebellion, from the moldering remains of which it sprung, could ever put into the field! An Invisible Empire, with a trained and disciplined army of masked midnight marauders, making war upon the weakling "powers" which the Wise Men had set up in the lately rebellious territory!

And then the defense!—no, not the *defense,*—the excuse. . . .

"We were rebels in arms: we surrendered, and by the terms of surrender were promised immunity so long as we obeyed the laws. This meant that we should govern ourselves as of old. Instead of this, they put military officers over us; they imposed disabilities on our best and bravest; they liberated our slaves, and gave them power over us. Men born at the North came among us, and were given place and power by the votes of slaves and renegades. There were incompetent officers. The revenues of the State were squandered. We were taxed to educate the blacks. Enormous debts were contracted. We did not do these acts of violence from political motives, but only because the parties had made themselves obnoxious. . . ." It was builded upon an ineradicable sentiment of hostility to the negro *as a political integer,* and a fierce determination that the white people of the South, or a majority of that race, should rule,—if not by the power of the ballot, then by force of skill, brain, and the habit of domination. The bravest and strongest and best of the South gave it their recognition and support,—in most cases actively, in some passively. Thousands believed it a necessity to prevent anarchy and the destruction of all valuable civilization; others regarded it as a means of retaliating upon the government, which they conceived to have oppressed them; while still others looked to it as a means of acquiring place and power. . . .

The revolution had been inaugurated, and its feasibility demonstrated. Henceforth it was only a question of time as to its absolute and universal success. The rule of the majority had been overthrown, the power of the Government boldly defied, and the penalties for crime successfully evaded, that the enfranchisement of the colored man might be rendered a farce; and the obnoxious Amendments and Reconstruction legislation had been shown to be practically nullified. Read by the light of other days, the triumph of the ancient South was incredibly grand; in the then present there was little lacking to give it completeness; in the future—well, that could take care of itself. . . .

7. The Road to Reunion

Northern and Southern whites did ultimately come to a national "reconciliation." Despite great bitterness after the War and the long-range smouldering of sectional animosities, a consensus evolved well before the end of the century. Northerners returned battle flags and paid their respects to the memory of Robert E. Lee, while Southerners gladly returned to old professions of patriotism. Ex-Confederate officials served in several cabinets and former Southern officers fought with their enemies of earlier years against the Spanish in 1898. However the price of reconciliation came high; and the new consensus involved the abandonment of the drive for full citizenship for the Negro. To the North, proponents of the "New South" promised national patriotism and a major effort to reform the Southern economy by pursuing commercial values, industrialism, and diversified agriculture; but Henry W. Grady, Southern editor and publicist, insisted on white supremacy accompanied by the rigid segregation and subordination of the Negro. In time the Northern clamor for Negro rights virtually ceased; indeed, Northerners could hardly afford to be very censorious of Southerners. Although most legal disabilities of the antebellum period were eventually eliminated and existence was usually not so desperate as in the South, institutionalized segregation and exposure to private violence continued to haunt most Northern Negroes. The Supreme Court seemed to lend approval to the new national consensus in a series of cases culminating in *Plessy v. Ferguson* (1896) which accepted the principle of "separate but equal" accommodations. Under these circumstances it was not surprising that the mantle of leadership passed from the militant Frederick Douglass to the patient and compromising Booker T. Washington. Yet even at the apex of his power as the chief of Federal patronage for Negroes, the leading Negro educator, and an influential figure in the Negro press, Washington aroused the enmity of young scholars and leaders such as W. E. B. DuBois. AUTHORS: Henry

W. Grady (1850–1889), the editor of the *Atlanta Constitution*, became the chief prophet of the "New South." Booker T. Washington (1856–1915), a former slave, became an educational leader, was consulted by several Presidents, controlled a measure of political patronage and was until his death undoubtedly the most influential Negro in America. SELECTIONS: "The New South: Industrialism and White Supremacy" from a Grady speech at the Dallas State Fair on October 26, 1887. "Northern Acquiescence" from *Plessy v. Ferguson* in 1896. "Accommodation for Limited Gains" from a Washington speech of 1895, published in *The Future of the Negro* (1899).

THE NEW SOUTH: INDUSTRIALISM AND WHITE SUPREMACY (1887): HENRY W. GRADY

What shall the South do to be saved? . . .

What of the negro? This of him. I want no better friend than the black boy who was raised by my side, and who is now trudging patiently with downcast eyes and shambling figure through his lowly way in life. I want no sweeter music than the crooning of my old "mammy," now dead and gone to rest, as I heard it when she held me in her loving arms, and bending her old black face above me stole the cares from my brain and led me smiling into sleep. . . .

The clear and unmistakable domination of the white race, dominating not through violence, not through party alliance, but through the integrity of its own vote and the largeness of its sympathy and justice through which it shall compel the support of the better classes of the colored race,—that is, the hope and assurance of the South. Otherwise, the negro would be bandied from one faction to another. His credulity would be played upon, his cupidity tempted, his impulses misdirected, his passions inflamed. . . .

It is a race issue. Let us come to this point and stand here. Here the air is pure and the light is clear, and here honor and peace abide. Juggling and evasion deceives not a man. Compromise and subservience has carried not a point. There is not a white man North or South who does not feel it stir in the gray matter of his brain and throb in his heart. Not a negro who does not feel its power. It is not a sectional issue. It speaks in Ohio, and in Georgia. It speaks wherever the Anglo-Saxon touches an alien race. It has just spoken in universally approved legislation in excluding the Chinaman from our gates, not for his ignorance, vice, or corruption, but because he sought to establish an inferior race in a republic fashioned in the wisdom and defended by the blood of a homogeneous people. . . .

What of the South's industrial problem? . . . There is a figure with which history has dealt lightly, but that, standing pathetic and heroic in the genesis of our new growth, has interested me greatly—our soldier-farmer of '65. What chance had he for the future as he wandered amid his empty barns, his stock, labor, and implements gone. . . . Who would have thought . . . [then] during those lonely and terrible days as he walked behind the plow, . . . [that] he would in twenty years, having carried these burdens uncomplaining, make a crop of $800,000,000. Yet this he has done, and from his bounty the South has rebuilt her cities, and recouped her losses. . . .

With amazing rapidity she [the South] has moved away from the one-crop idea that was once her curse. . . . Every train brings manufacturers from the East and West seeking to establish themselves or their sons near the raw material and in this growing market. . . .

The South, under the rapid diversification of crops and diversification of industries, is thrilling with new life. As this new prosperity comes to us, it will bring no sweeter thought to me, and to you, my countrymen, I am sure, than that it adds not only to the comfort and happiness of our neighbors, but that it makes broader the glory and deeper the majesty, and more enduring the strength, of the Union which reigns supreme in our hearts. In this republic of ours is lodged the hope of free government on earth. . . .

NORTHERN ACQUIESCENCE: *PLESSY V. FERGUSON* (1896)

The object of the [14th] amendment was undoubtedly to enforce the absolute equality of the two races before the law, but in the nature of things it could not have been intended to abolish distinctions based upon color, or to enforce social, as distinguished from political, equality, or a commingling of the two races upon terms unsatisfactory to either. Laws permitting, and even requiring their separation in places where they are liable to be brought into contact do not necessarily imply the inferiority of either race to the other, and have been generally, if not universally, recognized as within the competency of the state legislatures in the exercise of their police power. The most common instance of this is connected with the establishment of separate schools for white and colored children, which have been held to be a valid exercise of the legislative power even by courts of states where the political rights of the colored race have been longest and most earnestly enforced. . . .

The case reduces itself to the question whether the statute of Louisiana is a reasonable regulation. . . . In determining the question of reasonableness it [the state] is at liberty to act with reference to the established usages, customs, and traditions of the people, and with a view to the promotion of their comfort, and the preservation of the public peace and good order. Gauged by this standard, we cannot say that a law which authorizes or even requires the separation of the two races in public conveyances is unreasonable. . . .

We consider the underlying fallacy of the plaintiff's argument to consist in the assumption that the enforced separation of the two races stamps the colored race with a badge of inferiority. If this be so, it is not by reason of anything found in the act, but solely because the colored race chooses to put that construction upon it. . . .

ACCOMMODATION FOR LIMITED GAINS (1895): BOOKER T. WASHINGTON

. . . . Ignorant and inexperienced, it is not strange that in the first years of our new life we began at the top instead of at the bottom; that a seat in Congress or the state legislature was sought than real estate or industrial skill; that the political convention or stump speaking had more attractions than starting a dairy farm or truck garden. . . . Our greatest danger is that in the great leap from slavery to freedom we may overlook the fact that the masses of us are to live by the productions of our hands, and fail to keep in mind that we shall prosper in proportion as we learn to dignify and glorify common labour and put brains and skill into the common occupations of life; shall prosper in proportion as we learn to draw the line between the superficial and the substantial, the ornamental gew-gaws of life and the useful. No race can prosper till it learns that that there is as much dignity in tilling a field as in writing a poem. It is at the bottom of life we must begin, and not at the top. Nor should we permit our grievances to overshadow our opportunities. . . .

The wisest among my race understand that the agitation of questions of social equality is the extremest folly, and that progress in the enjoyment of all the privileges that will come to us must be the result of severe and constant struggle rather than of artificial forcing. No race that has anything to contribute to the markets of the world is long in any degree ostracized. It is important and right that all privileges of the law be ours, but it is vastly more important that we be prepared for the exercises of these privileges. The opportunity to earn a dollar in a factory just now is worth infinitely more than the opportunity to spend a dollar in an opera-house. . . . .

. . . I pledge that in your effort to work out the great and intricate problem which God has laid at the doors of the South, you shall have at all times the patient, sympathetic help of my race; only let this be constantly in mind, that, while from representations in these buildings of the product of field, of forest, of mine, of factory, letters, and art, much good will come, yet far above and beyond material benefits will be that higher good, that, let us pray God, will come, in a blotting out of sectional differences and racial animosities and suspicions, in a determination to administer absolute justice, in a willing obedience among all classes to the mandates of law. This, coupled with our material prosperity, will bring into our beloved South a new heaven and a new earth. . . .

Chapter VIII. REALISM AND NATURALISM

LITERARY INNOVATORS IN THE DECADES AFTER THE CIVIL WAR WERE somewhat more unpopular than usual. Americans willing to accept the Grants and the Garfields as statesmen and to ignore the rapacious aspects of a phenomenal economic expansion, wished to escape the "sordid" in leisure and eagerly sought the genteel exposition of sentimental and hyper-romantic fiction, which scrupulously avoided economic, social, ethnic, and racial conflicts, sensual passion, and, indeed, most disturbing and disreputable aspects of the social world. Writers with fresh visions had difficulty making themselves heard, and the old giants of the American Renaissance no longer commanded the literary scene. Thoreau died in 1862, Hawthorne in 1864, Emerson's closing years were not greatly creative, and Melville virtually disappeared from public view after the eighteen-fifties. Walt Whitman lived until 1892, but his passionately idealistic celebration of the democratic "Kosmos" no longer seemed very relevant to a nation governed by political mediocrities and "robber barons," and possessed by an almost universal mania for wealth. This later industrial America required the perceptive pen of Mark Twain in *The Gilded Age* or the rich, sprawling social details of Theodore Dreiser in *Sister Carrie*.

The best of the early realistic novels, *The Gilded Age*, held a mirror to commercial America, and presented an easily recognizable image in the "free-wheeling" financial speculator, Beriah Sellers. Unfortunately, Twain did not continue to work in this vein, and the honor of the first sustained career devoted to the realistic social novel belonged to William Dean Howells. While Howells was to an extent both a victim and an advocate of the genteel tradition with its insistence on the moral purity of young girls as a basic concern of literature, he nevertheless produced significant works of fiction with accurate portrayals of American domestic life. The social novel gained a larger scope and commanded a greater talent in the novels of Henry James. An artist's intense devotion to an authentic exploration

of the social world, a willingness to learn from a Flaubert or a Tur-
genev, and an insistence on the freedom of the novelist to work with
any aspect of human life, helped to make James a great writer. In
spite of his preference for the social *haute monde* and his customary
avoidance of the world of the flesh, he defended the right of the
novelist to deal with prostitutes or countesses, raw provincialism or
the cosmopolitan world.

Many pioneer realists were drawn by precisely those themes
which failed to attract James. The raw pungency and the provincial
earthiness of American life inspired the "local colorists" and the
regional writers to depict the humor of Georgia "crackers," the mores
of California mining camp prostitutes, the grotesque exaggerations of
Southwestern yarn spinners, or the speech of Ozark mountaineers.
The quality of this literature varied from the more banal *Pike County
Ballads* of John Hay to the one undisputed work of genius in the
genre, Mark Twain's *Huckleberry Finn*. Twain demonstrated the
potential value of dialect speech and "provincial" themes in writings
which are filled with the vitality of backwoods American life.

To another substantial body of American authors, the backwoods suggested bitter isolation or provincial barbarism rather than
freedom and vitality. Hamlin Garland recalled a desolate childhood
in the sod huts of the Great Plains, and other writers were even more
critical of the villages and towns which dominated the Midwest after
the passing of the frontier. This "revolt against the village" gathered
strength with Edgar Howe's early writings and reached its apex in the
twentieth century with Edgar Lee Master's *Spoon River Anthology*
and Sinclair Lewis's *Main Street*.

American literature appropriated new intellectual insights in the
"naturalistic" fiction of men such as Jack London, Frank Norris,
Stephen Crane, and Theodore Dreiser. These men varied a great deal
in temperament and artistic outlook, but a majority shared common
experiences and intellectual idols: they often had been journalists
with an intimate knowledge of commercial morality and of life
among the urban lower classes; they rejected the moralizing, sentimental pathos of popular American fiction and insisted on a "tough-
minded" study of human nature in which fear, hunger, and sex
played major roles; they admired the clinical detachment of European novelists such as Emile Zola, and studied the Darwinians to
exploit biological determinism or Nietzsche to learn about the will
to life and power. Jack London gave expression to a number of quasi-
scientific theories drawn from biology and philosophy. A socialist and

a student of Nietzsche who specialized in the portrayal of primitive instincts, biological struggle, and class war, London united Marx and the Superman with a boisterous "realism." The sustained celebration of power in *The Sea Wolf* or *The Call of the Wild* was inevitable in a writer for whom life was a struggle for survival and strength the only source of virtue. Frank Norris also regarded violence as characteristic in a human world driven by physical nature. Like his French literary master, Emile Zola, Norris was haunted by the animality of man, and in *McTeague* created the portrait of a "brute" dominated by his instinctive drives, victimized by economic deterioration, and ruined by an atavistic surrender to greed.

Stephen Crane and Theodore Dreiser were less doctrinaire and more talented. No subject was taboo for Crane, who presented a memorable gallery of prostitutes, adventurers, fear-ridden soldiers,— all helpless before human nature or social conditions and set adrift in a universe which was indifferent, yet somehow implacably hostile. Dreiser's favorite themes were the provincial man on the rise toward fortune or the successful man on the downgrade toward tragic failure. With a keen eye for realistic detail and a desire to describe exhaustively all that he observed, Dreiser created sprawling fictional canvasses of a disaster-ridden social world with a grimness only partly relieved by the author's compassion. Dreiser, like many other writers, lived in a "naturalistic" world of industrial and urban conflict, modern science and warfare, in the shadow of sensibilities shaped through a generation of violent proclamations by Social Darwinists.

1. New Approaches to Literature

William Dean Howells shared with his age an aversion for "gutter" literature, but a persistently troublesome aesthetic conscience led him away from "the genteel tradition" and toward the realistic portrayal of social types and relations. The careful presentation of the family life of a paint king, Silas Lapham, was a milestone in the development of American realism. Eventually Howells, troubled by urban slums and working-class poverty, became a socialist and attempted to advance the cause of reform through his novels. While Howells dealt with literary problems posed by a turbulently changing America, James sought an outlet for his more significant talent abroad. He became the most serious and skillful

American literary craftsman of his generation, and none of the "realists" could match his determination to present with artful precision and artless subtlety the shades of emotion and action in the social lives of the Englishmen, Frenchmen, and "international" Americans whom he observed. AUTHORS: Henry James (1843–1916), the son of a Swedenborgian reformer and the brother of a famous Pragmatic philosopher, did not find in America an acceptable literary haven, and wrote most of his novels while living in England. William Dean Howells (1837–1920), a native of Ohio, became one of the first citizens of Boston as editor of *The Atlantic Monthly*, a task which he eventually abandoned for life in New York and a more complete absorption in his own writing. SELECTIONS: "On the Art of Fiction" from James' *Partial Portraits* (1884). "The Simple, the Natural, the Honest" from Howells' *Criticism and Fiction* (1891).

ON THE ART OF FICTION (1884): HENRY JAMES

The old superstition about fiction being "wicked" has doubtless died out in England; but the spirit of it lingers. . . . Even the most jocular novel feels in some degree the weight of the proscription that was formerly directed against literary levity. . . .

The old evangelical hostility to the novel, which was as explicit as it was narrow, and which regarded it as little less favourable to our immortal part than a stage-play, was in reality far less insulting. The only reason for the existence of a novel is that it does attempt to represent life. When it relinquishes this attempt, the same attempt that we see on the canvas of the painter, it will have arrived at a very strange pass. . . .

A novel is in its broadest definition a personal, a direct impression of life: that, to begin with, constitutes its value, which is greater or less according to the intensity of the impression. But there will be no intensity at all, and therefore no value, unless there is freedom to feel and say. The tracing of a line to be followed, of a tone to be taken, of a form to be filled out, is a limitation of that freedom and a suppression of the very thing that we are most curious about. The form, it seems to me, is to be appreciated after the fact: then the author's choice has been made, his standard has been indicated; then we can follow lines and directions and compare tones and resemblances. Then in a word we can enjoy one of the most charming of pleasures, we can estimate quality, we can apply the test of execution. The execution belongs to the author alone; it is what is most personal to him, and we measure him by that. . . .

It goes without saying that you will not write a good novel unless you possess the sense of reality; but it will be difficult to give you a recipe for calling that sense into being. Humanity is immense, and reality has a myriad forms; the most one can affirm is that some of the flowers of fiction have the odour of it, and others have not; as for telling you in advance how your nosegay should be composed, that is another affair. . . . Experience is never limited, and it is never complete; it is an immense sensibility, a kind of huge spiderweb of the finest silken threads suspended in the chamber of consciousness, and catching every air-borne particle in its tissue. It is the very atmosphere of the mind; and when the mind is imaginative—much more when it happens to be that of a man of genius—it takes to itself the faintest hints of life, it converts the very pulses of the air into revelations. . . . Art derives a considerable part of its beneficial exercise from flying in the face of presumptions, and some of the most interesting experiments of which it is capable are hidden in the bosom of common things. Gustave Flaubert has written a story about the devotion of a servant-girl to a parrot, and the production, highly finished as it is, cannot on the whole be called a success. We are perfectly free to find it flat, but I think it might have been interesting; and I, for my part, am extremely glad he should have written it; it is a contribution to our knowledge of what can be done—or what cannot. Ivan Turgenieff has written a tale about a deaf and dumb serf and a lap-dog, and the thing is touching, loving, a little masterpiece. He struck the note of life where Gustave Flaubert missed it—he flew in the face of a presumption and achieved a victory. . . .

THE SIMPLE, THE NATURAL, THE HONEST, (1891): WILLIAM DEAN HOWELLS

The young writer who attempts to report the phrase and carriage of every-day life, who tries to tell just how he has heard men talk and seen them look, is made to feel guilty of something low and unworthy by the stupid people who would like to have him show how Shakespeare's men talked and looked, or Scott's, or Thackeray's or Balzac's, or Hawthorne's or Dickens's; he is instructed to idealize his personages, that is, to take the life-likeness out of them, and put the book-likeness into them. He is approached in the spirit of the wretched pedantry into which learning, much or little, always decays when it withdraws itself and stands apart from experience in an attitude of imagined superiority. . . .

As I said, I hope the time is coming when not only the artist, but the common, average man, who always "has the standard of the arts in his power," will have also the courage to apply it, and will reject the ideal [object] wherever he finds it, in science, in literature, in art, because it is not "simple, natural, and honest." . . . Now we are beginning to see and to say that no author is an authority except in those moments when he held his ear close to Nature's lips and caught her very accent. These moments are not continuous with any authors in the past, and they are rare with all. Therefore I am not afraid to say now that the greatest classics are sometimes not at all great, and that we can profit by them only when we hold them, like our meanest contemporaries, to a strict accounting, and verify their work by the standard of the arts which we all have in our power, the simple, the natural, and the honest. . . .

In life . . . [the realist] finds nothing insignificant; all tells for destiny and character; nothing that God has made is contemptible. He cannot look upon human life and declare this thing or that thing unworthy of notice, any more than the scientist can declare a fact of the material world beneath the dignity of his inquiry. He feels in every nerve the equality of things and the unity of men; his soul is exalted, not by vain shows and shadows and ideals, but by realities, in which alone the truth lives. In criticism it is his business to break the images of false gods and misshapen heroes, or take away the poor silly toys that many grown people would still like to play with. He cannot keep terms with Jack the Giant-killer or Puss in Boots, under any name or in any place, even when they reappear as the convict Vautrec, or the Marquis de Montrivaut, or the Sworn Thirteen Noblemen. He must say to himself that Balzac, when he imagined these monsters, was not Balzac, he was Dumas; he was not realistic, he was romantic. . . .

2. Revolt Against the Village

For many writers between 1880 and 1930, Mark Twain's presentation of the sweep, grandeur, and freedom of life on the frontier and the Mississippi must have seemed a swan song announcing the end of an age. If local colorists and regional novelists had found and continued to find rich literary materials in the backwoods farms and remote towns, other writers associated prairies and villages with sterile loneliness and hostile reactions against civilized values. Edgar Lee Masters attempted to demonstrate the prevalence of hostile attitudes toward aesthetic values and emotional authenticity; and Sinclair Lewis made "Main Street" and "Babbitt" terms of opprobrium throughout the Western world. AUTHORS: Edgar Lee Masters (1869–1950) practiced law successfully for twenty-four years before publishing Spoon River Anthology, which was followed by other volumes of poetry. Sinclair Lewis (1885–1951), born at Sauk Center, Minnesota and educated at Yale University, was the first American writer to earn a Nobel Prize. SELECTIONS: From Spoon River Anthology, Masters' collection of 1915. "Main Street" from Lewis' preface to Main Street (1920).

FROM SPOON RIVER ANTHOLOGY
(1915): EDGAR LEE MASTERS

SETH COMPTON

When I died, the circulating library
Which I built up for Spoon River,
And managed for the good of inquiring minds,
Was sold at auction on the public square
As if to destroy the last vestige
Of my memory and influence.
For those of you who could not see the virtue
Of knowing Volney's "Ruins" as well as Butler's
        "Analogy"
And "Faust" as well as "Evangeline,"
Were really the power in the village,
And often you asked me,
"What is the use of knowing the evil in the world?"
I am out of your way now, Spoon River,
Choose your own good and call it good.
For I could never make you see
That no one knows what is good
Who knows not what is evil;
And no one knows what is true
Who knows not what is false.

ARCHIBALD HIGBIE

I loathed you, Spoon River. I tried to rise above
        you,
I was ashamed of you. I despised you
As the place of my nativity.
And there in Rome, among the artists,
Speaking Italian, speaking French,
I seemed at times to be free
Of every trace of my origin.
I seemed to be reaching the heights of art
And to breathe the air that the masters breathed,
And to see the world with their eyes.
But still they'd pass my work and say:
"What are you driving at, my friend?
Sometimes the face looks like Apollo's,
At others it has a trace of Lincoln's."

There was no culture, you know, in Spoon
   River,
And I burned with shame and held my peace.
And what could I do, all covered over
And weighted down with western soil,
Except aspire, and pray for another
Birth in the world, with all of Spoon River
Rooted out of my soul?

MAIN STREET (1920): SINCLAIR LEWIS

This is America—a town of a few thousand, in a region of wheat and corn and dairies and little groves.

The town is, in our tale, called "Gopher Prairie, Minnesota." But its Main Street is the continuation of Main Streets everywhere. The story would be the same in Ohio or Montana, in Kansas or Kentucky or Illinois, and not very differently would it be told Up York State or in the Carolina hills.

Main Street is the climax of civilization. That this Ford car might stand in front of the Bon Ton Store, Hannibal invaded Rome and Erasmus wrote in Oxford cloisters. What Ole Jenson the grocer says to Ezra Stowbody the banker is the new law for London, Prague, and the unprofitable isles of the sea; whatsoever Ezra does not know and sanction, that thing is heresy, worthless for knowing and wicked to consider.

Our railway station is the final aspiration of architecture. Sam Clark's annual hardware turnover is the envy of the four counties which constitute God's Country. In the sensitive art of the Rosebud Movie Palace there is a Message, and humor strictly moral.

Such is our comfortable tradition and sure faith. Would he not betray himself an alien cynic who should otherwise portray Main Street, or distress the citizens by speculating whether there may not be other faiths? . . .

3. *Realistic and Naturalistic Literature*

William Dean Howells was determined to write realistically about the themes which he selected, but his range of interest was narrow, his taboos numerous, and the claims of the "genteel tradition" too influential to allow him full scope as a realist. Mark Twain's use of dialect speech and common social life enabled him to exploit his literary opportunities more effectively. The pessimistic determinism of Twain's later years linked him with the naturalists, but neither realism nor naturalism could lay full claim to his talent. The "revolt against the village" expanded the range of realistic fiction greatly. Through the naturalists—Stephen Crane, Frank Norris, Jack London, and Theodore Dreiser—Darwinian concepts as well as the ideology and the themes of French realism entered American literature. The naturalists made war on sexual taboos with particular relish: Crane's Maggie, Dreiser's Sister Carrie, Norris' Trina (in McTeague), London's Klondike women were offspring of Zola's Nana and ancestors of the "primitive," "elemental" women of popular twentieth-century fiction. To present men and women as hapless victims of an indifferent universe, of a brutalizing society, or of the animal essence of human nature were common naturalistic approaches. American and French writers were pleased by the concept of the writer as scientist, dispassionately examining human life under the microscope of an objective mind, and naturalistic heroes become recognizable types: Dreiser's tycoons and success-driven clerks, Crane's bewildered soldiers, Norris' helpless farmers imprisoned by their own wheatfields, and London's men and women who quickly shed the thin veneer of civilization to return to the conflicts "red of tooth and claw" which were the raw materials of biological evolution. AUTHORS: Stephen Crane (1871–1900) crowded into his short life experiences as a war reporter, an adventurer, and a successful writer. Theodore Dreiser (1871–1945), the son of a German immigrant business man, knew poverty in his youth, held a series of odd jobs in Chicago, and worked as a reporter before returning to serious writing and in time becoming the most celebrated of the American naturalists. SELECTIONS: "A Coldly Indifferent Universe" from Crane's The Black Rider (1895), and War Is Kind (1899). "An American Tragedy" from Dreiser's novel (1925).

A COLDLY INDIFFERENT UNIVERSE (1895, 1899): STEPHEN CRANE

1

God fashioned the ship of the world carefully.
With the infinite skill of an All-Master
Made He the hull and the sails,
Held He the rudder
Ready for adjustment.
Erect stood He, scanning His work proudly.

Then—at fateful time—a wrong called,
And God turned, heeding.
Lo, the ship, at this opportunity, slipped slyly,
Making cunning noiseless travel down the ways.
So that, for ever rudderless, it went upon the seas
Going ridiculous voyages,
Making quaint progress,
Turning as with serious purpose
Before stupid winds.
And there were many in the sky
Who laughed at this thing.

2

Should the wide world roll away,
Leaving black terror,
Limitless night,
Nor God, nor man, nor place to stand
Would be to me essential,
If thou and thy white arms were there,
And the fall to doom a long way.

3

Do not weep, maiden, for war is kind.
Because your lover threw wild hands toward the sky
And the affrighted steed ran on alone,
Do not weep.
War is kind.
    Hoarse, booming drums of the regiment,
    Little souls who thirst for fight,
    These men were born to drill and die.
    The unexplained glory flies above them,
    Great is the battle-god, great, and his kingdom—
    A field where a thousand corpses lie.
Do not weep, babe, for war is kind.
Because your father tumbled in the yellow trenches,
Raged at his breast, gulped and died,
Do not weep.
War is kind. . . .

4

The wayfarer,
Perceiving the pathway to truth,
Was struck with astonishment.
It was thickly grown with weeds.

"Ha," he said,
"I see that none has passed here
"In a long time."
Later he saw that each weed
Was a singular knife.
"Well," he mumbled at last,
"Doubtless there are other roads."

5

A man said to the universe:
"Sir, I exist!"
"However," replied the universe,
"The fact has not created in me
"A sense of obligation."

6

The trees in the garden rained flowers.
Children ran there joyously.
They gathered the flowers
Each to himself.
Now there were some
Who gathered great heaps—
Having opportunity and skill—
Until, behold, only chance blossoms
Remained for the feeble.
Then a little spindling tutor
Ran importantly to the father, crying:
"Pray, come hither!
See this unjust thing in your garden!"
But when the father had surveyed,
He admonished the tutor:
"Not so, small sage!
This thing is just.
For, look you,
Are not they who possess the flowers
Stronger, bolder, shrewder
Than they who have none?
Why should the strong—
The beautiful strong—
Why should they not have the flowers?"
Upon reflection, the tutor bowed to the ground,
"My lord," he said,
"The stars are displaced
By this towering wisdom."

AN AMERICAN TRAGEDY (1925):
THEODORE DREISER

Two incidents which occurred at this time tended still more to sharpen the contrary points of view holding between Clyde and Roberta. One of these was no more than a glimpse which Roberta had one evening of Clyde pausing at the Central Avenue curb in front of the post-office to say a few words to Arabella Stark, who in a large and impressive-looking car, was waiting for her father who was still in the Stark Building opposite. And Miss Stark, fashionably outfitted according to the season, her world and her own pretentious taste, was affectedly posed at the wheel, not only for the benefit of Clyde but the public in general. And to Roberta, who by now was reduced to the verge of distraction between Clyde's delay and her determination to compel him to act in her behalf, she appeared to be little less than an epitome of all the security, luxury and freedom from responsibility which so enticed and hence caused Clyde to delay and be as indifferent as possible to the dire state which confronted her. For, alas, apart from this claim of her condition [pregnancy], what had she to offer him comparable to all he would be giving up in case he acceded to her request? Nothing—a thought which was far from encouraging.

Yet, at this moment contrasting her own wretched and neglected state with that of this Miss Stark, for example, she found herself a prey to an even more complaining and antagonistic mood than had hitherto characterized her. It was not right. It was not fair. For during the several weeks that had passed since last they had discussed this matter, Clyde had scarcely said a word to her at the factory or elsewhere, let alone called upon her at her room, fearing as he did the customary inquiry which he could not satisfy. And this caused her to feel that not only was he neglecting but resenting her most sharply. . . .

On the other hand, Clyde, and at approximately this same time, was called upon to witness a scene identified with Roberta, which, as some might think, only an ironic and even malicious fate could have intended or permitted to come to pass. For motoring north the following Sunday to Arrow Lake, . . . the party on nearing Biltz, . . . was compelled to detour east in the direction of Roberta's home. And coming finally to a north and south road which ran directly from Trippettsville past the Alden farm, they turned north into that. And a few minutes later, came directly to the corner adjoining the Alden farm, where an east and west road led to Biltz. Here Tracy Trumbull . . . requested that some one . . . inquire . . . as to whether this road did lead to Biltz. And Clyde, being nearest to one door, jumped out. And then, glancing at the name on the mail-box which stood at the junction and evidently belonged to the extremely dilapidated old farm-house on the rise above, he was not a little astonished to note that the name was that of Titus Alden—Roberta's father. Also, as it instantly came to him, since she had described her parents as being near Biltz, this must be her home. . . . Again the mere identification of this lorn, dilapidated realm with Roberta and hence himself, was sufficient to cause him to wish to turn and run.

But Sondra, who was sitting next him in the car and now noting his hesitation, called: 'What's the matter, Clyde? Afraid of the bow-wow?' . . . But the effect of this house, once he contemplated it thoroughly, was sufficient to arouse in his brain the most troubled and miserable of thoughts. For what a house, to be sure! So lonely and bare, even in this bright, spring weather! The decayed and sagging roof. The broken chimney to the north—rough lumps of cemented field stones lying at its base; the sagging and semi-toppling chimney to the south, sustained in place by a log chain. The unkempt path from the road below, which slowly he ascended! He was not a little dejected by the broken and displaced stones which served as steps before the front door. And the unpainted dilapidated outbuildings, all the more dreary because of these others.

'Gee!' To think that this was Roberta's home. And to think, in the face of all that he now aspired to in connection with Sondra and this social group at Lycurgus, she should be demanding that he marry her! And Sondra in the car with him here to see—if not know. The poverty! The reduced grimness of it all. How far he had traveled away from just such a beginning as this!

With a weakening and sickening sensation at the pit of his stomach, as of some blow administered there, he now approached the door. And then, as if to further distress him, if that were possible, the door was opened by Titus Alden, who, in an old, thread-bare and out-at-elbows coat, as well as baggy, worn, jean trousers and rough, shineless, ill-fitting country shoes, desired by his look to know what he wanted. And Clyde, being taken aback by the clothes, as well as a marked resemblance to Roberta about the eyes and mouth, now as swiftly as possible asked if the east and west road below ran through Biltz and joined the main highway north. . . .

For, as he now recalled, and with an enormous sense of depression, Roberta was thinking and at this very time, that soon now, and in the face of all Lycurgus had to offer him—Sondra—the coming spring and summer—the love and romance, gayety, position, power—he was going to give all that up and go away with and marry her. Sneak away to some out-of-the-way place! Oh, how horrible! And with a child at his age! Oh, why had he ever been so foolish and weak as to identify himself with her in this intimate way? Just because of a few lonely evenings! Oh, why, why couldn't he have waited and then this other world would have opened up to him just the same? If only he could have waited!

And now unquestionably, unless he could speedily and easily disengage himself from her, all this other splendid recognition would be destined to be withdrawn from him, and this other world from which he sprang might extend its gloomy, poverty-stricken arms to him and envelop him once more, just as the poverty of his family had enveloped and almost strangled him from the first. . . . [Later Roberta drowns and Clyde is held responsible.]

Chapter IX. SOCIAL DARWINISM

WHILE THE ECHOES OF JOHN BROWN'S RAID WERE STILL REVERBERATING across the nation, New York, Boston, and Philadelphia booksellers received the first copies of a book which made all of nature resemble an eternal battlefield far bloodier than Bull Run or Antietam. The parade of violence and catastrophe lay partly concealed behind the precise terminology, the air of detachment, and the careful scientific reasoning of Charles Darwin's *Origin of Species*, and the Civil War absorbed too much energy and attention to allow time for debates over a monograph in biology. Yet Americans in the generation to come were to hear much about nature "red of tooth and claw" which bred creatures with reckless fecundity into a world able to support only the victorious survivors of the unrelenting struggle for existence. Darwin's scientific detachment seemed to keep the question distant from the daily concerns of men; and the intellectual pioneers who extended Darwin's ideas to history and politics began by assuring their readers that evolution constituted a benevolent force which inflicted pain on individuals here and there only in order to thrust the human race through social struggle and competition toward a future bright beyond all past speculations.

In the very beginning neither Darwin nor the Social Darwinists won many victories. Even some of the naturalists refused to concede the scientific case to Darwin. If American scientists such as Asa Gray, the Harvard botanist, came early into the fray on the side of evolution, other scientists followed the Harvard geologist and paleontologist, Louis Agassiz, in marshalling all the available scientific arguments against Darwin. Theologians and clerics in far higher percentages, fearful for the Book of Genesis, denounced the concept of the evolutionary emergence of species, and rushed to man the fundamentalist ramparts for the defense of Creation as God's special act. The literalists already faced external danger from the secular forces of industrialism and urbanism and the internal menace posed by the theological investigations of "the Higher Criticism" which threatened many traditional articles of faith. For all the impassioned attacks on Darwinism, many of the churches and clerics were vulnerable, and each decade increased the number of theologians who wished to reconcile evolution and theology. Often ministers, like other educated men, came to embrace the new ideas after reading the books and articles of proselytizers such as John Fiske. The popularizers set out to make converts for new ideas about man's origins, the beginnings of life on the planet, and the implications of Darwinism for economics, history, law, literature, philosophy, and religion. By the end of the nineteenth century, most educated Americans had quietly set aside Genesis or at least amended the theory of the special creation by God of Adam and Eve, the beasts, and the birds, so as to make possible the acceptance of cosmic and biological evolution. Darwinism fascinated thoughtful men much as the Newtonian explanation of the cosmos had a century and a half earlier. Few American theologians could remain completely indifferent to the victories of the popularizers and the scientists. Some, like the Presbyterian President of Princeton, James McCosh, accepted the new theories fairly early and set to work explaining how the evolutionary process expressed God's will and activity.

Economists and sociologists were more interested in the applications of Darwinism to their own disciplines and to anthropology, politics, and history. Many scholars joined William Graham Sumner, the Yale economics professor, in seeking intellectual guidance in the philosophical treatises of Herbert Spencer rather than in the monographs of Darwin. Spencer applied the evolutionary approach to the entire cosmos as well as to the human society. Spencer and Sumner defended "social selection" as the mechanism of progress, and argued for the competitive struggles of laissez-faire capitalism which allowed the economically "fit" to gain the rewards of victory and the "unfit" industrial poor to experience the penalties of defeat. Sumner was particularly insistent on allowing the industrial tycoon to enjoy his rich rewards and on rejecting the "irresponsible" interference of reformers and planners who proposed the impossible task of setting aside through legislation the iron laws of social evolution. Herbert Spencer, equally sympathetic toward the masters of capital, enjoyed an enormous popularity in America, and industrial magnates such as Andrew Carnegie and John D. Rockefeller commonly used the formula of Spencer and Sumner to justify wealth as the creation of the gloriously "fit" winners in the great economic competition, to ascribe long hours and short wages, unemployment, and high mortal-

ity rates among the industrial poor to their lack of moral and economic fitness. The notion that economic progress guaranteed the
progress of American society, and perhaps the progress of the entire
human race, became a very popular pattern of explanation among
upper- and middle-class Americans in the age of Social Darwinism.

The pervasive influence of evolutionary concepts conquered
great numbers of citizens as well as the scholarly elite, statesmen,
anthropologists, philologians, and jurists. Without evolutionary
thought one finds it difficult to imagine the emergence of pragmatic
philosophy, the new directions in American law initiated by Oliver
Wendell Holmes and others, and the emergence of anthropology
under the direction of men such as Lewis Henry Morgan. A native of
New York state, a lawyer as well as an anthropologist, and a coun-
selor to the Iroquois Indians, Morgan was particularly qualified to
apply the Darwinian approach to the historical evolution of cultures.
The Pragmatists spread their philosophical nets even more broadly by
placing philosophy, meaning, and even truth itself in an evolutionary
framework. A narrower application, but one of profound significance
to American society was the use of Spencer's philosophy by Justices
of the Supreme Court to defend the power and privileges of corporations. However, as reform theorists eventually discovered, the razor of
evolutionary thought could cut both ways. Oliver Wendell Holmes
reminded his fellow judges that opinions, ideas, and economic philosophies were themselves subject to the evolutionary process. If
Spencer argued that economic competition provided the mechanism
of social evolution, Holmes replied that other mechanisms might
emerge and that *laissez-faire* ideas had to struggle for survival against
reform concepts which might ultimately turn out to be victoriously
"fit."

Holmes' analogy was an apt one for an age which spawned a
great many versions of the social struggle. Negrophobes stressed racial
conflict and urged the need for white supremacy and purity; California politicians accepted the idea of racial struggle but argued that
the great danger came from the "yellow peril" of Oriental hordes
about to descend on America; and still other publicists warned of
racial dangers to the Anglo-Saxons, or Nordics, or old American
stock, or the superior American branch of the Anglo-German racial
defenders of liberty and pure Christianity. In time even the enemies
of corporate power, chauvinism, and racism discovered ways of using
evolutionary doctrine. Cooperation, they argued, characterized nature
more commonly than competition. Members of the same species did

not engage in a suicidal struggle for existence, but rather survived through cooperative techniques. In any case, man had an advantage over other species in his ability to control the process of social evolution. Classes, members of the same society, perhaps all of mankind, might by social planning and "controlled" evolution eliminate competition and poverty. After this fashion many social critics and reformers of the Progressive era were to argue their case.

1. The Scientific Background

A century of research and speculation in geology, biology, and philosophy came to a culmination in Charles Darwin's The Origin of Species. Evolution was to be the dominant idea in almost every intellectual realm between the Civil War and the First World War, and the singular importance of Darwin's book sprang from a weight of evidence so overwhelming as to make the rejection of biological evolution extremely difficult. The impressive quantity of data in The Origin of Species supported two major findings: (1) the Malthusian observation that population increases more rapidly than food supply, and that in the inevitable struggle of overly numerous creatures for the limited means of existence, those who are biologically the fittest survive; and (2) the biological process continually produces new variations and those variations persist through time which makes possible a superior adjustment to environment or successful competition against rival organisms. AUTHOR: Charles Darwin (1809–1882), a grandson of the eighteenth-century biologist, Erasmus Darwin, abandoned medical education to become the official naturalist on the celebrated voyage of the Beagle in South American and Pacific waters. This voyage and later investigations enabled Darwin to expound the concept of evolution in The Origin of Species and The Descent of Man. SELECTION: "Natural Selection" from Darwin's Origin of Species (1859).

NATURAL SELECTION (1859): CHARLES DARWIN

If during the long course of ages and under varying conditions of life, organic beings vary at all in the several parts of their organisation, and I think this cannot be disputed; if there be, owing to the high geometrical ratio of increase of each species, a severe struggle for life at some age, season, or year, and this certainly cannot be disputed; then, considering

the infinite complexity of the relations of all organic beings to each other
and to their conditions of existence, causing an infinite diversity in structure, constitution, and habits, to be advantageous to them, I think it
would be a most extraordinary fact if no variation ever had occurred
useful to each being's own welfare, in the same manner as so many
variations have occurred useful to man. But if variations useful to any
organic being do occur, assuredly individuals thus characterised will have
the best chance of being preserved in the struggle for life; and from the
strong principle of inheritance they will tend to produce offspring similarly characterised. This principle of preservation, I have called, for the
sake of brevity, Natural Selection; and it leads to the improvement of
each creature in relation to its organic and inorganic conditions of life.

Natural selection, on the principle of qualities being inherited at
corresponding ages, can modify the egg, seed, or young, as easily as the
adult. Amongst many animals, sexual selection will give its aid to ordinary
selection, by assuring to the most vigorous and best adapted males the
greatest number of offspring. Sexual selection will also give characters
useful to the males alone, in their struggles with other males.

Whether natural selection has really thus acted in nature, in modifying and adapting the various forms of life to their several conditions and
stations, must be judged of by the general tenor and balance of evidence
given in the following chapters. But we already see how it entails extinction; and how largely extinction has acted in the world's history, geology
plainly declares. Natural selection, also, leads to divergence of character;
for more living beings can be supported on the same area the more they
diverge in structure, habits, and constitution, of which we see proof by
looking to the inhabitants of any small spot or to naturalised productions.
Therefore during the modification of the descendants of any one species,
and during the incessant struggle of all species to increase in numbers, the
more diversified these descendants become, the better will be their
chance of succeeding in the battle for life. . . .

2. The Darwinian Impact on Religion

While a few scientists and theologians protested during the eighteen-
sixties, public controversy did not really begin until after Darwin brought
man into the context of biological struggle in *The Descent of Man*
(1871). Many American scientists felt the need to cope with the major
theological issues, particularly those related to God's creation of the
cosmos. Louis Agassiz bordered on heresy when he insisted that only
multiple creations by God could explain the great diversity of species, but

his attacks on Darwinian evolution still won a warm welcome in some religious quarters. Asa Gray, who argued for the acceptance of Darwin, insisted that evolution properly understood pointed to the existence of divine design in nature. The militant popularizer, John Fiske, wished to "consign" the idea of God's special creation "to oblivion" along with other Scriptural statements about "physics" and "biology." A more representative path to the acceptance of evolution was provided by James McCosh who argued for the evolutionary process as an instrument of God's purpose. Even McCosh, however, balked at the complete inclusion of man in the evolutionary process, and the general controversy continued for many decades in universities and theological seminaries, in press and pulpit, town hall and private parlor. AUTHORS: Louis Agassiz (1807–1873), Swiss-born scientist and educator, continued the work of his friends Cuvier and Humboldt when he came to the United States in 1846. He became professor of natural history at Harvard, exerted great influence as a teacher, and lectured to large audiences throughout the east. Asa Gray (1810–1888) was in his time the leading American botanist and Agassiz's foremost opponent in the debate over evolution. James McCosh (1811–1894), Scottish-born educator and philosopher and Princeton President, advocated belief in intuition and the philosophy of the Scottish school of Common-Sense. John Fiske (1842–1901), professor of History at Washington University, was the leading American popularizer of Darwinism. SELECTIONS: "The Book of Genesis Upheld" from an Agassiz article in *The Christian Examiner* (1860). "Darwinism Supports the Theistic View of Nature" from Gray's *Darwinia: Essays and Reviews Pertaining to Darwinism* (1876). "God Works Through Evolution" from McCosh, *The Religious Aspect of Evolution* (1888). "Consign the Special Creation Hypothesis to Limbo" from Fiske's "The Destiny of Man" in *The Writings of John Fiske*, XXI (1902).

THE BOOK OF GENESIS UPHELD (1860): LOUIS AGASSIZ

We know so little respecting the first appearance of organized beings in general. . . . Investigation into the ways of nature, into the ways of the Creator, and into the circumstances under which organized beings were created, is a question wholly disconnected with religion, belonging entirely to the department of natural history. But, at the same time, we deny that, in the view which we take of these questions, there is anything contradicting the records in Genesis.

We may go farther to show that a common character by no means proves common descent . . . by comparing the different species of that so large genus, the cats, in which the wild-cat, the panther, the leopard, tiger, lion, and all the numerous species of this group, having such similar natural dispositions, with the same structure, were yet constituted as so many distinct species, unconnected in their genealogy.

The comparisons made between monkeys and men by comparative anatomists, when tracing the gradations in nature, have been greatly misunderstood by those who have concluded that, because there were no other types between the highest monkeys and men, these highest monkeys were something intermediate between men and beasts; or that some race particularly disagreeable to those writers was something intermediate between monkeys and human beings. These links between mankind and the animal creation are only the great steps indicating the gradation established by the Creator among living beings and they no more indicate a relation between men and monkeys, than between monkeys and beasts of prey. . . .

DARWINISM SUPPORTS THE THEISTIC VIEW OF NATURE (1876): ASA GRAY

We have only to say that the Darwinian system, as we understand it, coincides well with the theistic view of Nature. It not only acknowledges purpose . . . but builds upon it, and if purpose in this sense does not of itself imply design, it is certainly compatible with it, and suggestive of it. Difficult as it may be to conceive and impossible to demonstrate design in a whole of which the series of parts appear to be contingent: the alternative may be yet more difficult and less satisfactory. If all Nature is of a piece—as modern physical philosophy insists—then it seems clear that design must in some way, and in some sense, pervade the system or be wholly absent from it. Of the alternatives, the predication of design—special, general or universal, as the case may be—is most natural to the mind; while the exclusion of it throughout . . . runs counter to such analogies as we have to guide us. . . . Design in Nature is distinguished from that in human affairs—as it fittingly should be—by all comprehensiveness and system. Its theological synonym is Providence. Its application in particular is surrounded by similar insoluble difficulties; nevertheless, both are bound up with theism. . . .

GOD WORKS THROUGH EVOLUTION (1888): JAMES McCOSH

I let it be known that while I thought there was truth, I believed there was error in the common expositions of evolution, and that the work of the common age must be to separate the truth, when it would be found, I was sure, that this, like every other part of God's work, would illustrate his existence and his wisdom. . . .

There is, or was, a wide-spread idea that the doctrine of development is adverse to religion. This has arisen mainly from the circumstance that it seems to remove God altogether, or at least to a greater distance from his works, and this has been increased by the circumstance that the theory has been turned to atheistic purposes. This impression is to be removed, first, by declaring emphatically that we are to look on evolution simply as the method by which God works. . . . A second erroneous impression needs to be effaced. Because God executes his purposes by agents, which it should be observed he has himself appointed, we are not therefore to argue that he does not continue to act, that he does not now act. He may have set agoing the evolution millions of years ago, but he did not cease from his operation, and sit aloof and apart to see the machine moving. He is still in his works which were created by him, but have no power without his indwelling. Though an event may have been ordained from all eternity, God is as much concerned in it as if he only ordained it now. God acts in his works now quite as much as he did in their original creation. The effects follow, the product is evolved, because he wills it, just as plants generate only when there is light shining on them; just as day continues only because the sun shines. A birth or a death may be brought about by a caused evolution, but the mother may rest assured that God is in both, rejoicing with her, or pitying her. . . .

The doctrine of evolution does not undermine the argument from Final Cause, but rather strengthens it by furnishing new illustration of the wisdom and goodness of God. The proof of design proceeds on the observation of things as adapted one to another to accomplish a good end, and is equally valid whether we suppose adjustment to have been made at once or produced by a process which has been going on for millions of years.

I am not prepared to prove that evolution is the best way in which God could have proceeded. . . . All that I propose to do is show that the method is not unworthy of God; that it is suited to man's nature; that it accomplishes some good ends. The present is evolved from the past, and is developed into the future. There is thus one orderly constitution of things from the beginning unto the end, making us feel how stable all things are as one generation succeeds another. . . .

We have to answer the question so often put: Did man come into the world by ordinary generation? Of course. From the lower animals? To this I answer that at first sight there is something special in the forthcoming of man, and this conviction is deepened the deeper we explore his nature, his intellectual, moral and spiritual faculties, his reason, his conscience, his free-will, which raise him far above the brutes. Your one-eyed evolutionists see only one side, and not the whole solid truth. Man is undoubtedly an animal; this of the highest, the mammalian form, the mammal standing upright and looking to heaven. But he is higher than the animals and is allied to God who made him and made all things. He discerns between truth and error, between good and evil; he sees distant consequences, and can rise to spiritual communion with God. . . .

CONSIGN THE SPECIAL CREATION HYPOTHESIS TO LIMBO (1902): JOHN FISKE

The overthrow of the dogma of fixity of species, and the consequent general displacement of the Doctrine of Creation by the Doctrine of Evolution, have made the scientific world familiar with the conception of the development of the more specialized forms of life from less specialized forms; and thus the development of the least specialized forms of life from the most complex forms of not-life ceases to seem absurd, and even acquires a sort of probability. . . .

We may thus picture to ourselves the earth's surface as at the outset composed only of uncombined elements, of free oxygen, hydrogen, nitrogen, carbon, sulphur, etc., and of iron, copper, sodium, and other metals in a state of vapour. With the lowering of this primitive temperature by radiation, chemical combinations of greater and greater heterogeneity became gradually possible. First appeared the stable binary compounds, such as water and the inorganic acids and bases. . . . As soon as it became cool enough for double salts to exist, then the mutual affinities of simple binary compounds and single salts . . . sufficed to produce double salts. And so on throughout the inorganic world.

Here we obtain a hint as to the origin of organic life upon the earth's surface. In accordance with the modern dynamic theory of life, we are bound to admit that the higher and less stable aggregations of molecules which constitute protoplasm were built up in just the same way in which the lower and more stable aggregations of molecules which constitute a single or a double salt were built up. . . . The case of living matter or protoplasm is in no wise exceptional.

According to the doctrine of derivation, the more complex plants and animals are the slowly modified descendants of less complex plants and animals, and these in turn were the slowly modified descendants of still less complex plants and animals, and so on until we converge to those primitive organisms which are not definable either as animals or as vegetal. . . . Obviously such a hypothesis is not only highly credible in itself, since it only alleges that the growth of a complex organism from a simple globule of protoplasm, which is accomplished in every case of individual evolution, has also been accomplished during the evolution of an immensely long series of individuals; but it is also a purely scientific hypothesis, since it appeals to no agencies save such as are known to be in operation, and involves no assumptions which cannot, sooner or later, be subjected to a crucial test. . . .

The presumption raised at the outset against the Doctrine of Special Creations is even superfluously confirmed by the testimony of facts. Not only is this doctrine discredited by its barbaric origin, and by the absurd or impossible assumptions which it would require us to make, but it utterly fails to explain a single one of the phenomena of the classification, embryology, morphology, and distribution of extinct and living organisms. While, on the other hand, the Doctrine of Derivation is not only accredited by its scientific origin, and by its appealing to none but verifiable processes and agencies, but it affords an explanation for each and all of the above-mentioned phenomena. I think we may, therefore, without further ado, consign the special creation hypothesis to that limbo where hover the ghosts of the slaughtered theories that were born of man's untutored intelligence in early times. . . .

3. Darwinism and the Evolution of Cultures

If Darwin's *The Descent of Man* set the stage for new advances in the social sciences, Lewis Henry Morgan exploited his intellectual opportunities efficiently in *Ancient Society* (1877) to establish himself as the foremost evolutionary anthropologist in America. Morgan believed that human history fell into grand periods of savagery, barbarism, and civilization (and the appropriate subdivisions of these three categories). Studying the whole history of the species from the "Lower States of Savagery" he described the leading inventions, the characteristic family and tribal organization, and the conception of property held by men in each stage. With technological advance as the primary criterion for measuring the transitions to "higher" cultural stages, he could easily "demonstrate" the decisive advantages of his own culture. Morgan argued that most cultures disintegrate before attaining civilization, and that his comparative evolutionary studies provided a method for measuring the precise level of accomplishment for any given society. AUTHOR: Lewis Henry Morgan (1818–1881), "the father of American anthropology," became interested in the subject because of his contacts with the Iroquois Indians. He wrote many tracts and articles on ethnology and did significant work on mental processes among simpler forms of organic life. SELECTION: "Evolutionary Origins of Civilization" from Morgan's *Ancient Society* (1877).

EVOLUTIONARY ORIGINS OF CIVILIZATION (1877): LEWIS HENRY MORGAN

The latest investigations respecting the early condition of the human race are tending to the conclusion that mankind commenced their career at the bottom of the scale and worked their way up from savagery to civilization through the slow accumulations of experimental knowledge. . . .

An attempt will be made . . . to bring forward additional evidence of the rudeness of the early condition of mankind, of the gradual evolution of their mental and moral powers through experience, and of their protracted struggle with opposing obstacles while winning their way to civilization. . . .

As we re-ascend along the several lines of progress toward the primitive ages of mankind, and eliminate one after the other, in the order in which they appeared, inventions and discoveries on the one hand, and institutions on the other, we are enabled to perceive that the former stand to each other in progressive and the latter in unfolding relations. While the former class have had a connection, more or less direct, the latter have been developed from a few primary germs of thought. Modern institutions plant their roots in the period of barbarism, into which their germs were transmitted from the previous period of savagery. They have had a lineal descent through the ages, with the streams of the blood, as well as a logical development.

The facts indicate the gradual formation and subsequent development of certain ideas, passions, and aspirations. Those which hold the most prominent positions may be generalized as growths of the particular ideas with which they severally stand connected.

First. Subsistence has been increased and perfected by a series of successive arts, introduced at long intervals of time, and connected more or less directly with inventions and discoveries.

Second. The germ of government must be sought in the organization into gentes in the Status of savages; and followed down, through the advancing forms of this institution, to the establishment of political society.

Third. Human speech seems to have been developed from the rudest and simplest forms of expression. Gesture or sign language, as intimated by Lucretius, must have preceded articulate language, as thought preceded speech.

Fourth. With respect to the family, the stages of its growth are embodied in systems of consanguinity and affinity, and in usages relating to marriage, by means of which collectively, the family can be definitely traced through several successive forms.

Sixth. House architecture, which connects itself with the form of the family and the plan of domestic life, affords a tolerably complete illustration of progress from savagery to civilization. Its growth can be traced from the hut of the savage, through the communal houses of the barbarians, to the house of the single family of civilized nations, with all the successive links by which one extreme is connected with the other.

Lastly. The idea of property was slowly formed in the human mind. . . . Its dominance as a passion over all other passions, marks the commencement of civilization. It not only led mankind to overcome the obstacles which delayed civilization, but to establish political society on the basis of territory and of property. A critical knowledge of the evolution of the idea of property would embody, in some respects, the most remarkable portion of the mental history of mankind. . . .

Out of a few germs of thought, conceived in the early ages, have been evolved all the principal institutions of mankind. Beginning their growth in the period of savagery, fermenting through the period of barbarism, they have continued their advancement through the period of civilization. The evolution of these germs of thought has been guided by a natural logic which formed an essential attribute of the brain itself. So unerringly has this principle performed its functions in all conditions of experience and in all periods of time, that its results are uniform, coherent and traceable in their courses. These results alone will in time yield convincing proofs of the unity of origin of mankind. The mental history of the human race, which is revealed in institutions, inventions and discoveries, is presumptively the history of a single species, perpetuated through individuals, and developed through experience. Among the original germs of thought, which have exercised the most powerful influence upon the human mind, and upon human destiny, are these which relate to government, to the family, to language, to religion, and to property. They had a definite beginning far back in savagery, and a logical progress, but they can have no final consummation, because they are still progressing, and must ever continue to progress. . . .

4. *The Economic and Social Struggle for Existence*

William Graham Sumner, a champion of big business, hard money, and free trade, grafted Darwinism to classical economics to provide a general defense for the power of the business community in industrial America. No other American scholar equated so closely wealth and "fitness," poverty and the lack of "fitness," or argued so forcefully for non-interference in *laissez-faire* economic competition. Sumner insisted that social progress could be made only through "natural" evolutionary processes, and that society should turn a deaf ear to reformers and social planners who wished to interfere with the competitive system which allowed the fit to rise to the top and thrust the unfit to the bottom. Naturally men of affairs such as Andrew Carnegie and John D. Rockefeller found the doctrines of Sumner and Herbert Spencer very palatable. Carnegie, the poor Scottish immigrant who became a great steel magnate, mixed the Darwinian concept of economic competition as "the law of life" with the American dream of success. AUTHOR: William Graham Sumner (1840–1910), professor of political and social science at Yale University, was born in Paterson, New Jersey, and began his professional life as an Episcopalian minister. Sumner's prodigious scholarly labors included work in economics, languages, Biblical criticism, and sociology. Andrew Carnegie (1835–1919), a young Scottish immigrant, began work in a cotton factory after his family moved to Pennsylvania. He gradually moved into the ranks of management, and built one of the largest fortunes in America. SELECTIONS: "No Natural Rights in the Social Struggle" from Sumner's *The Absurd Effort to Make the World Over* (1883). "Civilization Founded on Economic Competition" from Carnegie's "Wealth" in *The North American Review* (1889).

NO NATURAL RIGHTS IN THE SOCIAL STRUGGLE (1883): WILLIAM GRAHAM SUMNER

Certain ills belong to the hardships of human life. They are natural. They are part of the struggle with Nature for existence. We cannot blame our fellow-men for our share of these. My neighbor and I are both struggling to free ourselves from these ills. The fact that my neighbor has succeeded in this struggle better than I constitutes no grievance for me.

There is no possible definition of a "poor man." A pauper is a person who cannot earn his living; whose producing powers have fallen positively below his necessary consumption; who cannot, therefore, pay his way. A human society needs the active co-operation and productive energy of every person in it. A man who is present as a consumer, yet who does not contribute either by land, labor, or capital to the work of society, is a burden. On no sound political theory ought such a person to share in the political power of the State. . . .

The man who has done nothing to raise himself above poverty finds that the social doctors flock about him, bringing the capital which they have collected from the other class, and promising him the aid of the State to give him what the other had to work for. In all these schemes and projects the organized intervention of society through the State is either planned or hoped for, and the State is thus made to become the protector and guardian of certain classes. . . .

Society . . . does not need any care or supervision. If we can acquire a science of society, based on observation of phenomena and study of forces, we may hope to gain some ground slowly toward the elimination of old errors and the re-establishment of a sound and natural social order. Whatever we gain that way will be by growth, never in the world by any reconstruction of society on the plan of some enthusiastic social architect. The latter is only repeating the old error over again, and postponing all our chances of real improvement. Society needs first of all to be freed from these meddlers—that is, to be let alone. Here we are, then, once more back at the old doctrine—Laissez faire. Let us translate it into blunt English, and it will read, Mind your own business. It is nothing but the doctrine of liberty. Let every man be happy in his own way. If his sphere of action and interest impinges on that of any other man, there will have to be compromise and adjustment. Wait for the occasion. Do not attempt to generalize those interferences or to plan for them a priori. We have a body of laws and institutions which have grown up as occasion has occurred for adjusting rights. Let the same process go on. . . .

There is a beautiful notion afloat in our literature and in the minds of our people that men are born to certain "natural rights." If that were true there would be something on earth which was got for nothing, and this world would not be the place it is at all. The fact is, that there is no right whatever inherited by man which has not an equivalent and corresponding duty by the side of it, as the price of it. . . . If there were such things as natural rights, the question would arise, Against whom are they good? Who has the corresponding obligation to satisfy these rights? There can be no rights against Nature, except to get out of her whatever we can, which is only the fact of the struggle for existence stated over again. . . .

CIVILIZATION FOUNDED ON ECONOMIC COMPETITION (1889): ANDREW CARNEGIE

The price which society pays for the law of competition, like the price it pays for cheap comforts and luxuries, is also great; but the advantages of this law are also greater still, for it is to this law that we owe our wonderful material development, which brings improved conditions in its train. But whether the law be benign or not, we must say of it, as we say of the change in the conditions of men to which we have referred: It is here; we cannot evade it; no substitutes for it have been found; and while the law may be sometimes hard for the individual, it is best for the race, because it insures the survival of the fittest in every department. We accept and welcome, therefore, as conditions to which we must accommodate ourselves, great inequality of environment, the concentration of business, industrial and commerical, in the hands of a few, and the law of competition between these, as being not only beneficial, but essential for the future progress of the race. Having accepted these, it follows that there must be great scope for the exercise of special ability in the merchant and in the manufacturer who has to conduct affairs upon a great scale. That this talent for organization and management is rare among men is proved by the fact that it invariably secures for its possessor enormous rewards, no matter where or under what laws or conditions. The experienced in affairs always rate the MAN whose services can be obtained as a partner as not only the first consideration, but such as to render the question of his capital scarcely worth considering, for such men soon create capital; while, without the special talent required, capital soon takes wings. Such men become interested in firms or corporations using millions; and estimating only simple interest to be made upon the capital invested, it is inevitable that their income must exceed their expenditures, and that they must accumulate wealth. Nor is there any middle ground which such men can occupy, because the great manufacturing or commercial concern which does not earn at least interest upon its capital soon becomes bankrupt. It must either go forward or fall behind: to stand still is impossible. It is a condition essential for its successful operation that it should be thus far profitable, and even that, in addition to interest on capital, it should make profit. It is a law, as certain as any of the others named, that men possessed of this peculiar talent for affairs, under the free play of economic forces, must, of necessity, soon be in receipt of more revenue than can be judiciously expended upon themselves; and this law is as beneficial for the race as the others.

Objections to the foundations upon which society is based are out of order, because the condition of the race is better with these than it has been with any others which have been tried. Of the effect of any new substitutes proposed we cannot be sure. The Socialist or Anarchist who seeks to overturn present conditions is to be regarded as attacking the foundation upon which civilization itself rests, for civilization took its start from the day that the capable, industrious workman said to his incompetent and lazy fellow, "If thou dost not sow, thou shalt not reap," and thus ended primitive Communism by separating the drones from the bees. . . .

5. Social Darwinism and the Law

Most American jurists of the post-Civil War generation inherited a natural rights ideology which assured them that judicial decisions were objective reports on eternal essences in that high heaven of natural law. In post-Civil War America, those essences upheld property rights against the claims of planners and reformers and guaranteed *laissez-faire* economic competition against all challengers. Herbert Spencer seemed merely to confirm men of this temperament in their beliefs. Oliver Wendell Holmes, very much a Darwinist himself, arrived at substantially different conclusions. The judges who interpreted laws were men with varying capacities; laws merely reflected the strongly held opinions of the dominant forces in the society, and economic and political ideas like men and institutions generally struggled for ascendancy in the marketplaces of human activity. If the bearers of sovereignty insisted on laissez-faire, then the laws would reflect that belief; if power passed to social planners, they would express their power through legislation. AUTHOR: Oliver Wendell Holmes (1841–1935), professor of law at Harvard and Chief Justice of the Massachusetts Supreme Court, brought the experience of twenty years on the state bench to the U.S. Supreme Court in 1902. SELECTIONS: "Law and the Struggle for Life," from Holmes' comments on The Gas Stokers' Strike, *American Law Review* (1873). "Right of a Majority to Embody Their Opinions in Law" from Holmes' opinion in *Lochner v. New York* (1905).

LAW AND THE STRUGGLE FOR LIFE (1873): OLIVER WENDELL HOLMES

It has always seemed to us a singular anomaly that believers in the theory of evolution and in the natural development of institutions by successive adaptations to the environment, should be found laying down a theory of government intended to establish its limits once for all by a logical deduction from axioms. . . . The struggle for life, undoubtedly, is constantly putting the interests of men at variance with those of the lower animals. And the struggle does not stop in the ascending scale with the monkeys, but is equally the law of human existence. Outside of legislation this is undeniable. It is mitigated by sympathy, prudence, and all the social and moral qualities. But in the last resort a man rightly prefers his own interest to that of his neighbors. And this is as true in legislation as in any other form of corporate action. All that can be expected from modern improvements is that legislation should easily and quickly, yet not too quickly, modify itself in accordance with the will of the *de facto* supreme power in the community, and that the spread of an educated sympathy should reduce the sacrifice of minorities to a minimum. But whatever body may possess the supreme power for the moment is certain to have interests inconsistent with others which have competed unsuccessfully.

The more powerful interests must be more or less reflected in legislation; which, like every other device of man or beast, must tend in the long run to aid the survival of the fittest. The objection to class legislation is not that it favors a class, but either that it fails to benefit the legislators, or that it is dangerous to them because a competing class has gained in power, or that it transcends the limits of self-preference which are imposed by sympathy. Interference with contracts by usury laws and the like is open to the first objection, that it only makes the burden of borrowers heavier. The law brought to bear upon the gas-stokers is perhaps open to the second, that it requires to be backed by a more unquestioned power than is now possessed by the favored class; and some English statutes are also very probably open to the third. But it is no sufficient condemnation of legislation that it favors one class at the expense of another; for much or all legislation does that; and none the less when the *bona fide* object is the greatest good of the greatest number. Why should the greatest number be preferred? Why not the greatest good of the most intelligent and most highly developed? The greatest good of a minority of our generation may be the greatest good of the greatest number in the long run. But if the welfare of all future ages is to be considered, legislation may as well be abandoned for the present. If the welfare of the living majority is paramount, it can only be on the ground that the majority have the power in their hands. . . .

RIGHT OF A MAJORITY TO EMBODY
THEIR OPINIONS IN LAW (1905):
OLIVER WENDELL HOLMES

This case is decided upon an economic theory which a large part of the country does not entertain. If it were a question whether I agreed with that theory, I should desire to study it further and long before making up my mind. But I do not conceive that to be my duty, because I strongly believe that my agreement or disagreement has nothing to do with the right of a majority to embody their opinions in law. It is settled by various decisions of this Court that State constitutions and State laws may regulate life in many ways which we as legislators might think as injudicious or, if you like, as tryannical as this, and which equally with this interfere with the liberty to contract. Sunday laws and usury laws are ancient examples. A more modern one is the prohibition of lotteries. The liberty of the citizen to do as he likes so long as he does not interfere with the liberty of others to do the same, which has been a shibboleth for some well-known writers, is interfered with by school laws, by the Post Office, by every State or municipal institution which takes his money for purposes thought desirable, whether he likes it or not. The Fourteenth Amendment does not enact Mr. Herbert Spencer's *Social Statics*. The other day we sustained the Massachusetts vaccination law (*Jacobson v. Massachusetts*, 197 U.S. 11). United States and State statutes and decisions cutting down the liberty to contract by way of combination are familiar to this Court (*Northern Securities Company v. United States*, 193 U.S. 197). Two years ago we upheld the prohibition of sales of stock on margins or for future delivery in the constitution of California (*Otis v. Parker*, 187 U.S. 606). The decision sustaining an eight-hour law for miners is still recent (*Holden v. Hardy*, 169 U.S. 366). Some of these laws embody convictions or prejudices which judges are likely to share. Some may not. But a constitution is not intended to embody a particular economic theory, whether of paternalism and the organic relation of the citizen to the State of of laissez faire. It is made for people of fundamentally differing views. . . . Every opinion tends to become a law. I think that the word liberty in the Fourteenth Amendment is perverted when it is held to prevent the natural outcome of a dominant opinion, unless it can be said that a rational and fair man would admit that the statute proposed would infringe fundamental principles as they have been understood by the traditions of our people and our law. It does not need research to show that no such sweeping condemnation can be passed upon the statute before us. . . .

Chapter X. IMMIGRATION, RACISM, AND IMPERIALISM

DURING THE YEARS BETWEEN THE CIVIL WAR AND WORLD WAR I DAR-winian concepts of biological struggle were frequently used to justify racist, imperialist, and ultranationalist positions. Racist ideologies existed long before the arrival of the Darwinians—Southerners were particularly devoted to doctrines demonstrating the inferiority of the Negro—but evolutionary thought provided new energy and arguments for the justification of white supremacy over colored peoples. Several racist writers found valuable materials in William Z. Ripley's use of Darwinian concepts for the classification of races. The pioneer investigations of prehistoric man also provided relevant materials. Usually, however, racists preferred to concentrate on the recent past in order to reveal the "danger" in the biological "mixing" of modern human varieties. Madison Grant, who celebrated the greatness of "Nordics" at the expense of "mongrel" breeds beyond the pale, warned his readers that "degeneration" was the inevitable result when superiors breed with their inferiors. The dominant race was designated by various writers as "Caucasian," "Nordic," "Aryan," "North European," "Anglo-Saxon," and some thought that the Anglo-Saxons had attained their greatest development on the American scene.

The racist writers defended the virtues of Europeans in contrast to Asiatics and Africans and the superiority of North Europeans over Latin and Slavic peoples. This set of values helped create demands for the restriction of immigration around the turn of the century. Except for the Catholicism of the Irish and the "foreign" speech of the largely Protestant German groups, the bulk of immigrants before 1880 were Protestant in religion, North European by descent, and English speaking. After 1880 a growing majority of the new arrivals in the United States were Catholic and Eastern Orthodox peasants from Southern and Eastern Europe with little or no knowledge of English. Moreover, the immigration of the still more dissimilar Chinese and Japanese promised to reach substantial proportions. Advocates of the "melting pot" assured their fellow citizens that each new group would enrich and diversify the American mixture, but racist intellectuals from Josiah Strong to Henry Pratt Fairchild feared that the older American strains might be "swamped" by "the alien hordes."

Political writers who wished to prevent the free entry of "lesser breeds" into the United States often advocated the extension of republican blessings to those peoples through aggressive American foreign policies. A militant attitude toward the world and a restrictionist policy toward potential immigrants developed naturally in the minds of conservative nationalists who took a deep pride in the American past as they conceived it. These men did not wish to reject the republican intellectual heritage in toto; they merely wished to abandon some of its more generous aspects and adapt the remainder to their purposes. Republicanism and ultranationalism, Republicanism and imperialism, might have been their slogans. Intellectuals and politicians whose chauvinism and racism were not quite so militant reached far wider audiences than the extremist fringe. John Fiske joined a score of historians in tracing the towering virtues of the Anglo-Germanic peoples to the primitive Teutonic folk moot. Theodore Roosevelt, confident of the superiority of the American people and their institutions, advocated a free use of the "big stick" in foreign affairs, manipulated a revolution in Panama to obtain the Canal Zone, and thrust the United States into the center of international power politics. Roosevelt's predecessor, William McKinley (who presided over America's entry into the Spanish-American War) annexed the Philippines, Puerto Rico, and Hawaii to extend the blessings of Christianity and Republican institutions to peoples who presumably needed both. Roosevelt's successors abandoned most of his ventures in power politics and Woodrow Wilson denounced imperialism, but both Wilson and William Howard Taft sponsored imperialistic "dollar diplomacy" forays into Latin American countries, an approach used even more freely by the Republican Presidents of the nineteen-twenties.

Still, the golden years of American imperialist thought and action were from 1896 to 1908, when Alfred T. Mahan and Homer Lea mapped a strategy for the growth of American power in the Pacific; Henry Cabot Lodge constructed an economic rationale for imperialism; Albert Beveridge spun the rhetoric of "The White Man's burden"; and William McKinley went down on his knees to ask divine instruction on the annexation of new territories.

Imperialist spokesmen certainly did not have everything their own way, for a large and articulate group of anti-imperialists attempted to convince the public that annexation was wrong on a number of counts. William Graham Sumner argued that it would not profit the nation as a whole, and therefore made no economic sense. Carl Schurz's opposition rested on the more widely supported position that colonialism was inconsistent with the "American" belief in popular self-determination. His viewpoint was adopted by leaders of the American Anti-Imperialist League, who denounced national expansion because the process involved a morally dangerous abandonment of historic principles. Most anti-imperialists agreed that United States foreign policy ran counter to the ideals of both Christianity and humanitarianism. William Vaughn Moody, the leading poet of his age, brought a number of these arguments together in the most eloquent expression of anti-imperialism, "Ode in a Time of Hesitation."

1. Immigration and Nativist Reaction

Many middle-class persons as well as a scattering of bona fide aristocrats boarded ships for life in the New World, but the majority of immigrants were peasants, urban or rural working class, servants, bondsmen, convicts, or slaves. If removal to America sometimes meant a leisurely transfer of households, the search for a richer scene of operations for already prosperous persons, or the mildly trying transplantation of plain folk, the Amerian journey was also often a flight from actual or threatened European catastrophe which involved major hardships. Once in America most immigrants could expect a substantial measure of nativist hostility. The immigrant from a tradition-bound culture shaped in Eastern or Southern Europe by Eastern Orthodoxy or Catholicism, often suffering from Old World privations or the hardships of the journey, faced the enormous initial task of minimum adjustment to an English-speaking society which was largely oriented toward Protestantism, middle-class values, and republican institutions. Even when the immigrant was not subjected to criticism for his language, religion, political "irresponsibility," "false" morals, and "perverse" social habits, he might be attacked for the simple crime of coming to America in numbers large enough to drive wages down. Even Samuel Gompers, himself a Jewish immigrant labor leader, regarded Orientals as inherently inferior and denounced unrestricted immigration as the gravest danger to the American labor movement. AUTHORS: Emily Green Balch (1867–1953), educated at Bryn Mawr, Chicago, and Berlin, taught at Wellesley before she began a career in public service on educational and international boards. Samuel Gompers (1850–1924) who spent his early life in a London tenement, came to America at the age of thirteen, and later emerged from the ranks of the cigarmakers' union to lead the American Federation of Labor from 1886 to 1924 in every year except one. SELECTIONS: "Economic Disaster in Eastern Europe" from Balch's *Our Slavic Fellow Citizens* (1910). "Unrestricted Immigration a Threat to the American Worker" from Gompers' letter of May 16, 1902 to Representative James E. Watson of Georgia.

ECONOMIC DISASTER IN EASTERN EUROPE (1910): EMILY GREEN BALCH

Industry developed at the expense of agriculture. . . . As a money economy, with purchase and sale, extended, the dependence on household production diminished. Money was needed for taxes. The obvious economy of cheap factory textiles, the superiority of iron pots to earthen ones, indeed the temptation of novel wares of various kinds at low prices, all made new demands for money. With these changes went a rise in standards of living; new goods were available and new desires were contagious.

At the same time with the rise in demands, growth of population without growth of industry made an increased pressure on the land. . . . The old peasant economy had represented a fairly stable economic equilibrium. Population was kept more or less at a level by it, since only one son could take father's place, and consequently it was difficult for more than one to establish a family, unless, indeed, he went away to seek his fortune. It was the expectation that everything should go on as it had done. That is the essence of custom, and the peasant world is the world of custom.

The results of the breakup of the old system of land holding were often disastrous. The peasant being free to divide his land and feeling that his children all had equal claims, cut up land which was only sufficient to support one household among a number of descendants. The landholder unable to support himself from his own plot sought to eke out his living by working for wages in a population where few could afford to hire labor. In some districts debts, contracted under circumstances which put the borrower at the mercy of a creditor, worked havoc.

Thus the peasant with mortgage payments which he could not meet or with children for whom he could not provide an adequate patrimony, saw himself face to face with an intolerable decline of social status for

himself or for his children; namely, reduction to the position of a prop-
ertyless day laborer. This is the sting which induces many a man among
the Slovaks, the Poles, the Ruthenians, to fare overseas or to send out his
son to the new land from which men come back with savings.

In some cases the countryside had never supported its population;
there had always been an exodus, permanent or seasonal, of some of the
men and boys, as for instance in some Slovak counties. As the dislocation
of the old economy became more serious, and as mobility of population
increased, there was further overflow,—to Germany for the summer farm
work, to the cities, to less closely settled districts (e.g. to Southern
Hungary), to Russia, to Brazil, to the United States. Quicker transportation, and above all, knowledge of the facts, opened the way across the sea,
and all the requisites for a heavy emigration movement were present.
Sometimes the head of a family goes to retrieve the family fortunes,
sometimes he sends the most promising son. Or a brother goes hoping to
earn enough to pay off the inheritance of his co-heirs and buy the sole
right to the land which cannot support more than one family. . . .

UNRESTRICTED IMMIGRATION
A THREAT TO THE AMERICAN
WORKER (1902): SAMUEL GOMPERS

The organized workers of the country feel that the existing immigration
laws, while not without their value, are of trifling effect compared with
the needs and the just demands of American labor. . . .

The strength of this country is in the intelligence and prosperity of
our working people. But both the intelligence and the prosperity of our
working people are endangered by the present immigration. Cheap labor,
ignorant labor, takes our jobs and cuts our wages.

The fittest survive; that is, those that fit the conditions best. But it is
the economically weak, not the economically strong, that fit the conditions
of the labor market. They fit best because they can be got to work
cheapest. Women and children drive out men, unless either law or labor
organization stops it. In just the same way the Chinaman and others drive
out the American, the German, the Irishman. . . .

The Nashville convention of the American Federation of Labor, by a
vote of 1,858 to 352, pronounced in favor of an educational test for
immigrants. Such a measure would check immigration in a moderate
degree, and those who would be kept out by it are those whose competition in the labor market is most injurious to American workers. No other
measure which would have any important effect of this kind is seriously
proposed.

The need of regulation may be less sharply felt at the present time, when there are less men out of work than there were a few years ago. But the flood of cheap labor is increasing, and its effect at the slightest stagnation in industry or in any crisis will be fearful to the American workmen.

A fall in wages or a relative fall of wages makes the workers unable to buy as large a share as before of the goods they produce. This hastens the time when overproduction or underconsumption will show itself. That means hard times; and when hard times come, the mass of immigrants that prosperity attracted will be here to increase the burden of unemployment. . . .

2. The "Melting Pot" Debate

Toward the end of the nineteenth century the application of racist ideology to the immigration problem led to a score of re-evaluations of the immigrant impact on American society. A few writers, who advocated a kind of cultural federalism, believed that Italian, Polish, Russian, German, and English-speaking Americans might be bound by common national loyalty, tolerance, and a willingness to learn from others without losing ethnic identity, social customs, and cultural values. Immensely more popular was the "melting pot" idea which predicted the fusion of old and new stocks in a new national blend superior to all past and present nationalities. Advocates of the "melting pot" urged that the United States continue to serve without limitations as a refuge for the hungry and oppressed peoples of the world. A spokesman for nativist sentiment, Henry Pratt Fairchild, expressed the misgivings of those Americans of North European descent who feared that the new "alien swarms" would replace American democracy and the national character with a sterile "polyglot" society. Fairchild's point of view did not triumph completely, but it won impressive victories in the immigration legislation of the 1920's that reduced the great migrant flood to a small stream and tacitly accepted the notion that North Europeans were superior to the peoples of Southern and Eastern Europe, Africa, and Asia. AUTHORS: Emma Lazarus (1849–1887), a poet and essayist, was a native New Yorker born into a large and prosperous family of Sephardic Jewish origins. Several lines of her poem cited in this section were engraved on the base of the Statue of Liberty. Israel Zangwill (1864–1926), the son of a Russian Jewish immigrant to London, was an author, a philanthropist, and in later years a Zionist. Henry Pratt Fairchild (1880–1956) was a Professor of Sociology at New York University until his retirement.

SELECTIONS: "America: Refuge and 'Melting Pot' to the World" from Lazarus' *Poems* (1889) and Zangwill's *The Melting Pot* (1909). "The 'Melting Pot' Denounced" from Fairchild's *The Melting Pot Mistake* (1926).

AMERICA: REFUGE AND "MELTING POT" TO THE WORLD (1889, 1909): EMMA LAZARUS AND ISRAEL ZANGWILL

Not like the brazen giant of Greek fame,
With conquering limbs astride from land to land
Here at our sea-washed, sunset gates shall stand
A mighty woman with a torch, whose flame
Is the imprisoned lightening, and her name
Mother of Exiles. From her beacon-handed
Glows world-wide welcome; her mild eyes command
The air-bridged harbor that twin cities frame.
"Keep, ancient lands, your storied pomp!" cries she
With silent lips. "Give me your tired, your poor,
Your huddled masses yearning to breathe free,
The wretched refuse of your teeming shore.
Send these, the homeless, tempest-tost to me,
I lift my lamp beside the golden door!"

THE MELTING-POT

It is the fires of God round His Crucible.

There she lies, the great Melting-Pot—listen! Can't you hear the roaring and the bubbling? There gapes her mouth—the harbour where a thousand mammoth feeders come from the ends of the world to pour in their human freight. Ah, what a stirring and a seething! Celt and Latin, Slav and Teuton, Greek and Syrian,—black and yellow—

Jew and Gentile—

Yes, East and West, and North and South, the palm and the pine, the pole and the equator, the crescent and the cross—how the great Alchemist melts and fuses them with his purging flame! Here shall they all unite to build the Republic of Man and the Kingdom of God. Ah, Vera, what is the glory of Rome and Jerusalem where all nations and races come to worship and look back, compared with the glory of America, where all races and nations come to labour and look forward!

Peace, peace, to all ye unborn millions, fated to fill this giant continent—the God of our children give you Peace. . . .

THE "MELTING POT" DENOUNCED (1926):
HENRY PRATT FAIRCHILD

To live in America, then, is to live in the atmosphere of these immaterial standards and values, to possess them in one's own character, and to be possessed by them. This means to live in close, spontaneous, daily contact with genuine Americans. For the native-born American of American ancestry, as already stated, this is natural and automatic. What is it for the foreign immigrant? . . . The typical immigrant of the present does not really live in America at all, but, from the point of view of nationality, in Italy, Poland, Czecho-Slovakia, or some other foreign country. Let us look into the causes of this situation, and examine the barriers that keep the foreigner out of America. . . . During the century and a half of our independent national life we have developed from a simply organized, agricultural community into an elaborate, complicated, mechanical, and industrial society. The whole quality of our group life has altered correspondingly. Instead of homogeneity and essential equality have come heterogeneity and class distinctions. . . .

The great majority of immigrants come here as members of the wage-earning class, and most of them remain so. Most of them, also, are poor. So in their efforts to penetrate the stream of Americanizing influences they have to face the handicap not only of alien origin and character, but also of an inferior economic status and absolute poverty. To cap the climax, the differentiation of occupations has gone so far that to-day a large number of callings are almost completely given over to foreign workers, often of specific national groups. They have become "Wop labor," "Hunkie labor," "Kike labor," etc. Consequently the foreigner, not to speak of associating with "upper class" Americans, does not even have the opportunity of mingling with genuine Americans in his own walk of life. . . .

A second great cause of the change in the conditions of assimilation is found in the altered type of the immigrants themselves, as already pointed out in the distinction between the old and the new immigration. The typical immigrants of the first one hundred years of our national life came from the same nationalities as the ancestors of the native Americans. The change that they had to undergo in order to be assimilated was the same change that the ancestors of their associates had passed through. . . . To-day, the immigrants represent as diverse and inharmonious nationalities as are to be found among all the branches of the white race. The transformation necessary for assimilation is therefore both more sweeping and more difficult. . . .

These "foreign colonies," as they are commonly called, are living evidences of the tenacity of nationality. They show how vigorously every individual clings to his own original national traits, how choice and dear they seem to him, and how difficult it is for him to change them even if he wishes. There are many sections of the United States in which even the third generation of immigrants does not speak English.

The persistence of nationality, and the revolutionary nature of the transformation involved in a change of nationality, can hardly be comprehended by one who has never been called upon to undergo such a process. . . .

The process of Americanization, then, for the immigrant is infinitely more difficult than for the native because the former, during the years before his arrival in the United States, has already acquired more or less completely a foreign nationality. This nationality is dissimilar in most respects, and absolutely contradictory and inconsistent in many respects, to the American nationality. Yet to the foreigner it is his natural and authoritative spiritual tradition and social environment. He may hold a critical attitude toward certain aspects of it, just as most Americans are dissatisfied with some phases of the American nationality, but taken as a whole it represents to him truth, beauty, goodness, morality, justice, propriety, efficiency, custom, order, and—home. Let the critical and self-satisfied American of native birth reflect that in the process of Americanization this whole spiritual endowment must be abandoned, and another taken in its place, and it may help him dimly to perceive how tragic, how soul-wracking must be the experience of assimilation, though probably no one who has not actually gone through it can appreciate the stress and tragedy involved. . . .

3. Doctrines of Caucasian Superiority

Nineteenth-century opponents of immigration had cited the evils of Catholicism, Eastern Orthodoxy, and Judaism as well as the menace of Eastern and South European authoritarianism; Darwinian racists at the turn of the century discovered racial struggle as the basic law of life and added to the existing nativist arguments the malice of "polluting Nordic blood" with the lesser "stocks" of Europe and elsewhere. Madison Grant provided one of the most carefully prepared presentations of the menace to "Nordics" from immigration in The Passing of the Great Race. Thomas Dixon, Jr. was less concerned with denouncing the immigrant than with painting a portrait of the American Negro as a savage beast whose mere presence constituted an awful danger to the purity and supremacy of "white blood." Social Darwinism gave white supremacists new reasons for old prejudices. Dixon's novels provided popular vehicles for the fusion of old and new racisms, and the film *Birth of a Nation* (1915) gave Dixon's ideas a national hearing at a time when Americans were being told about the virtues of the "Great Race" and the vices of the inferior races by a variety of writers. Racist concepts played a major role in many areas of American thought and action, including foreign policy, war, and immigration legislation. AUTHORS: Madison Grant (1865–1937) was an anthropologist at the American Museum of Natural History and a leading popularizer of racist ideas. Thomas Dixon, Jr. (1864–1946), a North Carolina Baptist minister and an ardent defender of the Ku Klux Klan, wrote many widely read "romances of the white man's burden" with Southern settings. SELECTIONS: "The Immigrant Menace to Nordic Americans" from Grant's *The Passing of the Great Race* (1916). "The Racial Beast" from Dixon's *The Leopard's Spots* (1902).

THE IMMIGRANT MENACE TO NORDIC AMERICANS (1916): MADISON GRANT

In America we have nearly succeeded in destroying the privilege of birth; that is, the intellectual and moral advantage a man of good stock brings into the world with him. . . .

Mankind emerged from savagery and barbarism under the leadership of selected individuals whose personal prowess, capacity, or wisdom gave them the right to lead and the power to compel obedience. Such leaders have always been a minute fraction of the whole, but as long as the tradition of their predominance persisted they were able to use the brute strength of the unthinking herd as part of their own force, and were able to direct at will the blind dynamic impulse of the slaves, peasants, or lower classes. . . .

True aristocracy is government by the wisest and best, always a small minority in any population. Human society is like a serpent dragging its long body on the ground, but with the head always thrust a little in advance and a little elevated above the earth. . . .

The continuity of physical traits and the limitation of the effects of environment to the individual only are now so thoroughly recognized by scientists that it is at most a question of time when the social consequences which result from such crossings will be generally understood by the public at large. As soon as the true bearing and import of the facts are appreciated by lawmakers, a complete change in our political structure will inevitably occur, and our present reliance on the influences of education will be superseded by a readjustment based on racial values.

Bearing in mind the extreme antiquity of physical and spiritual characters and the persistency with which they outlive those elements of environment termed language, nationality, and forms of government, we must consider the relation of these facts to the development of the race in America. We may be certain that the progress of evolution is in full operation to-day under those laws of nature which control it, and that the only sure guide to the future lies in the study of the operation of these laws in the past.

We Americans must realize that the altruistic ideals which have controlled our social development during the past century, and the maudlin sentimentalism that has made America "an asylum for the oppressed," are sweeping the nation toward a racial abyss. If the Melting Pot is allowed to boil without control, and we continue to follow our national motto and deliberately blind ourselves to all "distinctions of race, creed, or color," the type of native American of Colonial descent will become as extinct as the Athenian of the age of Pericles, and the Viking of the days of Rollo. . . .

THE RACIAL BEAST (1902): THOMAS DIXON, JR.

What would happen to these fools [pro-Negro whites] when once they roused that thousand-legged, thousand-eyed beast with its thousand teeth and nails! He had looked into its face, and he shuddered to recall the hour.

He knew that this power of racial fury of the Anglo-Saxon when aroused was resistless, and that it would sweep its victims before its wrath like chaff before a whirlwind.

And then he thought of the day fast coming when culture and wealth would give the African the courage of conscious strength and he would answer that soul piercing shriek of his kindred for help, and that other thousand-legged beast, now crouching in the shadows, would meet thousand-legged beast around that beacon fire of a Godless revenge!

More and more the impossible position of the Negro in America came home to his mind. He was fast being overwhelmed with the conviction that sooner or later we must squarely face the fact that two such races, counting millions in numbers, can not live together under a Democracy.

He recalled the fact that there were more Negroes in the United States than inhabitants in Mexico, the third republic of the world.

Amalgamation simply meant Africanisation. The big nostrils, flat nose, massive jaw, protruding lip and kinky hair will register their animal marks over the proudest intellect and the rarest beauty of any other race.

The rule that had no exception was that one drop of Negro blood makes a Negro.

What could be the outcome of it? What was his duty as a citizen and a member of civilised society? Since the scenes through which he had passed with Tom Camp and that mob the question was insistent and personal. It clouded his soul and weighed on him like the horrors of a nightmare.

Again and again the fateful words the Preacher had dinned into his ears since childhood pressed upon him.

"You cannot build in a Democracy a nation inside a nation of two antagonistic races. The future American must be an Anglo-Saxon or a Mulatto." . . .

Suffrage in America has touched the lowest tide-mud of degradation. If our cities and our Southern civilization are to be preserved, there must be a return to the sanity of the founders of this Republic.

A government of the wealth, virtue and intelligence of the community, by the debased and the criminal, is a relapse to elemental barbarism to which no race of freemen can submit.

Shall the future North Carolinian be an Anglo-Saxon or a Mulatto? This is the question. . . .

4. *Imperialism and Anti-Imperialism*

The Reverend Josiah Strong provides an excellent example of the method by which the missionary impulse could be tied to racist and imperialist ideologies. According to Strong, the United States as the superior branch of the Anglo-Saxon racial bearers of "liberty" and "pure" Christianity, was destined to lead, perhaps to rule the world. White libertarian Christians had the mission of spreading their institutions around the globe. One did not, however, have to agree with Strong to be an expansionist, for the cause of American imperialism attracted several schools of thought.

While imperialism drew its greatest strength from the political right and anti-imperialism tended to rely on the left, Albert J. Beveridge and other reformers supported expansionist tendencies, and conservatives such as William Graham Sumner opposed them. The major thrust of American imperialism, the Spanish-American War of 1898, aroused widespread popular enthusiasm. President McKinley's politico-religious pieties along with Secretary of State Elihu Root's version of the white man's burden seemed to millions ample justification for a declaration of war against Spain and the postwar seizure of the Philippines. McKinley and Root, the war and the new possessions, aroused protests from the Democratic politician William Jennings Bryan, the poet William Vaughn Moody, the organizers of the Anti-Imperialist League, and many others. AUTHORS: Josiah Strong (1847–1916), a Congregational minister and a leader in the American Home Missionary Society, tried to draw attention to the areas in American culture which he considered to be danger spots for Protestantism. Elihu Root (1845–1937), Secretary of War and Secretary of State under Presidents McKinley and Roosevelt, won a Nobel Peace Prize in 1912. William Jennings Bryan (1860–1925), three times a candidate for the Presidency, served as Secretary of State under Woodrow Wilson. William Vaughn Moody (1869–1910) was perhaps the most accomplished lyric poet and dramatist of his generation. SELECTIONS: "A Religious Justification for Anglo-Saxon Domination of the World" from Strong's Our Country (1885). "The White Man's Burden; U.S. Occupation of the Philippines" from a Root speech of 1900. "Imperialism Incompatible with Christianity and American Democracy," a Bryan speech made in 1900, published in Speeches (1909). "A Poet's Protest" from Moody's Ode in a Time of Hesitation (1900).

A RELIGIOUS JUSTIFICATION FOR ANGLO-SAXON DOMINATION OF THE WORLD (1885): JOSIAH STRONG

Every race which has deeply impressed itself on the human family has been the representative of some great idea. . . . The noblest races have always been lovers of liberty. The love ran strong in early German blood, and has profoundly influenced the institutions of all the branches of the great German family; but it was left for the Anglo-Saxon branch fully to recognize the right of the individual to himself and formally to declare it the foundation stone of government.

The other great idea of which the Anglo-Saxon is the exponent is that of a pure *spiritual* Christianity. It was no accident that the great reformation of the sixteenth century originated among a Teutonic, rather than a Latin people. . . .

It is not necessary to argue to those for whom I write that the two needs of mankind, that all men may be lifted up into the light of the highest Christian civilization, are, first, a pure spiritual Christianity, and second, civil liberty. . . . It follows, then, that the Anglo-Saxon, as the great representative of these two ideas . . . is divinely commissioned to be, in a peculiar sense, his brother's keeper. Add to this the fact of his rapidly increasing strength in modern times, and we have well-nigh a demonstration of his destiny. . . . Does it not look as if God were not only preparing in our Anglo-Saxon civilization the die with which to stamp the peoples of the earth, but as if he were also massing behind that die the mighty power with which to press it? . . . There can be no reasonable doubt that North America is to be the great home of the Anglo-Saxon, the principal seat of his power, the center of his life and influence. . . .

America is to have the great preponderance of numbers and of wealth, and by the logic of events will follow the scepter of controlling influence. This will be but the consummation of a movement as old as civilization—a result to which men have looked forward for centuries. John Adams records that nothing was "more ancient in his memory than the observation that arts, sciences, and empire had traveled westward; and in conversation it was always added that their leap would be over the Atlantic into America." He recalled a couplet that had been inscribed or rather drilled, into a rock on the shore of Monument Bay in our old colony of Plymouth:

> " 'The Eastern nations sink, their glory ends,
>   And empire rises where the sun descends.' "

What is the significance of such facts? These tendencies infold the future; they are the mighty alphabet with which God writes his prophecies. . . . It seems to me that God, with infinite wisdom and skill, is training the Anglo-Saxon race for an hour sure to come in the world's future. Heretofore there has always been in the history of the world a comparatively unoccupied land westward, into which the crowded countries of the East have poured their surplus populations. There are no more new worlds. The unoccupied arable lands of the earth are limited, and will soon be taken. The time is coming when the pressure of population on the means of subsistence will be felt here as it is now felt in Europe and Asia. Then will the world enter upon a new stage of its history—*the final competition of races, for which the Anglo-Saxon is being schooled.* Long before the thousand millions are here, the mighty *centrifugal* tendency, inherent in this stock and strengthened in the United States, will assert itself. . . .

Whether the extinction of inferior races before the advancing Anglo-Saxon seems to the reader sad or otherwise, it certainly appears probable. . . . He is not, of course, superior to climatic influences; but even in warm climates, he is likely to retain his aggressive vigor long enough to supplant races already enfeebled. Thus, in what Dr. Bushnell calls "the out-populating power of the Christian stock," may be found God's final and complete solution of the dark problem of heathenism among many inferior peoples. . . .

Notwithstanding the great perils which threaten it, I cannot think our civilization will perish; but I believe it is fully in the hands of the Christians of the United States, during the next ten or fifteen years, to hasten or retard the coming of Christ's kingdom in the world by hundreds, and perhaps thousands, of years. We of this generation and nation occupy the Gibraltar of the ages which commands the world's future. . . .

THE WHITE MAN'S BURDEN: U.S. OCCUPATION OF THE PHILIPPINES (1900): ELIHU ROOT

What President McKinley has done in the Philippines has been to defend and assert the sovereignty of the United States. . . . What is charged against him is that he did not yield or procure Congress to authorize him to yield the sovereignty of the United States acquired by the cession of Spain with the assent of both parties, to the force of armed Tagalogs whose hands were red with the blood of American soldiers; place in their hands the government of the Philippine Islands, lower the American flag upon the walls of Manila and hurry away with our wounded and our dead from the bay made glorious by Dewey's victory.

The first specification under the charge is that it was unjust to the Filipinos not to do this. Of course it was impossible to do it. Self-respect forbade it, national honor forbade it; the whole world would have contemned and despised us if we had done it; the whole country would have risen in indignant protest against any President who dared to do it. . . .

The true question in the Philippines was, whether the withdrawal of the Spanish power which we had destroyed left a people capable of establishing and maintaining a free constitutional government; whether the humble and peaceable inhabitants, who constituted the great mass of the population, were competent to protect themselves; whether the wealth and commerce of Manila, the merchants from all the nations of Europe who were gathered there, the producers of hemp and tobacco and rice, would be protected by a rule of law and order and justice, or whether, on the other hand, the people, incapable of governing themselves, would become the subjects of a dictatorship, or the prey of bloody discord. . . .

The testimony is absolutely overwhelming that the people inhabiting the Philippine Archipelago are incapable of self-government, and that the fate here described would have befallen these islands of the tropics had American sovereignty been withdrawn. There is no Philippine people. The hundreds of islands which compose the Archipelago are inhabited by more than eighty different tribes, speaking more than sixty different languages. They have no common medium of communication, and they never had a government except the arbitrary rule of Spain. Most of them have not the first conception of what self-government means, or the first qualification for its exercise. . . .

IMPERIALISM INCOMPATIBLE WITH CHRISTIANITY AND AMERICAN DEMOCRACY (1900): WILLIAM JENNINGS BRYAN

The growth of the principle of self-government planted on American soil, has been the over-shadowing political fact of the nineteenth century. It has made this nation conspicuous among the nations and given it a place in history such as no other nation has ever enjoyed. Nothing has been able to check the onward march of this idea. I am not willing that this nation shall cast aside the omnipotent weapon of truth to seize again the weapons of physical warfare. I would not exchange the glory of this Republic for the glory of all the empires that have risen and fallen since time began. . . .

If true Christianity consists in carrying out in our daily lives the teachings of Christ, who will say that we are commanded to civilize with dynamite and proselyte with the sword? He who would declare the divine will must prove his authority either by Holy Writ or by evidence of a special dispensation. . . . I can conceive of a national destiny surpassing the glories of the present and the past—a destiny which meets the responsibilities of today and measures up to the possibilities of the future. Behold a republic, *resting securely upon the foundation stones quarried by revolutionary patriots from the mountain of eternal truth.* . . . Behold a republic standing erect while empires all around are bowed beneath the weight of their own armaments—a republic whose flag is loved while other flags are only feared. Behold a republic increasing in population, in wealth, in strength and in influence, solving the problems of civilization and hastening the coming of an universal brotherhood—a republic which shakes thrones and dissolves aristocracies by its silent example and gives light and inspiration to those who sit in darkness. Behold a republic gradually but surely becoming the supreme moral factor in the world's progress and the accepted arbiter of the world's disputes—a republic whose history, like the path of the just, "is as the shining light that shineth more and more unto the perfect day." . . .

A POET'S PROTEST (1900): WILLIAM VAUGHN MOODY

Before the solemn bronze Saint Gaudens made
To thrill the heedless passer's heart with awe,

And set here in the city's talk and trade
To the good memory of Robert Shaw,
This bright March morn I stand,
And hear the distant spring come up the land;
Knowing that what I hear is not unheard
Of this boy soldier and his Negro band,
For all their gaze is fixed so stern ahead,
For all the fatal rhythm of their tread.
The land they died to save from death and shame
Trembles and waits, hearing the spring's great name,
And by her pangs these resolute ghosts are stirred. . . .

Alas! what sounds are these that come
Sullenly over the Pacific seas,—
Sounds of ignoble battle, striking dumb
The season's half-awakened ecstasies?
Must I be humble, then,
Now when my heart hath need of pride?
Wild love falls on me from these sculptured men;
By loving much the land for which they died
I would be justified.
My spirit was away on pinions wide
To soothe in praise of her its passionate mood
And ease it of its ache of gratitude.
Too sorely heavy is the debt they lay
On me and the companions of my day.
I would remember now
My country's goodliness, make sweet her name.
Alas! what shade art thou
Of sorrow or of blame
Liftest the lyric leafage from her brow,
And pointest a slow finger at her shame?

Lies! Lies! It cannot be! The wars we wage
Are noble, and our battles still are won
By justice for us, ere we lift the gage.
We have not sold our loftiest heritage.
The proud republic hath not stooped to cheat
And scramble in the market-place of war;
Her forehead weareth yet its solemn star.
Here is her witness: this, her perfect son,
This delicate and proud New England soul
Who leads despised men, with just-unshackled feet,
Up the large ways where death and glory meet,
To show all peoples that our shame is done,
That once more we are clean and spirit-whole. . . .

Was it for this our fathers kept the law?
This crown shall crown their struggle and their ruth?
Are we the eagle nation Milton saw
Mewing its mighty youth,
Soon to possess the mountain winds of truth,
And be a swift familiar of the sun
Where aye before God's face his trumpets run?
Or have we but the talons and the maw,
And for the abject likeness of our heart
Shall some less lordly bird be set apart?—
Some gross-billed wader where the swamps are fat?
Some gorger in the sun? Some prowler with the bat?

Ah no!
We have not fallen so.
We are our fathers' sons: let those who lead us know!
'Twas only yesterday sick Cuba's cry
Came up the tropic wind, "Now help us, for we die!"
Then Alabama heard,
And rising, pale, to Maine and Idaho
Shouted a burning word.
Proud state with proud impassioned state conferred,
And at the lifting of a hand sprang forth,
East, west, and south, and north,
Beautiful armies. Oh, by the sweet blood and young
Shed on the awful hill slope at San Juan,
By the unforgotten names of eager boys
Who might have tasted girls' love and been stung
With the old mystic joys
And starry griefs, now the spring nights come on,
But that the heart of youth is generous,—
We charge you, ye who lead us,
Breathe on their chivalry no hint of stain!
Turn not their new-world victories to gain!
One least leaf plucked for chaffer from the bays
Of their dear praise,
One jot of their pure conquest put to hire,
The implacable republic will require;
With clamor, in the glare and gaze of noon,
Or subtly, coming as a thief at night,
But surely, very surely, slow or soon
That insult deep we deeply will requite.
Tempt not our weakness, our cupidity!
For save we let the island men go free,
Those baffled and dislaureled ghosts

Will curse us from the lamentable coasts
Where walk the frustrate dead.
The cup of trembling shall be drained quite,
Eaten the sour bread of astonishment,
With ashes of the hearth shall be made white
Our hair, and wailing shall be in the tent;
Then on your guiltier head
Shall our intolerable self-disdain
Wreak suddenly its anger and its pain;
For manifest in that disastrous light
We shall discern the right
And do it tardily.—O ye who lead,
Take heed!
Blindness we may forgive, but baseness we will smite.

Chapter XI. SOCIAL AND POLITICAL CRITICISM IN THE PROGRESSIVE ERA

BETWEEN THE CIVIL WAR AND THE TURN OF THE CENTURY SOCIAL DARwinism provided convenient sources of explanation and apologetics for a large variety of causes. The friends of imperialism, racism, corporate finance, ultra-nationalism, immigration restriction, *laissez-faire* government and economics exploited for two generations Darwinian metaphors on the "struggle for survival" and the "survival of the fittest." When the tide of public opinion began to turn during the Progressive era, social critics challenged the entire rationale of Social Darwinism. The new critics sometimes reinterpreted the Darwinian analogy, and sometimes denied that biological laws had any relevance whatsoever to the life of man. One approach taken by reform Darwinians noted that the "law of life" for the members of each single species was cooperation rather than competition; and a second approach, pioneered by Lester Frank Ward, accepted economic competition with the understanding that the state existed to regulate and mitigate the social struggle. For Emma Lazarus' defense of the American "melting pot," Darwinism had no relevance. For William Jennings Bryan's and William Vaughn Moody's attacks on imperialism, concepts of international struggle were even more beside the point; decent and humane people tried to substitute democratic cooperation at home and the rule of law abroad in place of internal strife and international conflict.

Reformer and "robber baron," the imperialist and his opponent could agree on one point: between the Civil War and the beginning of the twentieth century American society had been transformed. The remote world of Jefferson and Jackson, sometimes dimly remembered through a haze of nostalgia for its republican simplicity and staunch agrarian self-sufficiency, was becoming an industrial giant and a world power with a great network of factories, mines, and railroads. Cow pastures of yesterday became great cities fed by the steady flow of rural Americans as well as by immigrants from Sicily or the Ukraine; and a technological revolution with its ever-widening stream of new inventions promised to work an economic transformation of the society. In the new America the dynamic topics of conversation were the factory, the trust, the corporate-owned plantation, the immigrant political club, the city boss, the Americanization drive, the locomotive and the dynamo, the overnight organization of multimillion dollar city utility companies, Wall Street, and overseas markets.

For a few—and most of them were immigrant radicals—the new and thoroughly rotten society allowed the industrial plutocrats to live on the labor and blood of the working class. The great fortunes of the Rockefellers, the Morgans, the Carnegies presumably drew their substance from the labor of all elements in the proletariat including broken old men and women and young children, from the twelve-hour working day, the violent and festering slums, and all the other evils of a capitalist system which merited total opposition and complete destruction. For a radical anarchist such as Emma Goldman the organized and barbarous war of capitalism on mankind must be met by the militant members of the working class with violence. A few acts of terrorism did take place—Alexander Berkman shot Ford Frick of Carnegie Steel, Leon Czolgosz assassinated President McKinley, and the Molly McGuires in the Pennsylvania coal mines used terrorist attacks to repay the violence visited upon them by the Pinkerton detectives of the mine companies—but anarchism, terrorist or otherwise, won the loyalties of very few Americans. Considerably more popular in the early years of the twentieth century was Eugene Debs' domesticated version of Marxian socialism; at least the American Socialist Party seemed native enough to win almost a million votes for Debs as a Presidential candidate on a platform of "turn the great machines over to the people." Still, the Socialists never really got within striking distance of major party status, and the movement was shattered by the First World War and the political reaction which followed it.

Most critics of the economic system had a basic faith in the general soundness of the national society. Economic change, they reflected, represented the triumphant march of the common man toward greater liberty and prosperity through the continental railroads, the expanding West, the new machines and factories, all of which had once promised to bring the country closer to the fulfillment of the great promise of American life. Now in the midst of urban squalor and rural want, millions of Americans asked: what had gone wrong? How could the wrongs be undone? Reformers provided a torrent of answers to these questions. As early as 1879 Henry George analyzed the new anxieties of the middle class and the suffering of many working-class people; he proposed to remedy economic evils through social legislation and to finance his program through a single grand tax on the "unearned increments" on land. How simple, thought George, to tax the soaring "unearned" land values, particularly in the cities, and to apply the vast sums to welfare measures. George attracted attention for a generation, and gathered around him a small band of devoted disciples, but failed to develop a mass following.

American opinion, so hostile to reform in the years after the Civil War, gradually changed in the face of new conditions and the great flood of reform books, tracts, and articles. The literature of reform ranged from scholarly monographs to best selling Utopian novels and sensational exposes of political and industrial corruption by the "muckraking" journalists. Edward Bellamy won a large audience for his popular Utopian novel, *Looking Backward* (1888), in which he imagined men of the next generation organized into a cooperative socialist democracy, living in abundance, and looking backward with awe and wonder at the poverty, inequality, and fierce competition of the past. Economic criticism from more scholarly writers such as Thorstein Veblen had little initial impact. Even scholars paid little attention at first to Veblen's economic treatises, but time ultimately provided readers for his biting analysis of the "conspicuous consumption" of free spending millionaires for "honorific" purposes. Later, in the nineteen-twenties he published an interesting economic critique which described the engineers, technicians, and administrative specialists as the real source of industrial success, and relegated the financier and the business "owner" to largely parasitic roles. Veblen was only one member in a new generation of critical economists who objected to the ultra-capitalist stress of "classical economics" on unrestricted economic competition. Moreover, the change which transformed economic scholarship also took place in sociology, law, history, and other disciplines.

Critics of commercial America were particularly heartened by Charles Beard's historical investigations. In his most influential book, *An Economic Interpretation of the Constitution of the United States* (1913), Beard tried to show that the Constitution, so skillfully exploited by friends of corporate industry, expressed the economic interests of the property owners who created the document. Beard's book seemed to imply the existence of a conspiracy of commercial property against the great agrarian majority. The work of "Progressive" scholars in many fields supported Beard's line of thought; and scholars joined with publicists and reformers to assert a Progressive theory of society which postulated the struggle of the business man and "the people" as the central thread of American history. Progressives assumed the common fact of economic and political conspiracy: high courts and business heads might speak of "due process," "liberty of contract," "the iron law of wages," and city charters, but the real forces behind the abstract mask of conspiracy were the rough and sordid factors, the bribe, the rebate, and the shady deal.

Many Protestant leaders preferred to criticize industrial America in terms of social sin rather than economic conspiracy. Washington Gladden and other advocates of the "Social Gospel" used the pulpit and church publications to spread their ideas on Christian social responsibility. Advocates of the Social Gospel proposed to Christianize capitalism, to make men of modest and great wealth aware of their responsibility to the industrial poor, and to persuade American society of the need, not only for greater charity, but also for ameliorative legislation.

More influential than Social Gospellers or Single Taxers, scholars or political radicals, were the Muckrakers. Ostensibly, journalism rather than reform provided their reason for being, but they aroused a great deal of sentiment for social reform. Most of the Muckrakers used the mass circulation magazine or the best selling book as a medium of expression. Ida M. Tarbell exposed the Rockefeller "Octopus" of the oil industry which through ruthless, unrelenting, and often "unfair" competition drove thousands of competitors out of business and toward economic ruin. Upton Sinclair revealed the inhuman working conditions of the Chicago stockyards and the willingness of the packers to risk poisoning consumers for the sake of slightly higher profits. Lincoln Steffens visited city after city to demonstrate the shady connections between business and politics, policemen and vice, and to reveal the almost universal existence of corrupt bosses who had long since moved from illegal registration roles and stuffed ballot boxes to casting votes from deserted houses, graveyards, and even the Social Register.

Evidence for the reality of discontent in the Populist and Progressive eras can be found in many places from the mass circulation magazines to pulpit, podium, and political platform. At various times between 1890 and 1917, city, town, and country knew a fair measure of discontent. If the Populist movement of the eighteen-nineties had been largely an expression of agrarian displeasure over falling prices and "exploitation" by railroads and industry, the Progressive movement expressed the discontent in towns and cities during the early twentieth century over economic, political, and social conditions. The trust, the "robber baron," the urban boss, and the corruption of older codes of commercial ethics drove the Progressive into reform campaigns to "clean up" the city or the police, the national economy or the U.S. Congress. Theodore Roosevelt first emerged as a reform police commissioner who sought to smash corrupt connections of the police with vice and business; Woodrow Wilson came to general public attention as the man who "brought the government to the people" by replacing the rule of the New Jersey "bosses" with the enlightened Progressive "trustees" of the people; and Robert M. LaFollette made Wisconsin a "laboratory of democracy" with his reform experiments. Cities tried the city manager system, and many states in the effort to take power from the bars and give it to "the people" tinkered with the direct primary, the legislative initiative and referendum, the recall of elected officials, the "open" nominating convention, and other devices.

On the national scene the Progressive movement effected several significant changes. Under Theodore Roosevelt partial enforcement of the Sherman Anti-Trust Act began after more than a decade of neglect, and through the Elkins Bill and the Hepburn Act the railroads came under serious Federal regulation. Here and there in the national economy, bills such as the Pure Food and Drug Act brought about perceptible changes. Wilson sponsored a larger array of bills which strengthened anti-trust laws, made new regulations for railroads and banks, established the Federal Reserve system, and attempted to grant labor the right to organize, bargain, and strike. The list of Progressive legislation was, however, relatively brief, and a high percentage of that modest list did not survive the First World War and the postwar political reaction. The Progressive rhetoric expressed the commitment of millions to "public morality," "political honesty," and "economic opportunity," but after all the parades and speeches, American society in 1917—and in 1929—had been changed only in minor respects. Still, the Crash of 1929 and the New Deal were yet to come.

1. *The Reaction Against Social Darwinism*

The reaction against ruthless social struggle and those who defended it came from the pulpit, the reform platform, the politician, the market-place, and the university. Lester Frank Ward, sociologist, geologist, anthropologist, and president of The International Institute of Sociology in 1903, insisted that the qualities which enabled men to successfully compete with their fellow men were far from being the most useful to "society at large." Ward, refusing to accept the identification of the "fittest" and the wealthiest, urged Americans to realize that government should control social evolution through economic and political planning. AUTHOR: Lester Frank Ward (1841–1913), self-educated at great sacri-fice, became an outstanding American sociological scholar. SELECTION: "Plutocracy and Paternalism" from a Ward article in *The Forum* (1895).

PLUTOCRACY AND PATERNALISM (1895):
LESTER FRANK WARD

Justly or unjustly, society has made wealth a measure of worth. It is easy on general principles to prove that it is not such a measure. Every one is personally cognizant of numerous cases to the contrary. All will admit that, taken in the abstract, the principle is unsound, and yet all act upon it. Not rationally, not perhaps consciously, but still they do it. It is "human nature" to respect those who have, and to care little for those who have not. There is a sort of feeling that if one is destitute there must be a reason for it. It is inevitably ascribed to some personal deficit. In a word, absence of means is, in one form or another, made to stand for the absence of merit. Its cause is looked for in character. This is most clearly seen in the marked contrast between the indisposition to help the un-successful, and the willingness to help the successful. . . .

Modern society is suffering from the very opposite of paternalism,— from undergovernment, from the failure of government to keep pace with the change which civilization has wrought in substituting intellectual for physical qualities as the workers of injustice. Government to-day is pow-erless to perform its primary and original function of protecting society. There was a time when brigandage stalked abroad throughout Europe and no one was safe in life or property. This was due to lack of adequate government. Man's nature has not changed, but brigandage has suc-cumbed to the strong arm of the law. Human rapacity now works in subtler ways. Plutocracy is the modern brigandage, and can be dislodged only by the same power,—the power of the state. . . . Without stopping to show that, from the standpoint of a civilized society, the qualities which best fit men to gain advantage over their fellows are the ones least useful to society at large, it will be sufficient for the present purpose to point out that in the actual state of society it is not even those who, from this biological point of view, are the fittest, that become in fact the recipients of the greatest favors at the hands of society. This is due to the creation, by society itself, of artificial conditions that destroy the balance of forces and completely nullify all the beneficial effects that are secured by the operation of the natural law on the lower plane. . . .

And thus we have the remarkable fact, so persistently overlooked in all the discussions of current question, that government, which fails to protect the weak, is devoting all its energies to protecting the strong. It legalized and promotes trusts and combinations; subsidizes corporations, and then absolves them from their obligations; sustains stockwatering schemes and all form of speculation; grants without compensation the most valuable franchises, often in perpetuity; and in innumerable ways creates, defends, and protects a vast array of purely parasitic enterprises, calculated directly to foster the worst forms of municipal corruption. The proofs of each one of these counts lie about us on every hand. Only those who are blinded by interest or prejudice can fail to see them. . . .

2. The Radical Left: Socialists and Anarchists

Efforts to criticize, to amend, or to reform competitive American society seemed very frail responses to the minority radical factions. Capitalist oppression, socialists and anarchists believed, could be eliminated only by completely transforming the society. All of the major socialists agreed on the common goal. The socialism of Jack London was romantic, eccentric, and filled with what his critics might have called a "petty bourgeois" fear of personal ruin. The more significant leaders, Eugene V. Debs and Daniel DeLeon, differed from London a great deal and disliked the "romantic adventurism" for which he stood. Debs and DeLeon also shared a common opposition to the cautious craft-unionism of Samuel Gompers and the American Federation of Labor. Still, the two socialist leaders represented two very different approaches to social change. Debs had been a union leader long before he studied Karl Marx, and he was perfectly willing to ally himself with as broad a labor front as he could muster and to explore the tactics of evolutionary democratic socialism. The more militant DeLeon demanded revolutionary action and helped to found the International Workers of the World (Wobblies) as an instrument for the immediate implementation of his strategy. For a revolutionary anarchist like Emma Goldman, intent on terrorist warfare against capitalism, neither the "gradualism" of Debs nor the "immediatism" of DeLeon could provide adequate weapons for the struggle or an acceptable plan for the anarchistic future. AUTHORS: Jack London (1876–1916), an illegitimate child, after an erratic boyhood in San Francisco, led a colorful existence as a waterfront adventurer, oyster pirate, ordinary seaman, tramp, prospector for gold, and journalist, before turning to socialist agitation and adventure fiction. Eugene V. Debs (1855–1926) of Terre Haute, Indiana emerged from the ranks to become the first President of the American Railway Union. After being jailed for his part in the railroad strike of 1894, he read Karl Marx and took up the cause of socialism. He went on to run five times as the Presidential candidate on the Socialist Party ticket. Emma Goldman (1869–1940), a Russian-born radical, advocated feminism, birth control, and, most importantly, anarchism. SELECTIONS: "An Unscientific Socialist" from London's War of the Classes (1905). "We Will Own the Mammoth Machines" from a Debs speech at Girard, Kansas, 1908. "Anarchism Is the Only Philosophy" from Goldman's Anarchism (1910).

AN UNSCIENTIFIC SOCIALIST (1905): JACK LONDON AT THE BOTTOM OF THE SOCIAL PIT

It is quite fair to say that I became a Socialist in a fashion somewhat similar to the way in which the Teutonic pagans became Christians—it was hammered into me. Not only was I not looking for Socialism at the time of my conversion, but I was fighting it. I was very young and callow, did not know much of anything, and though I had never even heard of a school called "Individualism," I sang the paean of the strong with all my heart. . . .

And because of all this, exulting in my young life, able to hold my own at work or fight, I was a rampant individualist. It was very natural. I was a winner. Wherefore I called the game, as I saw it played, a very proper game for MEN. To be a MAN was to write man in large capitals on my heart. To adventure like a man, and fight like a man, and do a man's work (even for a boy's pay)—these were things that reached right in and gripped hold of me as no other thing could. . . . I could see myself only raging through life without end like one of Nietzsche's blond beasts, lustfully roving and conquering by sheer superiority and strength.

As for the unfortunates, the sick, and ailing, and old, and maimed, I must confess I hardly thought of them at all. . . .

I hope I have made it clear that I was proud to be one of Nature's strong-armed noblemen. The dignity of labor was to me the most impressive thing in the world. . . .

In short, my joyous individualism was dominated by the orthodox bourgeois ethics. I read the bourgeois papers, listened to the bourgeois preachers, and shouted at the sonorous platitudes of the bourgeois politicians. . . .

Just about this time, returning from a seven months' voyage before the mast, and just turned eighteen, I took it into my head to go tramping. . . . And on this new *blond-beast* adventure I found myself looking upon life from a new and totally different angle. I had dropped down from the proletariat into what sociologists love to call the "submerged tenth," and I was startled to discover the way in which that submerged tenth was recruited.

I found there all sorts of men, many of whom had once been as good as myself and just as *blond-beastly;* sailor-men, soldier-men, labor-men, all wrenched and distorted and twisted out of shape by toil and hardship and accident, and cast adrift by their masters like so many old horses. I battered on the drag and slammed back gates with them, or shivered with them in box cars and city parks, listening the while to life-histories which began under auspices as fair as mine, with digestions and bodies equal to and better than mine, and which ended there before my eyes in the shambles at the bottom of the Social Pit.

And as I listened my brain began to work. The woman of the streets and the man of the gutter drew very close to me. I saw the picture of the Social Pit as vividly as though it were a concrete thing, and at the bottom of the Pit I saw them, myself above them, not far, and hanging on to the slippery wall by main strength and sweat. And I confess a terror seized me. What when my strength failed? when I should be unable to work shoulder to shoulder with the strong men who were as yet babes unborn? . . . I think it is apparent that my rampant individualism was pretty effectively hammered out of me, and something else as effectively hammered in. But, just as I had been an individualist without knowing it, I was a Socialist without knowing it, withal, an unscientific one. I had been reborn. . . .

WE WILL OWN THE MAMMOTH MACHINES (1908): EUGENE DEBS

Yes, I am my brother's keeper. I am under a moral obligation to him that is inspired, not by any maudlin sentimentality, but by the higher duty I owe to myself. What would you think of me if I were capable of seating myself at a table and gorging myself with food and saw about me the children of my fellow beings starving to death?

Allow me to say to you, my fellow men, that nature has spread a great table bounteously for all of the children of men. There is room for all and there is a plate and a place and food for all, and any system of society that denies a single one the right and the opportunity to freely help himself to nature's bounties is an unjust and iniquitous system that ought to be abolished in the interest of a higher humanity and a civilization worthy of the name. . . .

The great majority of mankind have always been in darkness. The overwhelming majority of the children of men have always been their own worst enemies. In every age of this world's history, the kings and emperors and czars and potentates, in alliance with the priests, have sought by all the means at their command to keep the people in darkness that they might perpetuate the power in which they riot and revel in luxury while the great mass are in a state of slavery and degradation, and he who has spoken out courageously against the existing order, he who has dared to voice the protest of the oppressed and downtrodden, has had to pay the penalty . . . all the way from Jesus Christ of Galilee down to Fred Warren of Girard.

Nothing is more humiliating than to have to beg for work, and a system in which any man has to beg for work stands condemned. No man can defend it. Now the rights of one are as sacred as the rights of a million. Suppose you happen to be the one who has no work. This republic is a failure so far as you are concerned. . . .

How is it with the babe that is born in Mott street, or in the lower Bowery, or in the east side of New York City? . . .

These children by hundreds and thousands are born in sub-cellars, where a whole grown family is crowded together in one room, where modesty between the sexes is absolutely impossible. They are surrounded by filth and vermin. From their birth they see nothing but vice and immorality and crime. They are tainted in the cradle. They are inoculated by their surroundings and they are doomed from the very beginning. This system takes their lives just as certainly as if a dagger were thrust into their quivering little hearts, and let me say to you that it were better for many thousands of them if they had never seen the light.

Now I submit, my friends, that such a condition as this is indefensible in the twentieth century. . . .

Nature's storehouse is full to the surface of the earth. . . . Why should any man, woman, or child suffer for food, clothing or shelter? Why? . . . Your material interest and mine in the society of the future will be the same. Instead of having to fight each other like animals, as we do today, and seeking to glorify the brute struggle for existence—of which every civilized human being ought to be ashamed—instead of this, our material interests are going to be mutual. We are going to jointly own these mammoth machines, and we are going to operate them as joint partners and we are going to divide all the products among ourselves.

We are not going to send our surplus to the Goulds and Vanderbilts of New York. We are not going to pile up a billion of dollars in John D. Rockefeller's hands—a vast pyramid from the height of which he can look down with scorn and contempt upon the "common herd." John D. Rockefeller's great fortune is built upon your ignorance. When you know enough to know what your interest is you will support the great party that is organized upon the principle of collective ownership of the means of life. . . .

ANARCHISM IS THE ONLY PHILOSOPHY
(1910): EMMA GOLDMAN

Anarchism is the only philosophy which brings to man the consciousness of himself; which maintains that God, the State, and society are non-existent, that their promises are null and void, since they can be fulfilled only through man's subordination. Anarchism is therefore the teacher of the unity of life; not merely in nature, but in man. There is no conflict between the individual and the social instincts, any more than there is between the heart and the lungs: the one the receptacle of a precious life essence, the other the repository of the element that keeps the essence pure and strong. The individual is the heart of society, conserving the essence of social life; society is the lungs which are distributing the element to keep the life essence—that is, the individual—pure and strong . . .

Anarchism is the great liberator of man from the phantoms that have held him captive; it is the arbiter and pacifier of the two forces for individual and social harmony. To accomplish that unity, Anarchism has declared war on the pernicious influences which have so far prevented the harmonious blending of individual and social instincts, the individual and society.

Religion, the dominion of the human mind; Property, the dominion of human needs; and Government, the dominion of human conduct, represent the stronghold of man's enslavement and all the horrors it entails. . . .

Real wealth consists in things of utility and beauty, in things that help to create strong, beautiful bodies and surroundings inspiring to live in. But if man is doomed to wind cotton around a spool, or dig coal, or build roads for thirty years of his life, there can be no talk of wealth.

What he gives to the world is only gray and hideous things, reflecting a dull and hideous existence,—too weak to live, too cowardly to die. Strange to say, there are people who extol this deadening method of centralized production as the proudest achievement of our age. They fail utterly to realize that if we are to continue in machine subserviency, our slavery is more complete than was our bondage to the king. They do not want to know that centralization is not only the death knell of liberty, but also of health and beauty, or art and science, all these being impossible in a clock-like, mechanical atmosphere. . . .

"All government in essence," says Emerson, "is tyranny." It matters not whether it is government by divine right or majority rule. In every instance its aim is the absolute subordination of the individual. . . .

Direct action against the authority in the shop, direct action against the authority of the law, direct action against the invasive, meddlesome authority of our moral code, is the logical, consistent method of Anarchism. . . .

Anarchism, the great leaven of thought, is today permeating every phase of human endeavor. Science, art, literature, the drama, the effort for economic betterment, in fact every individual and social opposition to the existing disorder of things, is illumined by the spiritual light of Anarchism. It is the philosophy of the sovereignty of the individual. It is the theory of social harmony. It is the great, surging, living truth that is reconstructing the world, and that will usher in the Dawn.

3. Critical Analyses of Commercial America

Henry George and Thorstein Veblen represent two very different aspects of the new social criticism. George was constantly in the fray as a pamphleteer, journalist, reformer, and candidate for Mayor in New York City. Veblen lived not only at the fringe of American society but on the outer edge of academic life. A curious, involuted, and often unnecessarily obscure scholarly jargon veiled a devastating critique of the American businessman. Veblen and George were only two among hundreds of scholars, publicists, reformers, and journalists who subjected almost every aspect of modern commercial life to critical scrutiny. AUTHORS: Henry George (1839–1897), left a middle-class, devoutly Episcopalian home for a seaman's life and a variety of working-class jobs before settling down to economics and reform. Thorstein Veblen (1857–1929), the son of poor Norwegian immigrants to Wisconsin, took a doctorate at Yale in preparation for an academic career which provided few rewards and left him perpetually insecure. SELECTIONS: "Progress and Poverty" from George's book of the same title (1879). "Conspicuous Leisure and Consumption" from Veblen's *Theory of the Leisure Class* (1899). "Engineer vs. Captain of Industry" from Veblen's *The Engineers and the Price System* (1921).

PROGRESS AND POVERTY: THE SINGLE TAX (1879): HENRY GEORGE

At the beginning of this marvelous era it was natural to expect . . . that the enormous increase in the power of producing wealth would make real poverty a thing of the past. . . .

Now, however, we are coming into collision with facts which there can be no mistaking. From all parts of the civilized world come complaints of industrial depression; of labor condemned to involuntary idleness; of capital massed and wasting; of pecuniary distress among business men; of want and suffering and anxiety among the working classes. . . .

This association of poverty with progress is the great enigma of our times. It is the central fact from which spring industrial, social, and political difficulties that perplex the world, and with which statesmanship and philanthropy and education grapple in vain. . . . I propose to seek the law which associates poverty with progress and increases want with advancing wealth. . . .

Until its ownership will confer some advantage, land has no value. Thus rent or land value does not arise from the productiveness or utility of land. . . . I may have very rich land, but it will yield no rent and have no value so long as there is other land as good to be had without cost. But when this other land is appropriated, and the best land to be had for nothing is inferior, either in fertility, situation, or other quality, my land will begin to have a value and yield rent. And though the productiveness of my land may decrease, yet if the productiveness of the land to be had without charge decreases in greater proportion, the rent I can get, and consequently the value of my land, will steadily increase. Rent, in short, is the price of monopoly, arising from the reduction to individual ownership of natural elements which human exertion can neither produce nor increase. . . .

There is but one way to remove an evil—and that is, to remove its cause. Poverty deepens as wealth increases, and wages are forced down while productive power grows, because land, which is the source of all wealth and the field of all labor, is monopolized. To extirpate poverty, to make wages what justice commands they should be, the full earnings of the laborer, we must therefore substitute for the individual ownership of land a common ownership.

The equal right of all men to the use of land is as clear as their equal right to breathe the air—it is a right proclaimed by the fact of their existence. For we cannot suppose that some men have a right to be in this world and others no right . . .

But a question of method remains. How shall we do it? . . . *It is not necessary to confiscate land; it is only necessary to confiscate rent.* . . .

What I, therefore, propose, as the simple yet sovereign remedy, which will raise wages, increase the earnings of capital, extirpate pauperism, abolish poverty, give remunerative employment to whoever wishes, afford free scope to human powers, lessen crime, elevate morals, and taste, and intelligence, purify government and carry civilization to yet nobler heights, is—*to appropriate rent by taxation.*

In this way, the State may become the universal landlord without calling herself so, and without assuming a single new function. In form, the ownership of land would remain just as now. No owner of land need be dispossessed, and no restriction need be placed upon the amount of land any one could hold. For, rent being taken by the State in taxes, land, no matter in whose name it stood, or in what parcels it was held, would be really common property, and every member of the community would participate in the advantages of its ownership.

Now, insomuch as the taxation of rent, or land values, must necessarily be increased just as we abolish other taxes, we may put the proposition into practical form by proposing— *To abolish all taxation save that upon land values.* . . .

CONSPICUOUS LEISURE AND CONSUMPTION (1899): THORSTEIN VEBLEN

These lower classes can in any case not avoid labor, and the imputation of labor is therefore not greatly derogatory to them, at least not within their class. Rather, since labor is their recognized and accepted mode of life, they take some emulative pride in a reputation for efficiency in their work, this being often the only line of emulation that is open to them. . . .

But it is otherwise with the superior pecuniary class, with which we are here immediately concerned. For this class also the incentive to diligence and thrift is not absent; but its action is so greatly qualified by the secondary demands of pecuniary emulation, that any inclination in this direction is practically overborne and any incentive to diligence tends to be of no effect. The most imperative of these secondary demands of emulation, as well as the one of widest scope, is the requirement of abstention from productive work. This is true in an especial degree for the barbarian stage of culture. During the predatory culture labor comes to be associated in men's habits of thoughts with weakness and subjection to a master. It is therefore a mark of inferiority, and therefore comes to be accounted unworthy of man in his best estate. By virtue of this tradition labor is felt to be debasing, and this tradition has never died out. On the contrary, with the advance of social differentiation it has acquired the axiomatic force due to ancient and unquestioned prescription.

In order to gain and to hold the esteem of men it is not sufficient merely to possess wealth or power. The wealth or power must be put in evidence, for esteem is awarded only on evidence. . . .

We have a realizing sense of ceremonial uncleanness attaching in an especial degree to the occupations which are associated in our habits of thought with menial service. It is felt by all persons of refined taste that a spiritual contamination is inseparable from certain offices that are conventionally required of servants. Vulgar surroundings, mean (that is to say, inexpensive) habitations, and vulgarly productive occupations are unhesitatingly condemned and avoided. . . .

In order to avoid stultification he [the rich man] must also cultivate his tastes, for it now becomes incumbent on him to discriminate with some nicety between the noble and ignoble in consumable goods. . . . This cultivation of the aesthetic faculty requires time and application, and the demands made upon the gentleman in this direction therefore tend to change his life of leisure into a more or less arduous application to the business of learning how to live a life of ostensible leisure in a becoming way. Closely related to the requirement that the gentleman must consume freely and of the right kind of goods, there is the requirement that he must know how to consume them in a seemly manner. . . .

ENGINEER VS. CAPTAIN OF INDUSTRY (1921): THORSTEIN VEBLEN

In more than one respect the industrial system of today is notably different from anything that has gone before. . . . It is an organization of mechanical powers and material resource, rather than of skilled craftsmen and tools; although the skilled workmen and tools are also an indispensable part of its comprehensive mechanism. It is of an impersonal nature, after the fashion of the material sciences, on which it constantly draws. It runs to "quality production" of specialized and standardized goods and services. For all these reasons it lends itself to systematic control under the direction of industrial experts, skilled technologists, who may be better called "production engineers," for want of a better term. . . .

And for the due working of this inclusive going concern it is essential that that corps of technological specialists, who by training, insight, and interest make up the general staff of industry, must have a free hand in the disposal of its available resources, in materials, equipment, and man power, regardless of any national pretensions or any vested interests. Any degree of obstruction, diversion, or withholding of any of the available industrial forces, with a view to the special gain of any nation or any investor, unavoidably brings on a dislocation of the system; which involves a disproportionate lowering of its working efficiency and therefore a disproportionate loss to the whole, and therefore a net loss to all its parts.

And all the while the statesmen are at work to divert and obstruct the working forces of this industrial system, . . . and the captains of finance are working at cross-purposes and in collusion, to divert whatever they can to the special gain of one vested interest and another, at any cost to the rest. So it happens that the industrial system is deliberately handicapped with dissension, misdirection, and unemployment of material resources, equipment, and man power, at every turn where the statesmen or the captains of finance can touch its mechanism; and all the civilized people are suffering privation together because their general staff of industrial experts are in this way required to take orders and submit to sabotage at the hands of the statesmen and the vested interests. Politics and investment are still allowed to decide matters of industrial policy which should plainly be left to the discretion of the general staff of production engineers driven by no commercial bias. . . .

4. The Social Gospel

Antebellum clergymen such as Theodore Parker set notable precedents by preaching social reform from the pulpit. Washington Gladden and many other colleagues in the Protestant ministry during the eighteen-eighties and the nineties followed their predecessors by making serious efforts to cope with the evils created by industrialism and urban growth. Advocates of the Social Gospel generally took a moderate approach by calling for an awakened Christian social conscience and ameliorative legislation. The reform ministers generally spoke to their middle-class church members, but some clerics tried seriously to work among the urban working class. AUTHOR: Washington Gladden (1836–1918), a Congregationalist minister from Indiana, spoke for the social conscience of the urban middle class in stressing the social nature of righteousness. SELECTION: "Christian Social Duties" from Gladden's *Applied Christianity* (1886).

CHRISTIAN SOCIAL DUTIES (1886): WASHINGTON GLADDEN

Perhaps the question with which we are trying to grapple will be more easily handled if we divide it just here into two separate inquiries:

1. What ought Christians to ask the state to do toward a more equitable distribution of wealth? What should be attempted in this direction by political methods?

2. What should Christians teach that individuals ought to do to promote a more equitable distribution of wealth?

First, then, it is undoubtedly the duty of Christians to do what they can by means of law to secure a better industrial system. But this is not saying that Christians should ask the state to take the property of the rich and distribute it among the poor. . . .

There are, however, one or two things that he will insist upon as the immediate duty of the state. Certain outrageous monopolies exist that the state is bound to crush. . . . The coal barons must not be permitted to enrich themselves by compelling the miners to starve at one end of their lines and the operatives to freeze at the other. In like manner the great lines of transportation from the West are under the control of three or four men. . . . Even now the oil in the poor man's lamp is heavily taxed by a greedy monopoly. All these iniquitous encroachments upon the rights of the people must be arrested; and it is the duty of every Christian, as the servant of a God of justice and righteousness, to say so in terms that cannot be misunderstood. . . .

Beyond this they cannot go far in this direction. . . . If all the property of this country were equally divided to-morrow morning, before to-morrow night thousands would be penniless and some hundreds would already be well on the way to fortune. . . .

All that intelligent Christians will ask the state to do, therefore, toward promoting the distribution of wealth, is to provide for the general welfare, as it now does, by taxation; to protect all classes in the exercise of their rights; to strike down those foes that now clutch our industries by the throat, and then leave the natural laws of trade and the motives of humanity and goodwill to effect a more equitable distribution. . . .

What message has Christianity for those who are getting the lion's share of the profits of production, respecting their duties to those who are getting so small a proportion of it? . . .

The Christian moralist is bound to admonish the Christian employer that the wage-system, when it rests on competition as its sole basis, is anti-social and anti-Christian. "Thou shalt love thy neighbor as thyself" is the Christian law, and he must find some way of incorporating that law into the organization of labor. It must be something more than an ideal; it must find expression in the industrial scheme. God has not made men to be associated for any purpose on an egoistic basis; and we must learn God's laws and obey them. . . .

It is not a difficult problem. The solution of it is quite within the power of the Christian employer. All he has to do is to admit his laborers to an *industrial partnership* with himself *by giving them a fixed share in the profits of production*, to be divided among them, in proportion to their earnings, at the end of the year. . . .

The sum of all this discussion is that the possession of wealth is justified by the Christian ethics, but that it puts the possessor under heavy obligations to multitudes less fortunate. He could never have become rich without the co-operation of many; he ought not to hold his riches for his own exclusive benefit. The great inequalities arising from the present defective methods of distribution will only be corrected through a deepening sense of the obligations imposed by the possession of wealth. The economic law, like the moral law, can never be fulfilled without love. . . .

5. The Muckrakers

The "Muckrakers" were christened by the disapproving Theodore Roosevelt who compared them to the benighted souls in John Bunyan's *Pilgrim's Progress*, so obsessed with raking muck at their feet that they failed to see the stars. Through mass circulation magazines such as *McClure's*, *Cosmopolitan*, and *Munsey's*, the Muckrakers relentlessly pursued graft, police-protected vice, political corruption, bribes by businessmen, child labor, the ruthlessness of giant trusts such as Standard Oil, the U.S. Senate as a "millionaire's club," and dozens of similar themes. AUTHORS: Lincoln Steffens (1866–1936), born into a well-to-do Sacramento family, chose journalism as a career. He joined the staff of *McClure's* in 1902. Ray Stannard Baker (1870–1946), born in Lansing, Michigan, was best known for his articles on railroad and financial abuses in *McClure's* magazine. With a mixture of sympathy and prejudice he "followed the color line" in the fall of 1906 and the spring of 1907. SELECTIONS: "The

Shame of the Cities" from the Steffens book of the same title. (1904.) "Following the Color Line North" from Baker's *Following the Color Line* (1908).

THE SHAME OF THE CITIES (1904):
LINCOLN STEFFENS

There is hardly an office from United States Senator down to Alderman in any part of the country to which the business man has not been elected; yet politics remains corrupt, government pretty bad, and the selfish citizen has to hold himself in readiness like the old volunteer firemen to rush forth at any hour, in any weather, to prevent the fire; and he goes out sometimes and he puts out the fire (after the damage is done) and he goes back to the shop sighing for the business man in politics. The business man has failed in politics as he has in citizenship. Why? Because politics is business. That's what's the matter with everything,—art, literature, religion, journalism, law, medicine,—they're all business. . . .

Many politicians have gone out into business and done well (Tammany ex-mayors, and nearly all the old bosses of Philadelphia are prominent financiers in their cities), and business men have gone into politics and done well (Mark Hanna, for example). They haven't reformed their adopted trades, however, though they have sometimes sharpened them most pointedly. The politician is a business man with a specialty. When a business man of some other line learns the business of politics, he is a politician, and there is not much reform left in him. Consider the United States, and believe me.

And it's all a moral weakness; a weakness right where we think we are strongest. Oh, we are good—on Sunday, and we are "fearfully patriotic" on the Fourth of July. But the bribe we pay to the janitor to prefer our interests to the landlord's is the little brother of the bribe passed to the alderman to sell a city street, and the father of the air-brake stock assigned to the president of a railroad to have this life-saving invention adopted on his road. And as for graft, railroad passes, saloon and bawdy-house blackmail, and watered stock, all these belong to the same family. We are pathetically proud of our democratic institutions and our republican form of government, of our grand Constitution and our just laws. We are a free and sovereign people, we govern ourselves and the government is ours. But that is the point. We are responsible, not our leaders, since we follow them. We *let* them divert our loyalty from the United States to some "party"; we *let* them boss the party and turn our municipal democracies into autocracies and our republican nation into a plutocracy. We cheat our government and we let our leaders loot it, and we let them wheedle and bribe our sovereignty from us. True, they pass for us strict laws, but we are content to let them pass also bad laws, giving away public property in exchange, and our good, and often impossible, laws we allow to be used for oppression and blackmail. And what can we say? We break our own laws and rob our own government, the lady at the custom-house, the lyncher with his rope, and the captain of industry with his bribe and rebate. The spirit of graft and of lawlessness is the American spirit. . . .

FOLLOWING THE COLOR LINE NORTH
(1908): RAY STANNARD BAKER

Having followed the color line in the South, it is of extraordinary inter-est and significance to learn how the Negro fares in the North. Is he treated better or worse? Is Boston a more favourable location for him than Atlanta or New Orleans? A comparison of the "Southern attitude" and the "Northern attitude" throws a flood of light upon the Negro as a national problem in this country. . . .

I know of nothing more tragic than the condition of the swarming newer Negro populations of Northern cities—the more tragic because the Negro is so cheerful and patient about it all. I looked into the statistics closely in several of them, and in no instance does the birth-rate keep pace with the death-rate. Even allowing for the fact that birth statistics are not very accurately kept in most cities it is probable that if it were not for the immigration constantly rolling upward from the South the Negro population in Northern cities would show a falling off. Consumption and the diseases of vice ravage their numbers. . . .

A few years ago no hotel or restaurant in Boston refused Negro guests; now several hotels, restaurants, and especially confectionery stores, will not serve Negroes, even the best of them. The discrimination is not made openly, but a Negro who goes to such places is informed that there are no accommodations, or he is overlooked and otherwise slighted, so that he does not come again. A strong prejudice exists against renting flats and houses in many white neighborhoods to colored people. . . .

Even at Harvard, where the Negro has always enjoyed exceptional opportunities, conditions are undergoing a marked change. A few years ago a large class of white students voluntarily chose a brilliant Negro student, R. C. Bruce, as valedictorian. But last year a Negro baseball player was the cause of so much discussion and embarrassment to the athletic association that there will probably never be another colored boy on the university teams. The line has already been drawn, indeed, in the medical department. . . .

In Indianapolis the Negro comes in contact with the "bungaloo gangs," crowds of rough and lawless white boys who set upon Negroes and beat them frightfully, often wholly without provocation. Although no law prevents Negroes from entering any park in Indianapolis, they are practically excluded from at least one of them by the danger of being assaulted by these gangs.

The street cars are free in all Northern cities, but the Negro nevertheless sometimes finds it dangerous to ride with white people. . . .

6. Populism

The Populist Party was organized in 1891, won a million votes for presidential candidate James B. Weaver in 1892, captured scattered governorships as well as six U.S. Senators and seven Representatives in 1894, and accepted the Democratic Presidential nominee (William Jennings Bryan) in 1896. The Populists proposed the nationalization of communications and transportation, the graduated income tax, and other reforms. The eight-hour day and similar Populist proposals failed to draw Eastern workers into their Western-Southern farm movement, but in the South the Party represented the single serious attempt in American history to bring Negro and white voters into a party on the ground of common economic interests. White supremacists used the weapon of racism to defeat the movement, and after 1897 the Populist Party ceased to be an effective force in the South or the West. SELECTION: Selection from *The Preamble and Platform of the Populist Party* (1892).

PREAMBLE AND PLATFORM OF THE POPULIST PARTY (1892)

The conditions which surround us best justify our cooperation. We meet in the midst of a nation brought to the verge of moral, political and material ruin. Corruption dominates the ballot-box, the Legislatures, the

Congress, and touches even the ermine on the bench. The people are demoralized; most of the States have been compelled to isolate the voters at the polling places to prevent universal intimidation or bribery. The newspapers are largely subsidized or muzzled, public opinion silenced, business prostrated, our homes covered with mortgages, labor impoverished and the land concentrating in the hands of the capitalists. The urban workmen are denied the right of organization for self-protection; imported pauperized labor beats down their wages; a hireling army, unrecognized by our laws, is established to shoot them down, and they are rapidly degenerating into European conditions. The fruits of the toil of millions are boldly stolen to build up colossal fortunes for a few, unprecedented in the history of mankind, and the possessors of these in turn despise the Republic and endanger liberty. From the same prolific womb of governmental injustice we breed the two great classes—tramps and millionaires. . . .

A vast conspiracy against mankind has been organized on two continents, and it is rapidly taking possession of the world. If not met and overthrown at once it forbodes terrible social convulsions, the destruction of civilization, or the establishment of an absolute despotism.

We have witnessed for more than a quarter of a century the struggles of the two great political parties for power and plunder, while grievous wrongs have been inflicted upon the suffering people. We charge that the controlling influence[s] dominating both these parties have permitted the existing dreadful conditions to develop without serious effort to prevent or restrain them. Neither do they now promise us any substantial reform. . . .

We declare, therefore,

First—That the union of the labor forces of the United States this day consummated shall be permanent and perpetual; may its spirit enter into all hearts for the salvation of the Republic and the uplifting of mankind.

Second—Wealth belongs to him who creates it, and every dollar taken from industry without an equivalent is robbery. "If any will not work, neither shall he eat." The interests of rural and civic labor are the same; their enemies are identical.

Third—We believe that the time has come when the railroad corporations will either own the people or the people must own the railroads, and should the government enter upon the work of owning and managing all railroads, we should favor an amendment to the Constitution by which all persons engaged in the government service shall be placed under a civil service regulation of the most rigid character, so as to prevent the increase of the power of the national administration by the use of additional government employees. . . .

Land—The land, including all the natural sources of wealth, is the heritage of the people, and should not be monopolized for speculative purposes, and alien ownership of land should be prohibited. All land now held by railroads and other corporations in excess of their actual needs, and all lands now owned by aliens, should be reclaimed by the government and held for actual settlers only. . . .

7. *Progressivism*

The Progressive movement can be dated from about 1902 to 1917, but its roots go back into the eighteen-eighties and nineties. A generation ago, commonly accepted interpretations traced origins to Populism, but now-adays scholars present the movement as an urban middle-class phenome-non, and several writers insist that the urban masses also took part. Progressivism had too many ambiguities to be captured in a few pat phrases: the movement attracted some great financiers and industrialists as well as their bitterest enemies; the ardent social reformers and con-servative Americans of "old family" nostalgic for the good old days before trusts, "robber barons," and corrupt political machines; social workers with sympathy and understanding for the immigrant masses in the cities and politicians with fear and hostility for the immigrant "menace." Both Theodore Roosevelt and Woodrow Wilson tried to bridge the several major camps by devising policies which would serve as unifying forces. Roosevelt's "New Nationalism" proposed to accept industrial bigness and to control it. Woodrow Wilson's "New Freedom" implied the rejection of all "monopolistic" tendencies and a Federal drive to "restore" lost economic freedom and opportunity. Wilson carried Progressive idealism, and his own style of political moralizing, into international affairs. AUTHORS: Theodore Roosevelt (1858–1919), Progressive reformer and a Harvard graduate with a patrician background, hunter and amateur rancher, historian, and author of books on Western life, governor of New York and a "Rough Rider" who led his own regiment of Western ranch hands in the Spanish-American War, came to the Presidency after the assassination of President McKinley in 1901. Woodrow Wilson (1856–1924), the son of a Virginia Presbyterian minister, had a long career as Professor and President at Princeton before running for the New Jersey Governorship in 1910. SELECTIONS: "We Stand at Armaged-don and Battle for the Lord" from Roosevelt's Acceptance Speech in 1912. "No Compromise with Monopoly" (1912) from Wilson's The New Freedom (1913). "To Make the World Safe for Democracy" from Wilson's War Message to Congress, April 2, 1917, and the Four-teen Points of January 3, 1918.

WE STAND AT ARMAGEDDON AND BATTLE
FOR THE LORD (1912): THEODORE ROOSEVELT

The prime need to-day is to face the fact that we are now in the midst of a great economic evolution. There is urgent necessity of applying both common sense and the highest ethical standard to this movement for better economic conditions among the mass of our people if we are to make it one of healthy evolution and not one of revolution. . . . Our fight is a fundamental fight against both of the old corrupt party machines, for both are under the dominion of the plunder league of the professional politicians who are controlled and sustained by the great beneficiaries of privilege and reaction. . . .

The first essential in the Progressive programme is the right of the people to rule. . . . We should provide by national law for presidential primaries. We should provide for the election of United States Senators by popular vote. We should provide for a short ballot. . . . [and] stringent and efficient corrupt-practices acts. . . .

Industry . . . must submit to such public regulation as will make it a means of life and health, not of death or inefficiency. We must protect the crushable elements at the base of our present industrial structure. . . .

We hold that under no industrial order, in no commonwealth, in no trade, and in no establishment should industry be carried on under conditions inimical to the social welfare. The abnormal, ruthless, spend-thrift industry of establishment tends to drag down all to the level of the least considerate. . . .

We stand for a living wage. . . high enough to make morality possible, to provide for education and recreation, to care for immature members of the family, to maintain the family during periods of sickness, and to permit of reasonable saving for old age.

Hours are excessive if they fail to afford the worker sufficient time to recuperate and return to his work thoroughly refreshed. We hold that the night labor of women and children is abnormal, and we hold that one day of rest in seven should be provided by law. . . .

It is abnormal for any industry to throw back upon the community the human wreckage due to its wear and tear, and the hazards of sickness, accident, invalidism, involuntary unemployment, and old age should be provided for through insurance. This should be made a charge in whole or in part upon the industries, the employer, the employee, and perhaps the people at large to contribute severally in some degree. . . .

Working women have the same need to combine for protection that working men have; the ballot is as necessary for one class as for the other; . . . and therefore we favor woman suffrage. . . .

It is utterly hopeless to attempt to control the trusts merely by the anti-trust law, . . . The anti-trust law should be kept on the statute-books and strengthened so as to make it genuinely and thoroughly effective against every big concern tending to monopoly or guilty of anti-social practices. At the same time, a national industrial commission should be created which should have complete power to regulate and control all the great industrial concerns engaged in interstate business—which practically means all of them in this country. This commission should exercise over these industrial concerns like powers to those exercised over the railways by the Interstate Commerce Commission, and over the national banks by the comptroller of the currency, and additional powers if found necessary. . . .

Our cause is based on the eternal principle of righteousness; and even though we who now lead may for the time fail, in the end the cause itself shall triumph. . . . To you who strive in a spirit of brotherhood for the betterment of our nation, to you who gird yourselves for this great new fight in the never-ending warfare for the good of mankind, I say in closing: . . . We stand at Armageddon, and we battle for the Lord.

NO COMPROMISE WITH MONOPOLY (1912): WOODROW WILSON AND THE NEW FREEDOM

We are at the parting of the ways. We have, not one or two or three, but many, established and formidable monopolies in the United States. We have, not one or two, but many, fields of endeavor into which it is difficult, if not impossible, for the independent man to enter. We have restricted credit, we have restricted opportunity, we have controlled development, and we have come to be one of the worst ruled, one of the most completely controlled and dominated, governments in the civilized world —no longer a government by free opinion, no longer a government by conviction and the vote of the majority, but a goverment by the opinion and the duress of small groups of dominant men. . . .

The Roosevelt plan is that there shall be an industrial commission charged with the supervision of the great monopolistic combinations which have been formed under the protection of the tariff, and that the government of the United States shall see to it that these gentlemen who have conquered labor shall be kind to labor. I find, then, the proposition in be this: That there shall be two masters, the great corporation, and over it the government of the United States; and I ask who is going to be master of the government of the United States? It has a master now,— those who in combination control these monopolies. And if the government controlled by the monopolies in its turn controls the monopolies, the partnership is finally consummated. . . .

The great employers and capitalists of the country would be under a more overpowering temptation than ever to take control of the government and keep it subservient to their purpose. . . . You cannot use monopoly in order to serve a free people. . . .

I do not trust any promises of a change of temper on the part of monopoly. Monopoly never was conceived in the temper of tolerance. Monopoly never was conceived with the purpose of general development. It was conceived with the purpose of special advantage. Has monopoly been very benevolent to its employees? Have the trusts had a soft heart for the working people of America? Have you found trusts that were keen to protect the lungs and the health and the freedom of their employees? Have you found trusts that thought as much of their men as they did of their machinery? Then who is going to convert these men into the chief instruments of justice and benevolence? . . .

The reason that America was set up was that she might be different from all the nations of the world in this: that the strong could not put the weak to the wall, that the strong could not prevent the weak from entering the race. America stands for opportunity. America stands for a free field and no favor. America stands for a government responsive to the interests of all. And until America recovers those ideals in practice, she will not have the right to hold her head high again amidst the nations as she used to hold it.

It is like coming out of a stifling cellar into the open where we can breathe again and see the free spaces of the heavens to turn away from such a doleful program of submission and dependence toward the other plan, the confident purpose for which the people have given their mandate. Our purpose is the restoration of freedom. We purpose to prevent private monopoly by law, to see to it that the methods by which monopolies have been built up are legally made impossible. We design that the limitations on private enterprise shall be removed, so that the next generation of youngsters, as they come along, will not have to become proteges of benevolent trusts, but will be free to go about making their own lives what they will; so that we shall taste again the full cup, not of charity, but of liberty,—the only wine that ever refreshed and renewed the spirit of a people. . . .

TO MAKE THE WORLD SAFE FOR DEMOCRACY (1917, 1918): WOODROW WILSON

We have no quarrel with the German people. We have no feeling towards them but one of sympathy and friendship. It was not upon their impulse that their Government acted in entering this war. . . .

We are accepting this challenge of hostile purpose because we know that in such a government, following such methods, we can never have a friend; and that in the presence of its organized power, always lying in wait to accomplish we know not what purpose, there can be no assured security for the democratic governments of the world. We are now about to accept gage of battle with this natural foe to liberty and shall, if necessary, spend the whole force of the nation to check and nullify its pretensions and its power. We are glad, now that we see the facts with no veil of false pretence about them, to fight thus for the ultimate peace of the world and for the liberation of its peoples, the German peoples included; for the rights of nations great and small and the privilege of men everywhere to choose their way of life and of obedience. The world must be made safe for democracy. . . .

We entered this war because violations of right had occurred which touched us to the quick and made the life of our own people impossible unless they were corrected and the world secured once for all against their recurrence. What we demand in this war, therefore, is nothing peculiar to ourselves. It is that the world be made fit and safe to live in; and particularly that it be made safe for every peace-loving nation which, like our own, wishes to live its own life, determine its own institutions, be assured of justice and fair dealing by the other peoples of the world as against force and selfish aggression. All the peoples of the world are in effect partners in this interest, and for our own part we see very clearly that unless justice be done to others it will not be done to us. . . .

Chapter XII. FROM PROTESTANT POLITY

TO RELIGIOUS PLURALISM

IN THE BEGINNING THE AMERICAN POPULATION WAS OVERWHELMINGLY Protestant. Of all religious congregations in 1775, 98.4 per cent can be classified as Protestant, 1.4 as Catholic, and three-twentieths of one per cent Jewish—a much higher degree of religious homogeneity than existed in England, France, Germany, or Ireland. A religious consensus existed, although it was limited by the fact that Protestants gave their loyalties to dozens of different churches. By 1775 various Protestant groups had worked out a rough measure of mutual toleration, and even members of the twenty-six Catholic churches and five synagogues generally worshipped in peace along with the Congregationalists, Presbyterians, Anglicans, Methodists, Moravians, French Reformed, Congregationalists-Separatists, Dunkers, Mennonites, and adherents of several dozen small sects. For a thousand years before the American Revolution, the ideal of religious uniformity had been defended as a political necessity, and most political writers assumed that prince and subjects had to share a common religion to make political allegiance possible. Yet in 1789 American society could command the loyalties of citizens from many different sects as well as from the scattered Catholic and Jewish congregations; and three centuries of American experience ultimately transformed Protestant predominance into an authentic pluralism.

Neither the condition of diversity nor the belief in religious pluralism as a value came to exist in Colonial America with the willing consent of Crown, Church, or Parliament. The first charter of Virginia, like other documents of this kind, required that only "the true word and service of God" be allowed and the second charter explicitly banned the entry of heretics. Most of the major thrusts of anti-Catholicism in England also affected the Colonies. In New England and in other sections where religious leaders had the numerical strength and the institutional power to enforce uniformity, they vigorously persecuted Quakers, Baptists, Arminians, and Unitarians. How then, did diversity and pluralism develop? First of all England during the sixteenth and seventeenth centuries was in religious affairs a badly divided country, and immigration transported those divisions to America by bringing Puritans and Separatists to New England, Baptists to Rhode Island, Catholics to Maryland, and Presbyterians and Anglicans to most of the colonies. Secondly, the English monarchs sometimes granted charters to heretics; certainly the cause of religious uniformity suffered from the grant to the Penn family which made possible the Quaker colony in Pennsylvania, or the Calvert grant which brought Catholics to Maryland. Special historical conditions explain the presence of several religious groups: settlers from the Netherlands established the Dutch Reformed Church in New Amsterdam, the small Scandinavian settlements left Lutheran traces in the Middle Colonies, and members of scattered English and German Pietistic sects of the eighteenth century slipped into the colonies almost unnoticed. Moreover, colonies such as Rhode Island, Maryland, and New York developed a cosmopolitan religious community fairly early, and the simple fact of coexistence sometimes seemed to lend the stamp of approval to diversity. The colonial physical and social environment stimulated the growth of religious diversity in several ways. The wilderness provided a refuge for dissenters like Anne Hutchinson, Roger Williams, and the Baptists and the Quakers who fled the Massachusetts Bay Colony for religious liberty beyond the pale of settlement. Institutional weaknesses often made it difficult or even impossible to suppress "heretical" sects, and all the conditions of geography, space and time, which made the Colonial enforcement of British political or economic measures difficult, also created problems for the implementation of religious policies.

By the time of the Revolution, most Americans had come to accept a rough toleration of other "denominations." Part of the credit can be given to the seventeenth-century conviction of some Calvinists in the Puritan and Baptist camps that no mortal man and no human institution could be regarded as infallible, and that God might disclose or confirm truth through unfettered theological discussion. Since all men were enslaved by sin, man's churchly institutions must be limited in power, and each congregation must be left in relative freedom to follow God's truth. The evolution of these ideas in the context of the American environment thrust the Colonists toward denominational freedom. Protestants of the American Revolution, like their ancestors in earlier years, denounced "sectarianism" as a bitterly divisive force in Christendom. The new concept of denominational freedom postulated the existence of a Christian community manifesting itself through denominational instruments, which existed primarily to organize various outward forms of worship and organization. A loose but authentic unity helped to make a large measure of tolerance possible for a society in which most of the large churches shared common Calvinist theological beliefs. The two exceptions were more apparent than real: Colonial Anglicans, often very "low church" in inclination, were influenced by Calvinism; and Lutherans did not arrive in large numbers during the crucial period.

During the early national period competition for members was keen among the large denominations, but they cooperated reasonably well in facing the two great challenges of the age: the unchurched majority in the East, and the insatiable need for organization in the rapidly expanding West. Interchurch drives launched a number of Bible Tract, Home Mission, and Sunday School Societies, which achieved major successes in the East and the West. If, in time, several churches expressed dissatisfaction with group activities, it was partly because of the relative decline in strength of the "old" and the "new" churches. Well over half of all churched Americans in 1775 had been Congregationalists, Presbyterians, or Anglicans, but by 1830 the three "old" churches had fewer than eight hundred thousand members while the Methodists and Baptists could boast of well over two million members. Except for the later growth of the Lutherans and several Pentecostal sects, the patterns of 1830 persisted into the twentieth century.

Between 1775 and 1830 the Methodists and Baptists displayed much skill in attracting lower income groups in the East, but the really spectacular expansion came because of their greater institutional ability to cope with conditions on the frontier and in the back country. A stress on revivalism, emotionalism, and evangelism; the circuit rider and the camp meeting; a sermon style which provided a simplified "modernized" version of latter day Calvinism; the tendency to reduce theology to the fundamental drama of the individual struggling to escape sin and win salvation; few or no educational requirements for the clergy beyond "investiture by the Holy Spirit," (which made it possible to place a substantial number of ministers in the right place at the right time to gather converts)—all of these factors enabled the Methodist and Baptist Churches to exploit Western opportunities so as to win a very high percentage of total memberships. Life on the frontier was often raw, disorganized, lonely, and violent. Frontier conditions were not often fully grasped by Episcopal and Congregational leaders. Western expansion seemed to be a more difficult task for the older churches because of their greater rigidity of theological definitions, higher educational standards for the ministry, and their tendency to frown on the methods of the camp meeting and the revival which won so much favor in the back country.

Nevertheless, all Protestant churches prospered to some extent, and if the Episcopalians, Congregationalists, and Presbyterians gained less than other groups between the Revolution and the Civil War they could still find consolation in the steady and substantial growth of their own churches. By 1850 American Protestants had many reasons for confidence. The West had been saved for Christianity; the number of churched persons had nearly tripled since the Revolution and continued to rise; institutions such as Bible Tract Societies and Sunday School organizations existed across the country; and most churches displayed at least limited toleration toward other religious groups. At this juncture of affairs, two violent storms of emotion burst upon Protestants. The first controversy involved a great wave of nativist hostility against the Catholicism of the Irish immigrants; and the second controversy centered around slavery, an issue so bitterly debated that it led to the separation of many Protestant churches into Northern and Southern branches. The mere passage of time did not remove the roots of either controversy, but the abolition of slavery and the expansion of Negro Protestant churches moved the problem of race relations at least temporarily from the center of affairs. The anti-Catholic furor receded from the emotional peak of the fifties, but the forces which had created the Know-Nothing movement reappeared in the American Protestant Association of the eighteen-eighties, anti-Catholic drives of the Ku Klux Klan in the nineteen-twenties, and the wave of Protestant protest in 1928 against the Catholicism of the Democratic presidential candidate, Alfred E. Smith.

More than forty million immigrants entered the United States between the Civil War and the First World War, and a high percentage of them were Catholic peasants from Southern and Eastern Europe. The consequences for American society were large from the beginning, but it was not until after the First World War that the impact of the newcomers began to work substantial differences in the national society. At first only dimly aware of the newcomer, Protestants concentrated on their own numerical growth and on the attempt to cope with the rise of the city through such institutions as the Young Men's Christian Association and the community church.

In modern times the cities posed more baffling problems for Protestant churches, and with each decade of the twentieth century the percentage of urban Protestants has declined. Protestants, along with Catholics, Jews, and other religious groups, also began in the nineteen-twenties more serious efforts to find solutions for the problems posed by the reality of religious pluralism. The quest for tolerance without the loss of group integrity, the need for each religious body to exist in the company of many others and yet resist illegitimate demands from the currently dominant forces in the culture,—these were perhaps the basic problems for most religious Americans.

The Catholic Church demonstrated much solid strength and institutional vitality in the twentieth century after a long history which had often involved precarious or violent circumstances. Catholicism arrived in America with Columbus, and the Church planted its missions in what was to become California and Texas long before the United States became a political reality. Still, major confrontations of Protestants and Catholics did not often take place in early American history. In 1776 the new nation contained only twenty-six parishes. The Catholic Church was not very visible to most Protestants in the first generation or two; the official definitions of American society welcomed all comers; and the Protestant theory of denominational tolerance tended to throw a cloak of partial acceptance around Catholics. However the confrontation of middle- and working-class Yankee Protestants and Irish Catholic peasant immigrants in the eighteen-forties and -fifties led to street fighting in Boston, New York, Philadelphia, and elsewhere, to the burning of several convents and churches, to the Nativist "Know Nothing" movement, and to the continuing hostility of many native American Protestants. In antebellum America, Catholic leaders such as Bishop John Hughes of New York often fought to eliminate Protestant trappings from public school, but with only indifferent success, and as the century wore on many Catholics became persuaded of the need to build a parochial school system. The poverty of most immigrants made the task an extremely difficult one, and it was not until modern times that an adequate parochial school system came into being. Moreover the Protestants did not have a monopoly on internal factionalism. While the Catholic Church in America was to a certain extent shaped in the Irish image, it became by the end of the nineteenth century an institutional coalition of immigrants from Ireland, Italy, Poland, and elsewhere. Irish power had its challengers, and intergroup conflict posed many problems. The Catholic Church experienced more subtle difficulties in its attempts to keep the integrity of the faith in an American environment which encouraged careless-ness in theological distinctions, and manifested opposition to several basic Catholic ideas. Still, no problem seemed insoluble, and the Catholic Church grew in numbers and institutional strength during each decade of the twentieth century. The election of a Catholic president in 1960 demonstrated the decline of Protestant hostilities, and millions of Catholics felt confident enough about the state of the Union to indulge their personal preferences by voting against John F. Kennedy.

Like the Catholics, American Jews in the nineteen-sixties could point to many concrete social and economic gains. For a long time Judaism, represented in 1775 by only five synagogues, experienced a very slow institutional growth, despite the fact that American society showed little anti-Semitism. (But ghetto walls were also falling in many parts of Europe.) Early immigrants were mainly Sephardic Jews, originally from Spain and Portugal, and generally familiar with major trends of thought and life in the general Western society. Adjustment to American life did not involve insurmountable barriers, and a fairly high percentage of the small community achieved promi-nence in politics and other fields between the Revolution and the Civil War. The basic patterns of American anti-Semitism date only as far back as the eighteen-seventies and -eighties, and more particu-larly to the turn of the century when the major sources of immigra-tion shifted to Eastern Europe and the pace of migration increased at a fantastic rate. An upsurge of hostile feelings in the first quarter of the twentieth century was followed by a gradual but perceptible de-cline of anti-Semitism. The Nazi movement and the mass murders of the Second World War provided a sobering influence on many gen-tiles, gave some Jews new reasons for cosmic pessimism, and sug-gested to a great many Jews the value of the American refuge. Thus all major religious factions felt the thrust toward an exploration of the implications of religious pluralism. The Founding Fathers had intended to establish a cosmopolitan society which welcomed men and women of many faiths, but the increasing religious and ethnic diversification of the nineteenth and twentieth century made con-flicts in day-to-day life almost inevitable. Some gap between the open society proclaimed by the national ideology and the tensions of day-to-day living among diverse groups may be unavoidable, but by the middle of the twentieth century the gap of fifty or a hundred years earlier had been substantially narrowed. Despite the persistence of anti-Semitism, anti-Catholicism, and other forms of group hostility, members of these three faiths—and other churches such as the Eastern Orthodox—shared a common national society with a substantial store of mutual good will.

1. Evolving Protestantism

From the Great Awakening, Protestants tended to think of religion in two basic ways. The new evangelical approach of the seventeen-forties stressed revival methods, the central place of the emotions in religion, the need for the minister to be almost constantly moved by the Holy Spirit, and the necessity of attempting frequently to awaken the congregation to the joys of salvation and the awful imminence of damnation. Opponents of the Awakening emphasized a definition of religion in which a set of carefully defined, rationally defended theological beliefs played a central part; they clung to high standards of theological analysis by well-educated ministers who scorned the "wild" emotionalism of "misguided fanatics." Still the Calvinist Churches kept a measure of unity, and a battered but still active Calvinism moved into the nineteenth century. Antebellum America saw frequent conflicts of "Old Lights" who wished to preserve traditional Calvinism and "New Lights" who wanted to find modern formulas for modified Calvinism. After the Civil War, scientific developments such as evolution posed problems for the churches; and the "Higher Criticism" of the Bible proved even more corrosive to traditional beliefs. Twentieth-century "Fundamentalists" tried to save the belief in the literal truth of Scriptural "fundamentals," and the "liberal" advocates of "The New Theology" struggled to reconcile science and Biblical criticism with American Protestantism. In recent times, theologians such as Reinhold Niebuhr have abandoned "liberalism" as a danger to Christian faith, and sought an "orthodox" expression of tragic Christianity. AU-THORS: Horace Bushnell (1802–1876), a Yale graduate and a Congregational minister, tried to set aside both rigid rationalism and precise theological debate to re-express basic dogmas in a way that would reconcile faith and reason. William A. "Billy" Sunday (1862–1935) gave up a career in professional baseball to join the Chicago YMCA; in 1896 he began an independent evangelical mission and for decades to come made revival tours of the country. Theodore T. Munger (1830–1910), a Congregational minister, attempted to reorient Protestantism toward a full acceptance of science, evolution, and historical criticism. Reinhold Niebuhr (1892–   ), a leading theologian and an advocate of social justice,

has attracted much attention by his defense of neo-orthodoxy. SELEC-
TIONS: *Christian Nurture* (1847) from Bushnell's essay. "Urban Evangelism" from Sunday's *Sermons in Omaha as Reported by the Omaha Daily
News* (1915). "The New Theology" from Munger's *Freedom of Faith*
(1883). "A Protestant Return to Pessimism" from Niebuhr's *The Nature
and Destiny of Man*, 2 vols (1941, 1943).

CHRISTIAN NURTURE (1847): HORACE BUSHNELL

There is then some kind of nurture which is of the Lord, deriving a
quality and a power from Him, and communicating the same. Being
instituted by Him, it will of necessity have a method and a character
peculiar to itself, or rather to Him. It will be the Lord's way of education,
having aims appropriate to Him, and, if realized in its full intent, termi-
nating in results impossible to be reached by any merely human method.
. . . What is the true idea of Christian education? . . . *That the child
is to grow up a Christian, and never know himself as being otherwise.*

In other words, the aim, effort, and expectations should be, not, as is
commonly assumed, that the child is to grow up in sin, to be converted
after he comes to a mature age; but that he is to open on the world as one
that is spiritually renewed, not remembering the time when he went
through a technical experience, but seeming rather to have loved what is
good from his earliest years. . . .

This doctrine is not a novelty, now rashly and for the first time
propounded. . . . It is as old as the Christian church, and prevails extensively at the present day in other parts of the world. . . .

URBAN EVANGELISM (1915): BILLY SUNDAY

So, what's the nature of a revival? . . . As a nation we are facing the
danger of the domination of the material over the spiritual; we are com-
mercially drunk. Take a bushel of nickels and walk down the street of the
average town and you can lead that grasping bunch so close to hell they
can smell the brimstone and sulphur. . . . We have got a wonderful
country; wonderful. The American advances in industry, but I am mighty
sorry to say we have not had a corresponding advance in the morality and
decency of the country.

Andrew Carnegie can build libraries on every street; you can build
high schools in every block; you can build a university in every town, but
you cannot save the people or the country without religion.

If this country has the sins of Babylon, she will go to hell like Babylon. Education will not save you; nothing will save you but the gospel of Jesus Christ. . . .

This is the day of isms and schisms and ologies, fol-da-rols, tommy-rot and heresies to lead people astray. It is an axiom that the measure of your preparation will determine the measure of your success—in religion, politics, anything else. . . .

Listen to me. If in your city there are sins and immorality, drunkenness and crime; if you have seduction, pandering and white slavery, and your streets are filled with staggering, reeling drunkards, and girls losing their virtue, the responsibility for that state of things is not with God, but with the citizenship of Omaha. . . .

Martin Luther saved Europe from spiritual death—a spiritual revival under Martin Luther was the cause of the Reformation. . . .

Wesley and Whitefield saved England from the French Revolution. Edwards, Finney, and Moody lifted America from degradation by revivals of their day. . . .

You turn up your noses at a revival when the very religion which you love was born in a time of revival. I wonder God don't knock you over. Paul was an evangelist, and whenever Paul was to preach or wherever he went they had to call out the police to protect him; he had a revival or a riot everywhere he went. You cut the day of Pentecost off of history; you cut Peter, James and Paul out of history and what you have left would not make a decent rummage sale.

Any boy can throw a stone and break a stained glass window, but it takes an artist to make one; any fool can build a fire and burn a building, but it takes a skilled mechanic to reconstruct it; a mob crucified Christ, but it took God to raise him from the dead; any fool can sneer at a revival; any fool can do that, and you are a fool if you do. . . . The preacher has his place in God's economy and I have got mine. I believe God Almighty calls me to do what I am doing as much as any preacher. . . . A revival is a conviction of sin, a conviction of sin on the part of the church. . . .

THE NEW THEOLOGY (1883): THEODORE T. MUNGER

1. It does not propose to do without a theology. . . . If it finds itself driven into impenetrable mystery, as it inevitably must, it prefers to take counsel of the higher sentiments and better hopes of our nature. . . . While it believes in a harmony of doctrines, it regards with suspicion what have been known as systems of theology. . . .

2. The New Theology does not part with the historic faith of the church, but rather seeks to put itself in its line while recognizing a process of development.

3. It does not reject the specific doctrines of the church of the past. It holds to the Trinity, though indifferent to the use of the word, but not to a formal and psychologically impossible Trinity. . . .

4. It is not iconoclastic in its temper; it is not pervaded by a spirit of denial, but is constructive. . . .

5. It is not disposed to find a field and organization outside of existing churches. . . . I pass now to the positive features of the New Theology.

1. It claims for itself a somewhat larger and broader use of the reason than has been accorded to theology. . . .

2. The New Theology seeks to interpret the Scriptures in what may be called a more natural way, and in opposition to a hard, formal, unsympathetic and unimaginative way. . . .

3. The New Theology seeks to replace an excessive individuality by a truer view of the solidarity of the race. . . .

4. This theology recognizes a new relation to natural science; but only in the respect that it ignores the long apparent antagonism between the kingdoms of faith and of natural law. . . .

5. The New Theology offers a contrast to the Old in claiming for itself a wider study of man. . . .

6. The New Theology recognizes the necessity of a restatement of belief in Eschatology, or the doctrine of Last Things. . . .

A PROTESTANT RETURN TO PESSIMISM (1941, 1943): REINHOLD NIEBUHR

The idea of individuality which is the most unique emphasis of modern culture, is . . . a tragically abortive concept, which cannot be maintained as either fact or as idea within the limits of the cultural presuppositions of modernity. The social history of modern life moves from the individualism of the early commercial period to the collectivism of industrialism. The individual who emancipates himself from the social solidarities of agrarian feudalism and the religious authoritarianism of medievalism is, within a brief span of history, subjected to the mechanical solidarities of industrial collectivism. His revolt against this collectivism betrays him into the even more grievous tyranny of primitive racialism and imperial nationalism. . . .

Without the presuppositions of the Christian faith the individual is either nothing or becomes everything. In the Christian faith man's insignificance as a creature, involved in the process of nature and time, is lifted into significance by the mercy and power of God in which his life is sustained. But his significance as a free spirit is understood as subordinate to the freedom of God. His inclination to abuse his freedom, to over-estimate his power and significance and to become everything is under-stood as the primal sin. It is because man is inevitably involved in this primal sin that he is bound to meet God first of all as a judge, who humbles his pride and brings his vain imagination to naught. . . .

Protestantism, in spite of its more prophetic conception of the in-evitability of sinful pride in all the activities of mankind, allowed a vent for political arrogance of which the rising nation was to take full advan-tage.

As a consequence a culture, schooled by the Renaissance on the one hand and the Reformation on the other, has resulted in a contemporary period of decadence in which the collective will of man, particularly as embodied in the nation, has achieved heights of sinful pretension never before equalled. The nation is god. . . .

The pride of nations and the arrogance of self-deification of collec-tive man are the more extravagant for being expressed in and against a Christian culture in which it must consciously negate and defy the high-est insights of the faith which formed the culture of the western world.

The most daemonic form of nationalism today is expressed against rather than in a Christian culture. The German Nazis were quite right in regarding the Christian faith as incompatible with their boundless na-tional egoism. While Christianity may itself be made the tool of national-ism, the Christian faith, if it retains any vitality, is bound to mediate some word of divine judgment upon the nation, which the Nazis find intolerable. No nation is free of the sin of pride, just as no individual is free of it. . . . While all modern nations, and indeed all nations of history, have been involved in the sin of pride, one must realize, in this as in other estimates of human sinfulness, that it is just as important to recognize differences in the degree of pride and self-will expressed by men and nations, as it is to know that all men and nations are sinful in the sight of God. Here, as in individual life, the final sin is the unwillingness to hear the word of judgment spoken against our sin. By that criterion, the modern fascist nations have achieved a daemonic form of national self-assertion which is more dangerous even than that of the ancient religious empires because it is expressed within and against the insights of a Chris-tian culture. . . .

All the known facts of history verify the interpretation of human destiny implied in New Testament eschatology. Yet most of the philoso-phies of history, both ancient and modern, have sought to obscure either one or the other aspect of history which Biblical eschatology illumines. Ancient philosophies of history either denied the meaningfulness of his-tory entirely or they saw only the limited meaningfulness of its allegedly recurring cycles. Modern philosophies have emphasized the unity of history and its cumulative tendencies; but they sought to obscure and deny the perils and evils in the cumulations of history, so that they might regard history itself as the God of redemption.

If we inquire more closely why these mistakes were made, our consideration of the end of human destiny brings us back to the problems of the beginning. For the most plausible explanation of the mistakes is that they were prompted by the desire to find a way of completing human destiny which would keep man's end under his control and his power. The ancient world sought to do this by emancipating the spirit of man from the flux of finiteness or by subordinating his freedom to that flux. The modern world has sought redemption by regarding the process of history itself as a guarantor of the fulfillment of human life.

In every case the "vain imagination" of human pride entered into these calculations and determined the result. . . . The belief that man could solve his problem either by an escape from history or by the historical process itself is a mistake which is partly prompted by the most universal of all "ideological" taints: the pride, not of particular men and cultures, but of man as man. . . .

Thus wisdom about our destiny is dependent upon a humble recognition of the limits of our knowledge and our power. Our most reliable understanding is the fruit of "grace" in which faith completes our ignorance without pretending to possess its certainties as knowledge; and in which contrition mitigates our pride without destroying our hope. . . .

2. *Catholicism and Nativism*

In the seventeen-eighties John Carroll strove to organize a "National Catholic Church," the first Bishop of which might be elected by American priests. Bishop Carroll was appointed as the first American Catholic Bishop in 1789. Some of his suggestions were rejected by his ecclesiastic superiors, but he gave the American Church its initial direction, and his writings suggest some of the problems the Church was to encounter among Protestant Americans extremely suspicious of the international nature of Catholicism. Catholic spokesmen of the nineteenth century spent much time and energy in trying to answer the hostile attacks of Protestants. The Nativist-Catholic conflict involved more than religious issues, for it was also a cultural conflict between tradition-bound peasants and the mobile, restless citizens of a middle-class society, between Yankees and Irishmen. Many Catholics of the eighteen-forties and fifties were Irish immigrants who had arrived in poverty-stricken flight from catastrophe. The contrast of Irish poverty and Yankee prosperity tended to increase rather than diminish conflict. Even after anti-Catholic reaction retreated from the peak of the eighteen-fifties, churchmen such as Bishop Spaulding continued to grapple with problems raised by the Nativist accusation that Catholics could not be "good Americans." AUTHORS: Orestes A. Brownson (1803–1876) wandered restlessly through Presbyterianism, Universalism, Unitarianism, and agnosticism before becoming a Catholic. Samuel F. B. Morse (1791–1872), painter and inventor, produced characteristic propaganda pieces to express nativist hostility against immigrant Catholics. John Lancaster Spalding (1840–1916) of Lebanon, Kentucky, studied at St. Mary's College and the Louvain, was ordained in 1865, and became Bishop of Peoria in 1876. He served Theodore Roosevelt as an arbiter for the coal strike of 1902. SELECTIONS: The "Great Catholic Conspiracy Against the Republic" from Morse's *Imminent Dangers to the Free Institution of the United States Through Foreign Immigration* (1835). "Catholicism and Americanism" from Brownson's *The Convert* (1857). "Catholic Allegiance Not Divided" from Spalding's *Lectures and Discourses* (1882).

EARLY NATIVISM: THE "GREAT CATHOLIC CONSPIRACY" AGAINST THE REPUBLIC (1835): SAMUEL F. B. MORSE

Let me recapitulate the facts in the case, and see if any one of them can be denied; and if not, I submit it to the calm decision of every American, whether he can still sleep in fancied security, while incendiaries are at work; and whether he is ready quietly to surrender his liberty, civil and religious, into the hands of foreign powers.

　　1. It is a fact, that in this age the subject of civil and religious liberty agitates in the most intense manner the various European governments.

　　2. It is a fact, that the influence of American free institutions in subverting European despotic institutions is greater now. . . .

　　3. It is a fact that Popery is opposed in the very nature to Democratic Republicanism; and it is, therefore, as a political system, as well as religious, opposed to civil and religious liberty, and consequently to our form of government.

　　4. It is a fact, that this truth, respecting the intrinsic character of Popery, has lately been clearly and demonstratively proved in public lectures, by one of the Austrian Cabinet, a devoted Roman Catholic. . . .

　　5. It is a fact, that this Member of the Austrian Cabinet [Frederick Schlegel], in his lectures, designated and proscribed this country by name, as the "*great nursery of destructive principles; as the Revolutionary school for France and the rest of Europe.*". . .

6. It is a fact, that very shortly after the delivery of these lectures, a Society was organized in the Austrian capital, called the St. Leopold Foundation, for the purpose "of promoting the greater activity of Catholic Missions in America."

7. It is a fact, that this Society is under the patronage of the Emperor of Austria . . . that it is actively at work, collecting moneys, and sending agents to this country, to carry out into effect its designs. . . .

16. It is a fact, that the greater part of the foreigners in our population is composed of Roman Catholics. . . .

CATHOLICISM AND AMERICANISM (1857): ORESTES A. BROWNSON

I can say truly that, during the nearly thirteen years of Catholic experience, I have found not the slightest reason to regret the step I took. . . .

I do not pretend that I have found the Catholic population perfect . . . yet I have found that population superior to what I expected, more intellectual, more cultivated, more moral, more active, living, and energetic. Undoubtedly, our Catholic population, made up in great part of the humbler classes of the Catholic populations of the Old World, for three hundred years subjected to the bigotry, intolerance, persecutions, and oppressions of Protestant or quasi-Protestant governments, have traits of character, habits, and manners, which the outside non-Catholic American finds unattractive, and even repulsive. . . . This is certainly to be deplored, but can easily be explained without prejudice to the church, by adverting to the condition to which these individuals were reduced before coming here; to their disappointments and discouragements in a strange land; . . . and to our great lack of schools, churches, and priests. . . . Yet there is a respectable Catholic-American literature springing up among us, and Catholics have their representatives among the first scholars and scientific men in the land. In metaphysics, in moral and intellectual philosophy, they take already the lead; in natural history and the physical sciences, they are not far behind; and let once the barrier between them and the non-Catholic public be broken down, and they will soon take the first position in general and polite literature. . . . That the church serves the cause of patriotism; that, if embraced, it is sure to give us a high-toned and chivalric national character; that it enlists conscience in the support of our free institutions and the preservation of our republican freedom as the established order of the country, is a good reason why the American people should not oppose her, and why they should wish her growth and prosperity in our country; but the real reason why we should become Catholics and remain such, is, because she is the new creation, regenerated humanity, and without communion with her, we can never see God as he is, or become united to him as our supreme good in the supernatural order. . . .

CATHOLIC ALLEGIANCE NOT DIVIDED
(1882): BISHOP SPALDING

The Church is one, holy, Catholic, and apostolic. Its essential unity is derived from the Holy Ghost, who is its principle of life. "What the soul is to the body," says St. Augustine, "the Spirit of Jesus Christ is to the Church. He acts in the universal Church as the soul acts in the whole body. A limb that is cut off dies; life remains in the body, but not in the dissevered member; and so the Holy Ghost does not abide with those who have separated from the body of the Church." The Church, then, is one in its principle of life, from which it also derives its unity of organization, of government, of doctrine, and of worship. Opposed to unity are heresy and schism. Heresy violates unity of doctrine, and schism unity of organization and government. Doctrinal error, however, may exist without heresy. . . .

The perfect distinction between Church and state is perhaps the most striking peculiarity of Christian history. From the beginning Christians drew a line between God and Caesar, between fidelity to conscience and loyalty to the government.

The spiritual powers and political powers are both sovereign and separate. They differ from one another in their essence, in their constitution, in the end for which they exist, and in the means of which they make use. They are not, however, or ought not to be, enemies; and though each, in its own sphere, is independent of the other, the greatest good of the greatest number, whether here or hereafter, is attainable only when these two powers co-operate to this end. As the temporal and the eternal happiness of man are both ordered by God's law, the societies to which these interests are committed should work in harmony; and conflict can arise only when the one or the other is guilty of usurpation. Freedom of conscience, which is the mother of civil liberty, is protected and guarded by the separation of the religious and the civil authority; and this great fact, whose existence in history is due chiefly to the action of the Papacy, is thus the salvation and the glory of Christian civilization. . . . Neither the state nor the Church is permitted to absorb the whole man, and hence where the Church is free, absolutism cannot exist. The allegiance of the Catholic is not divided. He yields full and entire obedience to the state in all matters that are within the sphere of its competence, and he recognizes this duty as part of his religious faith. He obeys the Church in the same way, and finds that his devotion to his religion does not in the least interfere with his loyalty to the government. His allegiance is double and not divided. . . .

Liberty and toleration, which enter so largely into the constitution of civil society, especially in our day, cannot be left out of sight when there is question of the relations of Church and state. . . .

3. Judaism in America

The Reform movement to amend Orthodox Judaism had its roots in Germany and elsewhere, but the Conservative movement developed on the American scene, and occupied a medial position between Reform and Orthodox groups. As the essay by Solomon Grayzel indicates, a good many organizations sprang up to express Jewish beliefs, and not even all of these contained the activities of native-born and immigrant American Jews. AUTHOR: Solomon Grayzel (1920–   ), editor of the Jewish Publications Society of America and Corresponding Secretary of the American Jewish Historical Society, has published A History of the Jews as well as other works. SELECTION: "Orthodox, Reform, and Conservative Judaism" from a Grayzel essay in Harry Schneiderman, Two Generations in Perspective (1957).

ORTHODOX, REFORM, AND CONSERVATIVE JUDAISM (1957): SOLOMON GRAYZEL

Nowhere was religious division more apparent and more articulate than in the United States. The emergence of three distinct religious viewpoints by the beginning of the twentieth century has already been mentioned. Of the three, the Reform group alone was well organized. . . . In 1913, Schechter founded the United Synagogue of America, dedicated to what he preferred to call Historical Judaism, but which has come to be known as Conservative Judaism.

All of these religious movements and institutions combined, it must be remembered, did not command the adherence of all the Jews in the United States, any more than similar movements and institutions claimed the loyalty of all the countries of Europe. A substantial minority of the newly arrived immigrants as well as of the older residents were indifferent to affiliation with organized religion of any kind. This reflected the trend in the general population, though among Protestants more than among Catholics. That the lack of affiliation was more apparent in the Jewish group may be accounted for by a number of considerations; the impression that adjustment demands the obliteration of all differences, the special susceptibility of Jews to rationalist influences, the inability of immigrant parents to transmit their heritage in the terms of their new environment, and, finally, the patent fact that Jews can express their Jewishness in ways other than public or even private worship. Each of the numerous organizations which claimed the loyalty of Jews—B'nai B'rith lodges, landsmannschaften, the Workmen's Circle, Zionist clubs, or any number of others of a philanthropic nature—could claim to be an expression of the Jewish spirit.

This fragmentation of Jewish life may have made it colorful and interesting, but it also made it chaotic. . . .

The period of adjustment and conflict left its mark on the Judaism of western Europe and America. It emerged at the end of the half century different both from the Judaism which the immigrants had found on their arrival and from that which they had brought with them. A survey made in 1953, of an eastern American city with a Jewish population of several thousand, may be considered representative of the Jews in the United States in general, especially of those living away from the large centers of Jewish population. Only 30% of that city's Jews expressed strong objection to intermarriage, which had indeed, risen in that community to 7% of all marriages. Most Jews, however, were more or less conscious of their Judaism, its culture and its values. Far from being discouraging, this record must be considered very good in view of the attractiveness of the majority culture and the numerous problems and difficulties which the Jewish group has had to face under circumstances which made centralized control and direction impossible. That the internal ties would be weakened could have been and was foreseen; but that so many of the third, fourth, and sometimes even later generations, should still have strong attachments to the religion and way of life of a small minority is evidence of Judaism's vigor. . . .

Life in an environment which permits of cultural give and take is bound to be hazardous for a minority. Losses are to be expected. But the past sixty years, like other periods in Jewish history before, have proved the possibility of attaining integrated personality in which Judaism and western culture fuse harmoniously. The process will continue in the coming generations. If prejudices of various intensities do not intervene, the process will be a happier one than it has been in the generation here described. If the Jews are more careful to balance their general culture with a more ample supply of Jewish knowledge, experience, and spirituality, the results will be of even greater value to civilization. In any event, the continuance of Judaism and the Jewish people cannot be questioned. . . .

4. American Religion

Will Herberg has not been the only writer to warn religious groups of the danger of conquest by American culture. Catholic, Jewish, and Protestant theologians have insisted on the need to maintain the integrity of religious beliefs. Protestant churches have been particularly vulnerable; an observation which can be established by referring the reader to examples such as Henry Ward Beecher's efforts in the eighteen-seventies to make the Christian and the successful business entrepreneur one, or Bruce Barton's discovery in the nineteen-twenties that Jesus was essentially a good advertising man. AUTHOR: Will Herberg (1907—) holds A.B., A.M., and Ph.D. degrees from Columbia University, and is a Professor of Judaic Studies at Drew University. SELECTION: "A Curious Kind of Religion" from the Herberg essay in Thomas T. McAvoy, ed., *Roman Catholicism and the American Way of Life* (1960).

A CURIOUS KIND OF RELIGION (1960): WILL HERBERG

Well over 95 per cent of the American people identify themselves religiously, as Protestants, Catholics, or Jews—an incredibly high figure by all available standards of comparison. . . .

But it is a curious kind of religion. The very same people who are so unanimous in identifying themselves religiously, who are joining churches at an accelerating rate, and who take it for granted that religion is a "very important" thing, do not hesitate to acknowledge that religion is quite peripheral to their everyday lives; more than half of them quite frankly admit that their religious beliefs have no influence whatever on their ideas in economics and politics, and a good proportion of the remainder are obviously uncertain. . . . This is the problem: the religiousness of a secularist society, the "strengthening of the religious structure in spite of increasing secularization.". . . What, then, is it that strikes one about the new function of religion in the life of the American people today? It is, I think, that religion, in its tripartite form of Protestant-Catholic-Jew, is rapidly becoming the primary context of self-identification and social location in the present-day America. . . . Within the threefold American scheme of race, ethnicity, and religion, a shift took place, a shift is taking place, from ethnicity to religion as the dominant form of selfindentification—as the dominant way of answering the question, "What am I? how do I differ from 'one man's family'? where do I fit in the totality of American society?" Ethnic identifications and traditions have not disappeared; on the contrary, with the third generation, they are enjoying a lively popularity as symbols of "heritage." But now the relation between ethnicity and religion has been reversed: religion is no longer an aspect of ethnicity; it is ethnicity, or rather what remains of it, that is taken up, redefined, and expressed through religious identifications and institutions. Religion, or at least the tripartite differentiation of Protestant, Catholic, and Jew has (aside from race) become the prevailing form of defining one's identity as an American in contemporary American society. . . . "Our government," Mr. Eisenhower declared shortly after his election in 1952, "makes no sense unless it is founded in a deeply felt religious faith, *and I don't care what it is.*" . . . Mr. Eisenhower made another important pronouncement on religion. "I am the most intensely religious man I know," he declared. "Nobody goes through six years of war without faith. That does not mean that I adhere to any sect. (Incidentally, following the way of all flesh, he was soon to join a "sect," the Presbyterian.) A democracy cannot exist without a religious base. I believe in democracy." Here we have the entire story in a single phrase: "I believe in religion because I believe in democracy! . . ."

What I am describing is essentially the "Americanization" of religion in America, and therefore also its thorough-going secularization. This process is not a recent one. It began for Protestantism some time after the Civil War and proceeded apace in the latter decades of the nineteenth century. . . .

What does . . . [it] mean? It means that we have in America an invisible, formally unacknowledged, but very potent religion—the religion of democracy, the religion of the American Way of Life—of which the conventional religions are felt to be more or less adequate expressions. Americans do not put it that way in just so many words, but that is how they feel and behave. In effect, this means that they participate in an actual civic religion, very much like the civic religion of the Roman Empire in early Christian times. The authentic relation between religion and culture is subverted, of which the civic religion is the sanctification, is idolatrized by being made ultimate, which means divine. Judaism, and Christianity in its two forms, become subordinated to the culture and tend to lose all sense of uniqueness, universality, and special vocation. . . .

Chapter XIII. THE REVOLT OF
THE MODERNS

THE RISE OF THE INDUSTRIAL PLUTOCRACY IN THE GENERATION after the Civil War created an unfriendly social environment for artists and writers. The tired businessman, when he was not completely bored by art, wished to escape the dramatic clash and clamor of his daytime world to the solace of the tranquil landscape and the moral tale. The "genteel tradition" made literature and art the guardians of an abstract and bloodless moral "purity" in a world rife with pretentious prettiness and faceless mediocrity; and most of the new men of wealth could not even rise to the flimsy culture of "gentility." The millionaires looked upon art as another commodity to consume and display. They knew that "culture" was manufactured in Europe and that was where they went to buy it; Old Masters, the most expensive and therefore the most valuable did not exist in America, so the work of American painters did not interest the masters of capital. Gothic castles and Renaissance chateaux were taken apart stone by stone to be shipped and reassembled in America where they might visually compete with the brownstone and marble reproductions and confusions of all styles and tastes. Each of the fine arts had its own set of difficult conditions: in architecture the owner often wanted the architect to passively copy or recombine elements from the great grab bag of all styles; the daguerreotype threatened to destroy the demand for portrait artists; and America had never developed the institutions to support a vigorous national musical and theatrical life. Some artists, such as the painter James Whistler, went into permanent exile in Europe, and others floundered between Europe and America trying with great difficulty to establish a reputation in the New World.

Still, for all the adverse circumstances, great changes were in the making at the turn of the century in the field of fine arts. One by one art and music schools, museums and libraries, the Metropolitan Opera, the New York and Boston Symphony Orchestras achieved major status. Even during the most difficult times there were Americans in several of the fine arts who continued to function creatively. The Hudson River school of Romantic landscape painting aroused the hostility of many young artists of the eighteen-nineties; but, still, the group left a heritage which later landscape painters claimed. The "realist" Winslow Homer, attempted to purge the national heritage of excessively romantic and sentimental elements in order to create a new style of landscape with a firm sense of structure and a subdued palette. Homer, like his solitary contemporaries Thomas Eakins and Albert Ryder, painting at the peak of the Gilded Age, ignored the current of fashion and events. Each developed a singular style. At the turn of the century a growing number of artists called for common action and American aesthetic manifestoes; even a romantic individualist like Robert Henri joined the hue and cry, and a group called "The Eight" advanced common protests against the American art world and proposed to reject European studio art in favor of experimental themes and techniques related to the American scene. This trend produced early in the twentieth century the "Ash Can school" of John Sloan and George Bellows who plunged so wholeheartedly into bold portrayals of contemporary urban themes.

American architecture began also to develop substantial native talents toward the end of the nineteenth century. At first the leading architects confined themselves to the mastery of historical styles: Richard Hunt worked with French Renaissance design, H. H. Richardson revived French Romanesque, and Charles F. McKim gave great vogue to "monumental" classicism. Neoclassical banks, train stations, government edifices, and educational buildings, and even private homes dominated a large part of the new architectural landscape. Still, demands for a truly native style increased, and the advance of industrialism provided iron and steel, reinforced concrete, and new ways of using wood and brick, all of which opened new architectural possibilities. Louis Sullivan, who built many of the early skyscrapers, insisted on simplicity, strength, and the most effective use of the new materials; and his student Frank Lloyd Wright campaigned for the blending of building site, interior use, and exterior design into a single "organic" whole. Sullivan, Wright, their colleagues, and the influence of European architectural movements worked major changes in American cities and homes during the thirties and forties.

Although the celebrated New York Armory Show of 1913 was devoted primarily to painting, it gave the whole range of "modern" design an insight into the aesthetic revolution then taking place in Europe. The 1913 parade of new styles—Impressionism, Fauvism,

Cubism—was a preview to the march in the twenties of Surrealism, Expressionism, Dadaism, and Futurism from Europe to America. American artists such as the painters Georgia O'Keefe and Ben Shahn, and the sculptor Alexander Calder mastered the new insights and techniques and used them in the context of American sensibilities. In the fifties American painters presented to the world "Abstract Expressionism" and in the sixties "Pop Art." Meanwhile American art had been enriched by the arrival of a great wave of emigrés in flight from Nazism and war: in the field of music alone Darius Milhaud, Bela Bartók, Igor Stravinsky, Paul Hindemith, Arnold Schoenberg, and many more came. Twentieth-century America began to produce significant native composers, in men such as Charles Ives, Virgil Thomson, and Aaron Copland. American theater also began to exercise a world influence through the work of Eugene O'Neill, Tennessee Williams, and many others. Indeed, in most of the arts Americans displayed significant creativity long before the nineteen-sixties.

While the fine arts in modern times involve a great complex of variables, a large portion of artistic and literary efforts can be described as "the revolt of the moderns," the search for significant new forms to express the technological revolutions or the human tragedies of the twentieth century. Architects often used the slogan "form follows function" in the war on "sterile" imitation of styles and the "frivolous" decorations of Victorian "gingerbread" or Classical colonnade. The European slogan, the house as "a machine for living," won many American adherents, but even more influential were Wright's plans for joining interior decoration to external design and relating both harmoniously to the social and natural setting. Reacting against the graphic image of the camera and searching for the structure of inner or outer vision, painters occupied themselves with structure and form. They sought to take apart structural realities and psychological conditions and to reassemble the constituent parts on canvas abstractly, surrealistically, or expressionistically. Sculptors and painters often wished to capture the angularity, speed, and power of surfaces and shapes of modern industrial civilization, and many artists began to explore the new possibilities for design in metals and plastics, machines and industrial structures.

The "Moderns" issued aesthetic manifestoes in the realm of literature; poets, playwrights, and novelists clamored for experimentation. They were not usually "radicals" or reformers, and if they quarreled with Western bourgeois culture they also wished to leave behind social protest and socialism, realism and naturalism. French symbolism and imagism attracted the attention of T. S. Eliot, Ezra

Pound, and many other American poets bent on extending the devices and insight of modern poetry. Deeply pessimistic, the poets wished to rake the spiritual roots of Western culture, and if all was in decay to evoke that decay; but they were also moved by an eager desire to explore the older Christian world, medieval Provence, the mythical life of the Classical world, India, and China. In the field of the novel, Americans studied the grand experiments in the novel of the Irish writer James Joyce and the French novelist Marcel Proust. Then, during the nineteen-thirties, William Faulkner began to sound his magnificent rhetoric. A master of the new prose, Faulkner experimented with plot construction, point of view, the prose-poem, and the stream of consciousness technique. If the sin and guilt-ridden protagonist in his Mississippi nightmare of violence and racism, terror and tragedy, seemed remote from the visible forms of twentieth-century modernism, perhaps on a deeper plane he was no stranger to an age which has known historical catastrophe.

1. Revolt in Contemporary Art

"The Eight" as artist-advocates of "social realism" painted the face of urban life replete with barrooms, dance halls, and waterfronts. The show of 1908, sponsored by The Eight, was generally regarded as an unprecedented act of effrontery, but this exhibit merely marked a modest beginning of revolutionary change in art. The New York Armory Show of 1913 with its parade of new styles aroused much more irritation and perplexity. Still, as the twenties and thirties demonstrated, the new styles were all destined to win favor in America. AUTHOR: Leo Stein (1872–1947), after completing his education at Pittsburgh, Harvard, and Johns Hopkins, settled in Paris and with his sister Gertrude kept a salon which Cezanne, Picasso, Matisse and other notables attended. SELECTION: "Panic in Art" from a Stein essay in The New Republic (1914).

PANIC IN ART (1914): LEO STEIN

Once a year for the last six years art has been reborn and named successively: Post-Impressionism, Cubism, Futurism, Orphism, Synchronism and Vorticism. And each conception is assumed to have the finality of a miracle. . . . Painting, which began with Giotto, has completed its cycle, and a new art made possible by a new freedom is to begin.

We are faced with it, the freedom to paint hair green, thighs blue, and tables out of perspective; the further freedom to dismember any object and scatter its parts in dynamic rhythm; the ultimate right to evolve whirlpools of color splashed by flaming pinwheels in which the last traces of the object is inundated. . . . The new in recent art is the expression of two impulses, the first a panic-stricken attempt (Post-Impressionism) to recover our lost innocence of the eye, the second (Cubism, Futurism, etc.) a frantic endeavor to achieve forms so pure and beauty so abstract that they would be a new absolute. Both are ineffectual and both are significant because they are phases of an inevitable revolt against an unavoidable criticism growing every year more intolerable to the artist.

For the compilation of art history has grown so complete that no one can escape it. The process of enthusiastic allegiance to some historic type of beauty by which the artist educates his sense of design and form becomes an immense critical labor. Instead of an immediate native tradition there is a bewildering array of historic tradition to choose from. The sculptor, for instance, not only compares Greek statues with Egyptian, Hindu bronzes with Chinese monuments, but he must compare Phidian marbles with archaic Attic bas-reliefs, and later Egyptian monoliths with examples of the first dynasties. He cannot take Greek art in general, or any other art, as his model; his knowledge of it is already too complete. Forty years ago the mere sight of the first Japanese prints to reach Europe determined Whistler's sense of composition, Van Gogh's draughtsmanship, Monet's secession from the Barbizon School. But already the painter knows that Hokusai and Hiroshighe are decadent. . . .

Is it surprising that painters and sculptors ended with a forlorn sense of the wisdom of ignorance, that, utterly weary of the burden of sophistication, their only ultimate enthusiasm should be for every primitive period of art in which they could regain a sense of seeing with the uneducated gaze of the savage and the childlike eye? There followed ten or fifteen years in which every type of primitive simplicity was revived: the simplification of drawing, the distortion of the nude, the color schemes of pure reds, blues and yellows which raised shrieks of protest. . . .

As in all revivals, much was recovered that was permanently valuable. Color achieved a new splendor. Painting acquired an intrinsic beauty of material, a sheer loveliness of texture, . . . [but] the conviction grew more and more irresistible that everything had been done and there was no use doing it over again. . . . Significantly enough, Picasso, collector of death-masks and totem-poles, was the first to emancipate himself from the object.

So we have had the rise of five or six "Damn-the-Object" schools.

The cubists proclaim, "The mission of the artist is to divest objects of their banal appearance and to fashion the real image of the spirit." The painter is to search for "the plastic essence of the world," tending to express itself as "a colored mathematics of things." Observe the absolutist's contempt for the merely phenomenal world. Objects are appearances, thin and unreal things. Vision is only a form of illusion; reality is elsewhere. The artist pondering on the nature of his art begins to reflect on the nature of reality. And with phenomenal ingenuity he creates fantastic systems of graphic symbols to express naive systems of metaphysics. The cubists are particularly preoccupied with the nature of space and volume, . . . and they express their conviction in canvasses full of cones, cylinders and cubes. . . .

The second revolution, like the first, ends in the past. The revolutionary painter, seeking the most uniquely modern goal he can imagine, has fallen victim to an ancient hunger—a poetic impatience to rend the veil of appearance, a poignant eagerness to be one with the hidden essence of being. He has expressed again his own weariness, a desire to lose himself in a world his eye can no longer dominate or understand.

Yet there is no need of echoing Kenyon Cox that painting is going to the dogs, or of whimpering with all the instructors that that art is dead. Whatever you may mean by death, be certain of one thing: Art may die innumerable deaths, if that is the metaphor you choose to adopt. It will not stop. The twin impulse to ornament and to play is an eternal passion. This kneading, thumping, hammering, cutting and smearing of materials into shapes and patterns is an incessant energy, and the habit of making easel pictures is only one of its phases. For the moment, painting is sealed in a test-tube of aesthetic experiments where form and color gleam and float in fiery disintegration.

2. The Emergence of Modern Architecture

Louis Sullivan, the most original architect of his day, between 1880 and 1895 designed a high percentage of all American buildings of enduring interest. Keenly aware of the intimate connections between architecture, technology, and social change, he advocated the idea that form must follow function, and argued that the architect must serve his age creatively. To design a modern department store after a Greek temple seemed the height of folly; Sullivan began with the function of the building, tried to find the most suitable building materials, and throughout the entire process stressed strength and simplicity. His student, Frank Lloyd

Wright, adopted several of his teacher's ideas and added quite a few of his own. Wright went so far as to state that the design of a building should be completely determined by materials, site, and human use. His continuous stress upon the aesthetic principle of unity—on the "organic" —was a major contribution to the theory and practice of architecture. Wright's concern for space, Sullivan's plea for adaptation of techniques to the new materials available, their joint practice of wedding the functional and the aesthetic were maintained by the distinguished German-American architect, Walter Gropius. AUTHORS: Louis Sullivan (1856–1924), Boston-born, a student at M.I.T. as well as abroad in France and Italy, settled in Chicago where some of his best designs were conceived and executed. Frank Lloyd Wright (1869–1959) of Wisconsin studied civil engineering at the State University, became an apprentice-assistant to Sullivan in 1884, and began independent practice in 1894. Walter Gropius (1883—), was born in Germany and educated at Berlin, Hannover, and Harvard. He first won international fame as master of a school of design, the "Staatliche Bauhaus" in Weimar (later in Dessau). SELECTIONS: "Form Follows Function" (1881) from Sullivan's *Autobiography of an Idea* (1922). "Organicism, Simplicity, Plasticity" from Wright's *Autobiography* (1932). "The New Architecture" from Gropius' *The New Architecture and the Bauhaus*, trans. T. M. Sland (1935).

FORM FOLLOWS FUNCTION (1881):
LOUIS SULLIVAN

Now Louis felt he had arrived at a point where he had a foothold, where he could make a *beginning* in the open world. Having come into its responsibilities, he would face it boldly. He could now, undisturbed, start on the course of practical experimentation he long had in mind, which was to make an architecture that fitted its functions—a realistic architecture based on well defined utilitarian needs—that all practical demands of utility should be paramount as basis of planning and designing; that no architectural dictum, or tradition, or superstition, or habit, should stand in the way. He would brush them all aside, regardless of commentators. For his view, his conviction was this: That the architectural art to be of contemporary immediate value must be plastic; all senseless conventional rigidity must be taken out of it; it must intelligently serve—it must not suppress. In this wise the forms under his hand would grow naturally out of the needs and express them frankly, and freshly. This meant in his courageous mind that he would put to the test a formula he had evolved, through long contemplation of living things, namely that *form follows function*, which would mean, in practice, that architecture might again become a living art, if this formula were but adhered to.

The building business was again under full swing, and a series of important mercantile structures came into the office, each one of which he treated experimentally, feeling his way toward a basic process, a grammar of his own. The immediate problem was increased daylight, the maximum of daylight. This led him to use slender piers, tending toward a masonry and iron combination, the beginnings of a vertical system. This method upset all precedent, and led Louis's contemporaries to regard him as an iconoclast, a revolutionary. . . . As buildings varying in character came under his hand, he extended to them his system of form and function, and as he did so his conviction increased that architectural manipulation, as a homely art or a fine art must be rendered completely plastic to the mind and the hand of the designer; that materials and forms must yield to the mastery of his imagination and his will; through this alone could modern conditions be met and faithfully expressed. This meant the casting aside of all pedantry, of all the artificial teachings of the schools, of the thoughtless acceptance of inane traditions, of puerile habits of uninquiring minds; that all this mess, devoid of a center of gravity of thought, and vacant of sympathy and understanding, must be superseded by a sane philosophy of a living architecture, good for all time, founded on the only possible foundation—Man and his powers. . . .

And [Sullivan] amid the immense number and variety of living forms, he noted that invariably the form expressed the function, as, for instance, the oak tree expressed the function oak, the pine tree the function pine, and so on through the amazing series. And, inquiring more deeply, he discovered that in truth it was not simply a matter of form expressing function, but the vital idea was this: That the function *created* or organized its form. . . .

ORGANICISM, SIMPLICITY, PLASTICITY (1932): FRANK LLOYD WRIGHT

And at this time I saw a house primarily as liveable interior space under ample shelter. I liked the sense of "shelter" in the look of the building. I still like it. Then I went after the popular abuses. Eliminated odds and ends in favor of one material and a single surface as a flat plane from grade to eaves. I treated these flat planes usually as simple enclosing screens or else I again made a plain band around the second story above the window sills turned up over into the ceiling beneath the eaves. . . . The planes of the building parallel to the ground were all stressed—I liked to "stress" them—to grip the whole to Earth. This parallel plane I called, from the beginning,—the plane of the third dimension. The term came naturally enough: really a spiritual interpretation of that dimension. . . . The house began to associate with the ground and become natural to its prairie site. . . .

What I have just described was all on the *outside* of the house. But it was there, chiefly, because of what had happened *inside*.

Dwellings of that period were cut up, advisedly and completely, with the grim determination that should go with any "cutting" process. The "interiors" consisted of boxes beside boxes or inside boxes, called *rooms*. All boxes were inside a complicated outside boxing. Each domestic "function" was properly box to box.

I could see little sense in this inhibition, this cellular sequestration that implied ancestors familiar with penal institutions, except for the privacy of bedrooms on the upper floor. . . . Then I screened various portions of the big room for certain domestic purposes, like dining or reading—receiving callers. . . . Scores of unnecessary doors disappeared and no end of partition. Both clients and servants liked the new freedom. The house became more free as "space" and more liveable too. Interior spaciousness began to dawn. Thus an end to the cluttered house. Fewer doors; fewer window holes, though much greater window area; windows and doors lowered to convenient human heights. . . . When the handling of the interior had thus become wholly plastic instead of structural—a new element, as I have already said, had entered the prairie house architecture. . . .

THE NEW ARCHITECTURE (1935): WALTER GROPIUS

A breach has been made with the past, which allows us to envisage a new aspect of architecture corresponding to the technical civilization of the age we live in; the morphology of dead styles has been destroyed; and we are returning to honesty of thought and feeling. The general public, formerly profoundly indifferent to everything to do with building, has been shaken out of its torpor; personal interest in architecture as something that concerns every one of us in our daily lives has been very widely aroused; and the broad lines of its future development are already clearly discernible. It is now becoming widely recognized that although the outward forms of the New Architecture differ fundamentally in an organic sense from those of the old, they are not the personal whims of a handful of architects avid for innovation at all cost, but simply the inevitable logical product of the intellectual, social and technical conditions of our age. A quarter of a century's earnest and pregnant struggle preceded their eventual emergence.

But the development of the New Architecture encountered serious obstacles at a very early stage of its development. . . . That is why the movement must be purged from within if its original aims are to be saved from the strait-jacket of materialism and false slogans inspired by plagiarism or misconception. Catch phrases like "functionalism" (*die neue Sachlichkeit*) and "fitness for purpose = beauty" have had the effect of deflecting appreciation of the New Architecture into external channels or making it purely one-sided. . . .

For instance rationalization, which many people imagine to be its cardinal principle, is really only its purifying agency. The liberation of architecture from a welter of ornament, the emphasis on its structural functions, and the concentration on concise and economical solutions, represent the purely material side of that formalizing process on which the *practical* value of the New Architecture depends. The other, the aesthetic satisfaction of the human soul, is just as important as the material. Both find their counterpart in that unity which is life itself. What is far more important than this structural economy and its functional emphasis is the intellectual achievement which has made possible a new spatial vision. For whereas building is merely a matter of methods and materials, architecture implies the mastery of space.

For the last century the transition from manual to machine production has so preoccupied humanity that, instead of pressing forward to tackle the new problems of design postulated by this unprecedented transformation, we have remained content to borrow our styles from antiquity and perpetuate historical prototypes in decoration.

That state of affairs is over at last. A new conception of building, based on realities, has emerged; and with it has come a new conception of space. These changes, and the superior technical resources we can now command as a direct result of them, are embodied in the very different appearance of the already numerous examples of the New Architecture.

Just think of all that modern technique has contributed to this decisive phase in the renascence of architecture, and the rapidity of its development!

Our fresh technical resources have furthered the disintegration of solid masses of masonry into slender piers, with consequent far-reaching economies in bulk, space, weight, and haulage. New synthetic substances—steel, concrete, glass—are actively superseding the traditional raw materials of construction. Their rigidity and molecular density have made it possible to erect wide-spanned and all but transparent structures, for which the skill of previous ages was manifestly inadequate. This enormous saving in structural volume was an architectural revolution in itself. . . .

3. *The New Poetry*

On the eve of the First World War a burgeoning group of "little magazines," such as *Broom*, *Blaze*, and *Poetry* provided vehicles for poetic experiment. The quarterlies provided an outlet for cultural nationalists such as Carl Sandburg and made it possible for American poets to use the insights of European aesthetic movements such as French Symbolism. Certainly the American "Imagists" learned much from the Symbolists. Ezra Pound, the earliest Imagist poet, wrote a number of significant poems in the new vein and aroused widespread interest by editing *Des Imagistes* in 1914. Amy Lowell, John Gould Fletcher, and William Carlos Williams wrote Imagist poetry, but only Hilda Doolittle followed the new movement over a period of many years. AUTHORS: Ezra Pound (1885–   ), an Idaho-born poet and graduate of the University of Pennsylvania, ultimately drifted into expatriation, living first in England and France before settling in Italy. Harriet Monroe (1860–1936), herself a poet and playwright, founded *Poetry* magazine in 1912. SELECTIONS: "A Few Don'ts" from Pound's article in *Poetry* magazine (1913). "Imagist Credo," anonymous. "A Remarkable Renascence" from Monroe's article in *Poetry* magazine (1928).

A FEW DON'TS (1913):
EZRA POUND

Use no superfluous word, no adjective, which does not reveal something.
. . . Go in fear of abstractions. Don't retell in mediocre verse what has already been done in good prose. Don't think any intelligent person is going to be deceived when you try to shirk all the difficulties of the unspeakably difficult art of good prose by chopping your composition into line lengths.

What the expert is tired of today the public will be tired of tomorrow.

Don't imagine that the art of poetry is any simpler than the art of music, or that you can please the expert before you have spent at least as much effort on the art of verse as the average piano teacher spends on the art of music.

Be influenced by as many great artists as you can, but have the decency either to acknowledge the debt outright, or to try to conceal it.

"Don't allow "influence" to mean merely that you mop up the particular decorative vocabulary of some one or two poets whom you happen to admire. A turkish war correspondent was recently caught red-handed babbling in his dispatches of "dove-gray" hills, or else it was "pearl-pale," I can not remember.

Use either no ornament or good ornament.

Rhythm and Rhyme: Let the candidate fill his mind with the finest cadences he can discover, preferably in a foreign language so that the meaning of the words may be less likely to divert his attention from the movement; e.g., Saxon charms, Hebridean folk songs, the verse of Dante, and the lyrics of Shakespeare—if he can dissociate the vocabulary from the cadence. . . .

Let the neophyte know assonance and alliteration, rhyme immediate and delayed, simple and polyphonic, as a musician would expect to know harmony and counterpoint and all the minutiae of his craft. No time is too great to give to these matters or to any one of them, even if the artist seldom has need of them. . . .

Don't chop your stuff into separate *iambs.* Don't make each line stop dead at the end, and then begin every next line with a heave. Let the beginning of the next line catch the rise of the rhythm wave, unless you want a definite longish pause.

In short, behave as a musician, a good musician, when dealing with that phase of your art which has exact parallels in music. The same laws govern, and you are bound by no others.

Naturally, your rhythmic structure should not destroy the shape of your words, or their natural sound, or their meaning. It is improbable that, at the start, you will be able to get a rhythm-structure strong enough to affect them very much, though you may fall a victim to all sorts of false stopping due to line ends and caesurae.

The musician can rely on pitch and the volume of the orchestra. You can not. The term harmony is misapplied to poetry; it refers to simultaneous sounds of different pitch. There is, however, in the best verse a sort of residue of sound which remains in the ear of the hearer and acts more or less as an organ-base. A rhyme must have in it some slight element of surprise if it is to give pleasure; it need not be bizarre or curious, but it must be well used if used at all. . . .

IMAGIST CREDO (1915):
ANONYMOUS

The poets in this volume do not represent a clique. Several of them are personally unknown to the others, but they are united by certain common principles, arrived at independently. These principles are not new; they have fallen into desuetude. They are the essentials of all great poetry, indeed of all great literature, and they are simply these:—

1. To use the language of common speech, but to employ always the exact word, not the nearly exact, nor the merely decorative word.

2. To create new rhythms—as the expression of new moods—and not to copy old rhythms, which merely echo old moods. We do not insist upon "free-verse" as the only method of writing poetry. We fight for it as for a principle of liberty. We believe that the individuality of a poet may often be better expressed in free-verse than in conventional forms. In poetry, a new cadence means a new idea.

3. To allow absolute freedom in the choice of subject. It is not good art to write badly about aeroplanes and automobiles; nor is it necessarily bad art to write well about the past. We believe passionately in the artistic value of modern life, but we wish to point out that there is nothing so uninspiring nor so old-fashioned as an aeroplane in the year 1911.

4. To present an image (hence the name: "Imagist"). We are not a school of painters, but we believe that poetry should render particulars exactly and not deal in vague generalities, however magnificent and sonorous. It is for this reason that we oppose the cosmic poet, who seems to us to shirk the real difficulties of his art.

5. To produce poetry that is hard and clear, never blurred nor indefinite.

6. Finally, most of us believe that concentration is of the very essence of poetry. . . .

A REMARKABLE RENASCENCE (1928): HARRIET MONROE

During the last few years there has been a remarkable renascence of poetry in both America and England, and an equally extraordinary revival of public interest in the art. . . . The magazine *Poetry*, ever since its foundation in October, 1912, has encouraged this new spirit in the art. . . .

What is the new poetry? and wherein does it differ from the old? The difference is not in mere details of form, for much poetry infused with the new spirit conforms to the old measures and rhyme-schemes. It is not merely in diction, though the truly modern poet rejects the so-called "poetic" shifts of language—the *deems*, *'neaths*, *forsooths*, etc., the inversions and high-sounding rotundities, familiar to his predecessors: all the rhetorical excesses through which most Victorian poetry now seems "over-appareled," as a speaker at a *Poetry* dinner—a lawyer, not a poet—put it in pointing out what the new movement is aiming at. These things are important, but the difference goes deeper than details of form, strikes through them to fundamental integrities.

The new poetry strives for a concrete and immediate realization of life; it would discard the theory, the abstraction, the remoteness, found in all classics not of the first order. It is less vague, less verbose, less eloquent, than most poetry of the Victorian period and much work of earlier periods. It has set before itself an ideal of absolute simplicity and sincerity—an ideal which implies an individual, unstereotyped rhythm. Thus inspired, it becomes intensive rather than diffuse. It looks out more eagerly than in; it becomes objective. The term "exteriority" has been applied to it, but this is incomplete. In presenting the concrete object or the concrete environment, whether these be beautiful or ugly, it seeks to give more precisely the emotion arising from them, and thus widens immeasurably the scope of the art.

All this implies no disrespect for tradition. . . .

Great poetry has always been written in the language of contemporary speech, and its theme, even when legendary, has always borne a direct relation with contemporary thought, contemporary imaginative and spiritual life. It is this direct relation which the more progressive modern poets are trying to restore. In this effort they discard not only archaic diction but also the shop-worn subject of past history or legend, which have been through the centuries a treasure-trove for the second-rate. . . . The modern poets have studied the French *symbolists* of the 'nineties, and the most recent Parisian *vers-libristes*. Moreover, some of them have listened to the pure lyricism of the Provençal troubadours, have examined the more elaborate mechanism of early Italian sonneteers and canzonists, have read Greek poetry from a new angle of vision; and last, but perhaps most important of all, have bowed to winds from the East. . . .

Then a few airs from Japan blew in—a few translations of *hokku* and other forms—which showed the stark simplicity and crystal clarity of the art among Japanese poets. And of late the search has gone further: we begin to discover a whole royal line of Chinese poets of a thousand or more years ago; and we are trying to search out the secrets of their delicate and beautiful art. . . .

All these influences, which tend to make the art of poetry, especially poetry in English, less provincial, more cosmopolitan, are by no means a defiance of the classic tradition. On the contrary, they are an endeavor to return to it at its great original sources. . . .

Chapter XIV. MODERN PHILOSOPHICAL TRENDS: IDEALISM, PRAGMATISM, AND POSITIVISM

DURING THE FIRST THREE-QUARTERS OF THE NINETEENTH CENTURY most American thinkers followed either John Locke and British empiricism or Thomas Reid and the Scottish "common sensists." As late as 1875 the intuitionism and the "realism" of the Scots in versions prepared by James McCosh and other American scholars, commanded more disciples in the groves of academe than any other philosophical outlook. During the decades after the Civil War, however, the new surge of interest in German Idealism and the emergence of Herbert Spencer's deterministic materialism, attracted widespread academic attention to philosophical speculation. When the young Pragmatists began to write, Spencer and Hegel were the two most challenging voices of the age. For the Pragmatists, as for others, the central concept of the nineteenth century was evolution, and a generation before the publication of Darwin's *Origin of Species* Georg Friedrich Hegel (1770–1831) had advanced a general theory of cosmic "evolution." Hegel, who asserted that reality was ideal rather than material, described the essential history of the universe as a process whereby the world-mind evolved from a lesser consciousness toward the "Absolute" consciousness. Karl Marx rejected Hegel's idealism, but used his evolutionary process for a materialistic philosophy of history which explained social progress through economic change and class conflict. Marx, like other materialists of his generation, reduced all events to a natural, mechanical plane and made no allowances for "soul," "spirit," "God," or "ideality."

While British empiricism resisted German materialism and German idealism with reasonable success during the first two-thirds of the nineteenth century, both philosophies eventually won substantial followings in the Anglo-American intellectual world. In America William T. Harris, a leader of the "St. Louis Hegelians," and Josiah Royce of Harvard University led the effort to revise German idealism and to cope with the materialist threat posed by the triumphs of the physical sciences. Royce, who wished to root human values and emo-

tions in the very nature of things, rejected as intolerable the materialist conception of a universe in which only matter in motion really
existed,—how terrible to contemplate the cosmos after a thermo-
dynamic "heat death," devoid of life and demonstrating that all of
man's aspirations had been for nought!

Along with this deep concern for human values Royce brought
an American breath of variety and regard for experience to the rigid
abstractions of Hegel. Royce's brand of idealism was by no means an
alien ideology in America, for theologians and writers from Jonathan
Edwards to Ralph Waldo Emerson and Herman Melville had described physical nature as a symbolic mask covering a deeper reality.
It should be noted that Hegel played a role even in that most
characteristically American philosophy of Pragmatism. The German
influence is obvious in Charles Peirce's contention that the universe
develops gradually toward greater law, order, and coherence. Pragmatic debts to Hegel, significant as they were, went largely unacknowledged as did those to the leading advocate of evolutionary
materialism, Herbert Spencer.

The Pragmatists were annoyed with the air of finality which
seemed to permeate the writings of both Spencer and Hegel; and
Spencer was attacked with special relish for his determinism, his
dogmatism, his advocacy of a "closed universe"—and even for his
popularity. During the period between 1865 and 1895 when the Pragmatic school came into existence, ideas on biological evolution dominated the intellectual world, and the philosopher Spencer was even
more influential than the scientist Darwin. Yet even as the Pragmatists rushed to embrace some Spencerian ideas, they stressed the
magnitude of Spencerian errors; evolutionary processes, they insisted
took place in the chaotic complexity of an incredibly diverse world
rather than according to Spencer's stately march of pre-determined
patterns. Charles Peirce suggested that an omnipotent mind armed
with all information about the past and present still could not predict
the future with absolute certainty, since spontaneity, chance, coin-
cidence, and possibility were real factors in this "open" universe.
Peirce, Chauncy Wright, and William James made war upon abso-
lutes, emphasized experimentation above all else, and believed in
man's freedom as a scientific investigator and as a moral agent. This
line of thought, which insisted that the facts were not all in and that
the future was still open, came naturally to men who were citizens of
a mobile, restless, and optimistic society.

Charles Peirce, who had more of an inclination toward metaphysical speculation than his colleagues, provided the strongest defenses of "objective chance." Alleged "laws of nature" were to Peirce's way of thinking only statements of probability, and to attribute immutable destiny to natural events was to impose on the chaos of experience preconceptions of the human mind. Peirce argued that "reality" must be approached with clear ideas, and that the test of clarity was relevance to practical consequences. Chauncy Wright, who did not share his colleague's predilection for metaphysics, vigorously seconded Peirce's desire for scientific precision in philosophical statements. Wright wished to see propositions purged of all that was not a prescription for gaining a particular and definable end. Like Wright and Peirce, William James was an able scientist to whom the dominant trends of Western philosophy seemed corrupted by multitudes of vague or foolish abstractions. James particularly objected to the idea of absolute truth as something which was simply "out there," neither made nor unmade, and unaffected in any way by the perceiver. On the contrary, James insisted, truth was in some way a relationship between the knower and the known, a thing which was "made" by the investigator handling his materials properly.

While John Dewey agreed with James in regarding knowledge as practical rather than contemplative, he placed his own social emphasis on the Jamesian analysis of truth as the product of utility and desire. For Dewey ideas were "instruments" which could be used by "the creative intelligence" to re-make the social world. A passionate democrat and a constant enemy to injustice, Dewey urged men to use freely social engineering for the attainment of their ends. He was particularly concerned with establishing an educational system appropriate to an open society, to a community of free men applying intelligence for the achievement of personal goals and social ends. Education in the past had always been an aristocratic instrument for the education of a leisure class in a manner which divided intellectual and practical knowledge. Dewey advocated "learning by doing" to prepare children for life in a democratic and utilitarian society.

John Dewey attracted a number of able and energetic followers who continued the fight against traditional idealist or materialist approaches, but Pragmatism was in time to lose its dominant position. George Santayana, who gave an urbane and eloquent voice to the materialist point of view, had few converts and, while Alfred Whitehead attracted widespread attention with his brilliant blending of idealism and modern physics, twentieth-century idealism has retained only a modest following. After 1945 the European existentialists, Martin Heiddiger, Karl Jaspers, and Jean-Paul Sartre attracted wide attention with their attempt to bring philosophy back to a central concern with human destiny. The bitter voice of existentialist anguish was the natural outcry of a war devastated world; still, neither "existentialist" nor "essentialist" philosophies could successfully compete with logical positivism for the center of the American philosophical scene. Positivism originated durng the 1920's in "the Vienna Circle" of scientists and philosophers. For the Positivists the history of philosophy with its tangled web of conflicting metaphysical systems was more valuable as a source of aesthetic satisfaction than for its stock of reliable truths. To end the pursuit of pseudo-concepts and to reduce philosophy to limits within which certain knowledge could be attained—these were the central goals of the Positivists who began by asking whether a given proposition was nonsensical or meaningful. Ideas which could not be reduced to empirically verifiable predictions were cast away as objects of no concern to the serious philosopher. Many members of the Vienna Circle emigrated to America, and Positivism, an intellectual cousin of Pragmatism, received a sympathetic reception in America. Variants of Positivism such as Bertrand Russell's Logical Empiricism and P. T. Bridgeman's Operationalism helped to establish a position of dominance for positivist points of view. Advocates of the new approach usually abandoned metaphysical speculations for symbolic logic and semantics, and discussions about the nature of signs and symbols or the proper construction of scientific hypotheses became the characteristic American philosophical study.

1. Idealism

Spurred by the threat of scientific materialism, Josiah Royce of Harvard University and William T. Harris, a leader of "the St. Louis Hegelians," strove to make German idealism viable in America. The influence of Hegel was paramount, but the memory of Emerson's "oversoul" stood in the background. Indeed, an old associate of Emerson's and a co-founder of Transcendentalism, Bronson Alcott, joined forces with the St. Louis Hegelians to "naturalize" German idealism by producing a philosphical approach which seemed less awesomely abstract and remote from experience. The American idealists did not wish to see the individual reduced to insignificance by the massive, rigidly predetermined development of the world-mind, so they stressed the voluntary role of each moral will as a component of the Absolute. Royce gave particular attention to explaining the emotional fullness that might come to an individual contemplating his membership in the greatest of all communities, the commonwealth of minds in communion with the Absolute. AUTHOR: Josiah Royce (1815–1916), California born and reared, an associate of George Santayana and William James at Harvard, was the leading American idealist. SELECTION: "A Defense of Idealism" from *The Spirit of Philosophy*, (1892).

A DEFENSE OF IDEALISM (1892): JOSIAH ROYCE

Idealism has two aspects. It is, for the first, a kind of analysis of the world. . . . This idealistic analysis consists merely in a pointing out . . . that the world of your knowledge . . . is through and through such stuff as ideas are made of, that you never in your life believed in anything definable *but* ideas, that as Berkeley put it "this whole choir of heaven and furniture of earth" is nothing for any of us but [ideas]. . . . My reason for believing that there is one absolute World-Self . . . is simply that the profoundest agnosticism . . . already presupposes, implies, demands, asserts, the existence of such a World-Self. . . . Ignorant as I am about first causes, I am at least clear, therefore, about the Self. If you deny him, you already in denying affirm him. . . . Here is, in fact . . . the very presupposition of presuppositions.

The infinite Self, . . . is actually asserted by you in every proposition you utter. . . .

The other aspect of idealism is the one which gives us our notion of the absolute Self. To it the first is only preparatory. This second aspect is the one which from Kant, until the present time, has formed the deeper problem of thought. Whenever the world has become more conscious of its significance, the work of human philosophy will be, not nearly ended (Heaven forbid an end!) but for the first time fairly begun. For then, in critically estimating our passions we shall have some truer sense of whose passions they are. . . .

Here, then, is our so real world of the senses, full of light and warmth and sound. If anything could be solid and external, surely, one at first will say, it is this world. . . . Yet this world of facts is, after all, not entirely stubborn, not merely hard. The strenuous will can mould facts. We can form our world, in part, according to our ideas. . . .

The reality of the world, however, when thus defined in terms of its stubbornness . . . I say, is still something wholly unanalyzed. In what does this stubbornness consist? . . . Matter is stubborn when it stands in hard walls against us, or rises in vast mountain ranges before the path-finding explorer. . . . Minds can be stubborn also. . . . to the rejected lover the world of the heart is all, and that is just his woe. . . . Nay, it is just an idea that now opposes him. . . . Let those who have refuted Bishop Berkeley's idealism by the wonder why he did not walk over every precipice or into every fire if these things existed only in his idea, let such, I say, first try some of the fires and the precipices of the inner life, ere they decide that dangers cease to be dangers as soon as they are called ideal, or even subjectively ideal in me.

Many sorts of reality, then, may be existent at the heart of any world of facts. . . . Our present question is, what sort of reality? . . . So far as the sense-world is beautiful, is majestic, is sublime, this beauty and dignity exist only for the appreciative observer. If they exist beyond him, they exist only for some other mind, or as the thought and embodied purpose of some universal soul of nature. . . . The sum and substance of it all is, you see, this: you know your world in fact as a system of ideas about things, such that from moment to moment you find this system forced upon you by experience. Even matter you know just as a mass of coherent ideas that you cannot help having. Space and time, as you think them, are surely ideas of yours. Now, what more natural than to say that *if* this be so, the real world beyond you must in itself be a system of somebody's ideas? . . .

But with this result we come in presence of a final problem. . . . Such a world would have to be in essence a mind, or a world of minds. . . . My world is thus a world of ideas. . . .

This whole world of ideas is essentially *one* world, and so it is essentially the world of one self and *That art Thou*. . . . This, in fact, is the very nature of that curious relation of a thought to an object which we are now considering. The self that is doubting or asserting, or that is even feeling its private ignorance about an object, and that still, even in consequence of all this, is *meaning*, is *aiming* at such an object, is in essence identical with the self for which this object exists in its complete and consciously known truth. . . .

You, for instance, are part of one larger self with me, or else I can't even be meaning to address you as outer beings. You are part of one larger self along with the most mysterious or most remote fact of nature, along with the moon, and all the hosts of heaven, along with all truth and all beauty. Else could you not even intend to speak of such objects beyond you. For whatever you speak of you will find that your world is meant by you as just your world. "What is [the] deeper self?" And the only answer is, *It is the self that knows in unity all truth*. This, I insist, is no hypothesis. It is actually the presupposition of your deepest doubt. . . .

The world, then, is such stuff as ideas are made of. Thought possesses all things. But the world isn't unreal. It extends infinitely beyond our private consciousness, because it is the world of an universal mind. Absolutely the only thing sure from the first about this world, however, is that it is intelligent, rational, orderly, essentially comprehensible, so that all its problems are somewhere solved, all its darkest mysteries are known to the supreme Self. This Self infinitely and reflectively transcends our consciousness, and therefore, since it includes us, it is at the very least a person, and more definitely conscious than we are; for what it possesses is self-reflecting knowledge, and what is knowledge aware of itself, but consciousness? Beyond the seeming wreck and chaos of our finite problems, its eternal insight dwells, threfore, in absolute and supreme majesty. Yet it is not far from every one of us. There is no least or most transient thought that flits through a child's mind, or that troubles with the faintest line of care a maiden's face, and that still does not contain and embody something of this divine Logos. . . .

2. The Origins of Pragmatism

A few years after the end of the Civil War, Chauncy Wright, Charles Peirce, William James, John Fiske, Oliver Wendell Holmes, Jr. and other young Boston intellectuals began to meet periodically in a "Metaphysical Club" to discuss scientific and philosophical problems. Three members of this group, Wright, Peirce, and James, were the founders of Pragmatism. All of the early Pragmatists were scientists who disliked the neat, compact abstractions of the dominant schools of thought; they brought to philosophy the methods, the perplexities, and the advantages of the laboratory approach during an age of rapid scientific progress. It was both characteristic and revealing that the Pragmatists should reject Herbert Spencer, the philosophical theorist of evolution, and embrace Charles Darwin, its scientific exponent. Among the ranks of the pioneer Pragmatists, Peirce was closest to German philosophic trends, and Wright more narrowly concerned with problems of meaning and method, while James occupied a middle ground between his associates. AUTHORS: Chauncy Wright (1830–1875), a scientist and philosopher, had a short but brilliant career. He may not have been quite a "Pragmatist" himself, but he made the initial formulation of several key ideas which Peirce, James, and Dewey were to develop later. Charles Peirce (1839–1914), scientist, mathematician, and philosopher, who combined a laboratory spirit with the romantic idealism of Schelling, was the least known and perhaps the most creative of the Pragmatists. SELECTIONS: "Science and Progress" (1865) from Wright's *Philosophical Discussions* (1877). "An Intellectual Autobiography" from a Peirce essay (1897).

SCIENCE AND PROGRESS (1865):
CHAUNCY WRIGHT

Why the inductive and mathematical sciences, after their first rapid development at the culmination of Greek civilization, advanced so slowly for two thousand years,—why in the following two hundred years a knowledge of natural and mathematical science has accumulated, which so vastly exceeds all that was previously known that these sciences may be justly regarded as the products of our own times,—are questions which have interested the modern philosopher. . . .

The difference, then, between ancient and modern science is not truly characterized by any of the several explanations which have been proposed. The explanation, however, which, in our opinion, comes nearest to the true solution, and yet fails to designate the real point of difference, is that which the positivists find in the distinction between "objective method" and "subjective method." The objective method is verification by sensuous tests, tests of sensible experience,—a deduction from theory of consequences, of which we may have sensible experiences if they be true. The subjective method, on the other hand, appeals to the tests of internal evidence, tests of reason, and the data of self-consciousness. Whatever the origin, real or ideal, the value of these theories can only be tested, say the positivists, by an appeal to sensible experience, by deductions from them of consequences which we can confirm by the undoubted testimony of the senses. Thus, while ideal or transcendental elements are admitted into scientific researches, though in themselves insusceptible of simple verification, they must still show credentials from the senses, either by affording from themselves consequences capable of sensuous verification, or by yielding such consequences in conjunction with ideas which by themselves are verifiable.

It is undoubtedly true, that one of the leading traits of modern scientific research is this reduction of ideas to the tests of experience. . . .

We find, then, the explanation of the modern development of science in the accumulation of a body of certified knowledge, sufficiently extensive to engage and discipline a rational scientific curiosity, and stimulate it to act independently of other motives. . . .

Philosophy proper should be classed with the Religions and with the Fine Arts, and estimated rather by the dignity of its motives, and the value it directs us to, than by the value of its own attainments. . . .

[Many modern thinkers have been misguided by the idea of Progress] But there is a truth implied in this idea, and an important one,— the truth, namely, that the proper objects of scientific research are all of them processes and the results of processes; not the immutable natures which Plato sought for above a world of confusion and unreality, in the world of his own intelligence, but the immutable elements in the orders of all changes, the permanent relations of co-existences and sequences, which are hidden in the confusions of complex phenomena. . . .

AN INTELLECTUAL AUTOBIOGRAPHY (1897): CHARLES PEIRCE

The reader has a right to know how the author's opinions were formed. . . . From the moment when I could think at all, until now, about forty years, I have been diligently and incessantly occupied with the study of methods [of] inquiry. . . . For ten years before this study began, I had been in training in the chemical laboratory. . . . I am saturated, through and through, with the spirit of the physical sciences. I have been a great student of logic, having read everything of any importance on the subject . . . and have produced systems of my own both in deductive and in inductive logic. . . . The first strictly philosophical books that I read were of the classical German schools; and I became so deeply imbued with many of their ways of thinking that I have never been able to disabuse myself of them. Yet my attitude was always that of a dweller in a laboratory. . . . For about two years, I had long and almost daily discussions with Chauncy Wright, one of the most acute of the followers of J. S. Mill. The effect of these studies was that I came to hold the classical German philosophy to be, upon its argumentative side, of little weight; although I esteem it, perhaps am too partial to it, as a rich mine of philosophical suggestions. The English philosophy, meagre and crude as it is, in its conceptions, proceeds by surer methods and more accurate logic. . . . From the evolutionary philosophers, I have learned little; although I admit that, however hurriedly their theories have been knocked together, and however antiquated and ignorant Spencer's First Principles and general doctrines, yet they are under the guidance of a great and true idea. . . . The works of Duns Scotus have strongly influenced me. If his logic and metaphysics, not slavishly worshipped, but torn away from its medievalism, be adapted to modern culture, under continual wholesome reminders of nominalistic criticisms, I am convinced that it will go far toward supplying the philosophy which is best to harmonize with physical science. But other conceptions have to be drawn from the history of science and from mathematics. Thus, in brief, my philosophy may be described as the attempt of a physicist to make such conjecture as to the constitution of the universe as the methods of science may permit, with the aid of all that has been done by previous philosophers. . . . The demonstrations of the metaphysicians are all moonshine. The best that can be done is to supply a hypothesis, not devoid of all likelihood, in the general line of growth of scientific ideas, and capable of being verified or refuted by future observers. . . . Infallibility in scientific matters seems to me irresistibly comical. . . . In those sciences of measurement which are the least subject to error—metrology, geodesy, and metrical astronomy—no man of self-respect ever now states his result, without affixing to it its probability and if this practice is not followed in other sciences it is because in those the probable errors are too vast to be estimated.

I am a man of whom critics have never found anything good to say. . . . Only once, as far as I remember, in all my lifetime have I experienced the pleasure of praise—not for what it might bring but in itself. That pleasure was beatific; and the praise that conferred it was meant for blame. It was that a critic said of me that I did not seem to be absolutely sure of my own conclusions. . . . My book will have no instruction to impart to anybody. Like a mathematical treatise, it will suggest certain ideas and certain reasons for holding them true; but then, if you accept them, it must be because you like my reasons, and the responsibility lies with you. Man is essentially a social animal: but to be social is one thing, to be gregarious is another: I decline to serve as bellwether. My book is meant for people who want to find out; and people who want philosophy ladled out to them can go elsewhere. There are philosophical soup shops at every corner, thank God! . . . For years in the course of this ripening process, I used for myself to collect my ideas under the designation fallibilism; and indeed the first step toward finding out is to acknowledge you do not satisfactorily know already. . . . Indeed, out of a contrite fallibilism, combined with a high faith in the reality of knowledge, and an intense desire to find things out, all my philosophy has always seemed to me to grow. . . .

3. Pragmatism: Problems of Meaning and Truth

The Pragmatists wished to tie methods of inquiry and concepts of meaning, truth, and belief to the direct, practical consequences which sprang from them. William James had a measure of both epistemological condescension and affection toward modern philosophy. He noted that after Descartes and a score of later speculators had set out to construct a metaphysical system on absolutely clear ideas and certain methods, philosophy was still burdened with dozens of conflicting systems. The Pragmatists proposed to bring the procedures of science as they understood them to philosophy, and to measure ideas by their consequences. The concept of a tree, for example was a series of predictions,—if I act in a given fashion I will encounter certain sense data; if I touch the tree it will feel "solid," if I measure it I will obtain certain dimensions. When all predictions have been tabulated the concept of tree has been exhaustively described. Any idea is a bundle of expectations, and clear or true ideas are those in which expectations have been exposed to experience and fulfilled or discarded after "disappointment." James' notion that ideas had a biological role and were instruments of survival and adjustment inspired John Dewey's "instrumentalism." The preoccupation of James and Peirce with problems of meaning foreshadowed the twentieth-century concern with signs, symbols, and semantics. However, James in one respect was a "tender minded" spirit whose desire to justify religious beliefs led him to look back toward traditional religious philosophy and away from the Pragmatic impatience with theological questions. AUTHORS: Charles Peirce (1839–1914), was most perceptive in writing on belief, meaning, symbols, and similar topics. William James (1842–1910), the son of a noted reformer and the brother of a great novelist, was an extremely influential teacher at Harvard University, the ablest of the pioneer American psychologists, and one of the three or four most influential American philosophers of all times. SELECTIONS: "The Fixation of Belief" from Peirce's essay of the same title (1877). "How to Make Our Ideas Clear" from Peirce's essay of the same title. (1878). "The Meaning of Pragmatism" from James' essay of the same title (1907). "The Will to Believe" from James' essay of the same title (1897).

THE FIXATION OF BELIEF
(1877): CHARLES PEIRCE

Few persons care to study logic, because everybody conceives himself to be proficient enough in the art of reasoning already. But I observe that this satisfaction is limited to one's own ratiocination, and does not extend to that of other men.

We come to the full possession of our power of drawing inferences, the last of all our faculties; for it is not so much a natural gift as a long and difficult art. The history of its practice would make a grand subject for a book. The medieval schoolmen, following the Romans, made logic the earliest of a boy's studies after grammar, as being very easy. So it was as they understood it. Its fundamental principle, according to them, was, that all knowledge rests either on authority or reason; but that whatever is deduced by reason depends ultimately on a premise derived from authority. Accordingly, as soon as a boy was perfect in the syllogistic procedure, his intellectual kit of tools was held to be complete. . . .

The object of reasoning is to find out, from the consideration of what we already know, something else which we do not know. Consequently, reasoning is good if it be such as to give a true conclusion from true premises, and not otherwise. Thus, the question of validity is purely one of fact and not of thinking. . . . It is true that we do generally reason correctly by nature. But that is an accident; the true conclusion would remain true if we had no impulse to accept it; and the false one would remain false, though we could not resist the tendency to believe in it. . . . Logicality in regard to practical matters (if this be understood, not in the old sense, but as consisting in a wise union of security with fruitfulness of reasoning) is the most useful quality an animal can possess, and might, therefore, result from the action of natural selection; but outside of these it is probably of more advantage to the animal to have his mind filled with pleasing and encouraging visions, independently of their truth; and thus, upon unpractical subjects, natural selection might occasion a fallacious tendency of thought.

That which determines us, from given premises, to draw one inference rather than another, is some habit of mind, whether it be constitutional or acquired. The habit is good or otherwise, according as it produces true conclusions from true premises or not; and an inference is regarded as valid or not, without reference to the truth of falsity of its conclusion specially, but according as the habit which determines it is such as to produce true conclusions in general or not. . . . Our beliefs guide our desires and shape our actions. The Assassins, or followers of the Old Man of the Mountain, used to rush into death at his least command, because they believed that obedience to him would insure everlasting felicity. Had they doubted this, they would not have acted as they did. So it is with every belief, according to its degree. The feeling of believing is a more or less sure indication of there being established in our nature some habit which will determine our actions. Doubt never has such an effect. . . . Doubt is an uneasy and dissatisfied state from which we struggle to free ourselves and pass into the state of belief; while the latter is a calm and satisfactory state which we do not wish to avoid, or to change to a belief in anything else. On the contrary, we cling tenaciously, not merely to believing, but to believing just what we do believe. . . .

The irritation of doubt causes a struggle to attain a state of belief. I shall term this struggle Inquiry. . . . With the doubt, therefore, the struggle begins, and with the cessation of doubt it ends. Hence, the sole object of inquiry is the settlement of opinion. We may fancy that this is not enough for us, and that we seek, not merely an opinion, but a true opinion. But put this fancy to the test, and it proves groundless; for as soon as a firm belief is reached we are entirely satisfied, whether the belief be true or false. . . .

That the settlement of opinion is the sole end of inquiry is a very important proposition. It sweeps away, at once, various vague and erroneous conceptions of proof. . . .

1. Some philosophers have imagined that to start an inquiry it was only necessary to utter a question whether orally or by setting it down upon paper, and have even recommended us to begin our studies with the questioning everything! But the mere putting of a proposition into the interrogative form does not stimulate the mind to any struggle after belief. There must be a real and living doubt, and without this all discussion is idle.

2. It is a very common idea that a demonstration must rest on some ultimate and absolutely indubitable propositions. . . . But, in point of fact, an inquiry, to have that completely satisfactory result called demonstration, has only to start with propositions perfectly free from all actual doubt. If the premises are not in fact doubted at all, they cannot be more satisfactory than they are.

3. Some people seem to love to argue a point after all the world is fully convinced of it. But no further advance can be made. When doubt ceases, mental action on the subject comes to an end; and, if it did go on, it would be without a purpose. . . . The problem becomes how to fix belief, not in the individual merely, but in the community. . . . The willful adherence to a belief, and the arbitrary forcing of it it upon others, must . . . both be given up. A different new method of settling opinions must be adopted, that shall not only produce an impulse to believe, but shall also decide what proposition it is which is to be believed. Let the action of natural preference be unimpeded, then, and under their influence let men, conversing together and regarding matters in different lights, gradually develop beliefs in harmony with natural causes. . . .

To satisfy our doubts . . . it is necessary that a method should be found by which our beliefs may be determined by nothing human, but by some external permanency—by something upon which our thinking has no effect. Some mystics imagine that they have such a method in a private inspiration from on high. But that is only a form of the method of tenacity, in which the conception of truth as something public is not yet developed. Our external permanency would not be external, in our sense, if it was restricted in its influence to one individual. It must be something which affects, or might affect, every man. . . . Such is the method of science. Its fundamental hypothesis, restated in more familiar language, is this: There are Real things, whose characters are entirely independent of our opinions about them; those Reals affect our senses according to regular laws, and though our sensations are as different as are our relations to the objects, yet, by taking advantage of the laws of perception, we can ascertain by reasoning how things really and truly are; and any man, if he have sufficient experience and he reason enough about it, will be led to the one True conclusion. The new conception here involved is that of Reality. . . .

2. The feeling which gives rise to any method of fixing belief is a dissatisfaction at two repugnant propositions. But here already is a vague concession that there is some one thing which a proposition should represent. Nobody, therefore, can really doubt that there are Reals, for, if he did, doubt would not be a source of dissatisfaction. The hypothesis, therefore, is one which every mind admits. So that the social impulse does not cause men to doubt it.

3. Everybody uses the scientific method about a great many things, and only ceases to use it when he does not know how to apply it.

4. Experience of the method has not led us to doubt it, but, on the contrary, scientific investigation has had the most wonderful triumphs in the way of settling opinion. . . .

HOW TO MAKE OUR IDEAS CLEAR
(1878): CHARLES PEIRCE

Whoever has looked into a modern treatise on logic of the common sort, will doubtless remember the two distinctions between *clear* and *obscure* conceptions, and between *distinct* and *confused* conceptions. A clear idea is defined as one which is so apprehended that it will be recognized wherever it is met with, and so that no other will be mistaken for it. If it fails of this clearness, it is said to be obscure.

This is rather a neat bit of philosophical terminology; yet since it is clearness that they were defining, I wish the logicians had made their definition a little more plain. Never to fail to recognize an idea, and under no circumstances to mistake another for it, let it come in how recondite a form it may, would indeed imply such prodigious force and clearness of intellect as is seldom met with in this world. . . . I take it, however, that when the logicians speak of "clearness," they mean nothing more than such a familiarity with an idea, since they regard the quality as but a small merit, which needs to be supplemented by another, which they call *distinctness*.

A distinct idea is defined as one which contains nothing which is not clear. This is technical language; by the *contents* of an ideal logicians understand whatever is contained in its definition. So that an idea is *distinctly* apprehended, according to them, when we can give a precise definition of it, in abstract terms. Here the professional logicians leave the subject. . . . It is now time to formulate the method of attaining to a more perfect clearness of thought, such as we see and admire in the thinkers of our own time.

When Descartes set about the reconstruction of philosophy, his first step was to (theoretically) permit scepticism and to discard the practice of the schoolmen of looking to authority as the ultimate source of truth. That done, he sought a more natural fountain of true principles, and thought he found it in the human mind; thus passing, in the directest way, from the method of authority to that of a priority. . . . Self-consciousness was to furnish us with our fundamental truths, and to decide what was agreeable to reason. But since, evidently, not all ideas are true, he was led to note, as the first condition of infallibility, that they must be clear. The distinction between an idea *seeming* clear and really being so, never occurred to him. . . .

From all . . . sophisms we shall be perfectly safe so long as we reflect that the whole function of thought is to produce habits of action. . . . To develop [a thing's] meaning, we have, therefore, simply to determine what habits it produces, for what a thing means is simply what habits it involves. Now, the identity of a habit depends on how it might lead us to act, not merely under such circumstances as are likely to arise, but under such as might possibly occur, no matter how improbable they may be. What the habit is depends on *when* and *how* it causes us to act. . . . There is no distinction of meaning so fine as to consist in anything but a possible difference of practice.

To see what this principle leads to, consider in the light of it such a doctrine as that of transubstantiation. The Protestant churches generally hold that the elements of the sacrament are flesh and blood only in a tropical sense; they nourish our souls as meat and the juice of it would our bodies. But the Catholics maintain that they are literally just meat and blood; although they possess all the sensible qualities of wafer-cakes and diluted wine. But we can have no conception of wine except what may enter into a belief, either—

1. That this, or the other, is wine; or,
2. That wine possesses certain properties.

Such beliefs are nothing but self-notifications that we should, upon occasion, act in regard to such things as we believe to be wine according to the qualities which we believe wine to possess. The occasion of such action would be some sensible perception, the motive of it to produce some sensible result. Thus our action has exclusive reference to what affects the senses, our habit, our conception the same as our belief; and we can consequently mean nothing by wine but what has certain effects, direct or indirect, upon our senses; and to talk of something as having all the sensible characters of wine, yet being in reality blood, is senseless jargon. . . . Our idea of anything *is* our idea of its sensible effects; and if we fancy that we have any other we deceive ourselves, and mistake a mere sensation accompanying the thought for a part of the thought itself. It is absurd to say that thought has any meaning unrelated to its only function. It is foolish for Catholics and Protestants to fancy themselves in disagreement about the elements of the sacrament, if they agree in regard to all their sensible effects, here and hereafter.

It appears, then, that the rule for attaining the third grade of clearness of apprehension is as follows: Consider what effects, that might conceivably have practical bearings, we conceive the object of our conception to have. Then, our conception of these effects is the whole of our conception of the object. . . .

Different minds may set out with the most antagonistic views, but the progress of investigation carries them by a force outside of themselves to one and the same conclusion. This activity of thought by which we are carried, not where we wish, but to a fore-ordained goal, is like the operation of destiny. No modification of the point of view taken, no selection of other facts for study, no natural bent of mind even, can enable a man to escape the predestinate opinion. This great hope is embodied in the conception of truth and reality. The opinion which is fated to be ultimately agreed to by all who investigate, is what we mean by the truth, and the object represented in this opinion is the real. That is the way I would explain reality. . . .

We have, hitherto, not crossed the threshold of scientific logic. It is certainly important to know how to make our ideas clear, but they may be ever so clear without being true. How to make them so, we have next to study. How to give birth to those vital and procreative ideas which multiply into a thousand forms and diffuse themselves everywhere, advancing civilization and making the dignity of man, is an art not yet reduced to rules, but of the secret of which the history of science affords some hints. . . .

THE MEANING OF PRAGMATISM
(1907): WILLIAM JAMES

Some years ago, being with a camping party in the mountains, I returned from a solitary ramble to find every one engaged in a ferocious metaphysical dispute. The *corpus* of the dispute was a squirrel—a live squirrel supposed to be clinging to one side of a tree trunk; while over against the tree's opposite side a human being was imagined to stand. This human witness tries to get sight of the squirrel by moving rapidly round the tree, but no matter how fast he goes, the squirrel moves as fast in the opposite direction, and always keeps the tree between himself and the man, so that never a glimpse of him is caught. The resultant metaphysical problem now is this: *Does the man go round the squirrel or not?* He goes round the tree, sure enough, and the squirrel is on the tree; but does he go round the squirrel? In the unlimited leisure of the wilderness discussion had been worn threadbare. Every one had taken sides and was obstinate; and the numbers on both sides were even. Each side, when I appeared, therefore appealed to me to make it a majority. Mindful of the scholastic adage that whenever you meet a contradiction you must make a distinction, I immediately sought and found one, as follows; "Which party is right," I said, "depends on what you *practically mean* by 'going round' the squirrel. If you mean passing from the north of him to the east, then to the south, then to the west, and then to the north of him again, obviously the man does go round him, for he occupies these successive positions. But if on the contrary you mean being first in front of him, then on the right of him then behind him, then on his left, and finally in front again, it is quite obvious that the man fails to go round him, for by compensating movements the squirrel makes, he keeps his belly turned towards the man all the time, and his back turned away. Make the distinction, and there is no occasion for any further dispute. You are both right and both wrong, according as you conceive the verb 'to go round' in one practical fashion or the other."

Although one or two of the hotter disputants called my speech a shuffling evasion, saying they wanted no quibbling or scholastic hair-splitting, but meant just plain honest English "round," the majority seemed to think that the distinction has assuaged the dispute.

I tell this trivial anecdote because it is a peculiarly simple example of what I wish now to speak of as *the pragmatic method.* The pragmatic method is primarily a method of settling metaphysical disputes that otherwise might be interminable. Is the world one or many?—fated or free?—material or spiritual?—here are notions either of which may or may not hold good of the world; and disputes over such notions are unending. The pragmatic method in such cases is to try to interpret each notion by tracing its respective practical consequences. What difference would it practically make to anyone if this notion rather than that notion were true? If no practical difference whatever can be traced, then the alternatives mean practically the same thing, and all dispute is idle. Whenever a dispute is serious, we ought to be able to show some practical difference that must follow from one side or the other's being right. . . .

Theories thus become instruments, not answers to enigmas, in which we can rest. We don't lie back upon them, we move forward, and, on occasion, make nature over again by their aid. Pragmatism unstiffens all our theories, limbers them up and sets each one at work. . . .

So much for the pragmatic method! . . . Meanwhile the word pragmatism has come to be used in a still wider sense, as meaning also a certain *theory of truth.* . . . *Ideas (which themselves are but parts of our experience) become true just in so far as they help us to get into satisfactory relation with other parts of our experience.* . . . Any idea upon which we can ride, so to speak; any idea that will carry us prosperously from any one part of our experience to any other part, linking things satisfactorily, working securely, simplifying, saving labour—is true for just so much, true in so far forth, true *instrumentally*. . . .

The individual has a stock of old opinions already, but he meets a new experience that puts them to a strain. Somebody contradicts them; or in a reflective moment he discovers that they contradict each other; or he hears of facts with which they are incompatible; or desires arise in him which they cease to satisfy. The result is an inward trouble to which his mind till then had been a stranger, and from which he seeks to escape by modifying his previous mass of opinions. He saves as much of it as he can, for in this matter of belief we are all extreme conservatives. So he tries to change first this opinion, and then that (for they resist change very variously), until at last some new idea comes up which he can graft upon the ancient stock with a minimum of disturbance of the latter, some idea that mediates between the stock and the new experience and runs them into one another most felicitously and expediently. . . .

This new idea is then adopted as the true one. It preserves the older stock of truths with a minimum of modification, stretching them just enough to make them admit the novelty. . . . Time and space, cause and effect, nature and history, and one's own biography remain untouched. New truth is always a go-between, a smoother-over of transitions. It marries old opinion to new fact so as ever to show a minimum of jolt, a maximum of continuity. We hold a theory true just in proportion to its success in solving this "problem of maxima and minima." But success in solving this problem is eminently a matter of approximation. We say this theory solves it on the whole more satisfactorily than that theory; but that means more satisfactorily to ourselves, and individuals will emphasize their points of satisfaction differently. To a certain degree, therefore, everything here is plastic. . . .

See the exquisite contrast of the types of mind! The pragmatist clings to facts and concreteness, observes truth at its work in particular cases, and generalizes. Truth, for him, becomes a class-name for all sorts of definite working-values in experience. For the rationalist it remains a pure abstraction, to the bare name of which we must defer. When the pragmatist undertakes to show in detail just *why* we must defer, the rationalist is unable to recognize the concretes from which his own abstraction is taken. He accuses us of *denying* truth; whereas we have only sought to follow it. Your typical ultra-abstractionist fairly shudders at concreteness; other things equal, he positively prefers the pale and spectral. If the two universes were offered, he would always choose the skinny outline rather than the rich thicket of reality. It is so much purer, clearer, nobler. . . .

The true is the name of whatever proves itself to be good in the way of belief, and good, too, for definite, assignable reasons. . . . In this world, just as certain foods are not only agreeable to our taste but good for our teeth, our stomach, and our tissues, so certain ideas are not only agreeable to think about, or agreeable as supporting other ideas that we are fond of, but they are also helpful in life's practical struggles. If there be any life that it is really better we should lead, and if there be any idea, which, if believed in, would help us to lead that life, then it would be really *better for us* to believe in that idea, *unless, indeed, belief in it incidentally clashed with other greater vital benefits.* . . .

THE WILL TO BELIEVE
(1897): WILLIAM JAMES

Let us give the name of *hypothesis* to anything that may be proposed to our belief; and just as the electricians speak of live and dead wires, let us speak of any hypothesis as either *live* or *dead*. A live hypothesis is one which appeals as a real possibility to him to whom it is proposed. If I ask you to believe in the Mahdi, the notion makes no electric connection with your nature—it refuses to scintillate with any credibility at all. As an hypothesis it is completely dead. To an Arab, however (even if he be not one of the Mahdi's followers), the hypothesis is among the mind's possibilities: it is alive.

Next, let us call the decision between two hypotheses an *option*. Options may be of several kinds. They may be—1, *living* or *dead*; 2, *forced* or *avoidable*; 3, *momentous* or *trivial*; and for our purposes we may call an option a *genuine* option when it is of the forced, living, and momentous kind.

1. A *living* option is one in which both hypotheses are live ones. If I say to you: "Be a theosophist or be a Mohammedan," it is probably a dead option, because for you neither hypothesis is likely to be alive. . . .

2. Next, if I say to you: "Choose between going out with your umbrella or without it," I do not offer you a genuine option, for it is not forced. You can easily avoid it by not going out at all. But I say, "Either accept this truth or go without it," I put on you a forced option, for there is no standing place outside of the alternative. Every dilemma based on a complete logical disjunction, with no possibility of not choosing, is an option of this forced kind.

3. Finally, if I were Dr. Nansen and proposed to you to join my North Pole expedition, your option would be momentous; for this would probably be your only similar opportunity, and your choice now would either exclude you from the North Pole sort of immortality altogether or put at least the chance of it into your hands. He who refuses to embrace a unique opportunity loses the prize as surely as if he tried and failed. . . .

The thesis I defend is, briefly stated, this: *Our passional nature not only lawfully may, but must, decide an option between propositions, whenever it is a genuine option that cannot by its nature be decided on intellectual grounds; for to say, under such circumstances, "Do not de-*

cide, but leave the question open," is itself a passional decision—just like deciding yes or no—and is attended with the same risk of losing the truth. . . .

Moral questions immediately present themselves as questions whose solution cannot wait for sensible proof. A moral question is a question not of what sensibly exists, but of what is good, or would be good if it did exist. Science can tell us what exists; but to compare the *worths,* both of what exists and of what does not exist, we must consult not science, but what Pascal calls our heart. . . .

Turn . . . from . . . wide questions of good to a certain class of questions of fact, questions concerning personal relations, states of mind between one man and another. *Do you like me or not?*—for example. Whether you do or not depends, in countless instances, on whether I meet you half-way, am willing to assume that you must like me, and show you trust and expectation. The previous faith on my part in your liking's existence is in such cases what makes your liking come. But if I stand aloof, and refuse to budge an inch until I have objective evidence, until you shall have done something apt . . . ten to one your liking never comes. How many women's hearts are vanquished by the mere sanguine insistence of some man that they *must* love him! he will not consent to the hypothesis that they cannot. The desire for a certain kind of truth here brings about that special truth's existence; and so it is in innumerable cases of other sorts. . . .

In truths dependent on our personal action, then, faith based on desire is certainly a lawful and possibly an indispensable thing. . . .

Since belief is measured by action, he who forbids us to believe religion to be true, necessarily also forbids us to act as we should if we did believe it to be true. The whole defence of religious faith hinges upon action. If the action required or inspired by the religious hypothesis is in no way different from that dictated by the naturalistic hypothesis, then religious faith is a pure superfluity, better pruned away, and controversy about its legitimacy is a piece of idle trifling, unworthy of serious minds. I myself believe, of course, that the religious hypothesis gives to the world an expression which specifically determines our reactions, and makes them in a large part unlike what they might be on a purely naturalistic scheme of belief. . . .

4. Pragmatism and American Democracy

John Dewey described ideas as instruments for adjustment and survival, proposals for action, and tools for changing the world. For the instrumentalists, the validity of an idea was tested less by self-evidence or logical consistency than by successful practical application. In the crucial areas of politics and ethics, the instrumentalist rejected all absolute values in favor of "life" and "change." The rational and moral man had only one clue to the proper kind of practical action—he must accept as guides everything conducive to "growth" and "maturity," and he must always be willing to redefine his goals. Dewey brushed aside charges that his passionate devotion to social democracy and individual "growth" were inconsistent with the moral neutrality of an instrumentalist approach, and turned to a full application of his ideology to democratic education. According to Dewey education should deal only with problems which involve practical differences; teaching should be adjusted to the natural rhythms of the child; learning must exist as an active process rather than a passive absorption of information; and above all children should learn to attack social problems cooperatively. AUTHORS: John Dewey (1859–1952) as a writer and teacher at Johns Hopkins, Chicago, and Columbia Universities exercised an enormous influence on American thought, particularly in the field of education. SELECTIONS: "Democracy" from Dewey's *The Democratic Form* (1937). "Socializing Intelligence" from *Liberalism and Social Action* (1935). "Education" from *Education and the Social Order* (1922, 1934, 1938).

DEMOCRACY (1937): JOHN DEWEY

The foundation of democracy is faith in the capacities of human nature; faith in human intelligence and in the power of pooled and cooperative experience. It is not belief that these things are complete but that if given a show they will grow and be able to generate progressively the knowledge and wisdom needed to guide collective action. Every autocratic and authoritarian scheme of social action rests on a belief that the needed intelligence is confined to a superior few. . . . The democratic faith has emerged very, very recently in the history of mankind. . . .

Belief in equality is an element of the democratic credo. It is not, however, belief in equality of natural endowments. Those who proclaimed the idea of equality did not suppose they were enunciating a psychological doctrine, but a legal and political one. All individuals are entitled to equality of treatment by law and in its administration. . . .

While what we call intelligence may be distributed in unequal amounts, it is the democratic faith that it is sufficiently general so that each individual has something to contribute, and the value of each contribution can be assessed only as it enters into the final pooled intelligence constituted by the contributions of all. Every authoritarian scheme, on the contrary, assumes that its value may be assessed by some *prior* principle, if not of family and birth or race and color or possession of material wealth, then by the position and rank a person occupies in the existing social scheme. The democratic faith in equality is the faith that each individual shall have the chance and opportunity to contribute whatever he is capable of contributing and that the value of his contribution be decided by its place and function in the organized total of similar contributions, not on the basis of prior status of any kind whatever. . . .

SOCIALIZING INTELLIGENCE
(1935): JOHN DEWEY

Liberalism has to assume the responsibility for making it clear that intelligence is a social asset and is clothed with a function as public as is its origin, in the concrete, in social cooperation. . . . Consider also the development of the power of guiding ships across trackless wastes from the day when they hugged the shore, steering by visible sun and stars, to the appliances that now enable a sure course to be taken. It would require a heavy tome to describe the advances in science, in mathematics, astronomy, physics, chemistry, that have made these two things possible. The record would be an account of a vast multitude of cooperative efforts, in which one individual uses the results provided for him by a countless number of other individuals, and uses them so as to add to the common and public store. A survey of such facts brings home the actual social character of intelligence as it actually develops and makes its way. . . .

It is . . . said that intelligence is cold and that persons are moved to new ways of acting only by emotion, just as habit makes them adhere to old ways. . . .

Ideas that are framed to be put into operation for the sake of guiding action are imbued with all the emotional force that attaches to the ends proposed for action, and are accompanied with all the excitement and inspiration that attend the struggle to realize the ends. . . .

Again, it is said that the average citizen is not endowed with the degree of intelligence that the use of it as a method demands. . . . The last stand of oligarchical and anti-social seclusion is perpetuation of this purely individualistic notion of intelligence. The reliance of liberalism is not upon the mere abstraction of a native endowment unaffected by social relationships, but upon the fact that native capacity is sufficient to enable the average individual to respond to and to use the knowledge and the skill that are embodied in the social conditions in which he lives, moves and has his being. . . .

The indictments that are drawn against the intelligence of individuals are in truth indictments of a social order that does not permit the average individual to have access to the rich stores of the accumulated wealth of mankind in knowledge, ideas and purposes. . . . Back of the appropriation by the few of the material resources of society lies the appropriation by the few in behalf of their own ends of the cultural, the spiritual, resources that are the product not of the individuals who have taken possession but of the cooperative work of humanity. It is useless to talk about the failure of democracy until the source of its failure has been grasped and steps are taken to bring about that type of social organization that will encourage the socialized extension of intelligence. . . .

EDUCATION (1922, 1934, 1938): JOHN DEWEY

There is nothing new or striking in the conception of activity as an important educational principle. In the form of the idea of "self-activity" in particular, it has long been a name for the ultimate educational ideal. But activity has often been interpreted in too formal and too internal a sense, and hence has remained a barren ideal without influence on practice; sometimes it becomes a mere phrase, receiving the homage of the lips only.

To make the idea of activity effective, we must take it broadly enough to cover all the doings that involve growth of power—especially of power to realize the meaning of what is done. This excludes action done under external constraint or dictation, for this has no significance for the mind of him who performs it. It excludes also mere random reaction to an excitation that is finished when the momentary act has ceased—which does not, in other words, carry the person so habitual that it has become routine or mechanical. . . .

It is an old story that the human young have to *learn* most of the things that the young of other animals do instinctively or else with a slight amount of trying. Reflection on this fact shows that in learning these things human offspring are brought to the need of learning other things, and also to acquiring a habit of learning—a love of learning. While these considerations are fairly familiar, we often overlook their bearing upon the fact of physical activities. It follows from them at once that in so far as a physical activity has to be *learned*, it is not merely physical, but is mental, intellectual, in quality. . . . There is a genuinely intellectual factor when the child learns that one kind of eye-activity means a certain kind of moving of the arm, clasping of the fingers, resulting in experience of smoothness, etc. In such cases, there is not simply an acquisition of a new physical capacity; there is also learning in the mental sense; something has been found out. . . .

A higher form of activity involving the motor apparatus of the body is found when the control over external objects is achieved by means of tools of some sort, or by the application of one material to another. The use of a thread in sewing, the application of heat and moisture in cooking or other simple experimentations, illustrate the use of one thing (or mode of energy) to bring about a change in another thing. . . .

So far as . . . the interest in discovery or in finding out what happens under given circumstances, gains in importance, there develops a third type of interest—the distinctively intellectual interest. . . .

As there is no sharp line of division in theory, so there is none in practice. Planning ahead, taking notice of what happens, relating this to what is attempted, are parts of all intelligent or purposive activities. It is the business of educators to see that the conditions of expression of the practical interests are such as to encourage the developing of these intellectual phases of an activity, and thereby evoke a gradual transition to the theoretical type. . . .

We live in a world that is changing, not settled and fixed. Even the best established of the natural sciences, physics, is full of unsolved questions and charged with rapid change. But the obvious matter is that the social world is in a state of flux, and that we go on teaching as if the Constitution and our forefathers had finally determined all important social and political questions—a method that leaves pupils later in life ready victims of propaganda and publicity agents. Method is relative to subject-matter and not much of the subject-matter of actual economic and social facts and forces finds it way into even the average high school.

In short we teach the doings and impart the skills of the past, and severely leave alone the forces of the present that are creating the future in which the graduates of our school will some day find themselves. We educate for a static social order which does not exist. We educate for the *status quo* and when the students go forth they do not find anything so settled that it can be called anything of a static kind. What I have said about studying the past does not apply alone or even chiefly to history. In general the students are concerned to learn the *achievements* of the past, whether they be in history, geography, arithmetic, science or civics. They do not learn how these achievements were brought about nor do they learn the relation of the present to these achievements. . . .

Our public education is the potential means for effecting the transfiguration of the mechanics of modern life into sentiment and imagination. We may, I repeat, never get beyond the mechanics. We may remain burly, merely vigorous, expending energy riotously in making money, seeking pleasure and winning temporary victories over one another. Even such an estate has a virility lacking to a culture whose method is reminiscence, and whose triumph is finding a place of refuge. But it is not enough to justify a democracy as against the best of past aristocracies even though return to them is forever impossible. To bring to the consciousness of the coming generation something of the potential significance of the life of today, to transmute it from outward fact into intelligent perception, is the first step in the creation of a culture. The teachers who are facing this fact and who are trying to use the vital unspiritualized agencies of today as means of effecting the perception of human meaning yet to be realized are sharing in the act of creation. To perpetuate in the name of culture the tradition of aloofness from realistic science and compelling industry is to give them free course in their most unenlightened form. Not chiding but the sympathy and direction of understanding are what the harsh utilitarian and prosaic tendencies of present education require. . . .

5. *Logical Positivism and Logical Empiricism*

The "Vienna Circle" of Ludwig Wittgenstein, Rudolf Carnap, Morris Schlick, Herbert Feigl, and other Austro-German philosophers and scientists attempted to reform philosophy by eliminating pseudo-problems as well as by ending the pursuit of concepts which were essentially meaningless. Many members of the Vienna Circle eventually accepted posts in American universities where they continued to deal with problems of meaning and truth. American-born Positivists were to also make creative contributions to the movement. Charles Stevenson, for example, brought the Positivist approach to ethics by suggesting that the correct formulation of propositions provided the key for the discovery of all ethical meanings as expressions of personal preference, subjective values disguised as statements of objective fact. ("Theft is bad" must be translated into "I dislike stealing.") AUTHOR: Herbert Feigl (1896—) a member of the Vienna Circle, came to the United States in 1930 and continued his work as a physicist. SELECTION: "A Logical Positivist on the Construction of Theories" from Schlick's essay of that title (1935). "Logical Empiricism" from Feigl's essay in *Twentieth Century Philosophy* edited by Dagobert D. Runes (1947).

LOGICAL EMPIRICISM (1947):
HERBERT FEIGL

Probably the most decisive division among philosophical attitudes is the one between the worldly and the other-worldly types of thought. Profound differences in personality and temperament express themselves in the ever changing forms these two kinds of outlook assume. . . .

It seems likely that this situation in philosophy will continue as long as human nature in its relations to its cultural environment remains what it has been for the last three or four thousand years. The tough-minded and the tender-minded, as William James described them so brilliantly, are perennial types, perennially antagonistic. . . .

Empiricism, Skepticism, Naturalism, Positivism, and Pragmatism are typical thought movements of the worldly, tough-minded variety. Respect for the facts of experience, open-mindedness, an experimental trial-and-error attitude, and the capacity for working within the frame of an incomplete, unfinished world view distinguish them from the more impatient, imaginative, and often aprioristic thinkers in the tender-minded camp. Among the latter are speculative metaphysicians, intuitionists, rationalists, and absolute idealists. . . .

Throughout its history philosophy has been the particular stronghold of verbal magic. By purely verbal means it has tried to explain things which only science could explain or which cannot be explained at all. In the process it creates its own perplexities, and at its worst it attempts the "solution" of these pseudo-problems—problems arising only out of linguistic confusion—by means of pseudo-techniques—more verbal magic. Analysis teaches us that all this is altogether unnecessary. Thus, if a little levity be permitted, we may define philosophy as the disease of which it should be the cure.

The Analysis of Language and the Meaning of "Meaning"

The systematic pursuit of the problem of meaning by means of a logical analysis of language distinguishes Logical Empiricism from the earlier, more psychologically oriented types of Empiricism, Positivism, and Pragmatism. The imperative need for a logic of language was impressed upon scientists and logicians most poignantly in the last few decades. Just as the seminal ideas of some nineteenth-century philosophies originated in a scientific achievement (Darwin's theory of evolution) so twentieth-century Logical Empiricism was conceived under the influence primarily of three significant developments in recent mathematics and empirical science. These are the studies in the foundations of mathematics (led by Russell, Hilbert, and Brouwer), the revision of basic concepts in physics (advanced especially by Einstein, Planck, Bohr, and Heisenberg) and the reform of psychology by the behaviorists (Pavlov, Watson, et al). Though very different in context and subject-matter, these three developments focussed attention on the necessity for an inquiry into the limits and structure of meaningful discourse. . . .

Granting that language as used in common life serves in a fusion or a combination of various functions, it would seem imperative that some sort of theoretical separation of functions be undertaken for the sake of greater clarity and the avoidance of confusion. The list below is the result of such an analysis. Among the dozens of meanings of "meaning" we shall enumerate only those which are of prime importance for philosophical purposes.

The Functions of Language, or the Meaning of "Meaning"

Cognitive meanings (Informational function)	Non-cognitive meanings (Emotive expression and appeal function)
Purely formal	Pictorial (Imaginative)
Logico-arithmetical	Emotional (Affective)
Factual (= Empirical)	Volitional-motivational (Directive)

This table, correctly understood and properly used, is a powerful tool in the disentanglement and the traditional puzzles of philosophy. Many metaphysical "problems" and their "solutions" depend upon the erroneous presumption of the presence of factual meaning in expressions which have only emotive appeals and/or a formally correct grammatical structure. And many an epistemological question has been obscured by mistaking logico-mathematical for factual meanings. It is such confusion or erroneous pretense that is exposed to criticism on the basis of our table of meanings. No evaluation of the functions of language as such is implied. Emotive appeals are indispensable in the pursuits of practical life, in education, in propaganda (good or bad), in poetry, in literature, in religious edification and moral exhortation. Some of the highest refinements of our civilized existence depend upon the emotional overtones of spoken and written language. . . .

We may paraphrase [the problem of meaning] crudely: A difference that is to be a difference (i.e., more than a merely verbal or emotive one) must make a difference. Or, a little more precisely: If and only if assertion and denial of a sentence imply a difference capable of observational (experiential, operational, or experimental) test, does the sentence have factual meaning. Another useful formulation is [A. J.] Ayer's: "It is the mark of a genuine factual proposition . . . that some experiential propositions can be deduced from it in conjunction with certain other premises without being deducible from these other premises alone." This is simply empiricism brought up to date. . . .

In the light of the preceding distinctions, we may say that an expression is devoid of empirical meaning (i.e., of factual reference) or, briefly, is factually-meaningless, if it belongs to any one or several of the following five groups: (a) Expressions violating the syntactical formation-rules of a given language; (b) Analytic sentences; (c) Contradictory sentences; (d) Sentences containing extra-logical terms for which no experiential or operational definitions can be provided; (e) Sentences whose confirmability, i.e., even indirect and incomplete testability-in-principle, is logically excluded by the assumptions of the system of which they are a part. . . .

The question "How do we know?" presupposes the question "What do we mean?" and in the pursuit of both these questions we find ourselves urged to reconstruct our knowledge and to justify its truth-claims on a basis of observational evidence. Not the origin and psychological development of knowledge but its logical structure and empirical validation are the subject of a thus reformed epistemology. The psychology of knowledge (from the experimental study of discrimination behavior on the animal level to the scarcely begun investigation of the higher creative thought processes on the human level) is, after all, only one among the sciences and therefore, itself one of the subjects of epistemological analysis. . . .

As a consequence of all this, the concept of truth is disclosed to be ambiguous. In mathematical knowledge truth amounts to accordance with the formal (syntactical definitions, the postulates, of the system). In the factual context it means accordance with the empirical definitions, the semantical rules. Thus we call a sentence true if its terms are so applied to fact that none of the designation-rules of the language in question are violated. Error, whatever its source may be (illusion, misinterpretation of evidence, or only mis-speaking), simply consists in the disrupting of the one to one or many-one correspondence between the terms in the sentence and their referents, i.e., the constituents of the facts described. This version of the "correspondence" view of truth has none of the psychologistic inadequacies of the earlier "copy" or "picture" versions. . . .

A little reflection suffices to show that the meaning of the term "ethics" is highly ambiguous and that it designates at least five different types of endeavor: (1) Moral "vision," i.e., the recognition, discovery, or (alleged) demonstration of a "right" or "good" way of life or of an uppermost standard of moral evaluation; (2) Moral exhortation, education, and propaganda; (3) Empirical studies of actual moral evaluations, either descriptive or explanatory; (4) The technology of the "good" life—a branch of applied science concerned with the discernment and perfecting of means (instrumental values) in view of certain ends (terminal values); (5) The logical analysis of ethical terms and sentences—either by the casuistic Socratic method or by the elaboration of a hypothetico-deductive system of ethical norms. The five-fold division just outlined is itself a result of the Socratic type; of approach. . . .

Ethical norms or imperatives as discovered or intuited in (1), proclaimed and advocated in (2), factually studied in (3), practically implemented in (4), and subjected to a meaning analysis in (5) may be reconstructed as sentences referring to a possible (usually not actualized) state of affairs and expressed with an emotional-motivational appeal. In the use of such terms as "ought," "should," "right," "good," "duty," etc. lies the irreducibly directive component of moral value-judgments. An ethical imperative like the Golden Rule simply means: "Would that everybody behaved toward his fellowmen as he expects them to behave toward him." This sentence, having its accent in the emotive appeal, could not possibly be deduced from a knowledge of facts only; it is neither true nor false. It is rather an invitation (suggestion, request, exhortation, or command) to make the contained factual sentence true. In traditional metaphysically or theologically oriented moral philosophies the attempt was made to validate the fundamental standards on the basis of revelation, apriori intuition, or logical proof. Absolute values were thus either concretely specified and dogmatically proclaimed or merely abstractly assumed and their specific content left open. From the logico-empirical point of view all of these approaches involve confusions of meaning or assumptions incapable of test. Absolute values as well as categorical imperatives can be expressed only in emotive language.

Relative values in the sense of instrumental values which are determined by needs and interests and hypothetical imperatives which state empirically confirmable means-ends relations are factually-meaningful. Here the questions of truth or falsity make sense. As long as disagreement in morals depends upon differences in opinion or belief regarding the efficacy of contending means, such disagreement is in principle capable of settlement by the empirical method. . . .

The quest for certainty, here in the field of morals just as elsewhere, may lead to emotionally soothing or edifying results. But the acceptance of an absolute authority or extra mundane sanction for morality, like the belief in an absolute source of factual truth, manifests a not fully liberated, pre-scientific type of mind. A completely grown-up mankind will have to shoulder the responsibility for its outlook and conduct; and in the spirit of an empirical and naturalistic humanism it will acknowledge no other procedure than the experimental and by our own insights in the possibilities of improving human nature. . . .

Chapter XV. CRITICAL INTELLECTUALS IN A MASS CULTURE

IN PURITAN NEW ENGLAND OR IN THE AGE OF THE AMERICAN REV-
olution "intellectual," "politician," and "ruling elite" can be described as several roles for the same group of men rather than
different classes of persons. From the eighteen-forties, if not sooner,
one finds writers, scholars, and artists who function as "critical intellectuals"* by bringing both intellectual detachment and personal concern to a critical and creative scrutiny of some significant aspect of
American society. Twentieth-century intellectuals have generally displayed somber moods and a pessimism which can be traced back at
least as far as Edgar Allan Poe, Herman Melville, and Nathaniel
Hawthorne.

The pessimistic writer has rarely won public favor in the
United States, and in ante-bellum America the serene, hopeful attitude of a Ralph Waldo Emerson, a Henry Thoreau, or a Walt Whitman seemed to spring more naturally from the national character. A
young, self-confident democracy attached itself firmly to beliefs in the
goodness of human nature, the inevitability of social progress, and
the value of personal success. The intellectual who failed to embrace
these doctrines often experienced great difficulties in his career. Nathaniel Hawthorne was torn between a tragic perception of the Puritan past and a sense of personal irrelevancy in the bustling, utilitarian
society of his age. If Hawthorne never found the audience he sought,
Edgar Allan Poe and Herman Melville fared even worse. Melville
abandoned his career for nearly two decades, and Poe both lived and

---

* The relationships of the "intelligentsia" to the Tsarist regime in Russia or
of the Philosophes to the *ancien regime* in France are reasonably clear, but the
place of the "intellectual" in American society is much more difficult to
ascertain. The category "critical intellectual" must be understood to refer to those
who had insights and perceptions as well as concepts. (Men such as Henry James
and Ernest Hemingway were obviously not masters of abstract ideas.) The element
of detachment must be stressed, for we cannot assume that Woodrow Wilson or
Herbert Hoover functioned in the White House as critical intellectuals, even
though Wilson was a former professor and Hoover a reasonably good classical
scholar.

died tragically. Hawthorne, who deeply envied the English writed his social heritage, spent most of his later years abroad as a diplomat; and the alienation of Henry James from the American scene was nearly complete.

After the Civil War the intellectuals were faced with both the sterile, anti-aesthetic pieties of "the genteel tradition" and the disturbing consequences of the industrial revolution. Early in the twentieth century as a mass culture appropriate to the age of the machine and the assembly line developed, American intellectuals were affected by a malaise which also stirred European intellectuals to revolt against machines and materialism, progress, and bourgeois complacency. While Nietzsche pondered the profound implications of "the death of God" and Spengler wrote the early essays on the decline of Western civilization, Henry Adams—baffled by the complexities of the twentieth century—nostalgically contemplated the manner in which the Virgin Mother had given meaning and impetus to every aspect of life during the Middle Ages. Only the dynamo seemed to provide a force comparable to that of the Virgin, and Adams could not bring himself to worship at the shrine of this modern deity.

In the years before and during the First World War the mood of disenchantment deepened, and Adams' doubts settled in the minds of kindred intellectuals. Brooks Adams charted the laws of cultural decay, and the New Humanists under the leadership of Irving Babbitt assured their readers that the decline of Western culture was evident and could be arrested only through the preservation of traditional moral values, the construction of a lofty aestheticism, and the return to power of an authentic intellectual elite. A young Harvard poet from St. Louis, T. S. Eliot, who found no grounds at all for hope, portrayed a world of inconsequentiality without human values or religious solace. At opposite poles from Eliot in personality and manner was H. L. Mencken, who shared with the Adamses, Irving Babbitt, and Eliot a distaste for popular dogmas about democracy and progress. Mencken had been influenced by Nietzsche's exaltation of the superior man above the "contemptible" masses, but the Baltimore journalist bore his pessimism with the air of a rowdy Epicurean.

After the mass slaughter of World War I, T. S. Eliot's *The Wasteland* seemed an appropriate gospel for a time of despair. American artists and intellectuals became expatriates and gathered in the cafes and bistros of Paris where pessimism could at least be combined with an exuberant creativity. Paris was the locale for a fascinating if bewildering parade of aesthetic experiments—Dada, Expressionism,

Cubism, the "new" poetic symbolism, and so many more; the great works of Marcel Proust and James Joyce cast a very large shadow over the literary scene; and the activities of Ezra Pound, Ernest Hemingway, and Gertrude Stein suggested that the consolation of an enduring literature might be salvaged from a world in emotional ruins. The extraordinary E. E. Cummings and some of his poetic contemporaries in the Dada movement felt the impact of the modern crisis quite differently as a release from all the old inhibitions, a "time to murder and create," an opportunity to live completely in the present moment. Men and women without the talent of a Cummings or the catharsis of truly significant creative activity often fell into a round of cafes, cabarets, literary manifestoes, and drunken parties that suggested the feverish energy preceding the "crack-up"—a denouement so brilliantly described by F. Scott Fitzgerald. Hemingway's heroes were more stoic, and realized that the gaudier aspects of expatriatism simple mirrored the raucous vulgarity of American life in the age of the George Babbitts and Warren Hardings.

Ultimately the stance of despairing stoicism collapsed, and the lost generation struggled to find itself. T. S. Eliot retreated from the wasteland to Anglo-Catholicism, while Hemingway discovered that "no man is an island to himself" and made his way through several political novels toward engagement with humanity. The bitter depression years after 1929 affected the thinking of many intellectuals, usually helping to convert moods of despair or ironic detachment into anger against a social system which had brought forth so much misery. John Dos Passos' trilogy, U.S.A., presented a panoramic view of a disintegrating industrial society, and John Steinbeck's novels vividly portrayed the broken social patterns of "Okies" fleeing the Dust Bowl, farmers rich in rotting, unsalable crops, or striking workers struggling for economic existence. Literary currents moved stongly to the left, and the proletarian novel came into its own as Granville Hicks, Richard Wright, and other writers joined the movement for revolutionary Communism.

Affirmation often followed protest. Men who had believed themselves to be completely alienated from the American scene often came to see themselves as defenders of a national tradition against the threat of twentieth-century conditions. An American revival originated in the twenties and gained surprising momentum in the thirties. Scholars discovered that the nation possessed a great literature in the works of Melville, Hawthorne, Poe, Henry James, and others.

American scenes, sights, and history received more attention from intellectuals; the vogue of the folk song symbolized a change of temper; and dozens of writers such as Carl Sandburg celebrated the basic virtues of the American people. The sense of a heritage worth preserving grew as Stalin's ruthless maneuvers dissolved the Communist dream, and Hitler's aggressions revealed the extent of the Nazi threat.

Thomas Wolfe's descriptions of Nazi Germany and Archibald MacLeish's stern lectures to intellectuals on their responsibilities in the face of Hitler's war on civilization were among the writings which aroused men to the struggle against Nazi ideology and its manifestations in both Europe and America. The full horror of the Nazi holocaust was not realized until the end of the war when the victors captured the death camps where millions of Jews had been systematically murdered. Those intellectuals of the postwar period who sought grounds for pessimism could look backward to the Nazi debacle and forward to the terrible totalitarianism predicted by George Orwell. Certainly the twentieth-century chamber of horrors encouraged the postwar vogue of "conservatism." "New conservatives" such as Peter Viereck could denounce the ideas of progress and human goodness held by modern thinkers from Rousseau to John Dewey as guideposts pointing toward the sterility of a proletarian society, the terror of Nazi death camps, or the ruthlessness of Communist brainwashing techniques.

The dominant political mood of postwar America was often decried as conservative and conformist. The Cold War with Russia seemed to intensify this conformist trend and to create a political atmosphere in which many political intellectuals were accused of "disloyalty." Neither the loyalty controversy of the early fifties, nor any other aspect of the social and political scene, attracted the talents of many major American writers. Novelists may have reflected the inner anxieties of modern life in their concentration on themes of individual isolation and personal identity, but certainly they left the tasks of social interpretation largely to scholars and journalists such as David Riesman, C. Wright Mills, and William Whyte. The critical intellectuals suggested that the individual was threatened by the tendency of society to force the surrender of a constantly increasing measure of choice, freedom, and individuality. Whether the critics exaggerated or not, "suburban togetherness" had enough reality to stimulate the rise of a new generation of Bohemians, advocates of raw experience, "cool" jazz, speed, and sex. These were the "Beatniks," alienated outsiders, restless aesthetic and intellectual vagrants, perpetually "on the road." The Bohemian poets and the scholars were joined by theologians in the criticism of the mores of modern mass culture. The Catholic philosophers Jacques Maritain and Étienne Gilson made a deep impression on the American intellectual scene with their reinterpretations of the philosophy of St. Thomas Aquinas as the proper antidote to modern evils; European Christian Existentialists were widely read on this side of the Atlantic; and American Protestant theologians such as Reinhold Niebuhr and Paul Tillich, who wished to recover the tragic sense of Christianity, found a superabundance of spiritual sickness in both suburban "squares" and rebellious "beatniks," in nationalist fanatics and Communist "world menders." Finally, the essays and novels of Ralph Ellison and James Baldwin in the forties, fifties, and sixties, which displayed the terror and tragedy of the Negro "in white America," may have done much to signal "the end of innocence."

1. A Pale, Bleeding Past and a Coarse Modernity

Henry James objected very strongly to American indifference and hostility toward tradition; during a return visit to America after an absence of twenty-five years he was particularly struck by the way in which the "pale, bleeding past" suffered at the hands of the crude money-minded present. George Santayana, who lacked many of the American roots of a Hawthorne or James, joined his American mother at the age of eight for a future which revolved about the Boston Latin School, Harvard College, and Cambridge intellectual life. Although forty years in Boston left the stamp of New England on Santayana, he forcefully rejected the general Puritan-Yankee outlook. AUTHORS: Henry James (1843–1916) spent most of his adult life abroad, wrote his best novels in England, and became an English citizen in 1915. George Santayana (1863–1952), one of the greatest American philosophers, lived in the United States until 1912, but spent the last forty years of his life abroad. SELECTIONS: "The Exile Returns" from James' The American Scene (1907). "A Generation of Money Slaves" from Santayana's poem My Heart Rebels Against My Generation (1894).

THE EXILE RETURNS (1907):
HENRY JAMES

[New York City: Democracy and Progress] The will to grow was every-where written large, and to grow at no matter what or whose ex-pense. . . . The great presence that bristles for [the waiting observer] on the sounding dock, and that shakes the planks, the loose boards of its theatric stage to an inordinate unprecedented rumble, is the monstrous form of Democracy, which is thereafter to project its shifting angular shadow, at one time and another, across every inch of the field of this vision. It is the huge democratic broom that has made the clearance and that one seems to see brandished in the empty sky. . . .

As the usual, in our vast crude democracy of trade, is the new, the simple, the cheap, the common, the commercial, the immediate, and, all too often, the ugly, so any human product that those elements fail con-spicuously to involve or to explain, any creature, or even any feature, not turned out to pattern, any form of suggested rarity, subtlety, ancientry, or other pleasant perversity, prepares for us a recognition akin to rapture. These lonely ecstasies of the truly open sense make up often, in the hustling, bustling desert, for such "sinkings" of the starved stomach as have led one too often to have to tighten one's aesthetic waistband. . . .

[*Decay of the New England Countryside.*] Written over the great New Hampshire region . . . everywhere legible was the hard little his-toric record of agricultural failure and defeat. It had to pass for the historic background, that traceable truth that a stout human experiment had been tried, had broken down. One was in presence, everywhere, of the refusal to consent to history, and of the consciousness, on the part of every site, that this precious compound is in no small degree being in-solently made, on the other side of the continent, at the expense of such sites. . . . The appeal was thus not only from the rude absence of the company that had gone, and the still ruder presence of the company left, the scattered families, of poor spirit and loose habits, who had feared the risk of change, it was to a listening ear, directly—that of the "summer people," to whom, in general, one soon began to figure so much of the country, in New England, as looking for its future. . . .

There was the little white wooden village, of course, with its houses in queer alignment and its rudely-emphasized meeting-house, in particu-lar, very nearly as unconsecrated as the store or the town pump; but this represented, throughout, the highest tribute to the amenities. A sordid ugliness and shabbiness hung, inveterately, about the wayside "farms," and all their appurtenances and incidents—above all, about their inmates; when the idea of appearance was anywhere expressed (and its highest flights were but in the matter of fresh paint or a swept dooryard), a summer person was usually the author of the boom. The teams, the carts, the conveyances in their kinds, the sallow, saturnine natives in charge of them, the enclosures, the fences, the gates, the wayside "bits," of whatever sort, so far as these were referable to human attention or human neglect, kept telling the tale of the difference made, in a land of long winters, by the suppression of the two great factors of the familiar English landscape, the squire and the parson. . . .

The ugliness—one pounced, indeed, on this as on a talisman for the future—was the so complete abolition of forms; if, with so little reference to their past, present or future possibility, they could be said to have been so much honoured as to be abolished. . . .

[Mount Vernon.] It is for the same reason for which we are always inordinately moved, on American ground, I think, when the unconscious minor scale of the little old demonstrations to which we owe everything is made visible to us, when their disproportionate modesty is proved upon them. The reason worked at Mount Vernon, for the restless analyst, quite as it had worked a few months before, on the small and simple scene of Concord Fight: the slight, pale, bleeding Past, in a patched homespun suit, stands there taking the thanks of the bloated Present—having woundedly rescued from thieves and brought to his door the fat, locked pocket-book of which that personage appears the owner. The pocket-book contains, "unbeknown" to the honest youth, bank-notes of incredible figure, and what breaks our heart, if we be cursed with the historic imagination, is the grateful, wan smile with which the great guerdon of sixpence is received. . . .

A GENERATION OF MONEY SLAVES (1894): GEORGE SANTAYANA

> My heart rebels against my generation,
> That talks of freedom and is slave to riches,
> And, toiling 'neath each day's ignoble burden,
> Boasts of the morrow.
>
> No space for noonday rest or midnight watches,
> No purest joy of breathing under heaven!
> Wretched themselves, they heap, to make them happy,
> Many possessions.
>
> But thou, O silent Mother, wise, immortal,
> To whom our toil is laughter,—take, divine one,
> This vanity away, and to thy lover
> Give what is needful:—

A staunch heart, nobly calm, averse to evil,
The windy sky for breath, the sea, the mountain,
A well-born, gentle friend, his spirit's brother,
Ever beside him.

What would you gain, ye seekers, with your striving,
Or what vast Babel raise you on your shoulders?
You multiply distresses, and your children
Surely will curse you.

O leave them rather friendlier gods, and fairer
Orchards and temples, and a freer bosom!
What better comfort have we, or what other
Profit in living

Than to feed, sobered by the truth of Nature,
Awhile upon her bounty and her beauty,
And hand her torch of gladness to the ages
Following after?

She hath not made us, like her other children,
Merely for peopling of her spacious kingdoms,
Beasts of the wild, or insects of the summer,
Breeding and dying,

But also that we might, half knowing, worship
The deathless beauty of her guiding vision,
And learn to love, in all things mortal, only
What is eternal.

2. *Toward the Wasteland*

A descendant of John Adams, John Quincy Adams, and Charles Francis
Adams, Henry Adams seemed destined for a major role in American
politics, but the rowdy, materialistic age of Grant had no use for this
child of an earlier, more austere time of Republican simplicity and dignity. Confined to the role of spectator, Adams sought a key to modern
history, and brooded over the contrast between the power and complexity
of the twentieth century and the serene faith of the Middle Ages. AU-
THOR: Henry Adams (1838–1918), a disappointed statesman never called
to public office, made a brilliant career for himself in history and the
philosophy of history. SELECTION: "The Dynamo and the Virgin" from
Adams' *The Education of Henry Adams* (1907).

THE DYNAMO AND THE VIRGIN
(1907): HENRY ADAMS

Under the shadow of Boston State House, turning its back on the house of John Hancock, the little passage called Hancock Avenue runs, or ran, from Beacon Street, skirting the State House grounds, to Mount Vernon Street, on the summit of Beacon Hill; and there, in the third house below Mount Vernon Place, February 16, 1838, a child was born. . . .

What could become of such a child of the seventeenth and eighteenth centuries, when he should wake up to find himself required to play the game of the twentieth? . . .

For him . . . the old universe was thrown into the ash-heap and a new one created. He and his eighteenth-century, troglodytic Boston were . . . cut apart—separated forever. . . .

Already, at ten years old, the boy found himself standing face to face with a dilemma that might have puzzled an early Christian. What was he?—where was he going? Even then he felt that something was wrong. . . . Turn the dilemma as he pleased, he still came back on the eighteenth century and the law of Resistance; of Truth; of Duty, and of Freedom. He was a ten-year-old priest and politician. He could under no circumstances have guessed what the next fifty years had in store, and no one could teach him; but sometimes, in his old age, he wondered—and could never decide—whether the most clear and certain knowledge would have helped him. Supposing he had seen a New York stock-list of 1900, and had studied the statistics of railways, telegraphs, coal, and steel— would he have quitted his eighteenth-century, his ancestral prejudices, his abstract ideals, his semi-clerical training, and the rest, in order to perform an expiatory pilgrimage to State Street, and ask for the fatted calf of his grandfather Brooks and a clerkship in the Suffolk Bank?

Sixty years afterwards he was still unable to make up his mind. . . .

Until the Great Exposition of 1900 closed its doors in November, Adams haunted it, aching to absorb knowledge, and helpless to find it. He would have liked to know how much of it could have been grasped by the best-informed man in the world. While he was thus meditating chaos, Langley came by, and showed it to him. . . .

Langley, with the ease of a great master of experiment, threw out of the field every exhibit that did not reveal a new application of force. . . .

Then he showed his scholar the great hall of dynamos, and explained how little he knew about electricity or force of any kind. . . . To Adams the dynamo became a symbol of infinity. As he grew accustomed to the great gallery of machines, he began to feel the forty-foot dynamos as a moral force, much as the early Christians felt the Cross. The planet itself seemed less impressive, in its old-fashioned, deliberate, annual or daily revolution, than this huge wheel, revolving within arm's-length at some vertiginous speed, and barely murmuring—scarcely humming an audible warning to stand a hair's-breadth further for respect of power—while it would not wake the baby lying close against its frame. Before the end, one began to pray to it; inherited instinct taught the natural expression of man before silent and infinite force. Among the thousand symbols of ultimate energy, the dynamo was not so human as some, but it was the most expressive. . . . In . . . seven years man had translated himself into a new universe which had no common scale of measurement with the old. He had entered a supersensual world, in which he could measure nothing except by chance collisions of movements imperceptible to his senses, perhaps even imperceptible to his instruments, but perceptible to each other, and so to some known ray at the end of the scale. Langley seemed prepared for anything, even for an indeterminable number of universes interfused—physics stark mad in metaphysics. . . .

The rays that Langley disowned, as well as those which he fathered, were occult, supersensual, irrational; they were a revelation of mysterious energy like that of the Cross. . . .

The historian was thus reduced to his last resources. . . . He made up his mind to venture it; he would risk translating rays into faith. . . .

Before this historical chasm, a mind like that of Adams felt itself helpless. . . . On one side, at the Louvre and at Chartres . . . was the highest energy ever known to man, the creator of four-fifths of his noblest art, exercising vastly more attraction over the human mind than all the steam-engines and dynamos ever dreamed of; and yet this energy was unknown to the American mind. An American Virgin would never dare command; an American Venus would never dare exist. . . .

The [modern] revolution in attitude seemed voluntary, but in fact was as mechanical as the fall of a feather. Man created nothing. After 1500, the speed of progress so rapidly surpassed man's gait as to alarm every one. . . . Society knew better. Yet the telescope held it rigidly standing on its head; the microscope revealed a universe that defied the senses; gunpowder killed whole races that lagged behind; the compass coerced the most imbruted mariner to act on the impossible idea that the earth was round; the press drenched Europe with anarchism. Europe saw itself, violently resisting, wrenched into false positions, drawn along new lines as a fish that is caught on a hook; but unable to understand by what force it was controlled. The resistance was often bloody, sometimes humorous, always constant. . . .

Very slowly the accretion of these new forces, chemical and mechanical, grew in volume until they acquired sufficient mass to take the place of the old religious science, substituting their attraction for the attractions of the Civitas Dei, but the process remained the same. Nature, not mind, did the work that the sun does on the planets. Man depended more and more absolutely on forces other than his own, and on instruments which superseded his senses. . . .

Thought itself became tortured, suffering reluctantly, impatiently, painfully, the coercion of new method. Easy thought had always been movement of inertia, and mostly mere sentiment; but even the process of mathematics measured feebly the needs of force.

The stupendous acceleration after 1800 ended in 1900 with the appearance of the new class of supersensual forces, before which the man of science stood at first as bewildered and helpless, as in the fourth century, a priest of Isis before the Cross of Christ. . . .

3. The First World War and the Lost Generation

The War was for European and American intellectuals both a cause for despair and a time of liberation. In painting, poetry, drama, and the novel, artists developed a wide range of new techniques. E. E. Cummings conducted a private war against punctuation and common verbal patterns in the same spirit which led European Dada artists to paint mustaches on prints of the Mona Lisa, sculpt from mechanical debris, and discover admirable qualities in acts of random violence. However the richness of esthetic novelty could not relieve the despair felt by many writers over the war and the inhumanity of modern life. Ernest Hemingway was the poet laureate for "the lost generation" of men and women who lacked the illumination of faith, despised the past, scorned the future, and lived in the present—sometimes with reckless gaiety, but more often with stoic resignation.

Hemingway during the twenties worked in Paris as an American newsman and lived in an expatriate colony which at one time or another included a sizeable portion of leading American writers. The artists and intellectuals who chose to remain at home rather than to experiment with expatriation were not necessarily more positive minded about America in the age of Harding and Coolidge. H. L. Mencken, the author of the remark that one stayed in America for the same reason people visited the zoo, satirized the follies and stupidities of what he called the great American democratic "boobeoisie." In the celebrated Scopes trial which Mencken covered as a reporter, Scopes was a public school teacher charged with violating the Tennessee law against the teaching of biological evolution. William Jennings Bryan, three times the Democratic Presidential candidate, assisted the prosecution, and Clarence Darrow,

the most famous criminal lawyer of his generation, defended Scopes.
AUTHORS: Ernest Hemingway (1898–1961), a reporter, expatriate, and
sportsman, became an extremely influential novelist and a Nobel Prize
winner. Henry L. Mencken (1880–1956), the Baltimore journalist, essay-
ist, and scholar, edited *The Smart Set* (1914–1923) and *The American
Mercury*. His most notable book was *The American Language* (1919).
SELECTIONS: "A Farewell to Arms" from Hemingway's novel. (1929.)
"An American Scandal: The Scopes Trial" from a Mencken article in
The American Mercury (1925).

A FAREWELL TO ARMS (1929):
ERNEST HEMINGWAY

[Lt. Henry describes the War in 1917.] Sometimes in the dark we heard
the troops marching under the window and guns going past pulled by
motor-tractors. There was much traffic at night and many mules on the
roads with boxes of ammunition on each side of their pack-saddles and
gray motor-trucks that carried men, and other trucks with loads covered
with canvas that moved slower in the traffic. There were big guns too that
passed in the day drawn by tractors, the long barrels of the guns covered
with green branches and green leafy branches and vines laid over the
tractors. To the north we could look across a valley and see a forest of
chestnut trees and behind it another mountain on this side of the river.
There was fighting for that mountain too, but it was not successful, and
in the fall when the rains came the leaves all fell from the chestnut trees
and the branches were bare and the trunks black with rain. The vineyards
were thin and bare-branched too and all the country wet and brown and
dead with the autumn. There were mists over the river and clouds on the
mountain and the trucks splashed mud on the road and the troops were
muddy and wet in their capes; their rifles were wet and under their capes
the two leather cartridge-boxes on the front of the belts, gray leather
boxes heavy with the packs of clips of thin, long 6.5 mm. cartridges,
bulged forward under the capes so that the men, passing on the road,
marched as though they were six months gone with child.

There were small gray motorcars that passed going very fast; usually
there was an officer on the seat with the driver and more officers in the
back seat. They splashed more mud than the camions even and if one of
the officers in the back was very small and sitting between two generals,
he himself so small that you could not see his face but only the top of his
cap and his narrow back, and if the car went especially fast it was
probably the King. He lived in Udine and came out in this way nearly
every day to see how things were going, and things went very badly.

At the start of the winter came the permanent rain and with the rain came the cholera. But it was checked and in the end only seven thousand died of it in the army. . . .

[Rinaldi and Henry talk about the War.] "Yes, they give the battalions in the front line as much as they can but the ones in back are very short. They have eaten all the Austrians' potatoes and chestnuts from the woods. They ought to feed them better. We are big eaters. I am sure there is plenty of food. It is very bad for the soldiers to be short of food. Have you ever noticed the difference it makes in the way you think?"

"Yes," I said. "It can't win a war but it can lose one."

"We won't talk about losing. There is enough talk about losing. What has been done this summer cannot have been done in vain."

I did not say anything. I was always embarrassed by the words sacred, glorious, and sacrifice and the expression in vain. We had heard them, sometimes standing in the rain almost out of earshot, so that only the shouted words came through, and had read them, on proclamations that were slapped up by billposters over other proclamations, now for a long time, and I had seen nothing sacred, and the things that were glorious had no glory and the sacrifices were like the stockyards at Chicago if nothing was done with the meat except to bury it. There were many words that you could not stand to hear and finally only the names of places had dignity. Certain numbers were the same way and certain dates and these with the names of the places were all you could say and have them mean anything. Abstract words such as glory, honor, courage, or hallow were obscene beside the concrete names of villages, the numbers of roads, the names of rivers, the numbers of regiments and the dates. . . .

[After the disorderly Caporetto retreat Lt. Henry flees to escape a senseless execution.] I would like to have had the uniform off although I did not care much about the outward forms. I had taken off the stars, but that was for convenience. It was no point of honor. I was not against them. I was through. I wished them all the luck. There were the good ones, and the brave ones, and the calm ones and the sensible ones, and they deserved it. But it was not my show any more and I wished this bloody train would get to Mestre and I would eat and stop thinking. I would have to stop.

Piani would tell them they had shot me. They went through the pockets and took the papers of the people they shot. They would not have my papers. They might call me drowned. I wondered what they would hear in the States. Dead from wounds and other causes. Good Christ I was hungry. I wondered what had become of the priest at the mess. And Rinaldi. He was probably at Pordenone. If they had not gone further back. Well, I would never see him now. I would never see any of them now. That life was over. I did not think he had syphilis. . . . But he would worry. I would worry too if I had it. Any one would worry.

I was not made to think. I was made to eat. My God, yes. Eat and drink and sleep with Catherine. To-night maybe. No that was impossible. But to-morrow night, and a good meal and sheets and never going away again except together. Probably have to go damned quickly. She would go. I knew she would go. When would we go? That was something to think about. It was getting dark. I lay and thought where we would go. There were many places. . . .

AN AMERICAN SCANDAL : THE SCOPES TRIAL (1925): H. L. MENCKEN

Dayton, Tennessee, July 13—There is a Unitarian clergyman here from New York, trying desperately to horn into the trial and execution of the infidel Scopes. He will fail. If [Clarence] Darrow [the defense attorney] ventured to put him on the stand the whole audience, led by the jury, would leap out of the courthouse windows and take to the hills. Darrow himself, indeed, is as much as they can bear. The whisper that he is an atheist has been stilled by the bucolic make-up and by the public report that he has the gift of prophecy and can reconcile Genesis and evolution. Even so, there is ample space about him when he navigates the streets. The other day a newspaperwoman was warned by her landlady to keep out of the courtroom when he was on his legs. All the local sorcerers predict that a bolt from heaven will fetch him in the end. The night he arrived there was a violent storm, the town water turned brown, and horned cattle in the lowlands were afloat for hours. A woman back in the mountains gave birth to a child with hair four inches long, curiously bobbed in scallops.

The Book of Revelation has all the authority, in these theological uplands, of military orders in time of war. The people turn to it for light upon all their problems, spiritual, and secular. If a text were found in it denouncing the anti-evolution law, then the anti-evolution law would become infamous overnight. But so far the exegetes who roar and snuffle in the town have found no such text. Instead they have found only blazing ratifications and reinforcements of Genesis. Darwin is the devil with seven tails and nine horns. Scopes, though he is disguised by flannel pantaloons and a Beta Theta Pi haircut, is the harlot of Babylon. Darrow is Beelzebub in person. . . .

I have hitherto hinted that an Episcopalian down here in the Coca Cola belt is regarded as an atheist. It sounds like one of the lies that journalists tell, but it is really an understatement of the facts. Even a Methodist, by Rhea County standards, is one a bit debauched by pride of intellect. It is the four Methodists on the jury who are expected to hold out for giving Scopes Christian burial after he is hanged. . . .

It is not enough to accept the truth as a mere statement of indisputable and awful fact; it must be embraced ecstatically and orgiastically, to the accompaniment of loud shouts, dreadful heavings and gurglings, and dancing with arms and legs.

This craving is satisfied brilliantly by the gaudy practices of the Holy Rollers, and so the mountaineers are gradually gravitating toward the Holy Roller communion, or, as they prefer to call it, the Church of God. Gradually, perhaps, is not the word. They are actually going in by whole villages and townships. At the last count of noses there were 20,000 Holy Rollers in these hills. The next census, I have no doubt, will show many more. The cities of the lowlands, of course, still resist, and so do most of the county towns, including even Dayton, but once one steps off the state roads the howl of holiness is heard in the woods, and the yokels carry on an almost continuous orgy. . . .

All the usual rules were suspended and the curfew bell was locked up. The prophet Bryan, exhausted by his day's work for Revelations, was snoring in his bed up the road, but enough volunteers were still on watch to keep the battlements manned.

Such is human existence among the fundamentalists, where children are brought up on Genesis and sin is unknown. . . .

4. *Science and Modern Pessimism*

To Brooks Adams, Josiah Royce, and kindred intellectuals, the second law of thermodynamics forecast the "heat death" of the cosmos through the gradual diffusion of concentrations of energy. Those who could no longer believe in a "Christian Universe," or even in the tight and orderly ship of the Newtonian cosmos, saw the world as a bleakly neutral place of residence for a humanity moved from the center to the periphery of existence; and life itself appeared as a brief and transitory moment in the vast desert wastes of infinity. The pessimists found in biology little more than a blind, bloody, and perpetual struggle which involved man as well as all other creatures. Freud's theory of "the unconscious" with its seething bed of repressed impulse which determined in a thoroughly nonrational way most human conduct, strengthened the conviction of many intellectuals that the essence of human life was blind and futile striving. Of course, others read Freud differently and praised him as a source of new self-knowledge or as a sexual liberator. Moreover, the pessimists drew their ideas from the apparent implications of physics and biology, disciplines then changing at a revolutionary pace. Albert Einstein's special and general theories of relativity turned a great many notions about the universe upside down, and the subatomic exploration of "matter" and "energy" toppled more ideas from general acceptance. Science and technology promised more precise knowledge and an enormous increase in man's power to harness nature, but the new scientific explorations made verbal speculations about the physical universe extremely difficult and doubtful. AUTHORS: Sigmund Freud (1856–1939), a Viennese physician, was the founder of psychoanalysis as a method for treating mental illness. In later years he applied psychoanalytic theory to the study of history, art, and literature. Joseph Wood Krutch (1893–   ), for many years a Professor of English at Columbia University, published in 1929 The Modern Temper, a book accepted by many readers as a basic summary of the major threads of pessimism in the twenties. SELECTIONS: "Civilization and Its Discontents" from Freud's book of the same title (1930). "The Spiritual Iconoclasm of Modern Science" from Krutch's The Modern Temper (1929).

CIVILIZATION AND ITS DISCONTENTS (1930): SIGMUND FREUD

The bit of truth behind all this—one so eagerly denied—is that men are not gentle, friendly creatures wishing for love, who simply defend themselves if they are attacked, but that a powerful measure of desire for aggression has to be reckoned as part of their instinctual endowment. The result is that their neighbor is to them not only a possible helper or sexual object, but also a temptation to them to gratify their aggressiveness on him, to exploit his capacity for work without recompense, to use him sexually without his consent, to seize his possessions, to humiliate him, to cause him pain, to torture and to kill him. . . .

The existence of this tendency to aggression which we can detect in ourselves and rightly presume to be present in others is the factor that disturbs our relations with our neighbors and makes it necessary for culture to institute its high demands. Civilized society is perpetually menaced with disintegration through this primary hostility of men towards one another. . . . Civilization expects to prevent the worst atrocities of brutal violence by taking upon itself the right to employ violence against criminals, but the law is not able to lay hands on the more discreet and subtle forms in which human aggressions are expressed. . . .

If civilization requires . . . sacrifices, not only of sexuality, but also of the aggressive tendencies in mankind, we can better understand why it should be so hard for men to feel happy in it. In actual fact primitive man was better off in this respect, for he knew nothing of any restrictions on his instincts. . . .

In rightly finding fault, as we thus do, with our present state of civilization for so inadequately providing us with what we require to make us happy in life, and for the amount of suffering of a probably avoidable nature it lays us open to—in doing our utmost to lay bare the roots of its deficiencies by our unsparing criticisms, we are undoubtedly exercising our just rights and now showing ourselves enemies of culture. . . .

THE SPIRITUAL ICONOCLASM OF MODERN SCIENCE (1929): JOSEPH WOOD KRUTCH

Casually [man] . . . accepts the spiritual iconoclasm of science, and in the detachment of everyday life he learns to play with the cynical wisdom of biology and psychology, which explain away the awe of emotional experience just as earlier science explained away the awe of conventional piety. Yet, under the stress of emotional crises, knowledge is quite incapable of controlling his emotions or of justifying them to himself. In love he calls upon the illusions of man's grandeur and dignity to help him accept his emotions, and faced with tragedy he calls upon illusion to dignify his suffering; but lyric flight is checked by the rationality which he has cultivated, and in the world of metabolism and hormones, repressions and complexes, he finds no answer for his needs. . . .

Time was when the scientist, the poet, and the philosopher walked hand in hand. In the universe which the one perceived the other found himself comfortably at home. But the world of modern science is one in which the intellect alone can rejoice. . . .

Thus man seems caught in a dilemma which his intellect has devised. . . . Weak and uninstructed intelligence takes refuge in the monotonous repetition of once living creeds, or is even reduced to the desperate expedient of going to sleep amid the formulae of the flabby pseudo-religions in which the modern world is so prolific. But neither of these classes affords any aid to the robust but serious mind which is searching for some terms upon which it may live. . . .

5. *Protest and Affirmation in the Depression Years*

The crash of 1929 brought a good many expatriates home. During the twenties most of them had been anti-nationalists and thoroughly detached from the American political scene, but the near collapse of an economic system and the suffering of millions created a new concern for the society. The novels of John Dos Passos are a good illustration of the dominant trend. *Three Soldiers* (1921) was centrally concerned with a soldier-esthete in rebellion against the war, the American army, and the society which stood behind it; *Manhattan Transfer* (1925) dealt with the meaningless tangle of lives from several corners of a barren and sterile society; the trilogy *U.S.A.* (1930, 1932, 1936) portrayed people defeated by a social system, expressed sympathy with the industrial proletariat and socialism, and concluded with the bitter announcement by the disillusioned wanderer Vag, "All right we are two nations"; *The Ground We Stand On* (1941) discovered American values worth preserving and commented affirmatively on the Founding Fathers. Not many major writers of the thirties actually joined the Communist Party, but a considerable number had strong sympathies for the political left, and a few took up Marxist cudgels for the Communist Party, the Trotskyites, and other leftist groups. AUTHOR: John Dos Passos (1896–   ), moved from a mood of alienation in the twenties to savage social criticism in the thirties and to affirmation and celebration in the forties and fifties. His later work, and most particularly a series of books on Jefferson's America, were marked by a growing social and political conservatism. SELECTION: "Portrait of a Hero: Eugene Debs" from Dos Passos' *The 42nd Parallel* (1930).

PORTRAIT OF HERO, EUGENE DEBS (1930): JOHN DOS PASSOS

Debs was a railroad man, born in a weather-boarded shack
at Terre Haute.
He was one of ten children.
His father had come to America in a sailingship in '49,
an Alsatian from Colmar; not much of a moneymaker, fond
of music and reading,
he gave his children a chance to finish public school
and that was about all he could do.
At fifteen Gene Debs was already working as a machinist
on the Indianapolis and Terre Haute Railway.
He worked as locomotive fireman,
clerked in a store
joined the local of the Brotherhood of Locomotive Firemen,
was elected secretary, traveled all over the country as
organizer.

He was a tall shamblefooted man, had a sort of gusty
rhetoric that set on fire the railroad workers in their
pineboard halls
made them want the world he wanted,
a world brothers might own
where everybody would split even:
I am not a labor leader. I don't want you to follow me
or anyone else. If you are looking for a Moses to lead
you out of the capitalist wilderness you will stay right
where you are. I would not lead you into this promised
land if I could, because if I could lead you in, someone
else would lead you out.
That was how he talked to freighthandlers and gandywalkers,
to firemen and switchmen and engineers, telling them it
wasn't enough to organize the railroadmen, that all workers
must be organized, that all workers must be organized in
the workers' cooperative commonwealth.
Locomotive fireman on many a long night's run,
under the smoke a fire burned him up, burned in gusty words
that beat in pineboarded halls; he wanted his brothers to
be free men.
That was what he saw in the crowd that met him at the Old
Wells Street Depot when he came out of jail after the
Pullman strike,
those were the men that chalked up nine hundred thousand
votes for him in nineteen twelve and scared the frockcoats
and the tophats and diamonded hostesses at Saratoga Springs,
Bar Harbor, Lake Geneva with the bogy of a socialist
president.
But where were Gene Debs' brothers in nineteen eighteen
when Woodrow Wilson had him locked up in Atlanta for
speaking against war,
where were the big men fond of whisky and fond of each
other, gentle rambling tellers of stories over bars in
small towns in the Middle West,
quiet men who wanted a house with a porch to putter
around and a fat wife to cook for them, a few drinks and
cigars, a garden to dig in, cronies to chew the rag with
and wanted to work for it
and others to work for it;
where were the locomotive firemen and engineers when they
hustled him off to Atlanta Penitentiary?

And they brought him back to die in Terre Haute
to sit on his porch in a rocker with a cigar in his mouth,

beside him American Beauty roses his wife fixed in a bowl;
and the people of Terre Haute and the people of Indiana
and the people of the Middle West were fond of him and
afraid of him and thought of him as an old kindly uncle
who loved them, and wanted to be with him and to have him
give them candy,
and they were afraid of him as if he had contracted a
social disease, syphilis or leprosy, and thought it was
too bad,
but on account of the flag
and prosperity
and making the world safe for democracy,
they were afraid to be with him,
or to think much about him for fear they might believe him;
for he said:
While there is a lower class I am of it, while there is a
criminal class I am of it, while there is a soul in prison
I am not free. . . .

6. The Threat of Authoritarianism and the Experience of War

The rise of Fascism did much to crystallize a sense of commitment to American society and affirmation toward Western values. Even Ernest Hemingway and Thomas Wolfe, basically nonpolitical writers, saw a rising modern barbarism in the Spanish Civil War and in the emergence of Nazi Germany. Early warnings about the menace of Fascism were generally ignored; the dominant mood of the country tended toward neutralism, nationalism, and isolationism. After a firsthand experience with war and exposure to the postwar revelations on the death camps Americans could begin to grasp the dimensions of the Nazi terror. AUTHORS: Thomas Wolfe (1900–1938), a North Carolina novelist, visited Germany in the first glow of fame as a young novelist. His visit began with a great joy in his reception abroad; but "little by little the world came in. . . ." Randall Jarrell (1914–   ), poet, critic, and novelist, was possibly the most talented American poet to emerge from the Second World War. SELECTIONS: "Thomas Wolfe in Nazi Germany" from Wolfe's *You Can't Go Home Again* (1934). "A Bomber Pilot in World War II" from Jarrell's *Losses* (1945).

THOMAS WOLFE IN NAZI GERMANY (1934)

The weeks passed so—and then it happened. Little by little the world came in. At first it sifted in almost unnoticed, like dark down dropped in passing from some avenging angel's wing. Sometimes it came to me in the desperate pleading of an eye, the naked terror of a startled look, the swift concealment of a sudden fear. Sometimes it just came and went as light comes, just soaked in, just soaked in—in fleeting words and speech and actions.

After a while, however, in the midwatches of the night, behind thick walls and bolted doors and shuttered windows, it came to me full flood at last in confessions of unutterable despair. I don't know why it was the people so unburdened themselves to me, a stranger, unless it was because they knew the love I bore them and their land. They seemed to feel a desperate need to talk to someone who would understand. The thing was pent up in them, and my sympathy for all things German had burst the dam of their reserve and caution. Their tales of woe and fear unspeakable gushed forth and beat upon my ears. They told me stories of their friends and relatives who had said unguarded things in public and disappeared without a trace, stories of the Gestapo, stories of neighbors' quarrels and petty personal spite turned into political persecution, stories of concentration camps and pogroms, stories of rich Jews stripped and beaten and robbed of everything they had and then denied the right to earn a pauper's wage, stories of well-bred Jewesses despoiled and turned out of their homes and forced to kneel and scrub off anti-Nazi slogans scribbled on the sidewalks while young barbarians dressed like soldiers formed a ring and prodded them with bayonets and made the quiet places echo with the shameless laughter of their mockery. It was a picture of the Dark Ages come again—shocking beyond belief, but true as the hell that man forever creates for himself. . . .

Hitlerism, he saw, was a recrudescence of an old barbarism. Its racial nonsense and cruelty, is naked worship of brute force, its suppression of truth and resort to lies and myths, its ruthless contempt for the individual, its anti-intellectual and anti-moral dogma that to one man alone belongs the right of judgment and decision, and that for all others virtue lies in blind, unquestioning obedience—each of these fundamental elements of Hitlerism was a throwback to that fierce and ancient tribalism which had sent waves of hairy Teutons swooping down out of the north to destroy the vast edifice of Roman civilization. That primitive spirit of greed and lust and force had always been the true enemy of mankind.

But this spirit was not confined to Germany. It belonged to no one race. It was a terrible part of the universal heritage of man. One saw traces of it everywhere. It took on many disguises, many labels. . . . And America had it, too, in various forms. For wherever ruthless men conspired together for their own ends, wherever the rule of dog-eat-dog was dominant, there it bred. And wherever one found it, one also found that its roots sank down into something primitive in man's ugly past. And these roots would somehow have to be eradicated, George felt, if man was to win his ultimate freedom and not be plunged back into savagery and perish utterly from the earth. . . .

A BOMBER PILOT IN WORLD WAR II (1945): RANDALL JARRELL

> The ranges by the desert or the shore,
> Fired at towed targets, waited for our scores—
> And turned into replacements and woke up
> One morning, over England, operational.
> It wasn't different: but if we died
> It was not an accident but a mistake
> (But an easy one for anyone to make).
> We read our mail and counted up our missions—
> In Bombers named for girls, we burned
> The cities we had learned about in school—
> Till our lives wore out; our bodies lay among
> The people we had killed and never seen.
> When we lasted long enough they gave us medals;
> When we died they said, "Our casualties were low."
> They said, "Here are the maps"; we burned the cities.
>
> It was not dying—no, not ever dying;
> But the night I died I dreamed that I was dead,
> And the cities said to me: "Why are you dying?
> We are satisfied, if you are; but why did I die?"

7. *Another Postwar Generation*

In several respects the first post-war decade (1945–1955) seemed to be a repetition of patterns which had prevailed in the twenties. Peter Viereck's "new" conservatism obviously drew strength from Irving Babbitt's "new" humanism of earlier decades, and Senator Joseph McCarthy's "Communist hunt" reminded many observers of "the Red scare" and the Sacco-Vanzetti case which followed the First World War. The retreat into suburban "togetherness" so carefully reported by William Whyte and David Riesman bore a certain resemblance to the "normalcy" of the Harding era. However the forties and fifties contained a number of unique developments, the most important of which was the fact that America assumed global responsibilities in the conflict with Russian Communism instead of retreating into the isolationism of the twenties and thirties. The intellectuals were thoroughly committed to American society, but the Cold War affected the domestic scene and made the loyalty controversy far more bitter than its precursors of the twenties. The economic situation was much healthier in the recent past than in the twenties, but the rise of the mass media, the further growth of mass production, the problems of personal identity and social conformity suggested an age of greater psychological and social problems. The "Beatnik" outlook of Allen Ginsberg represented a different type of alienation than that experienced by the expatriate intellectuals. In general the response of intellectuals was far more complex in the recent past than in the earlier period. AUTHORS: Peter Viereck (1916–), poet, essayist, and historian, won several major prizes for his poetry and much attention for his fluent presentation of a conservative point of view. Allen Ginsberg (1926–), won fame as the "poet laureate" of the "beat" generation. William H. Whyte (1917–), has served as an editor of Fortune magazine and a contributor to leading American periodicals. C. Wright Mills (1916–1961), a Professor of Sociology at Columbia University, won a sympathetic hearing among American and European intellectuals for his books, The Power Elite, White Collar, and others. SELECTIONS: "The New Conservatism" from Viereck's The Unadjusted Man (1956). "A Beatnik Protest" from Ginsberg's Howl (1957). "Conformity and the Organization Man" from Whyte's The Organization Man (1956). "Problems of Personal Identity" from Mills' White Collar (1951).

THE NEW CONSERVATISM (1956):
PETER VIERECK ON EQUALITY

The two primary types of equality should not be confused, the first legal and objective, the second psychological and subjective. In the definable, tangible, explicit sphere of legal rights, equality is possible in a country like America and also desirable; inequality in that sphere weakens liberty by making it seem hypocritical. But in the indefinable, intangible, implicit sphere of cultural and social status, equality is impossible; it involves

too many insatiable, semiconscious cravings of pride. When these cravings are too narrowly egotistic and, so to speak, too visceral, they oscillate,
with ever more uncontrollable violence, between prestige-feelings and in-
feriority-feelings. That oscillation is dangerous to liberty because it leads
to the overadjusted leveling imposed by envious mass-mediocrity. . . .

Many eighteenth-century liberals refused to support the civil-libertarian aristocracy of England against the murderous new Jacobin egalitar-
ians. The democratic egalitarian terminology of the Jacobins, like that of
the communists in the 1930's, sometimes had a hypnotic attraction out-
weighing the despotic reality behind the terminology. Hence, Tom Paine,
founder of American progressivism, ended by offering to guide the anti-
civil-libertarian despot Napoleon against the relatively civil-libertarian
aristocracy of parliamentary England. Paine succumbed to this moral trap
because the egalitarian, plebiscitarian elements in a Napoleon (today
substitute Mao or Lenin) can often make a man of democratic credo
forgive a Napoleon his dictatorial methods. Paine's evolution was paral-
leled in our own century by that of the liberal reformer Lincoln Steffens;
he moved from a liberal egalitarian democracy to an amoral, pragmatic
pro-communism: "I have seen the future, and it works."

A liberal cliché in the 1930's was the notion that "economic democracy" was better than our political liberty because giving more "real"
equality. The equality was "real" enough: an equal opportunity for doing
slave-labor in Karaganda. . . .

In the 1920's the liberal Democrat Bryan, veteran of the old western
Populists, led his successful campaign to ban the teaching of evolution in
Tennessee; his law remains unrepealed. Here is a clear example of academic freedom being thought-controlled not by the usual reactionary
champion of privilege but by a champion of democratic equality. Those
eager to exonerate democratic egalitarianism from its threat to liberty may
retort: "Bryan's thought-control of schools in Tennessee (forbidding
them to teach evolution) is merely the embittered old age of our democratic egalitarian hero and should not be read back from the 1920's into
the saner Bryan and saner Populism of the 1890's." But already in the
1890's, the folksy religiosity of the Populists imposed a now-forgotten but
important thought-control upon western rural areas. The surface motive
was the old Bible-belt Fundamentalism. The deeper motive was the anti-
urbanism and anti-intellectualism by which rural westerners expressed
their status-insecurity in the presence of a city-slicker East. . . .

Out of the western Populist movement came such apostles of
thought-control and racist bigotry as Tom Watson, Cole Blease, Huey
Long, Father Charles Coughlin and his presidential candidate William
Lemke, and even the late Senator Pat McCarran. The demagogy of the
Populists and La Follette Progressives was partly preferable to the present
Republican nationalist demagogy because, unlike the latter, the former
occasionally really did help the underprivileged it promised to help. But

the fact that the Populists bled for widows and orphans does not exempt them from criticism for the harmful precedents they set for current thought-controllers. Let us hope one can be permitted to criticize those precedents without being accused by liberals of wanting to send widows and orphans back to sweatshops. The point is to distinguish between the valid social gains of America's various Jeffersonians, Jacksonians, and La Follettes and their invalid Rousseauist philosophy of human nature. Now that the social gains are safely rooted, is it not time to re-examine more rigorously the invalid philosophy? Cannot our aging New Deal liberals wake up to the fact that the child labor laws, the Wagner Act, and SEC have become victorious long ago and are no longer problem-number-one? The horse they ride is wood, the horse they flog is dead. Instead of trumpeting about the admitted need for those old, long-achieved battles, is it not time to ask why material social reforms have failed to do for man's spirit what they have done so ably for his body? . . .

A BEATNIK PROTEST (1957): ALLEN GINSBERG

I saw the best minds of my generation destroyed by madness, starving hysterical naked,

dragging themselves through the negro streets at dawn looking for an angry fix,

angelheaded hipsters burning for the ancient heavenly connection to the starry dynamo in the machinery of night,

who poverty and tatters and hollow-eyed and high sat up smoking in the supernatural darkness of cold-water flats floating across the tops of cities contemplating jazz,

who bared their brains to Heaven under the El and saw Mohammedan angels staggering on tenement roofs illuminated,

who passed through universities with radiant cool eyes hallucinating Arkansas and Blake-light tragedy among the scholars of war,

who were expelled from the academies for crazy and publishing obscene odes on the windows of the skull,

who cowered in unshaven rooms in underwear, burning their money in wastebaskets and listening to the terror through the wall,

who got busted in their pubic beards returning through Laredo with a belt of marijuana for New York,

who ate fire in paint hotels or drank turpentine in Paradise Alley, death, or purgatoried their torsos night after night

with dreams, with drugs, with waking nightmares, alcohol and cock and endless balls,

incomparable blind streets of shuddering cloud and lightning in the mind

leaping toward poles of Canada and Paterson, illuminating all the
motionless world of Time between,

Peyote solidities of halls, backyard green tree cemetery dawns, wind
drunkenness over the rooftops, storefront boroughs of teahead joyride
neon blinking traffic light, sun and moon and tree vibrations in the
roaring winter dusks of Brooklyn, ashcan rantings and kind king light
of mind. . . .

who vanished into nowhere Zen New Jersey leaving a trail of ambiguous
picture postcards of Atlantic City Hall,

suffering Eastern sweats and Tangerian bone-grindings and migraines of
China under junk-withdrawal in Newark's bleak furnished room,

who wandered around and around at midnight in the railroad yard won-
dering where to go, and went, leaving no broken hearts. . . .

who journeyed to Denver, who died in Denver, who came back to Denver
and waited in vain, who watched over Denver and brooded and loned
in Denver and finally went away to find out the Time, and now Denver
is lonesome for her heroes,

who fell on their knees in hopeless cathedrals praying for each other's
salvation and light and breasts, until the soul illuminated its hair for a
second. . . .

CONFORMITY AND THE ORGANIZATION MAN (1956): WILLIAM H. WHYTE

The corporation man is the most conspicuous example, but he is only
one, for the collectivization so visible in the corporation has affected
almost every field of work. Blood brother to the business trainee off to
join Du Pont is the seminary student who will end up in the church
hierarchy, the doctor headed for the corporate clinic, the physics Ph.D. in
a government laboratory, the intellectual on the foundation-sponsored
team project, the engineering graduate in the huge drafting room at
Lockheed, the young apprentice in a Wall Street law factory. . . .

Between themselves and organization they believe they see an ultimate harmony and, more than most elders recognize, they are building an
ideology that will vouchsafe this trust. . . .

The pressures of the group, the frustrations of individual creativity,
the anonymity of achievement: are these defects to struggle against—or
are they virtues in disguise? The organization man seeks a redefinition of
his place on earth—a faith that will satisfy him that what he must endure
has a deeper meaning than appears on the surface. He needs, in short,
something that will do for him what the Protestant Ethic did once. And

slowly, almost imperceptibly, a body of thought has been coalescing that does that.

I am going to call it a Social Ethic. . . . By social ethic I mean that contemporary body of thought which makes morally legitimate the pressures of society against the individual. Its major propositions are three: a belief in the group as the source of creativity; a belief in "belongingness" as the ultimate need of the individual; and a belief in the application of science to achieve the belongingness. . . .

De Tocqueville made a prophecy. If America ever destroyed its genius it would be by intensifying the social virtues at the expense of others, by making the individual come to regard himself as a hostage to prevailing opinion, by creating, in sum, a tyranny of the majority.

And this is what the organization man is doing. . . .

To preach technique before content, the skills of getting along isolated from why and to what end the getting along is for, does not produce maturity. It produces a sort of permanent prematurity, and this is true not only of the child being taught life adjustment but of the organization man being taught well-roundedness. This is a sterile concept, and those who believe that they have mastered human relations can blind themselves to the true bases of co-operation. People don't co-operate just to co-operate; they co-operate for substantive reasons, to achieve certain goals, and unless these are comprehended the little manipulations for morale, team spirit, and such are fruitless.

And they can be worse than fruitless. Held up as the end-all of organization leadership, the skills of human relations easily tempt the new administrator into the practice of a tyranny more subtle and more pervasive than that which he means to supplant. No one wants to see the old authoritarian return, but at least it could be said of him that what he wanted primarily from you was your sweat. The new man wants your soul. . . .

It is easy to fight obvious tyranny; it is not easy to fight benevolence, and few things are more calculated to rob the individual of his defenses than the idea that his interests and those of society can be wholly compatible. The good society is the one in which they are most compatible, but they never can be completely so, and one who lets The Organization be the judge ultimately sacrifices himself. . . .

The quest for normalcy, as we have seen in suburbia, is one of the great breeders of neuroses, and the Social Ethic only serves to exacerbate them. What is normalcy? We practice a great mutual deception. Everyone knows that they themselves are different—that they are shy in company, perhaps, or dislike many things most people seem to like—but they are not sure that other people are different too. Like the norms of personality testing, they see about them the sum of efforts of people like themselves to seem as normal as others and possibly a little more so. It is hard enough to learn to live with our inadequacies, and we need not make ourselves more miserable by a spurious ideal of middle-class adjustment. Adjustment to what? Nobody really knows—and the tragedy is that they don't realize that the so-confident-seeming other people don't know either. . . .

PROBLEMS OF PERSONAL IDENTITY (1951): C. WRIGHT MILLS

In the world of the small entrepreneur, men sold goods to one another; in the new society of employees, they first of all sell their services. The employer of manual services buys the workers' labor, energy, and skill; the employer of many white-collar services, especially salesmanship, also buys the employees' social personalities. Working for wages with another's industrial property involves a sacrifice of time, power, and energy to the employer; working as a salaried employee often involves in addition the sacrifice of one's self to a multitude of "consumers" or clients or managers. . . .

One knows the salesclerk not as a person but as a commercial mask, a stereotyped greeting and appreciation for patronage; one need not be kind to the modern laundryman, one need only pay him; he, in turn, needs only to be cheerful and efficient. Kindness and friendliness become aspects of personalized service or of public relations of big firms, rationalized to further the sale of something. With anonymous insincerity the Successful Person thus makes an instrument of his own appearance and personality. . . .

The smile behind the counter is a commercialized lure. Neglect of personal appearance on the part of the employee is a form of carelessness on the part of the business management. "Self-control" pays off. "Sincerity" is detrimental to one's job, until the rules of salesmanship and business become a "genuine" aspect of oneself. Tact is a series of little lies about one's feelings, until one is emptied of such feelings. "Dignity" may be used only to make a customer feel that she shouldn't ask the price too soon or fail to buy the wares. . . .

The salesgirl cannot form her character by promotional calculations and self-management, like the classic heroes of liberalism or the new entrepreneurs. The one area of her occupational life in which she might be "free to act," the area of her own personality, must now also be managed, must become the alert yet obsequious instrument by which goods are distributed.

In the normal course of her work, because her personality becomes the instrument of an alien purpose, the salesgirl becomes self-alienated. In one large department store, a planted observer said of one girl: "I have been watching her for three days now. She wears a fixed smile on her made-up face, and it never varies, no matter to whom she speaks. I never heard her laugh spontaneously or naturally. Either she is frowning or her face is devoid of any expression. When a customer approaches, she immediately assumes her hard, forced smile. . . ."

The personality market, the most decisive effect and symptom of the great salesroom, underlies the all-pervasive distrust and self-alienation so characteristic of metropolitan people. Without common values and mutual trust, the cash nexus that links one man to another in transient contact has been made subtle in a dozen ways and made to bite deeper into all areas of life and relations. People are required by the salesman ethic and convention to pretend interest in others in order to manipulate them. In the course of time, and as this ethic spreads, it is got on to. Still, it is conformed to as part of one's job and one's style of life, but now with a winking eye, for one knows that manipulation is inherent in every human contact. Men are estranged from one another as each secretly tries to make an instrument of the other, and in time a full circle is made: one makes an instrument of himself, and is estranged from It also. . . .

Chapter XVI. THE TWENTIETH CENTURY: INTERNATIONAL CONFLICTS AND INTERNAL CRISES

IN THE AGONY OF DECISION OVER GOING TO WAR, WOODROW WILSON expressed the fear that the conditions of total war in modern times might seriously damage or even destroy basic American freedoms. Wilson's fears may have been somewhat exaggerated, but they were not unrealistic: the "Creel Committee"—established by Wilson himself—deluged the United States and the world with billions of pieces of propaganda on the barbarism of "the Huns" and the wickedness of all things German, a propaganda drive which stimulated a domestic wave of private aggression in which school boards did away with German language courses, citizens' committees forced the removal of German music from symphony programs, chauvinists subjected German-American citizens to insult and intimidation, and state and municipal courts went so far as to imprison citizens for improper remarks about the flag or the draft. For the first time since the Alien and Sedition Acts of 1798 constitutional liberties were seriously abridged by such bills as the Espionage Act of 1918 (to be followed in later times of crisis by the Smith Act of 1940, the Communist Control Act of 1954, and other pieces of legislation). Victory and peace did not restore the country to temperate emotions. The Russian Revolution had taken place in 1917, several other "Red" regimes came to power briefly in Eastern and Central Europe, and the news from abroad tended to fan the coals of fear in America over Communists or anarchists, foreigners, or Catholics, and perhaps the modern world in general. Several "bomb scares" in 1919–1920 were followed by one very real bomb explosion during September, 1920 in the offices of the Morgan investment house which killed thirty persons, and talk of "Red" plots and conspiracies filled the newspapers and private conversations. Without waiting for overt actions, Wilson's Attorney-General, A. Mitchell Palmer, had set out nine months before the Morgan bombing to "save" the country from "Revolution" by making "Red raids" and arresting several thousand persons, most of whom professed neither anarchism nor Communism and had committed no crimes. The following year, two Italian anarchists, Sacco and Vanzetti, received death sentences for murder in a case which provoked the angry attacks of thousands of intellectuals, artists, and journalists who accused the court of having convicted innocent men in order to give vent to hostility toward "Reds" in particular and foreigners in general.

During this period public hostility toward the immigrant ran high and Congress in 1921 and 1924 passed restrictionist legislation which ultimately cut immigration from a million a year to a few thousand persons, favored British and North European peoples, and discriminated against South and East European peoples, Asians, and Africans. Group hatred in this era brought to life a second Ku Klux Klan of "white male persons, native-born gentile citizens" (one also had to be a Protestant), which began operations in 1920 and gained six million members by 1924. Negroes were the chief objects of hatred, but Jews, Catholics, the foreign-born in general, and "immoral" persons incurred the hatred of the Klan. If Klansmen burned crosses from New York to California and exercised much political power in the Midwest, their central bastion of strength lay in the South.

The nomination in 1928 by the Democrats of a Catholic for the Presidency, the jaunty New Yorker and progressive Governor, Alfred E. Smith, led to a new wave of hostility toward Catholics, city people, and enemies of Prohibition; but, generally speaking, group hostilities began to lessen from the middle of the decade. The "Red scares" diminished in number, the Klan began to fall apart after 1924, the repeal of the Eighteenth Amendment removed Prohibition as a divisive issue, and the political role of the urban "nationality" groups in the cities and in the nation continued to increase without arousing new upsurges of nativism. The "nationality groups" made large economic and social gains in the thirties, forties, and in the fifties, and in 1960 John F. Kennedy, a Catholic and the great-grandson of an Irish immigrant, not only won the Presidency but became one of the most popular chief executives in American history. In general, nativist sentiment declined rapidly, anti-Semitism receded perceptibly, and the relations of Protestants, Catholics, and Jews to each other were considerably improved.

Still, several basic issues relating to group conflict continued to plague the society. Despite the recommendations of Presidents Roosevelt, Truman, Eisenhower, Kennedy, and Johnson, Congress did not change the basic immigration policies established by the laws of 1921 and 1924. Moreover, professional "hate groups" displayed renewed strength in the early sixties. The most persistent and troublesome problems sprang from hostility toward the Negro. Two centuries of slavery left enduring "marks of oppression"; rigorous and persistent attempts to enforce the Fourteenth and Fifteenth Amendments would have removed many of them, but enforcement efforts virtually came to a halt in the eighteen-nineties. "Cradle to the grave" segregation ruled the Negro in the South; and the private discrimination which pervaded the North made his life burdensome there as well. The first signs of significant change came with the economic gains made during the New Deal and World War II years and with the gradual retreat by the Supreme Court from a long-standing tolerance of segregation. The new tendency in constitutional interpretation reached a point of no return with *Brown v. Board of Education* (1954) and later decisions which ruled against segregation in education and many other areas of public life. At least as important, and probably much more so, were the early Southern desegregation cases which aroused much mob violence; the Southern "sit-ins," boycotts, and freedom rides which were often brutally repressed; the urban demonstrations of the North which evoked a mixture of sympathy and hostility; and the march on Washington in 1963 which displayed great restraint and organizational strength,—all of which signalled a dramatic change in the political role of the American Negro and had much to do with the passage of the Civil Rights Act of 1964. By comparing the present with the past, it was possible to argue that much progress had been made, but the painful gap between Negro and white incomes, job prospects, educational opportunities, and death and disease rates continued to be alarmingly wide, and the majority of Negroes still lived in the rural poverty of the South or in the urban squalor of the great ghettoes in the North and the South.

Perhaps the most critical question in the Civil Rights crisis was whether or not the economy could produce enough jobs for everyone. The question went beyond Negro-white relations as the spectre of automation threatened an incredible output from the labor of a work force sharply declining in numbers, a situation which threatened to disrupt the traditional patterns of work, production, and income. The problem was merely the newest version of the old issue of jobs and production which had been central to the society since the twenties when the war boom tapered off. The nation was then even more industrial, urban, commercial, and dependent on mechanized agriculture than in the Progressive era and less psychologically prepared to cope with modern problems. The Progressives have been criticized by many scholars, but Roosevelt and Wilson did make serious attempts to cope with industrial problems and Warren Harding and Calvin Coolidge abandoned most of those efforts in the twenties.

The inability of party leaders to heal the Progressive-Regular split of 1912 coupled with events of the Wilson years and the war period left the Republican party in the twenties embracing the slogans of the McKinley years (and the postwar Democratic Party was only slightly better equipped to cope with basic economic problems). The administration of Warren G. Harding which came to power in 1920 set about to return the country to "normalcy" by staffing the modest number of regulatory agencies with executives from the industries to be regulated; by using the Attorney-General's office as a clearing house to give information on ways to shape new industrial combinations and escape the authority of the anti-trust laws; and by returning the railroads nationalized during the war to private ownership. The policies of Harding and Coolidge in lowering taxes, particularly those of the middle and upper groups, and raising tariffs encouraged the speculative boom in stocks and real estate that preceded the Crash of 1929.

The optimism of the twenties had some foundation in fact; economic growth in automobiles, chemicals, telephones, films, road construction, and other areas increased the national income by about sixty per cent between 1919 and 1929. The solid gains of the decade lent plausibility to pronouncements on the approaching end to poverty made by the Republican Presidential nominee in 1928, Herbert Hoover. Still, the economy displayed several very serious weaknesses. Working-class income increased less rapidly than middle- and upper-class income, and certainly not fast enough to insure a broad base of mass purchasing power for the increasing flow of products from the factories. Farm income, after a war boom, declined sharply, and farmers who concentrated on staples such as wheat, cotton, and corn experienced real hardship. Finally the savings of the prosperous piled up beyond opportunities for sound investment and continued to send stock market prices spiralling to higher and higher levels—until the Crash of 1929. Harding and Coolidge had not so much followed the classical capitalist role of noninterference as they had pursued a policy of aiding the business community and leaving other sectors of the economy alone. Although Hoover, in attempting to cope with the depression spent about three billions on public works, accepted special legislation to aid farmers, and used the Reconstruction Finance Corporation to lend money to railroads and financial institutions, he wished to rely more on the voluntary agreements of businessmen to sustain wages and on private charity for emergency relief. Hoover, obviously a more intelligent and enlightened man than his two predecessors, still could not escape *laissez-faire* ideology and the slogans about "balanced budgets" and "free enterprise." Compassionately but helplessly he watched the depression deepen until the jobless had grown to twelve million.

The presidential victor of 1932, the energetic and self-assured Franklin D. Roosevelt, brought to the White House an air of confidence and a determination to act. A pragmatic experimentalist rather than a doctrinaire ideologue, Roosevelt hoped to preserve the American economic system, but in any case he was determined to try device after device until he had found the means of restoring prosperity and employment. During the celebrated first "ninety days" of the new administration, F.D.R. sent to Congress a great welter of proposals which were promptly enacted. New banking, currency, and securities legislation met the immediate emergency and provided for reform and regulation; relief and public works programs created jobs for millions; and the Tennessee Valley Authority introduced an interesting social experiment in the plan to lift an entire region from hopeless poverty under the supervision of federal, state, and local authorities and citizens' groups. The National Recovery Authority and the Agricultural Adjustment Authority attempted to eliminate surpluses, raise prices, increase markets, and to stimulate cooperation in place of competition; but they met with only partial success and the Supreme Court challenged their constitutionality.

The major welfare measures establishing social security, federal housing programs for low- and middle-income groups, minimum wages and maximum hour regulations had more enduring significance as did the legislation which strengthened the labor movement and thus made possible wage and welfare gains through collective bargaining. By all these measures F.D.R. could claim major successes in meeting the immediate evils of the depression and in providing long needed welfare laws, but prosperity and full employment proved to be more elusive goals. Substantial gains in employment and business activity between 1934 and 1937 were partly destroyed by the recession of 1937, and full employment did not arrive until the war period.

In 1938 the Republicans made substantial Congressional gains, and foreign policy began to take an increasingly large portion of

F.D.R.'s time and attention. The stream of New Deal legislation slowed to a trickle. Still, those portions of the New Deal not struck down by the courts and not of an obviously temporary nature have endured in American politics. Wendell Willkie in 1940 and Thomas E. Dewey in 1944 and 1948 accepted F.D.R.'s basic accomplishments, and—despite some hostile campaign rhetoric—President Dwight D. Eisenhower allowed the most essential New Deal measures to stand between 1953 and 1961. (The charge of wishing to undo the gains of the thirties, however, was made against the Republican presidential nominee, Senator Barry Goldwater, in 1964.) The tone in the White House may have changed from the energetic but largely unsuccessful attempts of President Harry S Truman to get new social legislation (the "Fair Deal") to the decorous inactivity of Eisenhower, but Congress provided a dominant force for continuity and conservatism, and kept the country in the vicinity of dead center. F.D.R.'s welfare measures had become institutions which grew modestly now and then with an extension of social security coverage or a higher minimum wage. President John F. Kennedy, faced with a slow rate of economic growth and a substantial body of unemployed persons, tried to prod Congress into action to "get the country moving." If Kennedy enjoyed little immediate success, Congress in the wake of his assassination sent to President Johnson several major bills which promised to stimulate economic growth. Between 1932 and 1964 American productivity had grown enormously, but the periods of maximum increase came during the Second World War and the Korean War, with two major business recessions occurring during the post-war periods. The critics worried about a sluggish growth rate in the fifties and sixties (though the economy began to pick up in 1962) and about the quarter of the nation which knew poverty in the midst of general affluence. The optimists chose to stress soaring productivity and higher incomes.

Some Americans granted foreign policy primacy over domestic issues, and virtually all citizens agreed on America's permanent involvement in the major power struggles of the world. Such had not always been the case; for nearly a century, from the close of the Napoleonic Wars in 1815 to the First World War in 1914, diplomats seeking to avoid entanglement with European power politics had tried to confine America to action in the Western hemisphere and occasional forays into the Pacific. After the First World War and the U.S. rejection of the League of Nations, Harding, Coolidge, and Hoover felt that America had few basic international concerns beyond war debts and disarmament conferences; and in the critical years of the thirties America responded to the rise of Fascism in Germany, Italy, and Spain with neutrality laws so rigid that an application of these policies in 1917 might have kept the United States out of war. Franklin Roosevelt was sympathetic to the Western Alliance and many Americans expressed concern over the Nazi oppression and the fall of France in 1940, but not until the Japanese attack on Hawaii in December, 1941 did the nation go to war.

Even before the war began, President Roosevelt and Prime Minister Winston Churchill forged a close Anglo-American entente, and after 1941 both nations worked to establish patterns of cooperation with Russia against the common German enemy. In 1943 Roosevelt and Churchill met with Joseph Stalin at Teheran to discuss war operations. Deep-seated suspicions on both the Russian and the Western side created difficulties for the Alliance, and in the next major conference of February, 1945 at Yalta essential arrangements for war and peace were worked out only with great effort. If agreement on the closing operations of the war, the occupation zones in Germany, and the United Nations required much negotiation, other issues seemed even more difficult to resolve. American intelligence had informed the President that storming the home islands of Japan might take as many as a million casualties, and Roosevelt faced a difficult task in persuading the stubborn Stalin to join the war. In this endeavor he succeeded, but he and Churchill had to accept Russian claims to Outer Mongolia as well as the return of various Far Eastern territories and concessions lost by Russia to Japan after the defeat of 1905. The disposition of Eastern Europe raised even knottier problems. At the time Soviet troops held most of Eastern Europe, Stalin wished to establish Communist regimes from Poland to Yugoslavia, and the best that Roosevelt and Churchill could get from the Russians were promises of coalition governments and free elections.

With the collapse of the Nazi regime and the Japanese surrender, Allied cooperation became increasingly difficult. The United Nations did go into effective operation; treaties were signed with the Eastern European countries and Italy; and the Nuremberg trials of Nazi leaders did probe the execution of more than six million persons in the death camps; but disputes broke out over Greece, Germany, Poland, and Japan almost from the end of the war. In general each power dominated the territory she occupied. The United States managed the occupation of Japan as she pleased, and Russia pursued her own interests in Eastern Europe with arbitrary dispatch. By 1948 both major powers had begun to establish regimes to their respective liking in Eastern and Western Germany, and in 1948 the Russians took a dangerous step by blockading the Western sectors of Berlin, which promptly evoked a counteraction, the Berlin airlift, and the "Cold War" ("neither peace nor war") was launched. Between 1945 and 1948 "coalition" governments gave way to monolithic Communist regimes in all of Eastern Europe. In Czechoslovakia Russian interests triumphed when the Communist Party of that country staged a successful coup d'etat, and the West drew strength from the victory of the Anglo-American sponsored Greek Royalist government over the Communists after nearly three years of bitter civil war. In Asia the Communist conquest of China (1949) was undoubtedly a great victory for the Communist world movement, but beyond China and several small bordering states no other Communist Party succeeded in seizing power. President Truman adopted the strategy of containment, and transformed the Marshall Plan for economic reconstruction into military alliances to "contain" Russian expansion in key areas (Western Europe, Greece, Turkey, etc.). Stalin, for his part, followed a strategy of probing for weak points while avoiding actual war with the only nuclear power in the world. In 1946 Russian troops penetrated Iran, but ultimately withdrew in the face of strong and persistent diplomatic pressure; and the Berlin blockade seems to have been an "experiment," abandoned after nearly a year when no further advantage could be gained.

Possibly the Korean War of 1950 originated as the most daring of these "experimental probes." The remote country of Korea, divided after Japanese surrender in 1945 into a Russian zone in the North and an American zone in the South, experienced several years of military occupation before both nations withdrew their troops. The North Korean invasion of the South took the world by surprise (the United States had not even included South Korea in her defense plans as a "threatened" nation or an essential area). Fortunately the Americans caught the Russians temporarily boycotting the United Nations Security Council, and consequently succeeded in gaining U.N. sponsorship for the defense of South Korea. After the early defeats, the U.N. troops under General Douglas MacArthur, pushed North Koreans back into enemy territory toward the Chinese border. The Chinese entry into the War thrust the U.N. troops to the center of the peninsula, and a military stalemate gradually developed. General Dwight Eisenhower in his Presidential campaign of 1952 promised to do all in his power to "bring the boys back home from Korea" and advocated a strategy of liberation for eastern Europe. The military stalemate and the death of Stalin made possible an armistice in Korea, but the American failure to intervene even when the Russians suppressed the Hungarian Revolution of 1956 revealed the emptiness of the campaign rhetoric about "liberation."

American and Russian leaders grew increasingly conscious of the fact that general war could no longer be regarded as an instrument of national policy. In 1949 the Russians broke the American monopoly on nuclear arms and by the mid-fifties both nations had the nuclear capacity to annihilate any enemy population. The two great powers confronted each other in an atomic "balance of terror." It is likely that the Russians were able to intervene in Hungary during 1956 only because of Western embarrassment over the Anglo-French expedition sent to the Middle East to prevent the Egyptian nationalization of the Suez Canal. The limits of Russian power could be seen in the "missile confrontation" of 1962 when President John F. Kennedy forced the Russians to remove offensive missiles from Cuba. Gradually the Russians adjusted to new world conditions, and the death of Stalin followed the development of the nuclear stalemate made possible the rise of a new regime in Russia under Nikita Khrushchev which promised a policy of "peaceful co-existence," a challenge to the Western world to compete for supremacy by all means except war itself.

Russia and the United States had stood before all nations in 1945 as monolithic "super-powers," but with the passage of time a growing number of nations refused to commit themselves to either camp. The Second World War had blasted colonial power, and one new nation after another emerged in the Afro-Asian world with a neutral foreign policy. Neutralism, the nuclear stalemate, and the decline of Russian power within and beyond the Communist world reminded the Russians of the limits to their power in several ways. Communist political growth in the West virtually ceased and the Russians made only limited gains in the Afro-Asian world; Communist China persisted in "Stalinist error," rejected "peaceful co-existence," and openly defied Russia; Yugoslavia continued the independent policies which she had pursued even during the Stalin era. Albania and several other small national Communist parties followed the Chinese, and the Polish, Rumanian, and Italian Communist parties made unwelcome demands. The United States also experienced the frustrations of a "super-power" unable to deploy its power freely. President Truman saw the limits of nuclear power in the Korean crisis, and Cuban policies frustrated three Presidents. Russian industrial advances, the space advances which followed Sputnik, and the baffling war in South Vietnam created a clamor for "victories," but the nuclear stalemate allowed few clear-cut victories.

Both powers followed a policy of alternating power thrusts with probes for diplomatic agreement. In 1955 the Russians signed the Austrian peace treaty and the Geneva agreement on French Indo-China, then later created a crisis in Berlin. A Khrushchev tour of the United States, climaxed by a visit with President Eisenhower at Camp David in 1959, was followed by the angry denunciation of Eisenhower after the Russians downed a "U-2" spy plane on Russian soil. American diplomacy suggested a related approach when the United States explored the possibility of diplomatic agreement in 1962 (as in 1955 and 1959) while continuing to press the war in South Vietnam and to apply pressure on Cuba. In 1964 and 1965 President Lyndon B. Johnson continued to use the Kennedy approach in dealing with the new Soviet leaders who had risen to power after the downfall of Khrushchev.

1. Civil Liberties and National Crises

Lincoln's suppression of the writ of habeas corpus during the Civil War can be taken as a forecast on the future fate of civil liberties in time of war or national crisis. In modern times the approach of international conflict has invariably cast a portion of the Bill of Rights into limbo. The restrictive laws and orders of the First and Second Wars illustrate a trend which continued during the Cold War with the loyalty orders of Presidents Truman and Eisenhower and with bills such as the Communist Control Act of 1954. The Espionage Act of 1918, in effect, made anti-nationalist remarks about the government, or the flag or the Army uniform criminal; the Smith Act of 1940 accepted the once rejected notion of "guilt by association," and used the old common law concept of conspiracy to make it a crime to "conspire" or to "conspire to *advocate*" the violent overthrow of the government; and the Japanese Relocation order of 1942 violated the basic constitutional rights of many citizens of Japanese origin by taking them from private homes on the West Coast and placing them in interior "relocation camps." Each measure was taken with the plea that an internal or external enemy offered a threat so grave as to require the repression of speech or the restriction of actions. Justice Oliver Wendell Holmes agreed that "no one has the right to shout fire in a crowded theater," but he insisted that speech should be repressed only when its utterance expressed a "clear and present danger." The Supreme Court moved away from this principle in the early fifties and toward a doctrine which made the "gravity of the evil" the test of restriction; i.e., the Communist Party of the United States offered no immediate danger to the national government but the "gravity" of the "evil" in their goals justified its restriction. (A decade later the Supreme Court seemed to be in the process of taking a new position.)

The first three documents in this section provide instances of suppression which seems vastly disproportionate to any probable danger. The last three documents represent defensive positions taken by civil libertarians against both public and private attacks on free speech. Aside from the standard actions of legislatures and courts,—the silenced speaker, the banned book, overt and indirect economic and political pressure, and the vigilante patrols of unorthodox political action have been the usual instruments of repression. AUTHORS: Charles A. Beard (1874–1948) was probably the most influential historian of his generation. Books such as *An Economic Interpretation of the Constitution* and *Economic Origins of Jeffersonian Democracy* had a pervasive influence on the discipline of history. Alfred E. Smith (1873–1944), born in an East Side New York slum, became a New York legislator and governor as well as the Democratic candidate for the presidency in 1928. Oliver Wendell Holmes (1841–1935) served as one of the most eloquent voices of the Supreme Court for thirty years. Louis Brandeis (1856–1941) was Wilson's most important appointment to the Supreme Court. SELECTIONS: Espionage Act of 1918, 40, *U.S. Statutes* 217, 219, 230–231. Alien Registration Act of 1940, 54, *U. S. Statutes*, 670. Japanese Relocation Order from Franklin D. Roosevelt's Executive Order of February 19, 1942. "Charles Beard Resigns from the Columbia Faculty" from a statement in *The New Republic*, Dec. 29, 1917. "Against Loyalty Tests for Teachers" from a Smith statement of 1920 printed in *Up to Now* (1929). "Free Competition in Ideas" from *Gitlow v. New York* (1925). "Free Speech Limited Only by Clear and Imminent Danger" from *Whitney v. California* (1927).

ESPIONAGE ACT (1918)

Be it enacted, That section three of the Act . . . approved June 15, 1917, be amended so as to read as follows:

"Sec. 3. Whoever, when the United States is at war, shall wilfully make or convey false reports or false statements with intent to interfere with the operation or success of the military or naval forces of the United States, or to promote the success of its enemies, or shall wilfully make or convey false reports, or false statements, or say or do anything except by way of bona fide and not disloyal advice to an investor . . . with intent to obstruct the sale by the United States of bonds . . . or the making of loans by or to the United States, or whoever, when the United States is at war, shall wilfully cause . . . or induce . . . insubordination, disloyalty, mutiny, or refusal of duty, in the military or naval forces of the United States, or shall wilfully obstruct . . . the recruiting or enlistment service of the United States, and whoever, when the United States is at war, shall wilfully utter, print, write, or publish any disloyal, profane, scurrilous, or abusive language about the form of government of the United States, or the Constitution of the United States, or the military or naval forces of the United States, or the flag . . . or the uniform of the Army or Navy of the United States, or any language intended to bring the form of government . . . or the Constitution . . . or the military or naval forces . . . or the flag . . . of the United States into contempt, scorn, contumely, or disrepute . . . or shall wilfully display the flag of any foreign enemy, or shall wilfully . . . urge, incite, or advocate any curtailment of production in this country of any thing or things . . . necessary or essential to the prosecution of the war . . . and whoever shall wilfully advocate, teach, defend, or suggest the doing of any of the acts or things in this section enumerated and whoever shall by word or act support or favor the cause of any country with which the United States is at war or by word or act oppose the cause of the United States therein, shall be punished by a fine of not more $10,000 or imprisonment for not more than twenty years, or both. . . .

ALIEN REGISTRATION ACT (1940)

An act to prohibit certain subversive activities; to amend certain provisions of law with respect to the admission and deportation of aliens; to require the fingerprinting and registration of aliens; and for other purposes.

TITLE I

Section 1. (a) It shall be unlawful for any person, with intent to interfere with, impair, or influence the loyalty, morale, or discipline of the military or naval forces of the United States—

(1) to advise, counsel, urge or in any manner cause insubordination,

disloyalty, mutiny, or refusal of duty by any member of the military or naval forces of the United States; or

(2) to distribute any written or printed matter which advises, counsels, or urges insubordination, disloyalty, mutiny, or refusal of duty by any member of the military or naval forces of the United States.

Sec. 2. (a) It shall be unlawful for any person—

(1) to knowingly or willfully advocate, abet, advise, or teach the duty, necessity, desirability, or propriety of overthrowing or destroying any government in the United States by force or violence, or by the assassination of any officer of any such government;

(2) with the intent to cause the overthrow or destruction of any government in the United States, to print, publish, edit, issue, circulate, sell, distribute, or publicly display any written or printed matter advocating, advising, or teaching the duty, necessity, desirability, or propriety of overthrowing or destroying any government in the United States by force or violence;

(3) to organize help to organize any society, group, or assembly of persons who teach, advocate, or encourage the overthrow or destruction of any government in the United States by force or violence; or to be or become a member of, or affiliate with, any such society, group, or assembly of persons, knowing the purposes thereof. . . .

JAPANESE RELOCATION ORDER (1942): FRANKLIN D. ROOSEVELT

EXECUTIVE ORDER, AUTHORIZING THE SECRETARY OF WAR TO PRE-SCRIBE MILITARY AREAS.

Whereas the successful prosecution of the war requires every possible protection against espionage and against sabotage to national-defense materials, national-defense premises, and national-defense utilities. . . .

Now, therefore, by virtue of the authority vested in me as President of the United States, and Commander in Chief of the Army and Navy, I hereby authorize and direct the Secretary of War, and the Military Commanders whom he may from time to time designate, whenever he or any designated Commander deems such action necessary, or desirable, to prescribe military areas in such places and of such extent as he or the appropriate Military Commander may determine, from which any or all persons may be excluded, and with respect to which, the right of any person to enter, remain in, or leave shall be subject to whatever restrictions the Secretary of War or the appropriate Military Commander may impose in his discretion. The Secretary of War is hereby authorized to provide for residents of any such area who are excluded therefrom, such transportation, food, shelter, and other accommodations as may be necessary, in the judgment of the Secretary of War or the said Military Commander, and until other arrangements are made, to accomplish the purpose of this order. The designation of military areas in any region or locality shall supersede designations of prohibited and restricted areas by the Attorney General under the Proclamations of December 7 and 8, 1941, and shall supersede the responsibility and authority of the Attorney General under the said Proclamations in respect of such prohibited and restricted areas.

I hereby further authorize and direct the Secretary of War and the said Military Commanders to take such other steps as he or the appropriate Military Commander may deem advisable to enforce compliance with the restrictions applicable to each Military area. . . .

I hereby further authorize and direct all Executive Departments, independent establishments and other Federal Agencies, to assist the Secretary of War or the said Military Commanders in carrying out this Executive Order, including the furnishing of medical aid, hospitalization, food, clothing, transportation, use of land, shelter, and other supplies, equipment, utilities, facilities, and services. . . .

CHARLES BEARD RESIGNS FROM THE COLUMBIA FACULTY (1917)

Early in October, 1917, I was positively and clearly informed by two responsible officers of the University that another doctrinal inquisition was definitely scheduled for an early date. It was the evident purpose of a small group of the trustees (unhindered, if not aided, by Mr. [Nicholas Murray] Butler) to take advantage of the state of war to drive out or humiliate or terrorize every man who held progressive, liberal, or unconventional views on political matters in no way connected with the war. The institution was to be reduced below the level of a department store or factory and I therefore tendered my resignation.

I make no claims in behalf of academic freedom, though I think they are worthy of consideration. I have merely held that teachers should not be expelled without a full and fair hearing by their peers, surrounded by all of the safeguards of judicial process. Professors in Columbia University have been subjected to humiliating doctrinal inquisitions by the trustees, they have been expelled without notice or hearing, and their appointment and promotion depend upon securing, in advance, the favor of certain trustees. Without that favor scholarship and learning avail nothing. . . .

AGAINST LOYALTY TESTS FOR TEACHERS (1920): ALFRED E. SMITH

This bill [in the N.Y. state legislature] must be judged by what can be done under its provisions. It permits one man to place upon any teacher the stigma of disloyalty, and this even without hearing or trial. No man is so omniscient or wise as to have entrusted to him such arbitrary and complete power not only to condemn any individual teacher but to decree what belief or opinion is opposed to what he deems to be the institutions of the country.

The bill unjustly discriminates against teachers as a class. It deprives teachers of their right to freedom of thought, it limits the teaching staff of the public schools to those only who lack the courage or the mind to exercise their legal right to just criticism of existing institutions. The bill confers upon the Commissioner of Education a power of interference with freedom of opinion which strikes at the foundations of democratic education.

FREE COMPETITION IN IDEAS (1925): OLIVER WENDELL HOLMES

Mr. Justice Brandeis and I are of opinion that this judgment should be reversed. The general principle of free speech, it seems to me, must be taken to be included in the Fourteenth Amendment, in view of the scope that has been given to the word "liberty" as there used, although perhaps it may be accepted with a somewhat larger latitude of interpretation than is allowed to Congress by the sweeping language that governs, or ought to govern, the laws of the United States. . . . If what I think the correct test is applied, it is manifest that there was no present danger of an attempt to overthrow the government by force on the part of the admittedly small minority who shared the defendant's views. It is said that this Manifesto was more than a theory, that it was an incitement. Every idea is an incitement. It offers itself for belief, and, if believed, it is acted on unless some other belief outweighs it, or some failure of energy stifles the movement at its birth. The only difference between the expression of an opinion and an incitement in the narrower sense is the speaker's enthusiasm for the result. Eloquence may set fire to reason. But whatever may be thought of the redundant discourse before us, it had no chance of starting a present conflagration. If, in the long run, the beliefs expressed in proletarian dictatorship are destined to be accepted by the dominant forces of the community, the only meaning of free speech is that they should be given their chance and have their way.

FREE SPEECH LIMITED ONLY BY CLEAR AND IM-MINENT DANGER (1927): LOUIS BRANDEIS

The right of free speech, the right to teach and the right of assembly are, of course, fundmental rights . . . These may not be denied or abridged. But, although the rights of free speech and assembly are fundamental, they are not in their nature absolute. Their exercise is subject to restriction, if the particular restriction proposed is required in order to protect the State from destruction or from serious injury, political, economic, or moral. That the necessity which is essential to a valid restriction does not exist unless speech would produce, or is intended to produce, a clear and imminent danger of some substantive evil which the State constitutionally may seek to prevent has been settled. . . . They [the Founding Fathers] recognized the risks to which all human institutions are subject. But they knew that order cannot be secured merely through fear of punishment for its infractions; that it is hazardous to discourage thought, hope and imagination; that fear breeds repression; that repression breeds hate; that hate menaces stable government; that the path of safety lies in the opportunity to discuss freely supposed grievances and proposed remedies; and that the fitting remedy for evil counsels is good ones. . . . Those who won our independence believed that the final end of the state was to make men free to develop their faculties. . . . They believed that freedom to think as you will and to speak as you think are means indispensable to the discovery and spread of political truth. . . .

Fear of serious injury cannot alone justify suppression of free speech and assembly. Men feared witches and burnt women. It is the function of speech to free men form the bondage of irrational fears. To justify suppression of free speech there must be reasonable ground to fear that serious evil will result if free speech is practiced. There must be a reasonable ground to believe that the danger apprehended is imminent. There must be reasonable ground to believe that the evil to be prevented is a serious one. . . .

2. The Depression and the New Deal

Walter Lippmann described Franklin D. Roosevelt in 1932 as an affable fellow who, without any special qualifications, wished to be President of the United States. Politicians and writers sympathetic to Herbert Hoover have argued that Hoover was a "man of principle" and Roosevelt an "opportunist." In fact, Roosevelt shied away from ideology, had no precisely formulated set of plans during the summer and fall of 1932, and he did promise to cut the budget and reduce the Federal payroll in full sincerity. Lippmann, Hoover, and a good many others failed to appreciate that Roosevelt's determination to act and his willingness to abandon plans when they lost their utility were his chief assets. Hoover had principles (and certainly was not the cold-hearted villain of Democratic campaign propaganda), and those principles would have done a prosperous economy no great harm. As it was, he yielded enough to take several major steps toward using the Federal government as an instrument of national economic policy, but he could not really bring himself to compromise his ideology by making major adjustments in the classic doctrines of nineteenth-century laissez-faire capitalism. A history of Roosevelt's administrations on the other hand is an account of bold and confident experimentation. When the experiments turned out badly, Roosevelt was prepared to take another tack. F.D.R.'s respect for his Progressive predecessors, his notion that all citizens had basic economic rights and that the President bore a continuing responsibility for the protection of those rights as well as for the economy which sustained them,—all of these attitudes gave substance and continuity to the New Deal. Time, the hostility of the Supreme Court, the distractions of foreign policy, and the Congressional coalition of Southern Democrats and Republicans which developed after 1938, kept F.D.R. from adopting many policies which he considered. His successor, Harry S. Truman, after a hesitant start proposed in the "Fair Deal" a battery of legislative proposals to extend the policies of F.D.R. Most of Truman's measures failed in Congress; Dwight Eisenhower had no desire as President to walk in the path of Roosevelt and Truman; and John F. Kennedy experienced the same difficulties as Truman with Congress. Still the Full Employment Act of 1946 established continuing Federal responsibility for the economy; and bit by bit, even under Eisenhower, the welfare measures initiated by Roosevelt were slowly extended. After the election of Johnson, the legislative pace quickened briskly. AUTHORS: Herbert C. Hoover (1874–1964) became a wealthy mining engineer. From Food Administrator in

World War I, Hoover rose through a cabinet post to the Presidency in 1929. Franklin D. Roosevelt (1882–1945), a patrician New Yorker and Harvard graduate, served as a New York legislator, Assistant Secretary of the U.S. Navy, and New York Governor, before his Presidential victory of 1932. SELECTIONS: "A Spirit of Mutual Self-Help" (1931), and "The Spread of Government Destroys Initiative" (1931) from William Myers *The State Papers . . . of Herbert Hoover* I, 503; II, 13–15. "An Economic Declaration of Rights" from Roosevelt's Acceptance Speech of 1932, *The Public Papers . . . of . . . Roosevelt*, I, 750–754.

A SPIRIT OF MUTUAL SELF-HELP
(1931): HERBERT HOOVER

This broadcast tonight marks the beginning of the mobilization of the Nation for a great undertaking to provide security for those of our citizens and their families who, through no fault of their own, face unemployment and privation during the coming winter. Its success depends upon the sympathetic and generous action of every man and woman in our country. No one with a spark of human sympathy can contemplate unmoved the possibilities of suffering that can crush many of our unfortunate fellow Americans if we fail. . . .

Over a thousand towns and cities have well-organized and experienced unemployment relief committees, community chests, or other agencies for the efficient administration of this relief. With this occasion begins the nation-wide movement to aid each of these volunteer organizations in securing the funds to meet their task over the forthcoming winter. . . .

Our states, counties, and municipalities, through the expansion of their public works and through tax-supported relief activities, are doing their part. Yet, beyond all this, there is a margin of relief which must be provided by voluntary action. Through these agencies Americans must meet the demands of national conscience that there be no hunger or cold amongst our people. . . .

This task is not beyond the ability of these thousands of community organizations to solve. . . . To solve this problem in this way accords with the fundamental sense of responsibility, neighbor to neighbor, community to community, upon which our Nation is founded. . . . The maintenance of a spirit of mutual self-help through voluntary giving, through the responsibility of local government, is of infinite importance to the future of America. . . . The success and the character of nations are to be judged by the ideals and the spirit of its people. Time and again the American people have demonstrated a spiritual quality, a capacity for

unity of action, of generosity. . . . Our country and the world are today
involved in more than a financial crisis. . . . This civilization . . .
which we call American life, is builded and can alone survive upon the
translation into individual action of that fundamental philosophy announced by the Savior nineteen centuries ago. . . .

No governmental action, no economic doctrine, no economic plan or
project can replace that God-imposed responsibility of the individual man
and woman to their neighbors. That is a vital part of the very soul of the
people. If we shall gain in this spirit from this painful time, we shall have
created a greater and more glorious America.

THE SPREAD OF GOVERNMENT DESTROYS INITIATIVE (1931): HERBERT HOOVER

The whole of our governmental machinery was devised for the purpose
that through ordered liberty we give incentive and equality of opportunity
to every individual to rise to that highest achievement of which he is
capable. At once when government is centralized there arises a limitation
upon the liberty of the individual and a restriction of individual opportunity. The true growth of the Nation is the growth of character in its
citizens. The spread of government destroys initiative and thus destroys
character. Character is made in the community as well as in the individual by assuming responsibilities, not by escape from them. Carried to its
logical extreme, all this shouldering of individual and community responsibility upon the Government can lead but to the superstate where
every man becomes the servant of the State and real liberty is lost. . . .

AN ECONOMIC DECLARATION OF RIGHTS (1932): FRANKLIN DELANO ROOSEVELT

A glance at the situation today only too clearly indicates that equality of
opportunity as we have known it no longer exists. Our industrial plant is
built; the problem just now is whether under existing conditions it is not
overbuilt. Our last frontier has long since been reached, and there is
practically no more free land. More than half of our people do not live on
the farms or on lands and cannot derive a living by cultivating their own
property. There is no safety valve in the form of a Western prairie to
which those thrown out of work by the Eastern economic machines can
go for a new start. We are not able to invite the immigration from

Europe to share our endless plenty. We are now providing a drab living for our own people. . . .

Just as freedom to farm has ceased, so also the opportunity in business has narrowed. It still is true that men can start small enterprises, trusting to native shrewdness and ability to keep abreast of competitors; but area after area has been preempted altogether by the great corporations, and even in the fields which still have no great concerns, the small man starts under a handicap. The unfeeling statistics of the past three decades show that the independent business man is running a losing race. Perhaps he is forced to the wall; perhaps he cannot command credit; perhaps he is "squeezed out," in (Woodrow) Wilson's words, by highly organized corporate competitors, as your corner grocery man can tell you. Recently a careful study was made of the concentration of business in the United States. It showed that our economic life was dominated by some six hundred odd corporations who controlled two-thirds of American industry. Ten million small business men divided the other third. More striking still, it appeared that if the process of concentration goes on at the same rate, at the end of another century we shall have all American industry controlled by a dozen corporations, and run by perhaps a hundred men. But plainly, we are steering a steady course toward economic oligarchy, if we are not there already.

Clearly, all this calls for a re-appraisal of values. A mere builder of more industrial plants, a creator of more railroad systems, an organizer of more corporations, is as likely to be a danger as a help. The day of the great promoter or the financial Titan, to whom we granted anything if only he would build, or develop, is over. Our task now is not discovery or exploitation of natural resources, or necessarily producing more goods. It is the soberer, less dramatic business of administering resources and plants already in hand, of seeking to reestablish foreign markets for our surplus production, of meeting the problem of underconsumption, of adjusting production to consumption, of distributing wealth and products more equitably, of adapting existing economic organizations to the service of the people. The day of enlightened administration has come. . . .

As I see it, the task of Government in its relation to business is to assist the development of an economic declaration of rights, an economic constitutional order. This is the common task of statesman and business man. It is the minimum requirement of a more permanently safe order of things.

Happily, the times indicate that to create such an order not only is the proper policy of Government, but it is the only line of safety for our economic structures as well. . . .

Every man has a right to life; and this means that he has also a right to make a comfortable living. He may by sloth or crime decline to exercise that right; but it may not be denied him. We have no actual famine or dearth; our industrial and agricultural mechanism can produce enough and to spare. Our Government, formal and informal, political and economic, owes to everyone an avenue to possess himself of a portion of that plenty sufficient for his needs, through his own work. . . .

3. Communists and Fascists

Fascism of the kind represented by Lawrence Dennis never came close to constituting a serious threat to the Republic, but potential social materials for a Fascist movement can be seen in the group hatreds which have afflicted American society,—militant extremism in nativist movements, Negrophobia, and the anti-democratic authoritarianism of groups such as the Ku Klux Klan in the twenties or the John Birch Society in the sixties. The fates of Communist and Fascist factions have been intertwined in America; Communism in the thirties fed on the fear of rising Fascist power in Europe, and groups such as the Birch Society depended at least partly on anxieties aroused by the increase of Sino-Soviet power. Communists and Socialists won a million votes in 1932 because many citizens believed that American capitalism had collapsed, but New Deal reforms destroyed most of the left-wing vote. The ruthlessness of Stalin, the cynical division of Poland by Hitler and Stalin in 1939, and the coming of the Cold War reduced the Communist Party in the United States to inconsequential numbers in the fifties (less than 20,000). AUTHORS: Earl Browder (1891—) led the American Communist Party for many years until 1945. Lawrence Dennis (1893—) was a diplomat and a banker until 1930 when he turned to politics as an editor and writer. SELECTIONS: "A Communist Manifesto" from Browder's *Communism in the United States* (1935). "A Case for Fascism" from Dennis' *The Coming American Fascism* (1936).

A COMMUNIST MANIFESTO
(1935): EARL BROWDER

Only the Communist Party has consistently organized and led the resistance to the capitalist attacks. . . .

The Communist Party declares that wages must be maintained no matter what is the consequence to capitalist profits.

The Communist Party declares that unemployment insurance must be provided at the expense of capitalist profits.

The Communist Party declares that the masses of workers and farmers must not only fight against reduction in their living standards, but must win constantly increasing living standards at the expense of capitalist profits.

The Communist Party declares, if the continuation of capitalism requires that profits be protected at the price of starvation, fascism and war for the masses of the people, then the quicker capitalism is destroyed, the better. . . .

Only those can courageously lead and stubbornly organize the fight for the immediate interests of the toiling masses, who know that these things must be won even though it means the destruction of capitalist profits, and who draw the necessary conclusion that the workers and farmers must consciously prepare to overthrow capitalism.

The crisis cannot be solved for the toiling masses until the rule of Wall Street has been broken and the rule of the working class has been established. The only way out of the crisis for the toiling masses is the revolutionary way out—the abolition of capitalist rule and capitalism, the establishment of the socialist society through the power of a revolutionary workers' government, a Soviet government. . . .

This tremendous wealth, these gigantic productive forces are locked away from the masses who could use them. They are the private property of the small parasitic capitalist class, which locks up the warehouses and closes the factories in order to compel a growing tribute of profit. . . . There is no possible way out of the crisis in the interest of the masses except by breaking the control of the state power now in the hands of this small monopolist capitalist class. There is no way out except by establishing a new government of the workers in alliance with the poor farmers, the Negro people, and the impoverished middle class.

There is no way out except by the creation of a revolutionary democracy of the toilers, which is at the same time a stern dictatorship against the capitalists and their agents. There is no way out except by seizing from the capitalists the industries, the banks and all of the economic institutions, and transforming them into the common property of all under the direction of the revolutionary government. There is no way out, in short, except by the abolition of the capitalist system and the establishment of a socialist society. . . .

A CASE FOR FASCISM (1936): LAWRENCE DENNIS

The time has come when the limitations imposed by liberal theory on the sovereignty of the national State in respect of property rights, wealth, and economic activities generally, are no longer to be considered by a hard-thinking man of propety as calculated to protect his interests in the long run. The day has come when property must no longer assert any immunity from government taking and government commanding which a poor man cannot assert for his life or labor in war time when drafted for national defense. Fascism insists that property or capital and private economic enterprise must be called to the colors as well as conscripts in time of war. And fascism insists that the term of service for both capital and labor is not for an emergency but a new and permanent scheme of social organization and operation. Fascism insists that the new social adventure cannot be conducted on the good liberal principle of having the State always buy the co-operation of the owners and managers of property, as well as of the workers, by paying the price which any economic factor is able to hold out for, in a bargain in which there is great inequality of bargaining power as between different individuals and groups. . . .

The majority is purely a thing of assumption or definition on the occasion of some event, like an election, a Saar plebiscite, referendum vote on prohibition, or popular acclaim of a declaration of war. Minorities, on the other hand, are not just things of definition. They are active factors which, twenty-four hours of each day, are on the job of getting what they want. With minorities you can do things with majorities. Without minority initiatives you cannot get a majority act or expression. The minority is as real as an army in the field. The majority is real only as a definition of those who do some specific act, usually under minority pressure and direction. Fortunately for the advancement of the fascist case for responsible rule by the elite according to some idealized scheme of national interest, less argument is required in 1935 than would have been necessary in 1914. . . .

4. *The Cold War and the Loyalty Controversy*

In the postwar years the Communist Party in the United States was numerically insignificant, but the development of the Cold War almost inevitably led to American anti-Communist drives. Cold War conflicts, the death of the political left after the failure and subsequent collapse of Henry Wallace's Progressive Party in 1948, and the general drift of the country toward the right, all intensified American anti-Communism. The C.I.O. expelled the sprinkling of Communist leaders from their organization and the several unions in which Communist Party members had controlling power; liberals organized Americans for Democratic Action to combat Communists; and the federal government began to prosecute

Communists under the Smith Act of 1940. President Truman began in 1949 a "Loyalty Program" which was extended by Eisenhower until 6.6 million employees had been given "full field" security checks by the F.B.I. (No cases of espionage were detected and grounds for dismissal could be found for only 490 persons.) By 1950 it seemed extremely improbable that Communists held influential positions in any major field of American life, and the Communist Party, never large or powerful, had become a proscribed and dwindling band of isolated zealots. Yet 1950 was the year when anti-Communism began to assume the proportions of a mass movement. The Korean War, the sensational Alger Hiss spy case, and Senator Joseph McCarthy's elusive 205 or 81 or 57 "Communists in the State Department" got the newer anti-Communism off to a running start. State legislators, the film world, businesses, and many private agencies such as veterans groups and commercial associations soon joined in the search for Communists, and added their opposition to "Socialists," "fellow travellers," "pinks," "parlor pinks," "Communist dupes," and "anti-anti-Communists." The movement reached its peak with Senator McCarthy's investigation of Communist infiltration in that most improbable of all places—the U.S. Army. McCarthy over-reached himself and was censured by the U.S. Senate. The fall of McCarthy and the end of the Korean War helped to restore a more temperate climate of opinion, but professional anti-Communism gained new impetus in the late fifties with the rise of new groups on the radical right such as the John Birch Society. Leaders of the radical right went beyond "mere anti-Communism": some signed manifestoes demanding the impeachment of Chief Justice Earl Warren or the exposure of other famous "fellow travelers" and "willing Communist dupes" such as Roosevelt, Eisenhower, and Kennedy; others denounced the "Red fluoridation plot" or went into training for guerilla warfare. (The Communists, they said, had already seized control of the U.S. Government.) AUTHORS: J. Edgar Hoover (1895–   ) entered the Justice Department as a young lawyer in 1917 and became the Director of the F.B.I. in 1924. Henry S. Commager (1902–   ), scholar and editor, has been a history professor in recent years at Columbia and Amherst. SELECTIONS: "Menace of Communists and Fellow Travellers" from Hoover's testimony to the House Un-American Activities Committee on March 26, 1947. "Who is Loyal to America?" from a Commager essay of 1947 in *Living Ideas in America* (1951).

MENACE OF COMMUNISTS AND FELLOW TRAVELLERS (1947): J. EDGAR HOOVER

The Communist movement in the United States began to manifest itself in 1919. Since then it has changed its name and its party life whenever expedient and tactical. But always it comes back to fundamentals and bills itself as the party of Marxism-Leninism. . . . In recent years the Communists have been very cautious about using such phrases as "force and violence"; nevertheless, it is the subject of much discussion in their schools and in party caucus. . . .

The Communist Party of the United States is a fifth column if there ever was one. It is far better organized than were the Nazis in occupied countries prior to their capitulation. . . .

There is no doubt as to where a real Communist's loyalty rests. Their allegiance is to Russia, not the United States. . . .

What can we do? And what should be our course of action? The best antidote to communism is vigorous, intelligent, old-fashioned Americanism with eternal vigilance. I do favor unrelenting prosecution wherever they are found to be violating our country's laws.

. . . I do fear for the liberal and progressive who has been hood-winked and duped into joining hands with the Communists. I confess to a real apprehension so long as Communists are able to secure ministers of the gospel to promote their evil work and espouse a cause that is alien to the religion of Christ and Judaism. I do fear so long as school boards and parents tolerate conditions whereby Communists and fellow travelers, under the guise of academic freedom, can teach our youth a way of life that eventually will destroy the sanctity of the home, that undermines faith in God, that causes them to scorn respect for constituted authority and sabotage our revered Constitution. I do fear so long as American labor groups are infiltrated, dominated or saturated with the virus of communism. I do fear the palliation and weasel-worded gestures against communism indulged in by some of our labor leaders who should know better but who have become pawns in the hands of sinister but astute manipulators for the Communist cause. . . . The Communists have been, still are, and always will be a menace to freedom, to democratic ideals, to the worship of God and to America's way of life. . . .

WHO IS LOYAL TO AMERICA?
(1947): HENRY S. COMMAGER

What is the new loyalty? It is, above all, conformity. It is the uncritical and unquestioning acceptance of America as it is. . . . It is, it must be added, easily satisfied. For it wants not intellectual conviction, but mere outward conformity. In matters of loyalty it takes the word for the deed, the gesture for the principle. . . . It is designed neither to discover real disloyalty nor to foster true loyalty. . . .

Certainly it is a gross perversion not only of the concept of loyalty but of the concept of Americanism to identify it with a particular economic system. . . .

What do men know of loyalty who make a mockery of the Declaration of Independence and the Bill of Rights . . . ? What indeed do they know of America—the America of Sam Adams and Tom Paine, of Jackson's defiance of the Court and Lincoln's celebration of labor, of Thoreau's essay on Civil Disobedience and Emerson's championship of John Brown . . . ?

It is easier to say what loyalty is not than to say what it is. It is not conformity. It is not passive acquiescence in the status quo. It is not preference for everything American over everything foreign. It is not an ostrich-like ignorance of other countries and other institutions. It is not the indulgence in ceremony—a flag salute, an oath of allegiance, a fervid verbal declaration. It is not a particular creed, a particular version of history, a particular body of economic practices, a particular philosophy.

It is a tradition, an ideal, and a principle. It is a willingness to subordinate every private advantage for the larger good. It is an appreciation of the rich and diverse contributions that can come from the most varied sources. It is allegiance to the traditions that have guided our greatest statesmen and inspired our most eloquent poets—the traditions of freedom, equality, democracy, tolerance, the tradition of the higher law, of experimentation, co-operation, and pluralism. It is a realization that America was born of revolt, flourished on dissent, became great through experimentation. . . .

Every effort to confine Americanism to a single pattern, to constrain it to a single formula, is disloyalty to everything that is valid in Americanism. . . .

5. *The Civil Rights Struggle*

The Supreme Court in 1954 made clear its rejection of segregation in all basic areas of national life, yet the resistance of many Southern states and localities was bitter, determined, and violent. The history of school desegregation in the deep South yielded an annual September Saturnalia of violent and murderous mobs. If Southern politicians and mobs seized most of the headlines, it became increasingly difficult for Northerners to pretend that desegregation was merely a Southern problem. Each year saw a larger number of Negroes crowding into the squalor of urban ghettoes in ten or twelve Northern cities, and middle-class Negroes experienced great difficulties in penetrating most suburban areas.

In 1955 the focal point of the struggle shifted from the courts to political action with the organization of the bus boycott in Birmingham, Alabama under the leadership of Rev. Martin Luther King. Overnight King became nationally famous and his Southern Christian Leadership Conference (SCLC) organized Negro protest movements in other cities. In 1960 Southern students gave the movement new impetus with the lunch counter "sit-ins" and inspired the organization of the Student Non-Violent Co-ordinating Committee (SNICK). Excepting the Urban League which largely concentrated on finding jobs for Negroes, the National Association for the Advancement of Colored People (NAACP) had conducted the fight for equality in the courts almost unaided for a generation. Now other and more militant organizations took the lead, SCLC, SNICK, and the Congress of Racial Equality (CORE), a small group formed some twenty years earlier around a policy of nonviolent mass action. In 1961 James Farmer of CORE initiated a series of "freedom rides" to desegregate Southern bus stations; the CORE busses were met by hostile mobs, but the nation watched and the cause of civil rights moved perceptibly forward. Protest soon spread to the North as picketing, rallies, and mass demonstration became standard techniques for protesting against job discrimination, living conditions in the ghettoes, and de facto school segregation. In the South, voter registration drives and the desegregation of libraries, parks, court houses, train and bus stations, busses, restaurants, and other facilities took an increasing share of civil rights activity. Civil Rights leaders organized virtually the entire Negro community in Birmingham; Nashville; Albany, Georgia; Cambridge, Maryland; and other towns and cities. In the summer of 1964 the Mississippi Freedom Project organized voter registration drives and Freedom Centers as well as the Mississippi Freedom Democratic Party, the first state political movement in which Negroes could freely participate since Reconstruction days. All of these gains were painfully won, and many persons despaired of full equality. The Black Muslims reaped the harvest of despair and gained tens of thousands of working-class members in the fifties; the Muslims, asserting the collective guilt of white people in America for centuries of past violence and oppression against the Negro, reversed white supremacy attitudes by insisting that the "so-called Negroes" were the moral, physical, and mental superiors of their white oppressors. Virtually all middle-class Negroes and the great majority of working-class Negroes refused to answer the Muslim call to black unity, but a number of Negro leaders warned that time was running out for American society. Although enforcement of the Civil Rights Act of 1964 posed many serious problems, the Bill did strike at many of the chief sources of discontent in the South. The bill did not offer much to Northern Negroes, but President Johnson's "War on Poverty" provided at least an initial step toward the solution of several basic problems. AUTHORS: W. E. B. Dubois (1868–1962), historian, sociologist, editor, and champion of Civil

Rights, was associated for many years with Atlanta University and with the National Association for the Advancement of Colored People. Franz Boas (1858–1942) was educated at Heidelberg, Bonn, and Kiel Universities; in 1888 he came to America, and from 1896 to 1937 he served as a Columbia professor. He and his colleagues destroyed the last serious arguments for racism. SELECTIONS: "On the Despair and Courage of American Negroes" from Dubois' *Souls of Black Folk* (1902). "The Scientific Foundations of Modern Equalitarianism" from Boas' *Anthropology and Modern Life* (1928). "Separate Facilities are Inherently Unequal," Brown vs. Board of Education, 1954. "The U.S. Commission on Civil Rights: Police Brutality" from the Commission's *Report* (1961). The U.S. Civil Rights Commission: "School Segregation" from the Commission's *Report* (1963).

ON THE DESPAIR AND COURAGE OF AMERICAN NEGROES (1902): W. E. B. DUBOIS

The Negro is a sort of seventh son, born with a veil, and gifted with second-sight in this American world,—a world which yields him no true self-consciousness, but only lets him see himself through the revelation of the other world. It is a peculiar sensation, this double-consciousness, this sense of always looking at one's self through the eyes of others, of measuring one's soul by the tape of a world that looks on in amused contempt and pity. One ever feels his two-ness,—an American, a Negro; two souls, two thoughts, two unreconciled strivings; two warring ideals in one dark body, whose dogged strength alone keeps it from being torn asunder.

The history of the American Negro is the history of this strife,—this longing to attain self-conscious manhood, to merge his double self into a better and truer self. In this merging he wishes neither of the older selves to be lost. . . . He simply wishes to make it possible for a man to be both a Negro and an American, without being cursed and spit upon by his fellows, without having the doors of Opportunity closed roughly in his face.

This, then, is the end of his striving: to be a coworker in the kingdom of culture, to escape both death and isolation, to husband and use his best powers and his latent genius. These powers of body and mind have in the past been strangely wasted, dispersed, or forgotten. The shadow of a mighty Negro past flits through the tale of Ethiopia the Shadowy and of Egypt the Sphinx. . . . The Nation has not yet found peace from its sins; the freedman has not yet found in freedom his promised land. Whatever of good may have come in these years of change, the shadow of a deep disappointment rests upon the Negro people,—a disappointment all the more bitter because the unattained ideal was unbounded save by the simple ignorance of a lowly people. . . .

A people thus handicapped ought not to be asked to race with the world, but rather allowed to give all its time and thought to its own social problems. But alas! while sociologists gleefully count his bastards and his prostitutes, the very soul of the toiling, sweating black man is darkened by the shadow of a vast despair. . . .

Merely a concrete test of the underlying principles of the great republic is the Negro Problem, and the spiritual striving of the freedmen's sons is the travail of souls whose burden is almost beyond the measure of their strength, but who bear it in the name of an historic race, in the name of this the land of their fathers' fathers, and in the name of human opportunity. . . .

THE SCIENTIFIC FOUNDATIONS OF MODERN EQUALITARIANISM: CULTURE NOT TIED TO RACE (1928): FRANZ BOAS

There is little clarity in regard to the term "race.". . . We are easily misled by general impressions. . . .

It is well to remember that heredity means the transmission of anatomical and functional characteristics from ancestors to offspring. . . . All we know is that the children of a given family represent the hereditarily transmitted qualities of their ancestors. Such a group of brothers and sisters is called a fraternity. . . .

We have found that the term "racial heredity" is strictly applicable only when all the individuals of a race participate in certain anatomical features. In each race taken as a whole the family lines differ considerably in their hereditary traits. The distribution of family lines is such that a considerable number of lines similar or even identical in one or many respects occur in contiguous territories. The vague impression of "types," abstracted from our everyday experience does not prove that these are biologically distinct races, and the inference that various populations are composed of individuals belonging to various races is subjectively intelligible, objectively unproved. It is particularly not admissible to identify types apparently identical that occur in populations of different composition. Each individual can be understood only as a member of his group.

These considerations seem necessary, because they clear up the vagueness of the term "race" as usually applied. When we speak of heredity we are ordinarily concerned with family lines, not with races. The hereditary qualities of families constituting the most homogeneous populations differ very much among themselves and there is very little, if anything, that these family lines have in common and they are not sharply set off from neighboring populations that may give a quite distinctive impression. . . .

The differences between races are so small that they lie within the narrow range in the limits of which all forms may function equally well. . . .

So far as our experience goes we may safely say that in any given race the differences between family lines are much greater than the differences between races. . . .

Students of ethnology have always been so much impressed by the general similarity of fundamental traits of human culture that they have never found it necessary to take into account the racial descent of a people when discussing its culture. . . . In [cultural] study we are compelled to disregard the racial position of the people we study, for similarities and dissimilarities have no relation whatever to racial types.

It does not matter how the similar traits in diverse races may have originated, by diffusion or independent origin. They convince us of the independence of race and culture because their distribution does not follow racial lines. . . .

SEPARATE FACILITIES ARE INHERENTLY UNEQUAL: BROWN V. BOARD OF EDUCATION (1954)

We come then to the question presented: Does segregation of children in public schools solely on the basis of race, even though the physical facilities and other "tangible" factors may be equal, deprive the children of the minority group of equal educational opportunities? We believe that it does. . . .

We conclude that in the field of public education the doctrine of "separate but equal" has no place. Separate educational facilities are inherently unequal. Therefore, we hold that the plaintiffs and others similarly situated for whom the actions have been brought are, by reason of the segregation complained of, deprived of the equal protection of the laws guaranteed by the Fourteenth Amendment. . . .

THE U. S. COMMISSION ON CIVIL RIGHTS: POLICE BRUTALITY (1961)

Brazier died 5 days later at a hospital in Columbus, Ga. from brain damage and a fractured skull. He had four to six bruised spots on his scalp from a blunt instrument which apparently also caused the skull fracture. The police claimed that Brazier was hit only once or twice at the time of the arrest.

In a sworn statement to Commission representatives, Mrs. Hattie Bell Brazier, widow of the victim, claimed that this affair had actually started months earlier. Mrs. Brazier explained that she and her husband had purchased a new Chevrolet in 1956—and another in 1958. In November of 1957, James Brazier had been arrested on a speeding charge. According to Mrs. Brazier, her husband told her that Dawson Officer "Y" took him to jail, and that:

> When I first entered the door of the jail, ['Y'] hit me on the back of the head and knocked me down and said, 'You smart son-of-a-bitch, I been wanting to get my hands on you for a long time.' I said, 'Why you want me for?' ['Y'] said, 'You is a nigger who is buying new cars and we can't hardly live. I'll get you yet.'

Officer "Y" then allegedly hit Brazier several more times, put his foot on the small of the prostrate Negro's back (Mrs. Brazier said she saw the footprints there later), and warned him, "You'd better not say a damn thing about it or I'll stomp your damn brains out." After his release from jail, Brazier was bleeding from his ear and vomiting blood. From this time in the fall of 1957 until the second incident in April of 1958 James Brazier was under the care of a local white doctor because of these injuries. Officer "X", the policeman who accompanied "Y" during the arrest in April 1958, also allegedly made a remark about the new car at some time previous to the fatal incident. It appears that James Brazier of Terrell County like Bobby Hall of Baker County, was considered an "uppity" Negro. . . .

From the complaints and reports reviewed by the Commission it appears that there are more incidents in this category—police brutality occurring in the moments of initial contact between the police officer and the victim—than in any other. . . .

Prejudice and the desire for respect also play a part. . . . Indeed, some policemen seem to view lack of respect in and of itself as sufficient justification for violence. There are reports that some policemen in the South have used violence when a Negro responded to a question simply by a "No" or "Yes" without the addition of a "Sir". . . .

THE U. S. COMMISSION ON CIVIL RIGHTS: SCHOOL SEGREGATION (1963)

Nearly 10 years after the Supreme Court decision in the *School Segregation Cases*, Negro schoolchildren still attend segregated schools in all parts of the Nation.

In the South, most schools continue to be segregated by official policy, notwithstanding the Supreme Court's finding that segregation on the basis of race cannot constitutionally be enforced. But in the North and West, school segregation is widespread because of existing segregated housing patterns and the practice of assigning pupils to neighborhood schools. . . . In the North and West, Negro protests until recently took the form of petition and personal appearance before school boards. However, segregated schools have now become targets of public demonstrations. . . . Negroes have picketed in suburban Philadelphia and in Boston, Chicago, and St. Louis. In Boston, some 3,000 junior and senior high school students stayed out of school for a day and attended workshops in neighborhood churches and social centers where they were instructed in Negro history, U.S. government and civil rights, and the principles of nonviolence. In St. Louis, 30 parents and ministers blocked the departure from a West End school of 12 buses containing about 500 children who were being transported to under-utilized white schools miles away, where they would attend all-Negro classes. Two weeks later 2,000 Negroes marched on the board of education headquarters carrying signs saying "Freedom Now" and "Don't Teach Segregation.". . .

The proportionate size of the minority group enrollment does not entirely determine the percentage of segregated schools. At the elementary level, Chicago, with the same proportional minority group enrollment as New York, has over 60 per cent more segregated schools. Chicago has tenaciously confined its Negro pupils to neighborhood schools, refused to rezone attendance areas on the fringe of the concentrated Negro residential areas, and declined to relax its rules forbidding transfers from area of residence. In contrast, New York City has made strenuous efforts to limit segregation in its schools. . . .

The determination of most southern school boards to employ every contrivance to evade or avoid desegregation continues to thwart implementation of the *School Segregation Cases*. Even token desegregation usually has come only after a lawsuit is threatened or prosecuted. The Commission has found no evidence that this resistance is dissipating.

In the North and West, commitment to the neighborhood school plan for both theoretical and practical reasons is being pitted against Negro demands for the end of de facto segregation. . . .

6. The Democratic Order and the Threat of Nuclear War

The United States initiated the atomic age in 1945 with the "A" bombs dropped on Hiroshima and Nagasaki. Influenced by the awesome power of the bomb, President Truman sent Bernard Baruch in 1946 to the United Nations with a proposal to grant a monopoly of controls to an International Atomic Development Authority. The Russians, fearing that the Baruch Plan might in effect give the United States permanent control over atomic weapons, insisted on the cessation of production and the destruction of the "A" weapon stockpile *before* the establishment of international controls. The production of the much more powerful Hydrogen bomb (1952), the Russian development of both types of bombs (1949, 1953), and the gradual emergence of missile delivery systems all increased the danger of nuclear catastrophe. In the early fifties, nuclear weapons testing began to arouse much criticism around the world, and Democratic Presidential candidate Adlai Stevenson during the 1956 campaign proposed a ban on testing. The acquisition of H-bombs by Britain in 1957 and the atomic armament program announced by President Charles deGaulle of France in 1960 raised the spectre of the possible proliferation of atomic weapons until war would become increasingly difficult to avoid.

Even if war could be averted could American democracy survive a long-range Cold War? Truman and Eisenhower were optimistic, but political conservatives such as Robert A. Taft and Barry Goldwater, while conceding the need for "effective" defense, insisted that "big" government and high Federal budgets (needed to administer and pay for the Cold War) imperiled basic American traits and beliefs. Other critics, less concerned with business values, feared that democratic social and political values might ultimately succumb to Cold War conditions. President Kennedy, who cultivated a thoughtful realism, believed that Americans could both preserve their society and conduct foreign policy successfully in the Atomic Age. Moreover, Kennedy was willing to explore every possible area of agreement with the Russians. The Kennedy speech cited in this section marked the beginning of the negotiations which led to the Test Ban Treaty of 1963. AUTHORS: Bernard Baruch (1870–   ), a graduate of the City College of New York and a wealthy financier, served Presidents from Wilson to Eisenhower as a diplomat, a financial consultant and a special advisor. Harry S. Truman (1884–   ), a Missouri-born lawyer and judge, rose through state politics to the Senate, the Vice-Presidency, and the Presidency. Robert A. Taft (1888–1953), the son of President Taft and several times a Presidential contender himself, was for almost a decade one of the most powerful members of the Senate. John F. Kennedy (1917–1963) had a brilliant rise to power through the House and the Senate on to the Presidency, a career ended abruptly by assassination. SELECTIONS: "The Choice Between the Quick and the Dead" (1946) from a speech by Baruch to the U.N. in *The United States and the United Nations* (U.S. Dept. of State, 1947). "Western Democracy vs. Soviet Communism" from Truman's Address to Congress, *Congressional Record* XCV, January 20, 1949. "A Republican Version of Democracy and World Conflict" from Taft's "The Republican Party" *Fortune* (April, 1949). "The Journey of a Thousand Miles" from a Kennedy speech (1961) to the U.N., *To Turn the Tide* (1962).

THE CHOICE BETWEEN THE QUICK AND THE DEAD (1946): BERNARD BARUCH

We are here to make a choice between the quick and the dead.

That is our business.

Behind the black portent of the new atomic age lies a hope which, seized upon with faith, can work our salvation. If we fail, then we have damned every man to be the slave of Fear. Let us not deceive ourselves: We must elect World Peace or World Destruction.

Science has torn from nature a secret so vast in its potentialities that our minds cower from the terror it creates. Yet terror is not enough to inhibit the use of the atomic bomb. The terror created by weapons has never stopped man from employing them. For each new weapon a defense has been produced, in time. But now we face a condition in which adequate defense does not exist.

Science, which gave us this dread power, shows that it *can* be made a giant help to humanity, but science does *not* show us how to prevent its baleful use. So we have been appointed to obviate that peril by finding a meeting of the minds and hearts of our people. Only in the will of mankind lies the answer.

It is to express this will and make it effective that we have been assembled. We must provide the mechanism to assure that atomic energy is used for peaceful purposes and preclude its use in war. . . .

WESTERN DEMOCRACY VS. SOVIET COMMUNISM (1949): HARRY S. TRUMAN

The American people stand firm in the faith which has inspired this Nation from the beginning. We believe that all men have a right to equal justice under law and equal opportunity to share in the common good. We believe that all men have the right to freedom of thought and expression. We believe that all men are created equal because they are created in the image of God.

From this faith we will not be moved. . . .

Communism is based on the belief that man is so weak and inadequate that he is unable to govern himself, and therefore requires the rule of strong masters. . . .

Communism maintains that social wrongs can be corrected only by violence. . . .

First, we will continue to give unfaltering support to the United Nations. . . .

Second, we will continue our programs for world economic recovery. . . .

Third, we will strengthen freedom-loving nations against the dangers of aggression. . . .

Fourth, we must embark on a bold new program for making the benefits of our scientific advances and industrial progress available for the improvement and growth of underdeveloped areas. . . .

A REPUBLICAN VERSION OF DEMOCRACY AND WORLD CONFLICT (1949): ROBERT A. TAFT

What is liberty? It is freedom of speech and of the press, as the President said in his inaugural—but it is much more. It is the freedom of the individual to choose his own work and his life occupation, to spend his earnings as he desires to spend them, to choose the place where he desires to live, to take the job that fits him whether some union official is willing that he get it or not. It is the freedom of the local community to work out its own salvation when it has the power to do so. It is the freedom of cities, of counties, of school districts; the freedom to educate one's own children as one thinks best. It is the freedom of thought and experiment in academic institutions. It is the freedom of men in industry to run their businesses as they think best so long as they do not interfere with the rights of others to do the same. . . .

It is tragic that our people in recent elections have tended to support the theory that the government should be the source of all planning, of all control, and of bread and circuses for the multitude. It is tragic because at this very moment we see the magnificent success of a system of liberty in the U.S. as contrasted with the comparative poverty and dissatisfaction of many foreign nations. . . .

Nor do [Americans] yet realize the threat contained in the program that is now presented by the Democratic party. That program, if fulfilled, would soon bring a federal-tax burden of $60 billion, subject all business to detailed controls, extend the federal welfare bureaus into every home, and extend actual government operation of business into the larger industries. It would subject America to a totalitarian government. . . .

THE JOURNEY OF A THOUSAND MILES
(1961): JOHN F. KENNEDY

For in the development of this organization [the U.N.] rests the only true alternative to war, and war appeals no longer as a rational alternative. Unconditional war can no longer lead to unconditional victory. It can no longer serve to settle disputes. It can no longer be of concern to great powers alone. For a nuclear disaster, spread by winds and waters and fear, could well engulf the great and the small, the rich and the poor, the committed and the uncommitted alike. Mankind must put an end to war or war will put an end to mankind. . . .

It is therefore our intention to challenge the Soviet Union, not to an arms race, but to a peace race: to advance with us step by step, stage by stage, until general and complete disarmament has actually been achieved. We invite them now to go beyond agreement in principle to reach agreement on actual plans. . . . This generation learned from bitter experience that either brandishing or yielding to threats can only lead to war. But firmness and reason can lead to the kind of peaceful solution in which my country profoundly believes.

We are committed to no rigid formula. We see no perfect solution. . . .

I come here today to look across this world of threats to the world of peace. In that search we cannot expect any final triumph, for new problems will always arise. We cannot expect that all nations will adopt like systems, for conformity is the jailer of freedom, and the enemy of growth. Nor can we expect to reach our goal by contrivance, by fiat or even by the wishes of all.

But however close we sometimes seem to that dark and final abyss, let no man of peace and freedom despair. For he does not stand alone. If we all can persevere, if we can in every land and office look beyond our own shores and ambitions, then surely the age will dawn in which the strong are just and the weak secure and the peace preserved.

Ladies and gentlemen of this Assembly, the decision is ours. Never have the nations of the world had so much to lose or so much to gain. Together we shall save our planet or together we shall perish in its flames. Save it we can, and save it we must, and then shall we earn the eternal thanks of mankind and, as peacemakers, the eternal blessing of God.